Tightrope

Tightrope

Six Centuries of a Jewish Dynasty

Michael Karpin

John Wiley & Sons, Inc.

This book is printed on acid-free paper. ♾

Published by John Wiley & Sons, Inc., Hoboken, New Jersey
Published simultaneously in Canada

Library of Congress Cataloging-in-Publication Data:

Karpin, Michael I.
Tightrope : Six centuries of a Jewish dynasty / Michael Karpin.
p. cm.
Includes bibliographical references and index.
ISBN 978-0-470-17373-2 (cloth : alk. paper)
1. Backenroth family. 2. Jews—Poland—History. 3. Jews—Poland—Genealogy. 4. Poland—Ethnic relations. I. Title.
DS134.7.B33K37 2008
929'.209438—dc22

2008000977

Printed in the United States of America

10 9 8 7 6 5 4 3 2 1

Contents

Preface

I started to research the history of the Backenroth clan approximately twenty years ago, in response to an offer from Allan Kahane, a young Brazilian-born businessman. He had just settled in New York, and good friends introduced us. Later, in October 1987, while Allan was visiting his relatives in Jerusalem, he called me in London, where I was vacationing. He had an unusual request. "Michael," he said, "I would like you to write my father's life story."

His South American accent was unfamiliar, and because journalists sometimes find peculiar ways to amuse themselves, I was sure that one of my newsroom colleagues in Jerusalem was pulling my leg. I replied, "It's not April first, is it?"

But soon it became clear that his proposal was authentic.

Allan's father, Israel Kahane, whom everyone called Ullo, had died recently. Ullo had rescued some of his family members from the Nazi inferno in Eastern Europe and then immigrated to Brazil. He arrived penniless and ended up a millionaire several times over.

Nothing immediately enthralled me about his story. A Holocaust survivor who migrated to South America and succeeded in business was a common enough tale. Then Allan mentioned that his family's origins had been in Germany and its history went back to the Middle Ages. My ears pricked up. On Allan's father's side, Allan said, the story was unique, but the family chronicles of his mother, Hanna Backenroth, whom everybody called Nushka, were even more engrossing. Allan enumerated some of the family's exceptional characters and aroused my journalistic curiosity.

This surprising call produced an outstanding friendship and also an endeavor in genealogical-historical research that yielded this book.

My sources consisted of personal journals and letters, books, recordings, genealogies handed down from parents to children, and, primarily, scores of interviews that totaled hundreds of hours. Over the years, in the course of my journalistic travels, I interviewed family members whenever and wherever I came across them. Sometimes I made special trips to meet them. I conducted interviews in Vienna, London, Paris, Warsaw, Kraków, Rio de Janeiro, and New York City, and in several Israeli cities. Just before the breakup of the Soviet Union, when I was serving as Israel TV's correspondent in Moscow, I traveled to Ukraine to visit a number of towns: Lvov, Bolechow, and Sanok. The latter is on the San River, and the Backenroths had an oil refinery there. I also visited Drohobych, Schodnica, and Boryslav at the foot of the Carpathian Mountains, where oil was discovered in the late nineteenth century, enriching the Backenroth clan. Now, all that remains of the field are rusty iron grasshoppers. They had pumped out every drop of oil until the wells ran dry.

Over the years, certain family members had maintained an awareness of history and had written down accounts of their lives. Others preserved the writings and the correspondence of their forefathers.

I located a great deal of material in various archives. At the Institute for Jewish Research (YIVO) in New York City, I found the original report of an international committee that investigated the 1919 pogrom that took place in Lvov. At the end of World War I, a civil war broke out in Ukraine. Ukrainian militias rebelled against the Polish army and, incidentally, killed seventy Jews. Lvov's pogrom changed the worldview of Yerahmiel Kahane, Allan's grandfather.

In the government archives in Vienna, I found the first reports on oil prospecting in Galicia. I also located professional reports about those first oil wells in Poland in the New York Public Library, as well as reports in Philadelphia on the discovery of the first oil fields in the United States during the exact same period. John D. Rockefeller's Standard Oil of Ohio was a competitor of the Backenroths' company.

But the most significant document I found was in the library of the rabbinical seminary in London: the diary of Dov Ber Birkenthal that had come to light in London in 1912, titled the *Memoirs of Rabbi Dov from Bolechow*. Birkenthal was born in 1723, and in his youth he began to keep a journal in the Hebrew language. He left behind a vivid and detailed testimony of everyday life. His journal is a historical rarity because in the eighteenth century, Jews who wrote almost never mentioned secular matters. They devoted their time to study and to composing religious works in order to strengthen the faith, whereas Birkenthal's testimony gives us a glimpse into the life of a Jewish community to which several generations of Backenroths belonged.

This link between the annals of the Backenroths and historical events offers us an opportunity to weave the private and personal tales of family members into the known historical tapestry, giving us new perspectives and insights. It is a mirror in which almost any family can find its own historical reflection, a mirror that enables each of us to look back and observe our antecedents against the backdrop of their period and to see how our own values and beliefs have derived from them.

Acknowledgments

This epic tale of the Backenroth clan was shaped by real people—talented and creative women and men swept into distant regions and complex situations by the dramatic tides of the history of the Jews. They were forced to display resourcefulness and courage in order to survive. Some of them fought a battle for life that seems no less than miraculous. This saga reveals a family of rare vitality, many of whose members underwent extreme hardship or enjoyed affluence. Time and again they slid from prosperity and opulence to profound distress, and time after time they managed to surmount the crises by virtue of their personal abilities, a tenacious belief in their values, and family solidarity.

As I gathered the details of the Backenroth narrative, many of their scions and numerous acquaintances allowed me to pester them for hours in interviews. I thank them from the bottom of my heart. Many of the interviewees are dead now; may they rest in peace.

I am especially grateful to two descendants of this book's protagonists, Ullo Kahane and Naftali Bronicki: Ullo Kahane's son, Allan, and Naftali Bronicki's son, Lucien. Their contributions were essential for my research.

My good friend Abraham Kushnir read the manuscript. He was a steady source of wise counsel, and I owe him many thanks. Ronnie Hope, the chief copy editor of the *Jerusalem Report*, gave me advice on both language and content. My literary agent, Regina Ryan, in New York City, enthusiastically encouraged me and led the way to my publisher, John Wiley & Sons. I am especially grateful to Regina. My editor, Hana Lane, handled the manuscript with forbearance and professionalism. I am profoundly appreciative. Many thanks to Lisa Burstiner, who managed the production stages with talent and devotion, and to copy editor Patti Waldygo, whose contribution to the manuscript's precision and clarity was significant.

I was sustained throughout this project by the encouragement of my family: my wife, Pnina; my daughter, Maya; and my two sons, David and Daniel. All of these people have been loyal partners in my work, but the responsibility for any flaws in the finished product is mine alone.

The history of the Backenroths exemplifies the history of the Jews. The experiences the Backenroths went through as a family are the same ones the Jews went through as a people. Although my family is not related by blood to the Backenroths, their story is mine, too.

Go to my Web site, www.michaelkarpin.com, for more information.

PART ONE

High Hopes

1

Transfer

Dawn breaks over the great plain north of the city of Kraków, Poland. At the edge of the plain flows the Vistula River. A dirt road runs along its bank. The morning mists rise, revealing two dozen wagons scattered on a lush green meadow between the road and the river. Horses and mules graze, while scores of adults and children mill around among them, preparing to set out on their journey. It is early autumn in the year 1350, and these are the members of the Backenroth clan. They began their trek the previous winter from the land the Jews called Ashkenaz, known today as Germany.[1]

Vigorous young men saddle the horses and the mules and harness them to the wagons. Young women in long dark dresses bake bread in make-shift field ovens and feed the fire with dry twigs. Three mothers sit separately, nursing their babies. The older men gather around the venerable Rabbi Elimeilech Backenroth (they usually pronounced his name using the Ashkenazi accent—Eli*mei*lech—or abbreviated it to Meilech). He is the head of the family, whose word is law; he is the final, indeed the only, arbiter.[2] Not one action is taken during the trek without his being asked to determine whether it is correct and desirable.

Before the wagon train moves out, a few women extinguish the embers of the campfires. Men hurriedly load the baggage onto the carts. Someone calls out to the children in Yiddish, "*Gikh yetst, zum boyd arayngeyn!*" (Quickly now, get onto the wagons!)[3]

The sunrise illuminates a striking panoramic scene: dozens of wagons in a long train moving slowly eastward across the plain along a wide dirt road. From the drivers' seats, men urge the horses on. Behind them, on the

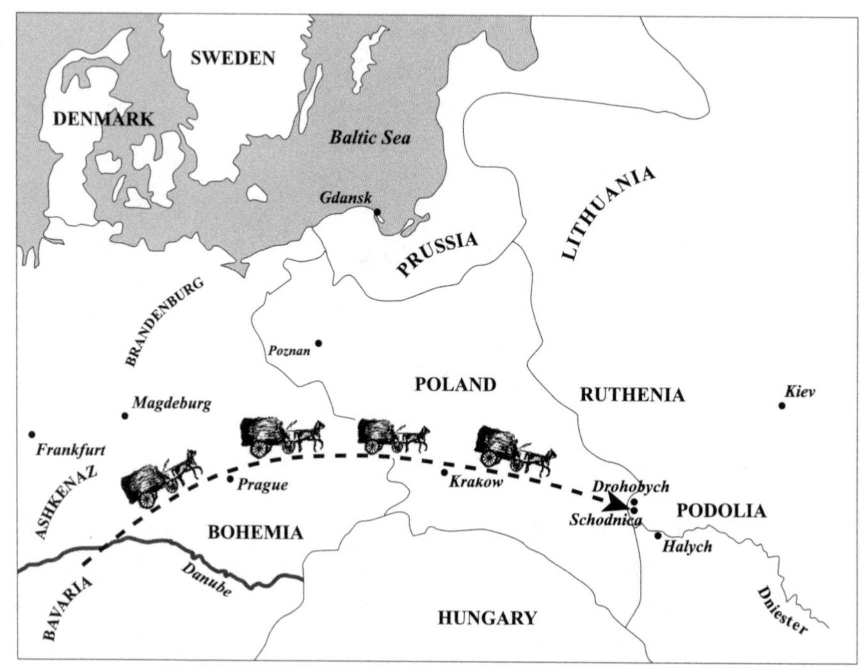

The path of the Backenroth clan on their journey east, 1350.

flat wagon beds, the women and the children are crowded together amid the baggage. Taking up the rear is a band of young men carrying axes, with daggers strapped to their waists. The men are bearded, long-haired, and covered with the dust of the journey. On their heads are hats with huge brims—not the three-cornered hats seen in depictions of Jews in Christian religious paintings of the era, but the headgear of German peasants. Some of the men have crude leather boots on their feet, but most have wrapped their feet and calves in cloth leggings, which are bound tightly with cords. On the far southeastern horizon the high ridges of the Carpathian mountain chain gradually come into view. This is their destination.

The idyllic picture, painted in the gentle autumnal colors of the Polish countryside, seems reminiscent of old photographs of early settlers in the western United States. In truth, however, the reality is depressing, even tragic, because the migration was caused by a cruel historical event. Members of the Backenroth family have departed from their home of the last several centuries, the land of Ashkenaz, to escape the horrors of the Black Death. This monstrous epidemic of bubonic plague swept Western Europe in the years 1347 to 1351. The Backenroths are making their way to Galicia, in eastern Poland (today part of Ukraine).

This was the second great migration undertaken by the clan. The first took place a thousand years earlier, after the failure of the Jewish rebellion against the Roman Empire, during the first century, had compelled their forefathers to abandon the land of Israel and go into exile.[4] Since that first uprooting, Jews had always prayed facing the direction of Jerusalem, and in every home they inhabited they always left one corner in one room unpainted, as a reminder of their destroyed homeland.

The historical memory was a harsh one. In the summer of 70 CE, at the height of a bloody civil war between extremist Jews, named the Sicarii (Latin for "daggers"), and their moderate brethren, the Roman army conquered Jerusalem and laid waste the temple that had been built by Herod the Great.[5] Jerusalem was in the eye of the storm, and its inhabitants suffered a great catastrophe: Most of their homes were set alight and gutted, and among the ruins lay tens of thousands of unburied bodies. Those who remained alive lost all of their belongings and were left to starve. A severe crisis also prevailed in other parts of the land of Israel.

As was the custom of the time, many Jewish prisoners of war were enslaved and carried off to Rome. They were forced to leave their country and to march behind the imperial army. Everywhere that a Roman soldier trod, he was followed by a Jewish slave, who settled near the army's fortress and became a member of the proletariat. The Jewish civilians who remained in the province of Judaea, as the land of Israel was called by the Roman imperial administration, lost most of their rights. Hundreds of thousands of Jews were left destitute and homeless.

The Romans kept up their harsh rule in every part of the country. The emperor Hadrian changed Jerusalem's name to Aelia Capitolina in the year 131 and forbade Jews to enter the city. The following year, the Jews rebelled again. Their leader was Bar Kokhba, and the rash, imprudent uprising that he declared was named after him. It lasted three years, and the loss of Jewish life was catastrophic. Historians' estimates of the death toll among Jews in the rebellions against the Roman Empire range from 600,000 to 1,200,000.

After the Romans suppressed the second rebellion, the Jews' plight became even worse. The foreign rulers decreed more severe measures against certain practices of the Jewish religion, including a ban on circumcision. At the same time, the Romans expelled entire communities of Jews, dispersing them throughout the Roman provinces in the Middle East, North Africa, and Europe.

In the coming years, an economic crisis forced many more Jews to migrate out of Israel. Hundreds of thousands fled to cities around the Mediterranean, and large areas of Palestine were totally deserted. The first to leave were the landowners and the merchants who had lost all of their possessions, and among them were the forefathers of the Backenroths.

Even before the fall of the Roman Empire in 476, Jews lived in almost all of the Roman provinces around the Mediterranean, usually along the imperial supply routes and close to the fortresses. Around 800 CE, Jewish settlements spread to Central and Western Europe (today's Germany and France), and by the end of the first millennium, the majority of the world's Jews were living in Europe. In Ashkenaz, where most of them had concentrated, they were mainly peddlers and craftsmen. Some engaged in international trade. In documents of the time, the words *Jew* and *merchant* were almost synonymous.

Jewish communities were established along the big rivers: the Rhine, the Main, the Mosel, and the Danube. Bohemia in Central Europe, today's Czech Republic, was the easternmost point of Jewish settlement. Eastern Europe was in those days considered wild and dangerous, and in the early Middle Ages, only a few adventurous merchants risked traveling there. People who considered themselves civilized were not drawn to those remote areas, which were said to be "beyond the mountains of darkness" by the Jews of Ashkenaz. These locales were considered to be practically another planet.

Indeed, around 1000 CE, Poland, where the Backenroths were heading, was a lot like the western United States when the first European settlers arrived there. Permanent settlements were scarce and had very little infrastructure. A small number of dirt roads crossed the countryside, some of them dangerous because of the harsh winters and the brigands. Way stations were few and far between, mainly at important junctions. Here there were inns, taverns, restaurants, and services for repairing wagons and looking after horses and mules. The way stations were inhabited primarily by nomadic tribes, Slavs and Russians, Finns and Mongols, who fought one another over territory. For hundreds of years, these tribes had come and gone, conquering and retreating.

It was only around 800 CE that the Slavs established the first political entity in Eastern Europe; they were not yet an actual nation-state, but they were no longer merely nomadic tribesmen without their own territory. They had a skeletal structure of political and economic institutions, but no bureaucracy to speak of, no organized administration, and very few officials. At the same time, the Slavs were spinning trade connections with people in the Byzantine Empire and the Islamic caliphate to the south, and the emerging Kuzari kingdom to the east.

While primitive nomadic tribes in Poland and other regions of Eastern Europe battled over territory and set up rudimentary and tenuous governmental frameworks, for hundreds of years the Jews had lived in an advanced state of civilization. They inhabited cities or villages and worked as merchants, officials, teachers, and scholars. In medieval times, most Poles were pagan idol worshippers, while the Jews were monotheists. Christianity, and with it the belief in one God, reached Poland for the first time in 966. In church documents of the time, Poland was called Nova Plantatio or "new plant." At the beginning of the second millennium, almost all Poles were illiterate, whereas 90 percent of Jewish men could read at least the *siddur*, the Jewish prayer book. The gender gap limited Jewish women's achievement, however; 90 percent of them were illiterate.

In the annals of Polish history, Jewish merchants are mentioned a few times before the Middle Ages and the establishment of the first Polish "state" in 936. While passing through Poland on their way east, to the Caucasus or to China, some of these itinerant merchants settled in Poland. After leaving Spain or Francia (today's France), they stopped for a few days at the city of Verdun, the location of the main slave market of Western Europe, and then traveled east in their wagons, along the banks of the great rivers.

One such route, called by merchants "the short route," led south along the Rhine, with a way station at the city of Mainz, which is known in Jewish history as Magenza. The route then led south to Strasbourg, the capital of the Alsace region, through the Black Forest, and along the Danube to Moravia and Hungary.

Another route, known as "the dangerous track," led along the Danube to Bohemia, to the city of Prague, and from there to Kraków, in southern Poland of today. In the eyes of the civilized Jewish people of Ashkenaz, Kraków was where the "Wild East" began and the law of the jungle prevailed. Apart from nomadic tribesmen, only the bravest of merchants dared to travel east on the swampy roads that were known as "the King's Highway to Kiev." Most of these merchants usually stopped overnight in Kraków.

Imagine a summer's evening in southern Poland, at Kraków's small way station. From the public house, loud sounds of merriment and shouting can be heard. The merchants are imbibing spirits and regaling one another with tales of their journeys' adventures. They trade valuable information about the state of the roads and their dangers and try to persuade young women to come and keep them warm in their beds. Outside, in the inn's courtyard, the merchants' apprentices are watering and feeding the horses, repairing horseshoes, hammering and straightening out the iron wagon wheels that have buckled, and loading supplies onto the wagons. Tomorrow at dawn the merchants will set out again. From Kraków, they will head due east and will ford the San River, a tributary of the Vistula. Then they will cross the Carpathian range and follow the Dniester River to the city of Kiev.[6]

What were those Jewish merchants doing there? Exactly what Jews have always done: buying and selling. They purchased goods in the relatively advanced state of Kievan Rus (the ancient Slavic Empire, circa 880 to 1250, from which three countries emerged: Russia, Byelorussia, and Ukraine), as Russia was known in those days, and sold them in the west. These were mostly expensive consumer goods—silken fabrics; carpets; and silver; lumber; horses; weaponry such as swords, daggers, and knives; and exotic foodstuffs. Some of the Jewish traders supplied Western Europe with male and female slaves from the east.

During the early Middle Ages, the Jewish merchants did not leave much of a mark in Poland. They passed through the land once or twice a year. As far as is known, there were no Backenroths among these merchant adventurers. At the start of the second millennium, the Backenroths were still securely ensconced in Ashkenaz. According to family tradition, one branch of the clan lived in southern Germany in the territory known today as Bavaria, and its members were engaged in commerce. They lived among their own people and managed most of their affairs themselves. Although the local Germans considered them unbelievers, as they did all the Jews in Ashkenaz, the Backenroths were nevertheless granted the protection of the German emperors. This status gave them both security and trading rights.

The Jews enjoyed many centuries in Ashkenaz, but this beneficent period came to an end as the first millennium drew to a close. Large areas of Europe entered a period of severe economic crisis, which resulted in political and social upheaval. Emperors and princes who had previously bestowed their protection upon the Jews lost power, while the Catholic popes gained strength. A dramatic turning point had been reached in the lot of the Jews in Europe.

From April to June 1096, the First Crusade stunned the Jews of Western Europe. As the Christian armies marched toward Jerusalem, they massacred many of the Jews they encountered on the way. For the first time in the history of their exile in Europe, the Jews felt that they had become fair game. Their collective sense of security was destroyed. Until that time, victimization of Jews had occurred mainly in France and usually took the form of economic sanctions or temporary banishment. Cases of mass murder of Jews were rare. But early in the second millennium and primarily in the mid-twelfth century, persecution by the church increased, and the existence of entire communities in Ashkenaz, along the Rhine, Mosel, and Danube rivers, was threatened. The heads of the church demanded that the Jews convert, forcing them to choose between baptism or death. Others were compelled to emigrate. Those who hesitated and neither converted nor fled were slaughtered in cold blood by the mobs.

The Second Crusade in 1146 prompted a mass migration of Jews eastward, and this exodus continued over hundreds of years. The Jews went east because they had no other choice. They couldn't go south because the Italian aristocracy didn't want them. They did not dare to go to the Holy Land, lest they be massacred by the crusaders or by Muslim armies that had invaded the land from the east. The Jews' only real option was to flee to the empty expanses of Eastern Europe. The men loaded their families and their possessions onto horse- or mule-drawn wagons and formed convoys. At first, only a few youngsters, brave unmarried men, or couples ventured beyond the mountains of darkness. They left Ashkenaz in small groups and made their way eastward on foot, crossing Bohemia into southern Poland and settling on the agricultural estates established by Polish noblemen in western Galicia, on the vast plains and the low hills between the city of Kraków and the Carpathian Mountains. Later, when the Black Death struck and spread through Europe, the flow of Jewish migrants surged eastward to undeveloped lands.

The Black Death was a historical watershed for the entire population of Europe because it turned the social and economic structures upside down. The epidemic weakened the feudal regimes, which eventually vanished altogether, and produced the first shoots of the Industrial Revolution. At the same time, faith in the Catholic Church declined, and the era of the Renaissance and the Reformation dawned.

For the Jews of Ashkenaz, however, the Black Death was more than a historical watershed. For them, it was an utter catastrophe, whose outcome was no less terrible than the Holocaust perpetrated by the Nazis in the twentieth century. No accurate statistics exist for the number of Jews who died of the plague or were murdered as a result of blood libels that blamed Jews for spreading the disease. There are detailed accounts of those who perished in certain communities—Cologne, Mainz, Frankfurt, Augsburg, Speyer, Strasbourg, and other cities and towns—but no statistics for all of the settlements. It is therefore difficult to accurately estimate how many Jews died. Nevertheless, there is some basis for the belief that proportionately, the number of Jews killed by the plague or murdered was no smaller than of those who died at the hands of the Nazis. It also seems likely that just as many Jews were murdered because of the blood libels as those who died of the plague. They were the scapegoats. "The Jews spread the plague," went the rumor from mouth to ear, from town to town. "The Jews poisoned the wells; let's get rid of them." And indeed, in the fifth decade of the fourteenth century, during the years of the Black Death (1347–1350), huge masses of Jews were expelled from Western and Central Europe: from northern Italy, Alsace Lorraine, the Rhine Valley, the banks of the Danube, and even Bohemia. In this way, most of the Jewish communities of Western and Central Europe were doomed to extermination or expulsion.

This was not the first blood libel in history, but it clearly was the cruelest and the most devastating. It apparently began in the town of Chillon, then in the duchy of Savoy (which today is in Switzerland). The police arrested several Jews and questioned them about the source of the plague. Under torture, one of them told his interrogators that a group of Jews from the south of France had poisoned the water supply. He testified that these Jews had murdered some innocent Christians, ripped out their hearts, and used them to make poison. According to the police record, the man said that the Jews had ground up the Christians' hearts and mixed them with "the flesh of lizards and spiders and strips of Christian holy bread." The Chillon police leaked his statement, and the story spread throughout Central and Western Europe.[7] The masses turned violent, and some three hundred Jewish communities suffered, with most settlements being obliterated. Tens of thousands of Jews were exterminated and hundreds of thousands driven away.

The cries of the Jews, and the Muslims who were similarly persecuted during the plague, were drowned out in the general clamor. Europe was in the throes of a terrible crisis. There is no parallel in history that can be used to depict the chaos and the anxiety of those years; it was veritably Dante's Inferno. The Black Death took millions of lives everywhere, and there was no way to escape it. It entered every home. Entire families were wiped out. Health officials working on behalf of the authorities burned the houses of those who had been infected. Whole neighborhoods were set alight, and entire communities ceased to exist. Rats gnawed at dead bodies lying in the streets of the big cities. Gravediggers could not bury all of the dead. The economy came to a halt, the supply of raw materials dried up, production ceased, and the fields lay desolate. A great famine broke out, and people fought one another over a loaf of bread. Despair and panic prevailed in the streets, and false prophets found willing followers. Then government collapsed, and bands of hooligans ran wild, killing, pillaging, and raping. Within less than four years, twenty-five million people perished from the plague, the famine, and the cold, about a quarter of the population of Central and Western Europe. In England, between half and two-thirds of the population died.

Europe had been laid to waste, and the suffering of the survivors was terrible. Everywhere, the picture was one of total devastation, poverty, and terrible desolation. In twentieth-century terms, it was comparable to what European survivors of World War II had witnessed. These two catastrophes—the Black Death, perpetrated by nature, and the war, by man—were the most horrific traumas inflicted on Europe. In both of these disasters, the suffering of the Jews was particularly acute. And both times, the Backenroth clan found itself in the eye of the storm.

In the aftermath of the plague, with the old order toppled, the dirt roads of Europe were full of refugees. Not only Jews headed east. While Jews had been driven from their homes, German migrants were also seeking fresh pastures for settlement.

The Jewish refugees behaved as their brethren had when fleeing from the many horrors of this people's history, beginning with the Exodus from Egypt. They left their places of abode in groups and moved together on the roads, each family close to another, led by their spiritual leaders, the rabbis. It was a somewhat raucous scene because they were noisy and energetic by nature. Three times a day, they paused by the wayside and the men gathered for prayers. First, they were obliged to locate the east, the direction of their homeland, of Jerusalem. They argued among themselves, with plenty of hairsplitting and nitpicking and gesticulating, until the rabbis deigned to intervene and made a decision. Then the group fell silent and faced the direction set by the rabbis. They huddled tightly together and for several minutes recited prayers in Hebrew, which they called the "holy tongue." It was the language they always prayed in, but for everyday discourse they used a dialect of German mixed with Hebrew words and phrases known as Yiddish. This "Jews' German" was the language they took to Poland.

The migration eastward continued until around 1450. A whole nation was on the move, community after community, family after family. The first rivulets heralding the flood had reached Poland around 1150, and the flow became a mighty stream by the fourteenth century, during the reign of King Casimir the Great of Poland (1333–1370). By the middle of the fifteenth century, the largest Jewish community in the world, consisting of some five hundred thousand souls, lived in Poland. Thus Germany, together with the rest of Central and Western Europe, was *Judenrein,* ethnically cleansed of Jews, for the first time.

The Backenroths were one of the clans that took part in this epic migration. Like the other Jewish families of Ashkenaz, they were compelled to leave their homes en masse for the second time, after their forefathers had been driven out of the land of Israel together with the other exiles of Zion hundreds of years earlier. We do not know what the original Hebrew name of the family had been, but it is clear that the German principality official who registered the family members when they arrived in the early days of the Middle Ages determined that henceforward they would be called Backenroth, or "red cheeks." Was this a translation of their Hebrew name, which could well have been Admoni—"red headed," or "of ruddy complexion" in Hebrew? Or was it Pnei-Edom, which means "facing Edom," the red-hued land across the Jordan River from Judaea, because of their place of residence?

It is interesting that the Hebrew name of the family was forgotten, never surviving the trials of the dramatic events in the early period of their European sojourn, whereas the German name has lasted, with a vengeance, to this day. Although in the Ashkenaz of the medieval era few people had family names (most people were known by their given names together with their place of residence, such as Jacob Berliner, or the name of their father, such as Moses Josephson), nevertheless, according to the Backenroth family tradition, that is when their name originated. Despite their having been forced out of Germany, their German name survived in Poland. The Polish princes' officials who received them and listed them in the population registries never bothered to translate their name into Polish. Apparently, the cachet of names from the more advanced west appealed to the Poles.

Indeed, the Polish hosts were very happy to welcome the new settlers into their midst. The Jewish immigration was a blessing for Poland, which was in the very early stages of political and economic development. Compared to Spain, Francia, Italy, and even the German principalities, Poland lagged behind. It did not have a true urban civilization or a middle class. A few noblemen, known in Poland as the *szlachta,* owned most of the land and ruled millions of illiterate, possessionless serfs. Eastern Poland, farther from western influence, was particularly backward.

Very quickly, the Polish ruling class discovered that the Jews were a positive social element. They knew about commerce and craftsmanship. They were industrious and reliable, with highly developed family values, and very few were drunkards. This, incidentally, had also been the impression the Jews made on the people of Gaul and Germany after first appearing in those countries following their forced exile from Israel by the Romans. They had arrived from the more civilized East, and the orderly code of laws by which they conducted their family and communal lives served as an example to the people of Central and Western Europe, most of whom were still cave dwellers at the time.

The kings and the princes of Poland thus opened their gates wide to the Jews, determined not to pass up this opportunity to develop their country. They took an unprecedented step in publishing an invitation to Jews (and Germans) to come and settle in Poland, to build cities and villages, to develop crafts and commerce, to establish guilds and banks, and to import and export goods.[8]

History has its surprises. Generally, most nations and states closed their gates to Jews. In many cases, Jews were forced to wander because they were not wanted. But now Poland wanted them, badly. And this was why the Backenroths, led by Rabbi Elimelech, made their way into Galicia. In a few days' time, they would reach the foot of the eastern slopes of the Carpathian Mountains and would choose a place to settle down.

2

The Tavern Keeper

THE TOWN OF DROHOBYCH first appear in an official document in 1375, about twenty-five years after the Backenroths settled nearby. The first houses had been built at the edge of a salt mine, during the period when Galicia was part of the kingdom of Kievan Rus, the medieval state of the Eastern Slavs. This state flourished from the tenth to the thirteenth centuries and was the predecessor of today's Russia, Belarus, and Ukraine. At the time, salt was a valuable commodity and was traded ounce for ounce for gold. To facilitate its marketing, the founders of the town widened the ancient roads that led from Drohobych northward, in the direction of Lvov, Galicia's capital city, and southward, toward Hungary.

Why had the Backenroth wagon train stopped here, on the banks of the Tysmenytsia River, near the Drohobych salt mine? There is no information from this era that could supply an answer. Possibly, the Backenroths believed that they could make a living from mining the salt; maybe they were enchanted by the peace, the serenity, and the captivating scenery of the wooded foothills of the Carpathian range; or perhaps they were simply exhausted after their long trek. According to one source, Jews who had settled in the town before the Backenroths were not eager to welcome the newcomers into their community. The mine and the lands surrounding it belonged to the noble Polish Lubomirski family, which eventually became one of the most influential aristocratic dynasties in Polish history.[1] In exchange for the right to mine the salt, the Jewish families paid a great deal of money and a percentage of the revenue to the Lubomirski family. But even after deducting these expenditures, the salt miners made a healthy profit, and it is no wonder that they were reluctant to take in new partners.

That was the reality in those days. New Jewish communities usually sprang up in the wake of a privilege that the local rulers granted to the first settlers, just as the Lubomirski family had allowed the Jews of Drohobych to mine salt. And according to custom, shaped first in Ashkenaz and transferred to Eastern Europe, no automatic right enabled either individuals or families to join existing communities. Due to the expulsion and the persecution of Jews, however, their movement from one community to another was a constant phenomenon. To ease the plight of those compelled to roam, the rabbis demanded that their settled brethren help the newcomers.[2] As a rule, those who agreed to pay the community's membership dues and conform to its rules were allowed to join. There were cases, however, where the existing members either feared business competition or suspected that the candidates would not be easily assimilated into the community, and they closed the gates to new arrivals. This appears to have happened in Drohobych.

And this was why the Backenroth wagon train was forced to move away from the little town and to continue a few miles southward. There, among the pine trees, the Backenroths came across a large and peculiar outcropping of rocks dotted with caves and crannies (the place is known today as Urycze Rock). Hundreds of years later, geologists would identify this location as a geological fault, indicating that in our planet's early days the Earth's crust had cracked open and a gigantic wave of lava had erupted from the core and solidified there. But on that day, late in the autumn of 1350, the caves and the hollows in the huge, strange rocks offered a temporary shelter where the Backenroths could set up camp until they built their first homes.

So the wagons drew to a halt, and the head of the family, Rabbi Elimeilech, declared, "This is where we shall settle." They began to build, and a few months later a new neighborhood had arisen on the outskirts of Drohobych. It gradually expanded and in the course of time became a village in its own right, which eventually acquired the name of Schodnica (located forty-four miles southwest of Lvov). It is not known whether the aristocratic Lubomirski landowners were asked for permission to call the village Backenroth. If they had been asked, it is doubtful that they would have consented, but that name would have been appropriate because there is no doubt that the Backenroths established this village in Galicia. Later, they opened a public house there; this institution provided food and drink for generations of Ruthenians, Poles, Germans, and Jews and was well known throughout the entire district.

Looking back from the perspective of almost seven hundred years, one could say that the Backenroths arrived in Galicia at the right time. A stormy era of war and terror had just ended, after lasting nearly a hundred years.

In the year 1240, Mongol tribes led by Subutai, the son of Genghis Khan, had invaded Kievan Rus from the east and conquered it in a lightning campaign.[3] The Mongols wiped out the armies of Poland and Hungary and aspired to advance into Central Europe. They were not interested in permanent settlement and took little responsibility for governing the areas they captured. This situation was exploited by the local elite, a group of princes of Slavic and Nordic origins, who carved up among themselves the former Kievan Rus territory, stretching for almost five hundred miles from Kiev to Kraków. In the southwestern area, they established a new principality named Galicia-Volhynia (one of more than ten separate principalities) and handed it over to Ruthenian-Ukrainian princes of the district, who were members of the aristocratic Romanovychi Dynasty. The rule of this dynasty, known as the Kings of Galicia, lasted a little more than a hundred years, until 1340.[4]

Then the army of Casimir the Great (with the help of Hungary's army) invaded Galicia under the pretext that it was the duty of Roman Catholic Poland to restore stability and protect the Christian populace from the depredations of the pagan Mongol hordes. Galicia fell to Casimir and was annexed as part of the Polish kingdom.[5] This was a dramatic change and the start of a new era. Exactly ten years later, the Backenroths settled on the northern slopes of the Carpathians.

Casimir, the new ruler of Galicia, was one of the first Eastern European monarchs who understood the global economy. In order to develop his country to the level that countries such as Italy and France had attained, he planned to establish an urban-capitalist class and to deepen Poland's involvement in international commerce. From this point of view, the grand-national strategy of the king and the circle of noblemen around him and the modest family strategy of the Backenroths dovetailed perfectly. The Polish aristocracy, the *szlachta*, for its part, saw Galicia as Poland, and so did the Backenroths. In the eyes of these natural partners, the local Ruthenian population, devoid of privileges, was the source of cheap labor. Its role was to occupy the lowest layer of the feudal pyramid.

But the Polish victory never eliminated the Ruthenians' national aspirations; it only postponed their achievement. Their basic differences with the Poles would eventually fuel a bitter conflict that had religious, ethnic, and social roots and would drag on for six hundred years (indeed, until Ukraine won its independence after the fall of the Soviet empire at the end of the twentieth century). As time passed and the feudal regime weakened, the Ruthenians audaciously challenged the Polish rulers and tried to unseat them. Jews often found themselves occupying the uncomfortable middle ground between the two sides of the conflict.

In 1385, just thirty-five years after the Backenroths had settled in this area, another event occurred that helped to stabilize Galicia. The kings of Poland and Lithuania signed a pact known as the Union of Krevo, which determined that Poland would rule Galicia "for all eternity."[6] The hitherto pagan Lithuania became Roman Catholic and united with Poland. As a result, "the lost Polish lands"—as Galicia was defined in the treaty—were restored.[7] In effect, the relatively advanced Poland, with its Western orientation, swallowed Lithuania (although the latter's territory was larger than Poland's). Now, the noise of war was muted. The Polish nobility, with the help of recently arrived migrants, mostly Jews and Germans, energetically set about developing the newly acquired territory.

Indeed, in the forthcoming two hundred years (1385–1570), Galicia, like many other parts of Poland, underwent a renaissance. New cities were built, roads paved, and infrastructures installed. Openness prevailed in politics, and there appeared the first signs of a state of law and of civil representation in government.[8] In Kraków, the first national university was founded. Citizens with access to sources of knowledge—Poles, Germans, and Jews, but almost no Ruthenians—learned French and Italian. Culture flourished, the Polish language developed, and Polish literature blossomed. The violent and reactionary reality of the Dark Ages gave way to a sense of intellectual awakening and religious freedom.

The golden age instituted by Casimir the Great was also an era of prosperity for the Backenroths. The beginning had been difficult, mostly because of the business competition. Almost all of the commerce, both wholesale and retail, had already been controlled by hundreds of Jewish families who resided in the vicinity when the Backenroths arrived. The first Jewish settlers owned shops, warehouses, market stalls, and public eating and drinking houses. Many were peddlers who traveled from village to village with their wares, and the Backenroths had to make an official request to establish themselves.

Drohobych was a district capital. In charge was an official appointed by Count Lubomirski with the title of *starosta*, "community head." He was a lesser nobleman, and his task was to manage the local bureaucracy and oversee the economy. Every day, heads of newly arrived Jewish families showed up in his offices to apply for permits, or "privileges," as they were called then. They wanted to mine salt, sell alcoholic beverages, cut down trees, and open shops. The Backenroths had to make a major effort to persuade the *starosta* to grant them a permit to sell strong drink.

Successful in their request, the Backenroths set up their public house on the southern outskirts of Drohobych, at the side of the road to Schodnica. It would remain the Backenroths' main business for hundreds of years. In a family record of the mid-eighteenth century, the name of Abraham Backenroth appears, and his occupation is given as bartender. There are no other details about him, no date of birth or date of death. The records do show that around the year 1745, his son, Shmuel Leib, was born in Schodnica. He married Silke Kupermann (or Kuperberg, according to another source), whose nickname was Babe, and who ran the tavern with her husband. According to family tradition, the Backenroth family had held the license to sell alcoholic drinks for at least six generations, and the public house evolved into an impressive establishment. In the early eighteenth century, it included a wayside restaurant, a grocery store, a real estate office, and a type of small bank or money-lending bureau.

The Jewish publican in Poland of the time was, first of all, a middleman and a merchant. He served as a bridge between the local Ruthenian population and the outside world. His tavern was a meeting place for villagers and town dwellers, as well as for local and visiting merchants.

In this class-conscious society, Ruthenian farmers and Polish officials lived in different worlds. The classes were completely segregated, and there was virtually no contact between noblemen and commoners or between educated government officials and agricultural workers. The only place where they could meet was at the public house. Here, thanks to the Jewish publican and the influence of intoxicating beverages, the class distinctions blurred.

In Polish history, the figure of the Jewish innkeeper evolved into something of a stereotype.[9] On a practical level, he was a key member of the community because of his activities as a middleman and a trader, but on the mythological spiritual plane, he was perceived as a medium with occult powers. People in the closed and devout Ruthenian peasant society related to the Christian saints in the same way that in earlier times they had given human qualities to their pagan idols. Now they ascribed unrealistic attributes to the Jewish publican, positioning him between the actual world and the other, intangible world. Apart from his mundane activities, selling liquor and foodstuffs, trading and acting as a middleman in transactions, the Jewish innkeeper had another role, an impossible one to fulfill. He was the earthly representation of the dark forces of the world of the dead: the evil, the wicked, the demons, and the ghosts. These very figures and characteristics are associated with the life of the public house, with the brandy and the vodka that enable men to get drunk and pass into other worlds, at least temporarily. In his tavern, the Jew represented occult forces, and in the eyes of Ruthenians and Poles, these forces were often identified with Satan himself.[10] The Jewish publican is frequently depicted in Polish folklore and literature as a cripple. He may be missing a limb or might be lame or one-eyed, and his character evolved into an emblem of evil: an ugly and nefarious moneylender.

Shmuel Leib Backenroth did not lack any of his limbs, and he was neither lame nor one-eyed. He was a whole Jew, tall, broad-backed, and bearded. He wore a white robe—the *kittel* of the Orthodox Jew—and a black *yarmulke,* a skullcap, on his head. Although he served his guests pork and nonkosher liquor and kept his establishment open for business on the Sabbath, he was nevertheless considered a pious man by his community.[11] Each morning he donned his phylacteries, and he prayed three times a day. The rabbis of the time were realistic and drew a distinction between a man's internal spiritual life and his external activities. Within the confines of the home and the institutions of the community, Jewish law, the *halakha*, was strictly observed. In the outside world, the constraints of real life dictated conduct. If the Jews had not compromised and separated the two worlds, they would not have been able to earn a living. Their shops and taverns were open on the Sabbath, and they sold nonkosher foodstuffs, as part of their obligation to provide services to the entire population. Closing a public house on a Jewish holy day would have entailed the loss of the license.

Several generations before Shmuel Leib, the Backenroth family had taken on a particularly profitable new business: leasing agricultural lands. Once a year, at the end of the summer, they leased some of Count Lubomirski's land from his local representative and then subleased it to Ruthenian farmers, in exchange for half of their produce. When the year was over and the crops were harvested, the accounts would be settled and glasses raised in a toast. Mostly, the results were good. In the family, they used to say that one year's good crop was enough to fill their coffers for many years to come.

The years of plenty continued for another two centuries, from the start of the great era of construction launched by King Casimir in the mid-fourteenth century until the end of the Jagiellon Dynasty's reign, at the close of the sixteenth century, when economic prosperity reached its height. All this time, the Poles and the foreigners among them prospered, but the Ruthenians, who considered themselves the owners of the land, remained oppressed, existing at the lowest rung of the socioeconomic ladder. The Polish *szlachta* strengthened its grip on the reins of power and helped itself freely to the fruits of economic abundance. The clergy enjoyed the benefits that accrued from serving the nobility. The Jewish and German entrepreneurs received their due. But the Ruthenian peasantry remained wretchedly poor and increasingly embittered. Their anger simmered slowly over the generations, but the Polish and even their own Ruthenian noblemen simply ignored them.[12]

There were three root causes of the tension that built up: the nationalist resentment of the Ruthenian natives against their foreign rulers, the Poles; the religious antagonism between the Roman Catholic Church of the Poles and the Orthodox Christianity of the locals; and the economic friction between poverty-stricken peasants and the landowners and their Jewish agents who managed their businesses and collected their debts. It all blew up in the middle of the seventeenth century, in the Cossack Uprising of 1648, under the leadership of the charismatic and forceful Ruthenian feudal landowner Bogdan Khmelnytsky, whose oratory powers enthused the masses.

This was a classic rebellion of serfs against their subjugators. The sworn aim of Khmelnytsky was to rid the land of its foreign occupiers and their cohorts. The leader of the uprising declared that the Poles had enslaved the Ruthenians and delivered them "into the hands of the accursed Jews." He recruited bands of Tatars from the Crimean Peninsula and Cossacks from the banks of the Dniester River, and together they set out to slaughter the Polish rulers.

At first, the Poles were pushed back, but they counterattacked and forced Khmelnytsky and his minions to retreat. He called for assistance from the Russian czar, and Russia invaded Poland in 1655, conquering Warsaw and Kraków. This war between Russia and Poland, and the Swedish invasion of Poland in 1656, known to the Poles as the *potop*, or "deluge," wrought great devastation and impoverished the Polish state.[13] When, however, Khmelnytsky's rebels retreated in the face of the powerful Polish armies, it turned out that most of their victims had been Jews. (The traditional Jewish narrative relates that three hundred Jewish communities were hit, including some in the Lvov area, and a hundred thousand Jews were murdered. The Ukrainian narrative says that fewer than fifty thousand were killed. Independent historians have concluded that there were somewhere between thirty and fifty thousand Jewish fatalities.)

Schodnica was on the sidelines during these events. According to family tradition, the Khmelnytsky depredations never really harmed the Backenroths. Perhaps even the opposite was true, because Drohobych's businessmen had taken advantage of the chaos and enlarged their trade activities. The city and its environs became a place of refuge for thousands of fleeing Lithuanians, as well as hundreds of families of various persecuted minorities in Lvov: Germans, Jews, Armenians, Hungarians, Greeks, and even some remnants of Kuzars. Indeed, the whole of Ukraine had been in a state of anarchy for ten years, and from May to November 1648, all work there had come to a standstill. Immediately after the city of Lvov was rescued from the rebels, however, a tense quiet reigned in Galicia, and life gradually returned to normal.[14]

The Jewish leaders in Poland took a lenient view of the massacres of Jews perpetrated by the Ruthenians. They believed that the rebellion's instigators had never intended to launch a campaign against the Jews in particular (the term anti-Semitism had not yet been coined) but had adopted a nationalist policy aimed at harming Poles and Germans. Therefore, even in the wake of the Khmelnytsky depredations, Jews continued to move to Ukraine from the west.[15]

These were the last waves of the great Jewish migration from Ashkenaz eastward. At that time, the west was already in the throes of economic upheavals brought about by the Industrial Revolution. In Western and Central Europe, factories were being established with production lines, and hundreds of thousands of poor peasants streamed into the big cities to become factory workers. Poland, however, with its millions of Jewish inhabitants, was left behind, beaten and bleeding, as its situation degenerated into a deep crisis. The decline lasted for roughly a hundred years. Governance collapsed, and anarchy reigned throughout the land. This ultimately led to Poland's territory being carved up among its neighbors three times, in the years 1772, 1793, and 1795. Each country took a voracious bite out of the areas of Poland that abutted its territory: Prussia helped itself in the west, Russia in the east, and what was left, including Galicia, was grabbed by Hapsburg Austria.

In the annals of the Backenroths, the economic crisis started during the lifetime of the great-grandfather of Shmuel Leib, in the middle of the seventeenth century. The crisis reached its height during the lifetime of Shmuel Leib and his wife, Silke ("Babe"), and their daughter, Tsiril, and son-in-law, Elimeilech, toward the middle of the eighteenth century. From this time onward, detailed records exist.

Tsiril was born around 1780. When she was fifteen, she married Elimeilech Epstein, nicknamed Meilech, a sixteen-year-old youth from a wealthy and pious family in Kraków. He was more observant than his father-in-law, Shmuel Leib. From the time that Elimeilech arrived in Schodnica, the only milk he allowed into his home was from the dairies of neighboring Drohobych because he knew that properly pious Jews lived there. Milk from the cows of Schodnica was not kosher by his standards. In Kraków, members of the Epstein family had their own synagogue. They were Hasidim, followers of the Admor (an acronym for the Hebrew words for "our master, teacher, and rabbi", which was a title bestowed on leading rabbis) of Chortkov. From the time that Elimeilech married a Backenroth, however, he adopted his father-in-law's family name and also the Backenroths' fidelity traditions and went to consult at the court of the rabbi of Zhidachov (whose life will be covered in the next chapter).

Four years after Elimeilech's marriage to Tsiril, when he was twenty, his father-in-law died and bequeathed him the public house. Times were hard. The economic crisis had become more severe, and the tavern hardly provided a living for the family. But a few years later, in the second decade of the nineteenth century, a miracle occurred.

3

The Miracle

THE HARSH WINTER OF 1817 left Elimeilech and Tsiril Backenroth in desperate straits, and they sought the advice of Rabbi Tzvi Hirsch Eichenstein for a way out of their despair. Elimeilech was thirty-eight, and Tsiril was a year younger. There was nothing remarkable in their requesting an audience with the rabbi of Zhidachov, for at one time or another each of his Hasidim had asked the rabbi for his advice and his blessing. Nevertheless, the outcome of their visit was highly unusual: in the rabbi's message was a revelation that would change the course of their lives in a truly miraculous fashion.

The men of the Backenroth family had joined the court of the Eichenstein rabbinical dynasty between 1795 and 1800, during the lifetime of the dynasty's founder. Rabbi Yitzchak Isaac Eichenstein (1740–1800) had established his court in the Hungarian village of Safrin, on the southern side of the Carpathian range.[1] Tsiril Backenroth's father, Shmuel Leib, traveled to Safrin twice a year, before "the Days of Awe"—the Jewish New Year and the Day of Atonement—and before Passover. For this three-day journey, Shmuel Leib hitched two horses to a wagon and crossed the mountains to arrive at the Hungarian village and the rabbi's court. He spent about two weeks there, rubbing elbows with the Hasidim, absorbing the interpretations of the Torah, and, on the Sabbath, joining the others in a meal consisting of remnants of the *challah* broken by the rabbi at his *tish*, or table.[2] After the festive season, Shmuel Leib again harnessed his horses to the wagon and returned home to Schodnica. In those days, Galicia was annexed to Austria, and thus there were no restrictions on travel between its territory and Hungary.

The founder of the Eichenstein dynasty died in 1800. Tzvi Hirsch was Rabbi Eichenstein's firstborn son.[3] He set up his own Hasidic court at Zhidachov, a small rural town south of Lvov.[4] Tsiril and Elimeilech now had no need to travel to Hungary for their audience with the Admor. Rabbi Tzvi Hirsch's court was a modest one, and he was neither a garrulous nor a gregarious man. He devoted most of his time to thinking and writing, and whenever he opened his mouth, he spoke laconically, telegraphically. A renowned kabbalist, he knew how to connect the material world with the divine, hidden world. Before being declared an Admor, he had studied with two of Poland's most prominent Hasidic leaders, Rabbi Elimeilech of (the Polish city of) Lizhensk and Rabbi Yaakov Yitzchak, known as the "seer" of Lublin. A prolific writer, Tzvi Hirsch became famous as a mystic and a miracle worker. Throughout the years, Hasidim flocked to his court to ask him questions and get his advice.

Why had Tsiril persuaded her husband to seek the rabbi's counsel? Well, why does any Jew go to his rabbi? Generally, when he has troubles: with making a living, with rebellious children, with a barren wife, and so on. And the Backenroths, like most of the Jews of Galicia, were beset with troubles.

Since the Khmelnytsky rebellion in 1648, the residents of Galicia had enjoyed very few years of peace and prosperity. War had followed war, and the territory had been divided up time after time. The Russian czar's army had invaded Poland, only to be followed by the Swedish army, and between the wars, several Ruthenian uprisings occurred. As for the Jewish residents, on more than twenty occasions between 1700 and 1760, Poles and Ruthenians had libeled them, saying that they had murdered Christian children and used the children's blood for their religious rituals.

Important figures in the Polish government hated the Jews.[5] In 1780, the chancellor, Andrzei Zamoyski, submitted bills in the Polish parliament, the Sejm, that would have changed civil rights laws in ways that would have segregated the Jews from other Poles and housed them in special ghettos, while unemployed Jews would be expelled from the country. Both proposals were rejected by the Sejm. Earlier, in 1764, the parliament had issued a decree abolishing the Council of the Four Lands that had been the central institution of Jewish self-government in Poland and Lithuania since 1580 and was the tangible expression of Jewish social and cultural autonomy.[6] For generations, the council had shaped the form of the community, known by the Hebrew term *kahal*, in each city as well as in the united and autonomous Jewish communal administration.[7]

The hopelessness that pervaded Jewish communities reached a peak following the Congress of Vienna, which assembled in 1814. The French Revolution (1789–1799) and the Napoleonic Wars (1803–1815) had obliterated many national boundaries in Europe, and the Vienna Congress was called by the major European powers to redraw the countries' demarcation lines. In the new map, independent Poland was entirely removed and its territory partitioned for the fourth time, among Russia, Prussia, and Austria.

At that time, Galicia was made part of the Austro-Hungarian Empire, and its inhabitants sensed that at last a new era of prosperity and well-being was about to dawn. Yet this hope was soon dashed because the crisis only deepened. Violent gangs of starving Ruthenian youths roamed the streets of Lvov, attacking citizens, then murdering and robbing them.

In Drohobych, Ruthenian children died of hunger and diarrhea, and children from impoverished Jewish families begged in the streets. A high proportion of the two hundred thousand Jews of Galicia were unemployed and became known as *luftmentschen*, or "air people," who lived from hand to mouth. Many suffered from exhaustion and disease; the average life expectancy was no more than forty years of age.

The Backenroth family somehow managed to keep the wolf from the door until 1816; the sales turnover from the tavern and the store gradually shrank, but the bank still functioned. Tsiril and Elimeilech lent money to the nobles of the district and to Polish officials living in Drohobych. As long as the debtors paid their loan installments and interest more or less on time, the family could make ends meet, but early in 1817, the monetary system collapsed.

The crisis spread, as people simply stopped paying their debts. It was a chain reaction. Prominent noblemen went bankrupt because of the high interest rates they had to pay on the funds they had borrowed to finance the wars. At the same time, the government had no money to pay the officials' salaries because most of the citizens of Galicia never paid taxes. Most important, the Ukrainian serfs were not earning enough to purchase seeds, so many of them ceased to work the land. Because the fields were not sown, crops never grew, and as there was no harvest, the entire land-leasing system, known in Polish as *arenda,* fell apart. This was the last straw. Elimeilech Backenroth had to admit that he would not be able to fulfill the quota that he had undertaken to pay the noble landowner from whom he had leased the fields.

Deprived of these revenues, the nobleman himself was now on the verge of bankruptcy. Who would have to pay the price? The middlemen, of course, Elimeilech and Tsiril, because the Ukrainian peasants were already barefoot and penniless. The Poles had borrowed and borrowed until they were unable to repay the loans, then had declared bankruptcy. The nobles' solution was to squeeze their tax collectors, the Jews.

The nobles held absolute power over the Jews, who called them by the pejorative Hebrew word for "powerful magnate," *paritz* (or *pooritz* in Yiddish). The Jews were so subservient to them that in 1740, a group of Polish noblemen tried to have a law enacted that would declare the Jews property that the noblemen could bequeath from father to son. The proposal was rejected, but nevertheless, in most cases the Jews were in fact considered no more than the private property of their *paritz*.

A shocking story about a member of the noble Radziwill family originated in Lithuania in the fourteenth century.[8] During a bout of drinking with his cronies, this nobleman told his Jewish land leaser to climb onto a fence on his estate and then shot him dead.[9] Another landowner, the Graf Basil Potocki, is said to have shot Jews and to have imprisoned another Jew in a pit after he was late with his payments. A legend that was handed down from generation to generation related, "[A]nd there he remained for many days and months until the birthday feast of the *paritz*. When the *paritz* was merry with wine he ordered that the Jew be brought before him and commanded him to dance dressed in a bearskin to the delight of the guests."[10]

The Backenroths' *paritz* was Count Lubomirski, the ruler of the district, the sheriff, and the judge, and his agent squeezed and threatened until, after he had completely emptied the Backenroth family coffers, he said that he would have Elimeilech arrested and thrown into the dungeon on the estate until the family could come up with the remainder.

Ostensibly, the profits from the public house should have been enough to rescue the family from catastrophe, for in times of economic crisis the numbers of the unemployed and the bankrupt multiply, and they tend to drink themselves into oblivion to forget their troubles. But in this case, the Ukrainian peasants took the initiative and manufactured alcoholic beverages, using home stills, from potatoes and barley that they had stored in their cellars. The Backenroths' tavern was deserted. For days on end, there were no customers, and the family's livelihood dwindled to nothing. All that remained of their assets was a plot of land, a defunct tavern, some stocks of goods in the store, a few furs, several pairs of shoes, and tools, which they tried to barter for food with the local peasantry.

Some of the Backenroths' Jewish neighbors chose to migrate westward. The rulers of the German principalities—Prussia, Brandenburg, and Pomerania—and of the free-trading city-states of Hamburg and Bremen had rediscovered the value of the Jews' entrepreneurial ability and had invited them to settle in German territories. The rulers granted the Jews commercial privileges but took care to keep out poor Jews. The Germans adopted a policy of keeping a very close eye on the movement of Jews and their employment, so those without capital or lacking in skills found it difficult to get permits for residence, for the acquisition of apartments, or for marriage. Many were thus forced to wander from community to community, giving birth to the legend of the "Wandering Jew."

The migration westward more typically consisted of Jews with some wealth, established merchants, and artisans who specialized in essential crafts.[11] The Backenroths, however, did not take part in these travels. The family did not even consider the option of moving back to Germany because the rabbis did not encourage their flocks to leave Poland. The Admor of Zhidachov, the Backenroths' spiritual leader, warned that families moving away would be cut off from their religion, and those whose faith dwindled would be liable to convert. It never crossed the mind of a Backenroth to do anything contrary to the rabbi's advice. The family was very observant and had been among the first to join the Hasidic courts when they were initially established, in the middle of the eighteenth century. At that time, enthusiasm over Hasidism had erupted like a volcano in Galicia. This mass support sprang from two sources, which were intimately connected by virtue of the circumstances: the severe economic and social crisis and the spread of belief in the kabbalah.

The esoteric teachings of the kabbalah developed within the Jewish faith at the beginning of the medieval era, but the Jewish masses in Poland became acquainted with it only in the early seventeenth century, as the distribution of printed books began to influence European life and society. The kabbalah reflected an attempt to define and describe the divine and to explain how it works and when it reveals itself to humankind. Rationality, as we know it today, is not a dominant element in the kabbalistic way of thinking. On the contrary, kabbalism is a mystical process whose essence lies in the effort to achieve unity between man and God.

The main stream of kabbalah flows from the work of Rabbi Yitzhak Luria, known as Ha'ari, or the Ari (the acronym made from the Hebrew Ashkenazi Rabbi Yitzhak), who lived in the sixteenth century in Cairo and later in the Galilee town of Safed, which has been home to kabbalists ever since. The Safed school of kabbalah is built around the concept of *tikun*, Hebrew for "repair," as the basis for the redemption of the world. According to Ha'ari, the messiah will come when the "repair of the world" is complete, both in the earthly sphere of man and in the heavenly world of God. And when Ha'ari declared, back in the sixteenth century, that the repair was almost complete and the messiah was to be expected forthwith, a great hope was aroused among the Jews of Eastern Europe that their salvation was just around the corner, that hardship and war would be a thing of the past, and that they would be elevated from degradation and poverty to ease and prosperity.

Before the seventeenth century, kabbalah was an esoteric theory, known only to a small minority of intellectuals, but when the grip of social crisis tightened, some religious leaders seized the opportunity to exploit the mystical doctrine in a populist manner for their own political advantage among the ignorant, impoverished, naive, and panic-prone Jewish masses.

According to the kabbalists' "calculations of the End," it was precisely the year of the Khmelnytsky uprising, 1648, that was destined to be the time of redemption for the People of Israel. In the *Book of the Zohar,* the kabbalist work composed in Spain probably in the thirteenth century, it is written that "in the sixth millennium in the time of four hundred and eight years [according to the Jewish calendar], all those who dwell in dust will arise, as it is written, 'And in this year of jubilee each man will return to his possession.'" The kabbalists interpreted this to mean that in 1648, the resurrection of the dead would happen, as predicted by the prophet Ezekiel in his Vision of the Dry Bones (Ezekiel, chapter 37).

Renowned rabbis, among them the greatest sages of Poland, as well as Christian scholars, repeated this prophecy from the Zohar and bolstered people's belief in it. Reality, however, confounded their calculations. The year 1648 turned out to be not the year of redemption but a year of disaster, in the wake of which the Jews of Poland faced a century and a half of severe tribulations. Nevertheless, the greater the hardships and the catastrophes that befell the Jews, the more they tended to seek salvation in mysticism.[12]

So severe were their troubles, with so many Jews being massacred, maimed, and taken hostage by Khmelnytsky's Cossacks, and so oppressive was the poverty that the cords that bound the Jewish community in Poland came undone. For the first time since the Jews had arrived in Poland, divisions appeared in their sense of unity. The internal social tension arose, first and foremost, because of the widening gap between rich and poor. Many Jews were newly impoverished. Their lives were unbearable, and the traditional leaders had no real solutions to offer. Numerous individual members of the community had lost faith in the rabbis and the synagogue leaders. Replacing them as voices of authority were populist leaders promoting revolutionary ideas. Some of these men were kabbalists who evoked extreme emotions among the Jews. The destitute masses were looking for a quick remedy for their troubles, and these new leaders offered them an instant messiah who would bring redemption to the Jews, carry them to the land of Israel, and solve all of their problems in one fell swoop.

The most prominent among the false messiahs was Shabbetai Tzevi, who aroused unprecedented fervor among the masses in Galicia, as well as in the entire Jewish world.[13] He was a self-proclaimed messiah and the founder of the Dönmeh sect (also known as the Shabbatean movement), which tied together components from Judaism, Christianity, and Islam and gathered hundreds of thousands of followers in the Middle East and Europe. Never before had a messianic movement arisen in Jewry that attracted the masses as powerfully as the Shabbatean movement did. Shabbetai Tzvi named the year 1666 as the millennium and built up enormous expectations in his followers.[14] When the day appeared and nothing happened, he was put in prison in Constantinople by the Turkish sultan Mehmed IV. To escape death, Shabbetai Tzevi embraced Islam, which devastated his followers and created a substantial crisis of faith among Jews.

Notwithstanding the disillusionment of Shabbetai Tzvi's followers, even after they dwindled, many kabbalist circles remained active in Poland. Some of the members were simply weird, others were ascetics and hermits, while some became famous preachers, teachers, or scholars. They continued to wait impatiently for redemption and took steps to hasten its coming. They spent their time in ascetic practices and praying in strange new ways. Sometimes they used loud voices, shouting, singing, and dancing with total devotion, moving their bodies in ecstasy, and exerting themselves to the utmost in their efforts to make contact with the heavens. Other times, their prayers were whispers, as Ha'ari of Safed had taught, and they mortified their flesh in punishment and purification, rolled naked in the freezing snow, performed calculations and numerological exercises, and conversed with animals and plants.

Certain eccentric, kabbalistic characters had enough power to influence the masses. One of them, Rabbi Yehuda Hassid of Shedlitz—a charismatic preacher and orator—went from community to community in Poland and Germany, persuading the congregations to believe in the coming redemption, to purify themselves, and to leave for the land of Israel. Some seventeen hundred Jews gathered around him, swathed themselves in white shrouds, and set off on their journey. Misfortunes and difficulties beset these pilgrims, and about five hundred died on the way before the survivors passed through the gates of Jerusalem in autumn 1700. They were exhausted and broken. One of them, the kabbalist rabbi Nathan Mannheim, described their entry into the Holy City in scriptural terms: "And all the people were in awe, and the old men rejoiced and trembled."

Two hundred years later, a member of the Backenroth clan, Moshe Heller (nicknamed Moye), at age fourteen, gathered hundreds of Jews and led them on a similar journey from Galicia to Jerusalem. That remarkable story will be told later in this book.

There is no doubt that Hasidism was the most important new sect to arise in Judaism's history before the nineteenth century. It became a way of life for the majority of Jews in Eastern Europe and changed the way that millions worshipped and believed.[15] It even dramatically transformed the appearance of many Jewish men in Eastern European *shtetls*: Hasidic men ceased to cut their sideburns (called *payoth*), shaved off all the hair on top of their heads, and wore a kind of uniform. It consisted of an oriental-type black caftan that covered the entire body, knee breeches, a white shirt, a sash, white socks, and a black fedora hat.

The sect's founder was Rabbi Israel ben Eliezar, known as the Baal Shem Tov (Master of the Good Name), whose life story is like a fairy tale. He became famous as a miracle worker and developed a revolutionary doctrine for life, which attracted the masses of uneducated Jews in the villages and the townships of Eastern Europe and slum dwellers who envied wealthy, educated urban Jews. A prominent Hasidic story teller, Yudel Rosenberg, related how these crude and uncultured Jews were viewed:

> All the town-dwellers were total ignoramuses. Their Judaism was very debased. They knew naught of laving hands before the meal. They had

> no ritual baths. The *shofar*—a Ram's horn that is used in prayers at the high holidays of Yom Kippur and Rosh Hashanah, the Jewish New Year—was so terrible a thing to them that they feared to gaze on it and it was their belief that he who blew it would die that same year.

The revolution manifested itself in the very fact that the Baal Shem Tov addressed the *luftmentschen,* the uneducated, destitute "air people." A Jew is entitled to worship God even if he lacks knowledge of the Torah, Baal Shem Tov told them, because the most important part of faith is in the heart, in goodwill, and in yearning for the Creator, not necessarily in study of the Torah and the Talmud. There is no need for you to delve into the texts and to learn them, he said. It is enough if you show God your joy, enthusiasm, and love. There is a whole world within the soul of every Jew, and it is not learning but doing that is most important. Joy at being alive is essential because despair prevents people from reaching spiritual ecstasy. It is fitting to merge with nature, not only to appreciate divine creation, but also to elevate the spirit.

The world outlook of Hasidism placed the individual, not the Torah, at its center. The two main properties required of the Hasid did not depend on study and education but on personal behavior: spiritual purification, reached through inner devotion and faith, and physical purification, through immersion in a Jewish ritual bathing pool, a *mikveh.*

Hasidism elevated the status of the *tzaddik,* the righteous man who had reached such a level of spiritual and physical purity that the Holy Spirit dwelled within him. The tzaddik could establish direct contact with the divinity and understand the messages it wanted to convey to mortals. "Tzaddikim deliver supplications to God, and He immediately fulfills them," The Baal Shem Tov's followers quoted him as saying. The following observation is attributed to Rabbi Elimelech of Lizhensk: "The Holy One, Blessed be He, decrees, and the tzaddik annuls; the Holy One, Blessed be He, annuls, and the tzaddik decrees and fulfills." The poor were indeed enthusiastic because the Baal Shem Tov enabled them to straighten their backs in pride, to rise above the dismal gloom of their lives, and to feel themselves the equals of middle-class urban Jews who sent their sons to study at yeshivas.

With the passage of time, a large popular movement evolved from the naive faith. Inevitably, at the same time, a movement of its opponents, Mitnagdim in Hebrew, developed, which was centered in Lithuania.

The Mitnagdim saw in Hasidism a dangerous trend that belittled the importance of studying the Torah and was liable to produce and encourage false messiahs, such as Shabbetai Tzevi. At the head of the Mitnagdim stood Rabbi Elijah ben Solomon Zalman, known as the Genius from Vilnius (in Hebrew, HaGaon m'Vilna), who condemned the ideas of the Baal Shem Tov, disparaged the new customs adopted by his followers, and insisted on the supremacy of Torah study.

The struggle between the Hasidim and the Mitnagdim was replete with antagonism, both verbal and physical. The Mitnagdim published vicious leaflets against the Hasidim, imposed bans on them, and closed their synagogues to them. Hasidim were detained by order of the heads of the communities, which in most cases were controlled by the conservatives. In Vilna in 1772, the *kahal* sentenced two Hasidim to be whipped.

Inside the Backenroth family, Hasidism generally ruled. The elders of the family joined the movement. In later generations, however, when the tension between the two sects lessened, the family allowed its daughters to marry into Mitnagdim families.

The founder of Hasidism, the Baal Shem Tov, had many followers, the first of whom was Rabbi Dov Ber, the Maggid (preacher) of Mezeritch. He had studied in Lvov and was considered a genius, and he broadened the Hasidic movement to many communities in Eastern Europe. His most famous pupil was Rabbi Elimelech of Lizhensk, who spread Hasidism throughout Galicia and who was the teacher of Rabbi Yitzchak Isaac Eichenstein, Shmuel Leib Backenroth's rabbi and the father of the Admor of Zhidachov, the esteemed rabbi Tzvi Hirsch of Zhidachov, to whom Tsiril and Elimeilech went for guidance.

When a Hasid wanted to see his rabbi, he did not make an appointment because the rabbi had no set timetable. Instead, the Hasid whispered in the ear of the synagogue's *gabbai*, or sexton, or handed him a note and then waited patiently. Sometimes the rabbi summoned him on the same day. Sometimes two weeks went by before the rabbi deigned to grant the man an audience. And there were also rare cases when the *gabbai* came back to the Hasid and told him quietly, "The rabbi doesn't want to see you. Come back in half a year. He may agree to see you before Passover."

The court of Tzvi Hirsch was modest in the extreme, and his personal chamber starkly austere: it contained a bed, a table, and two chairs. His world outlook was strictly kabbalistic—that is, mystical and based on the teachings of Rabbi Yitzhak Luria, the Ari of Safed, the greatest of the kabbalists. Tzvi Hirsch kept strange hours and had no regular daily schedule. He spent most of his time teaching and studying, slept little, and ate frugally. The pleasures of the world were foreign to him. He was an ascetic who lived by the power of his faith, and all of his being was devoted to one thing: solving the problems of his followers, by contacting supernatural forces and working miracles on their behalf. His servants were the *gabbais,* the officials of his court, who provided for his meager needs. His followers, the Hasidim, financed the court with their donations. Sometimes he woke up in the middle of the night and sat down to write. At other times, before daybreak, he summoned his Hasidim for a talk. His audience with Elimeilech and Tsiril also took place at dawn, as the sun was rising.

It started with a long silence. The elderly rabbi stood there in silence, brooding. His face was pale, his lips mumbled a prayer. Elimeilech sat on the guest's chair and Tsiril on the edge of the bed. Elimeilech looked around in wonder, amazed by the frugality. The little room was dark. The floor was bare. On the simple table was a jumble of books, some of them open, others with slips of paper inside them, and an inkwell with a quill inside it. The rabbi was short, his face wrinkled with age. On his head was a large black yarmulke. He was wrapped in a white *kittel,* the cloth coat worn by Orthodox Jews.

Until the rabbi opened his mouth, the couple was silent, and only after he mumbled, "*Nu . . . nu,*" Well . . . well, as if to ask, "Why are you here?" did Elimeilech dare to speak up and relate his troubles. As he talked, the rabbi took his seat, with his head bowed and his body bent forward. His fingers twisted his beard impatiently.

Elimeilech delivered his prepared, organized, and reasoned speech, and the rabbi nodded in silence. He was used to hearing such accounts of his followers' travails from their ordeals. They all had cruel extortionate feudal lords, large families to support, and dwindling incomes. When Elimeilech had finished, Tsiril sighed and spoke briefly about their son, Shmuel Leib. He was sixteen years old and was very talented, but the family lacked the means to send him to study at a yeshiva in Kraków.

On hearing Tsiril, the rabbi raised his head and mumbled a few words, not at all clearly, and then ponderously removed his hands from his beard, stretched his arms downward to their full length, and pointed his thumbs at the floor. Elimeilech looked on intensely and wrinkled his brow in wonder.

"What does the rabbi mean?" he asked out loud and glanced at his wife. The rabbi went on pointing at the floor and said nothing.

"To plant?" asked Elimeilech. "To sow crops?"

The rabbi said nothing.

"Must we dig for water?" asked Tsiril. "Sink a well on our land?"

Still the rabbi kept silent, his arms stretched downward, his thumbs pointing at the floor. Elimeilech and Tsiril were mystified, but the rabbi still didn't speak. When his lips moved without making a sound, Elimeilech put his head close to the rabbi's mouth but couldn't grasp what the rabbi was trying to tell him.

Then suddenly the rabbi bellowed, "You shall have a livelihood, the Backenroths shall have a livelihood, a livelihood there will be! You shall have wealth, immense wealth!" Thus shouted Rabbi Tzvi Hirsch of Zhidachov, his arms still stretched and his thumbs pointing downward.

Elimeilech sighed. He drew close to the rabbi, took his hand, and kissed it. Tsiril rose and bowed in gratitude. Elimeilech, exhilarated, blessed the rabbi hurriedly: "May you live to one hundred twenty years, one hundred twenty years of bliss, good years may you have, and thank you for the blessing, thank you, rabbi."

But the rabbi rose from his seat and impatiently shooed Elimeilech away with both hands, as if he were chasing away a fly. He said only, "Enough, enough, go now."

All of a sudden, the door opened, and the *gabbai* motioned them out.

Was there a note of anger or irritation in the way that the rabbi took leave of the couple? It's hard to tell. Tzvi Hirsch used to preach frugality to his followers. Even on weekdays, not only on the holy Sabbath, he strictly forbade members of the congregation to enter the synagogue with money in their pockets. Your wealth is not in material things, but in the spirit, he taught them. This was how he conducted his own life, making do with the minimum and avoiding material wealth. A parsimonious life, in his opinion, was nothing to be ashamed of, but rather something to aspire to. And now he, the penurious tzaddik, was blessing the Backenroths with the very material wealth that he rejected and despised. Surely, he would have preferred to bless them with spiritual riches, rather than gold and silver.

Either way, Elimeilech and Tsiril left the rabbi, stunned. Until that day, Elimeilech had adhered to his strict orthodoxy, but when it came to choosing between the two major camps in Judaism at that time, Hasidism and those opposed to that new mystical trend—the rational Mitnagdim, who stressed learning—Elimeilech had stayed on the fence since leaving his parents' home in Kraków and coming to Schodnica at age fifteen. His wife, on the other hand, had been brought up by a Hasidic father. She believed in the tzaddik of Zhidachov and had talked her husband into consulting with him.

Now, Elimeilech felt his hands trembling. The very presence of Rabbi Tzvi Hirsch had filled him with excitement, and the signs that the rabbi had made with his arms had utterly perplexed Elimeilech. What had the miracle maker meant? he asked Tsiril over and over. What did the arms stretched downward mean? Why had he pointed at the floor with his thumbs?

4

Oil Fever

WHEN TSIRIL AND ELIMEILECH BACKENROTH returned to Schodnica, they were convinced that Rabbi Tzvi Hirsch had advised them to give up commerce and begin farming. Elimeilech called three of his sons, Shmuel Leib, Zvi Hersh, and Itzig, handed them picks and shovels, and went out with them to dig a water well on their land.[1] After two days of digging, a dark, thick, malodorous liquid oozed into the pit they had excavated. The boys screwed up their faces in disgust. Elimeilech filled a small earthenware flask with the yellowish-black substance and dispatched it to Vienna for analysis. A month later, his courier returned with the results: the substance was a mixture of paraffin and asphalt, a mineral wax called in Latin *ozokerite* or *ozocerite* and known in Yiddish as *kefitzke,* or "boiling," because of its high boiling point.[2]

Elimeilech and Tsiril didn't know whether to rejoice or weep. They undoubtedly would have been happier if the well had produced water, for in those days paraffin was of little value. It served as a lubricant (or *shmeer*, in Yiddish) for wagon wheels.[3] In a few places near Drohobych and Schodnica, ozokerite (in local lingo it was sometimes called *ropa*), which was the most basic and crudest thick oil, seeped from the Carpathian Mountains' rocks. Often, it was stuck to the rocks. Ozokerite was gathered in small pits and could be dipped out by hand. Scavengers and idlers, both Jews and Ruthenians, called *lepak* in Polish and *lepakys* in Yiddish, collected the ozokerite in buckets from these small pools and sold it for pennies on market day in Drohobych.

Backenroth Ancestors

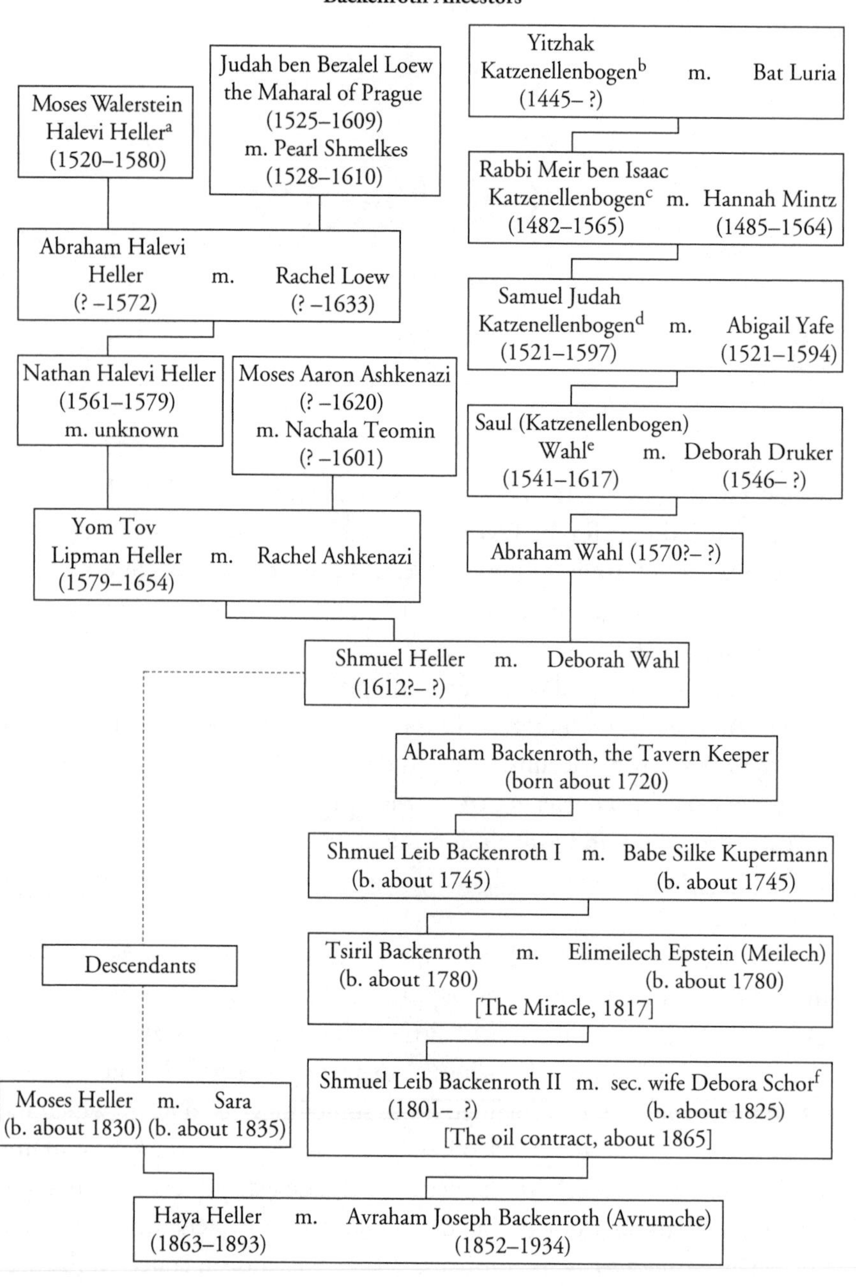

[a]The chief rabbi of Germany.

[b]The Katzenellenbogen family line leads back directly to Rashi (1040–1105) and Rabbenu Tam (1096–1171) and to the Kalonymus family (which had settled in Lucca, Italy, in the second half of the eighth century and, around 920, spread to Mainz and Speyer in Ashkenaz). This line is considered one of the most aristocratic in Jewish chronicles.

[c]Known as MaHaRam Padua, he was the chief rabbi of Padua and Venice and a well-known *halakha* authority.

[d]The rabbi of Venice, who was distinguished for his scholarship.

[e]According to a common legend, he was elected by the Polish Diet (parliament) to hold the throne of Poland for a single night, August 18, 1578, and therefore is known in Jewish history by his nickname "king for a night." *Wahl* means "elected" in German. The story goes that in 1586, when King Bathori died, the Polish aristocracy was divided into factions, and the contending parties in the Diet could not agree on anyone until Prince Nicholas Radziwill made a proposal to honor one of his closest advisers, Saul Katzenellenbogen, with a temporary title of king. Indeed, he was elected to be king for one night. Another legend says that many years earlier, in Padua, Italy, Prince Radziwill found himself in trouble, and Saul's father, Samuel Judah Katzenellenbogen, borrowed for him a substantial amount of money and saved him from harm.

[f]The Schors (also spelled Schorr, Szor, Szorer, and Szoor) are descendants of Joseph ben-Isaac Bechor-Shor, a twelfth-century scholar of Orléans, France.

Although family tradition relates that Elimeilech Backenroth was the first to sink an oil well in Galicia, it is doubtful. There was no gusher of oil on Elimeilech's land, just a puddle of paraffin at the bottom of a pit. All indications are that another Jew, whose name is unknown, was the first to strike oil one year earlier, in 1816, in the neighboring village of Boryslav.

Almost two years after the visit to the Rabbi of Zhidachov, the Backenroths closed their tavern and established in that location a modest family factory to manufacture paraffin and a small store next to it. Elimeilech sold wooden barrels full of paraffin to the Ukrainian peasants, who used it to grease their wagon wheels, and to the urban Poles he sold paraffin jelly, which is similar to modern-day petroleum ointment, for the treatment of abrasions and other skin ailments.

When Elimeilech died (in 1840?), he bequeathed to his oldest son, Shmuel Leib, a small family industry, with a limited sales turnover, enough for the household needs and a little extra to go toward savings. Shmuel Leib hired a chemist to teach him how to refine the murky paraffin and produce kerosene, which could be used for both lighting and heat.[4] In those days, the technology required to distill gasoline or diesel fuel hadn't been invented yet, but people knew how to separate kerosene from paraffin. Shmuel Leib sold the kerosene to farmers as fuel for the oil lamps they used to light their houses. At first, the income was hardly adequate, but the family had great hopes. The first signs of an economic miracle were becoming evident.

Today we're aware that places where precious resources are discovered—gold, diamonds, oil, uranium—undergo a rapid transformation, but Shmuel Leib, despite his great faith in the validity of Rabbi Tzvi Hirsch's blessing, could not imagine that his family would be thrust into a new reality. The last valuable discovery in the Drohobych district had been salt, but the excitement over that had long been forgotten, and the commodity's value had declined as well, since methods of extracting salt from seawater had been developed.

All that the Backenroths knew about the slimy liquid discovered on their land was that it smelled bad and had limited uses. Even though cloth wicks for lighting lamps had been invented by the end of the eighteenth century, people did not begin to use kerosene commercially for light until the middle of the nineteenth century.[5] Most important, the internal combustion gasoline engine was still a far-off dream. The futurologists of the era, among them Jules Verne, could have predicted where all of this was leading, but

The Galician Oil Belt.

an ordinary citizen like Shmuel Leib, up to his neck in day-to-day work, was not blessed with prophetic vision. In addition, from 1830 to 1860, as Europe enjoyed the beginning of a new era of advancement and modernization, the remote region in Galicia, in which oil was discovered, was undergoing a period of confusion and chaos.

Nevertheless, the Backenroths didn't miss the chance to bring their share of the opportunity to fruition. Of course, the rabbi of Zhidachov's blessing had spiritually led them to their destined treasure, yet for the ultimate magnitude of that bounty, they would always credit Shmuel Leib's second wife.

Shmuel Leib married twice. His first wife, Esther (there is no record of her family name), died young. His second wife was Debora Schor, who was known in the family as a powerful woman and to whose name in the future there would always be added the epithet "the wise." She was blessed with a sharp mind and was the first one to accurately assess the potential of the oil rush. It was thanks to her that the Backenroths' small kerosene business blossomed into an economic empire.

The strip of land in Galicia where oil was found measured only about ten miles long by six miles wide, but the social changes that resulted from this discovery were enormous. Black gold flowed out from family plots of land, and the wealth that it produced completely transformed the lives of people in this region. Europe had never experienced such an upheaval, as this backward provincial district moved suddenly into the center of the contemporary economic stage. Would rural, God-fearing folks who had only a basic education and restricted knowledge of the world, folks who were thrown off balance by every slight innovation, be able to cope with such an extreme change, one not of their own design? Could their society survive a revolution that would rock their staid way of life, which had taken generations to develop? Lacking the necessary professional knowledge, what chance did they have of planning their moves in a logical and orderly way, evaluating the risks and the prospects, in order to take advantage of the opportunity that had befallen them?

Within the next half-century, tens of thousands of families living in this oil belt, among them the Backenroths, would be at the forefront of a global energy revolution. The world's technological progress and ability to transport people and goods would depend on the amount of oil the Galicians could extract from their lands.

The remote neighboring village of Boryslav was the hub of the activity. Most of the future high-producing wells were dug in and around that community. Like Boryslav, nearby Schodnica was also thoroughly dotted with wells, but unlike that village, Schodnica's residents managed to preserve their town's bucolic character. To the north, the district capital of Drohobych served as the administrative center that provided the landowners and the entrepreneurs with the political, legal, and banking services they required.[6]

None of the developments were anticipated or planned. The greater the pace of change, the more the community leaders lost control over the direction that events would take. Exposure to the world was harsh. It was as if, all of a sudden, thousands of spotlights were turned upon a tiny island. With the light came a swarm of motley characters, like moths to a flame: entrepreneurs seeking to promote deals even before they had permits; profit-hungry real estate middlemen; smartly turned-out lawyers attempting to give the bizarre reality a respectable image; chemists and engineers who spoke in technical jargon; crowds of brawny young laborers, gleeful at this opportunity that had turned up during their wandering search for work; and, of course, prostitutes and their pimps, journalists documenting the new scene, politicians calculating what advantages they could glean from it, and thousands of curious sightseers who stood around holding their noses and watching as the murky liquid was pumped up out of the earth.

The new era began with a brutal assault of oil prospectors, entrepreneurs, and contractors on the land. They dug thousands of wells, pits, and shafts that changed a tranquil, pleasant landscape into a maze of dirty ditches and trenches. The environmental damage was irreparable. Then hundreds of thousands of workers flowed into the region from every direction, and long rows of ugly wooden huts were constructed to house them. A workers' political party arose, the likes of which Galicia had never known (because the Industrial Revolution had passed it by, and there were no local factories that employed masses of workers). The party was compartmentalized into various ideological cells, each with its sharp-tongued orators, radical handwritten newspapers, and political polarization. During the first decade or so, imperial officials in Vienna ignored the challenges and the difficulties that the outlying province faced. The capital's politicians and bureaucrats woke up to the new reality only when they discovered that vast oil revenues had begun to flow into the entrepreneurs' purses, while the empire had no stake in the new wealth.

All of these issues were addressed at length in the newspapers of the period, but most important matters were decided behind the scenes, away from the scrutiny of the press. Local politics was a lively scene, and interested parties, often bitter rivals, formed secret coalitions. In makeshift temporary laboratories that were set up in Lvov, chemists studied samples of the substances taken from the earth and invented groundbreaking formulas and technologies. In the main street of Drohobych, in offices whose rents kept soaring, engineers tested different types of blocks, pulleys, and cranes and built models of drilling towers. In nearby premises, lawyers framed contracts. And in the congested shacks of the workers' quarters that surrounded Boryslav on all sides, labor union officials formulated pamphlets condemning the employers as exploiters.

The more oil production expanded, the more the gap widened between rich and poor. At the same time, charlatans and gamblers of every type converged on the Galicia Oil Belt. And then angry voices were heard—voices of those to whom the oil rush was not a blessing but a curse. First and foremost were farmers whose agricultural land had been requisitioned from them and leased to oil entrepreneurs. Equally embittered were the families who owned land where no oil was found or those who had not grown rich from the boom. Religious leaders—Orthodox and Catholic, Christians and Jews—complained in their sermons about the loss of morality and modesty.

As is often the case, some people accurately predicted where this rapid "progress" was leading, and others got it all wrong. There were those who had no qualms about dipping their hands into the inky black liquid, and those who recoiled from it. Not a few families missed the opportunities that had opened up before them, for various reasons: ignorance, laziness, fear of the risks, incorrect calculations, and, of course, family squabbles and disputes with neighbors. Many families from among the Ruthenian population not only failed to make any money but lost everything they possessed, including their land. They lacked the resourcefulness to take advantage of the treasure bubbling up from the ground, and there was no one to help them.

The first people to grasp the true significance of the discovery of oil were certain families of the Polish nobility, who were excellently positioned to exploit the economic boom, and Jewish families, who were skilled at entrepreneurship. A few foreigners became involved early on, including some Germans and at least one Paris-based French investment company, but, not being familiar with Galicia's chaotic ways, they found it difficult to conduct business and achieve financial success. Several Hungarian investors joined forces with Jewish or Polish families and made fortunes. The locals, the Ruthenians, were generally left on the sidelines of the economic miracle, and they blamed everyone else for their plight.[7]

For the Jewish communal leadership, the main issue had nothing to do with the commercial or professional aspects of the boom, even though the political and economic upheaval happened so suddenly that they had only a brief period to adjust. What worried Jewish leaders most was whether the younger generation would be tempted to assimilate into Christian society after being exposed to the extravagant lifestyles of the newly wealthy; engaging in partnerships with Poles, Hungarians, and Germans; studying secular sciences; and taking on modern professions. Would young Jews manage, the rabbis agonized, to block the assault of modernity and stay within the bosom of tradition?

From the very beginning, greed and the desire for power motivated many founders of the oil industry. This lust for power by the nouveaux riches sharply collided with the community and family values that Jewish spiritual leaders and educators in Galicia had tried to inspire over the generations. Yet Jewish leaders were determined to meet the challenge, and among the richest strata of the community, only a few individuals ignored moral principles and professional ethics.

Years later, Galicia's inhabitants realized that they were not alone in dealing with an oil rush. During that same period, in the middle of the nineteenth century, the petroleum industry was developing rapidly in several locations: Pennsylvania in the United States, Romania, and Russia.[8]

The world's first oil company, Pennsylvania Rock Oil, was founded in 1854 by a New York lawyer named George Bissel. The process of drilling oil wells had not yet been invented, and Bissel's oil came out of the ground on its own (and in some places was extracted from bitumen). This is exactly what happened on the Backenroths' plot of land in Schodnica in Galicia and on neighboring plots. It was enough to dig a shallow pit in the ground for the crude oil to well up.

Almost at the same time, at a coal mine in Derbyshire, Scotland, the black oily liquid that seeped out of the rocks aroused the curiosity of a chemist named James Young. He had managed to distill the liquid and patented his invention as kerosene for lighting. This is exactly what happened in Galicia as well. According to the Austrian Empire's official chronicles, in July 1853, a Lvov pharmacist, Ignacy Lukasiewicz (1822–1882), invented the kerosene distillation process and for the first time derived commercial profit from the modern kerosene lamp. Lukasiewicz was asked by surgeons of a local hospital to provide light for an emergency surgery. After Lukasiewicz successfully lit the operation, he registered his distillation process with the Viennese government on December 31, 1853.

The first actual drilling for oil was carried out near Titusville in northwestern Pennsylvania in August 1859, by Edwin Laurentine Drake. Less than three years later, the first drilling machine was brought to Boryslav. It took quite a long time for Galician entrepreneurs to fit the new machine to the local land conditions and to pinpoint an area that produced oil. Then, in the spring of 1862, when the new drilling machine had reached a depth of only sixty-six feet, a mighty stream of oil spurted skyward. The gusher was so astounding that news spread quickly and thousands of curious individuals poured into the town from all over Galicia. They stood around the well for hours and watched the liquid as it spurted out of the ground and sprayed black rain all around. Many people came close and touched the oil with their fingers or even tasted it.

At the time, few people knew how to cap a gusher, and no one knew the exact chemical composition of the oil and all of its many applications. Nevertheless, oil fever struck Galicia. Landowners in the entire district, from Boryslav to Stanislav (which the Ukrainian government renamed Ivano-Frankivs'k), hired laborers to dig pits on their property, and they danced for joy whenever pools of oil appeared. Everyone sensed the tremendous economic potential that lay in their future. The people of Drohobych said that never in recorded history had there been such exciting times as during those spring days in 1862, when upstanding citizens were drunk at noon and covered in oil as they pranced around crazily in the black mud. This was also the first time in Galician history that people stopped dwelling on the rivalry between Poles and Ukrainians and took a rest from complaining about "the Jewish problem." In view of the great abundance all around them, Galicians managed to find it within themselves to love their neighbors. The mood was jolly, and people laughed with pleasure. Politicians and public figures promised them prosperity and power. Entrepreneurs' fantasies soared to the sky.

There was no need to dig deep to hit oil. Thirty to sixty feet was enough, sometimes even less. Often, a narrow shaft was dug and a bucket lowered down on a rope. When it was pulled up, it was generally full of paraffin, asphalt, thick crude oil, or a mixture of all three, covered by a thin layer of water. And when the water was removed with a tin cup and the sediment of earth that had sunk to the bottom was cleared away, heavy oil remained. Some landowners planned to go into independent oil production on their own. Others, who chose to lease their oil-bearing land, divided their plots into narrow strips and rented them out. Sometimes one plot was divided between four or five oil producers. The landowners obligated the lessees to pay a basic sum for the oil production rights, on top of which landowners would collect between a quarter and a third of the revenues from the sales. It was necessary to delineate the limits of the strips of land with agreed-on borders, and in order to calculate the revenues, the oil producers had to keep books. Many disputes broke out over both of these matters. Lawyers and legal advisers were in great demand. The official legal bureau in Drohobych expanded—by the end of the nineteenth century, it was the largest legal bureau in the entire Austro-Hungarian Empire—as did the district court.[9]

In the 1850s and the early 1860s, the imperial administration in Vienna was openly disdainful toward the oil fever that had infected Galicia. "A provincial fuss over nothing," wrote a senior Ministry of Mines official in a report, adding that "[t]he naptha discovered in Galicia has no use. Instead of developing oil fields, it is worthwhile to develop energy from peat and coal."[10]

Only in 1863 did a special committee of geologists, engineers, and chemists travel to Galicia to look into the situation on the emperor's behalf. In Lvov, two local experts were co-opted to join the committee, an engineer named Leon Syroczynski and a geologist, Dr. Rudolf Zuber, of Lvov University, who spoke fluent German and who in coming years would publish geological surveys and maps of the Galician oil fields. The committee did a thorough job. For several weeks, the members toured the area, checked the excavations and the wells, measured and sketched, conferred with landowners, extracted samples, consulted experts, and ultimately presented the Austrian government with a scholarly report that caused great excitement in Galicia. The committee had determined that the oil fields in the saline Miocene soil of Galicia's narrow strip of land, starting at Drohobych and accumulating primarily within the main reservoir under Boryslav and Schodnica, were far larger than had been previously thought and that they would produce oil for hundreds of years.[11]

The hysteria spread, and a cry of joy went up from the populace that could be heard in Lvov. "A new epoch has begun," people said to one another, and they were right. The publication of the report prompted a new flow of speculators to the area, and whenever oil gushed out of some well, by the next day the price of the surrounding land reached new peaks. In the Backenroth family, there was no doubt that with God's grace, the rabbi of Zhidachov had proved to be a miracle worker.

A few months later, agents working on behalf of the imperial government began to negotiate with owners of the land where oil had been discovered. They offered to pay fifty thousand golden coins, approximately $1 million in today's currency for each oil well. Some of the well owners immediately agreed and sold the land and the wells to the government, but the Backenroths never did because a sharp dispute broke out within the family. Shmuel Leib's position was: "Let's sell now! Fifty thousand gold coins will set us up for life, and I, Shmuel Leib, can't fight the kaiser." But his second wife, Debora Schor, was dead set against him. "What's good for the kaiser is good for me, too," she told her husband, and she proposed a partnership: the Backenroths would give the government 50 percent of the oil produced on their land if the government would cover the costs of infrastructure and development.

The negotiations went on for two months, and finally a contract was signed. The land, the well that had been sunk there, and the oil it produced would remain the property of the Backenroth family. The government would erect the required infrastructure: that is, would pave roads and lay pipelines. The profits from the oil produced by the well would be divided equally between the family and the government.

Debora Schor had triumphed, as usual. Shmuel Leib gave in. That's the way it was with the Backenroths; the women always displayed acumen in business. Most important, the plot of land containing the oil wells remained the family's exclusive property.

The day that the contract with the government was signed (in 1868, according to the family), was the thirteenth birthday of Debora and Shmuel Leib's son Avraham Yosef, nicknamed Avrumche. His parents' quarreling over the deal left its mark on his memory. Thirty years later, toward the end of the nineteenth century, when Avrumche headed the Backenroth Brothers oil consortium, he would recall his mother's amazing astuteness and be grateful for it.

5

Backenroth the Hasid

DEBORA SCHOR PICKED AN EXCELLENT MATCH for Avrumche, her oldest son: Haya Heller, the great-granddaughter of Rabbi Yom Tov Lipman Heller, who was known by the nickname Rital, an acronym of his name.[1] He had attained renown among the Jews of Europe in the first half of the seventeenth century for two reasons: his arrest and imprisonment and the outstanding commentary that he authored on the Mishna, the authoritative Jewish oral law.

The course of Rital's life brought him to the most important junctions in the history of the Jews in Ashkenaz, Bohemia, and Poland in the seventeenth century. In his childhood, Rital was recognized as a prodigy, and when he was seventeen, a wealthy Jewish merchant, Moses Aaron Ashkenazi, invited him to study in Prague, granted him an allowance, and gave him his daughter Rachel as a wife. (After Rachel passed away, Rital married Nechle Teomin.)

Rital's mentor in Prague was Rabbi Yehuda Loew, who was considered the wisest sage of his generation. He became famous as the Maharal of Prague.[2] His name was linked to the legend of the Golem of Prague.[3] Studying with Rital in Prague were students who later filled the highest spiritual roles in the Jewish communal establishment in Europe at the end of the Middle Ages and the beginning of the Renaissance (among them David Ganz, Eliyahu Luanz, and Shlomo Efraim of Lunshitz).[4]

This group of Jewish intellectuals had gathered in Prague during the second half of the sixteenth century and the beginning of the seventeenth century because the capital of Bohemia willingly took in many of the outcasts of Europe, including "unbelievers," as the Jews were considered to be. Prague also welcomed heretics or innovators who dared to disagree with church teachings, especially people whom the tolerant and learned Emperor Rudolf II von Hapsburg considered worthy of his protection.[5] Rudolf invited intellectuals, astronomers, and scientists to visit his court, as well as writers, thinkers, and artists. They read philosophical works together and gazed at the stars.

The Maharal—who had studied Aristotle and Plato, was knowledgeable about the natural sciences, and took an interest in alchemy—was a member of this circle. Rudolf invited him to his court on February 23, 1592.[6] The emperor asked about kabbalah, and the Maharal expounded on the theories of the Ari (Ha'ari) of Safed.[7] Together with his student Ganz, the Maharal was in touch with the Danish astronomer Tycho Brahe, who had built instruments for observing the stars and who had recourse in his research to the work of the blind German mathematician Johannes Kepler, the formulator of the three laws of planetary motion.

The Maharal was a controversial figure among Jewish leaders of his generation, mainly because he had given the German Enlightenment movement,

Rabbi Yom Tov Lipman Heller's grave in the Jewish cemetery of Kraków.

then still in its infancy, a foothold in Orthodox Judaism. His emphasis on the individual's right to make independent spiritual and materialistic decisions was regarded by his colleagues as too permissive. His interest in secular sciences and his intimacy with Christian intellectuals annoyed the conservative rabbis. They did not deny his talents but were highly critical of his world outlook, which was far too pluralistic for their tastes. He was considered an inveterate oppositionist by his community because he censured leaders who amassed wealth and lived in luxury, claiming that they did not serve as models for their congregations.

In the field of education, the Maharal was an innovator. He ruled out the accepted method of learning Talmud by means of *pilpul*, which in Hebrew means "sharp analysis" and which characterizes one of the most important techniques in Judaism. *Pilpul* is a dialectical way of studying the Talmud through intense, sometimes fervent, textual analysis in an attempt to explain perceptual differences between the rulings of various rabbinical authorities. It stands in opposition to the literary method of study, which emphasizes the narrative and its historical background. The controversy between supporters of these two methods has accompanied Jewish education ideologists since the Talmud was compiled probably at the end of the fifth century CE.

The Maharal insisted on returning to the literal basic meaning of the sources of the *halakha*.[8] In secular studies, he distinguished between what he called the "external wisdom," mathematics, astronomy, and the natural sciences, the teaching of which he permitted, and "Greek wisdom"—philosophy, literature, and the Greek language—which he outlawed because in his opinion they contradicted the principles of Judaism.

The Maharal rejected the rationalist Aristotelian view, in contrast to the Rambam, or Maimonides.[9] Aristotle taught that man reached perfection through the profundity of his thought. The Maharal believed that human perfection was not a function of rationality because only a minority of human beings were given the amount of wisdom that could bring them to such perfection and an understanding of the concept of divinity.

The Maharal asked whether it was possible that only a few were able to attain a grasp of the supreme, divine perfection, and he answered his own query in the negative. He explained that from Judaism's point of view, the Aristotelian theory had no validity because the secret of comprehending "supreme perfection" was not to be found in rational acumen. Rather, any person who studies the Torah for the sake of study and who observes the practical *mitzvoth*, or precepts, approaches divinity, adheres to it, and discovers its secrets. It is therefore not in rational understanding that perfection is to be found, but in the sense of adherence and piety. In other words, amassing knowledge and wisdom does not guarantee that one will understand the divine, but one acquires such understanding through studying the Torah and keeping the *mitzvoth*. Even if you do not understand the Talmud, the Maharal contended, your study of it brings you closer to an understanding of God. Several of his philosophical formulations were hundreds of years before their time, and his influence on Judaism became significant only several generations later, mainly in the Hasidic movement.[10]

The Maharal's educational innovations and biblical interpretations also aroused criticism. His commentaries introduced three things that in his era were considered an inappropriate oversimplification of the Scriptures: First, in order to give the biblical texts more mass appeal, he added color and illustrative details, in the manner of modern literature. Second, under the influence of the kabbalah, he added a mystical quality to the dry biblical text.[11] Third, he created links between things that were apparently unconnected, links that existed in another plane of thought. It is not surprising that for decades, community leaders tried to keep the Maharal away from influential positions. In order to attain the post of chief rabbi of Prague, he had to wait until he was eighty-five years old.

His student, Rital, did not have to wait this long. In 1627, he was appointed chief rabbi of the city at age forty-eight, and two years later he became entangled in a grave affair that caused distress in the Jewish communities of Eastern Europe and Ashkenaz.

During the Thirty Years' War (1618–1648), the Hapsburg emperor Ferdinand II imposed a tax on the Jews of Bohemia to help finance the war.[12] In order to collect its share, the Jewish community in Prague instructed the city's rabbi, Rital, to set a quota for each family. But some poor families accused the rabbi of favoring the wealthy, and they would not pay. Rital denied the allegations, and when the controversy sharpened and his opponents demanded that he resign, he refused. Someone informed on him, telling the emperor that he had taught the Mishna and the Talmud, which had been forbidden after both books were banned by the pope and ordered to be destroyed in bonfires.[13] At the urging of the church, the emperor ordered Rital's arrest on July 8, 1629, and his incarceration in Vienna. Under interrogation, Rital argued that he had no choice but to teach the Mishna and the Talmud because it was his duty. Jews are obliged to learn the six books of the Mishna, Rital explained, because they are the Oral Law and contain most of the precepts of the Jewish religion.

"Without Mishna and Talmud, there are no Jews," he told his interrogators, and he would not recant. Because of his obstinacy, he was put on trial before a tribunal of Catholic clergymen and charged with showing contempt for the pope and insulting the Catholic faith. He was sentenced to death. Influential Viennese Jews intervened on his behalf, however, and the emperor commuted his sentence. A heavy fine was imposed on him, his books and essays were banned, and he was forbidden to serve as a rabbi throughout the Austrian Empire. After a while, his sentence was commuted again, when Prague's Jews petitioned on his behalf. His works could be published again, and the ban on his serving as a rabbi was restricted to Prague alone. Rital had been imprisoned for forty days in Vienna, and at the end of August 1629 he returned to Prague. He described the entire affair in a manuscript in the Hebrew language titled "The Scroll of Hatred."[14]

When Rital's life returned to normal, he composed one of the most renowned commentaries on the Mishna, *Tosafot Yom Tov* (Yom Tov Commentaries). He used the word *addenda* out of modesty, to stress that he did not claim to be breaking new ground, but had only added to existing commentaries. The distinction of his work lies in its simplicity and his avoidance of *pilpul* and sophistry. His commentaries set out to reconcile contradictions between sections of the Mishna and to make literal elucidations, while taking great care not to complicate matters or to base any ideas on marginal interpretations. Although he tended toward kabbalistic thinking, like his teacher the Maharal, his own interpretation was by no means mystical. On the contrary, he resorted to pure logic and never deviated from the original intention of the Mishna. He followed a clear path, saying that the *pshat*, or literal meaning, in the Mishna was the foundation of the laws. His style is astoundingly lucid. When it came to formulations, he outdid the Maharal, whose wording is sometimes difficult to understand. This cannot be said about Rital's clear writing style. An abbreviated version of his book, titled *Yom Tov's Main Addenda*, was published in Lvov in 1790 by the printer Meshulam Ben Yoel Katz, and it found its way into many Jewish homes.

As mentioned previously, Rital's great-granddaughter Haya Heller, with her impeccable pedigree, married Avrumche Backenroth, the oldest son of Shmuel Leib and Debora Schor, the smart woman who resisted her husband's attempt to sell the family's land to the empire—an act that was praised by future generations of Backenroths. Nevertheless, the credit for actually founding the family's business belonged to her son, Avrumche. Together with his two brothers, Avrumche set up the Backenroth Brothers firm, which became the family's flagship business. Backenroth Brothers, as majority shareholders, established a partnership with five others in a new company named Nafta Petroleum Corporation.

Backenroth Brothers brought the family's land holdings to this partnership. Their property contained ozokerite, the waxy mineral paraffin that their grandparents Tsiril and Elimeilech Backenroth, together with their three sons, had discovered in the well they dug in the wake of the "Miracle Worker" of Zhidachov's blessing, and from which the family had manufactured candle wax, lamp oil, paraffin ointment, and grease for lubricating wagon wheels.

The remaining partners in Nafta Petroleum were two other Jews, a Polish baroness, a Polish prince, and a Hungarian nobleman. The corporation had a seat on the European oil cartel and took part in the discussions in which the prices of crude oil and its products were set.

The two Jewish partners were *Die Rebbetzin* ("the rabbi's wife," in Yiddish) Panzer and Rabbi Abraham Schreiber-Sofer. (Abraham Schreiber-Sofer, 1815–1872, was known as Ktav Sofer, "author's message," in Hebrew. *Schreiber* in German and *sofer* in Hebrew mean "author.") The rebbetzin was the wife of Rabbi Yossele Panzer. Avrumche greatly admired her business skills and made her a partner in most of the family's ventures. Her daughter Pearl married Avrumche's grandson Shmuel Yitzhak. As for Rabbi Schreiber-Sofer, he was the head of the Yeshiva of Pressburg, in Hungary.[15] His father, Moses Sofer-Schreiber, who was known by the epithet Hatam Sofer, was the leader of Orthodox Jewry in Hungary.[16] He was also an uncompromising fighter against Reform Judaism, whose first beginnings had appeared in Berlin and Hamburg, as well as in Vienna and some cities in Hungary.[17]

Until around 1880, most of the entrepreneurs in the Galicia Oil Belt were Jewish. This is no surprise because Jews could lean on their rich commercial experience. For them, the marketplace was not a new sphere. Just give them a chance to do business, and they will know how to make the most of it. This is precisely what happened with the Backenroth brothers, most of whom were local residents and who were among the pioneers of the petroleum industry in Galicia. Apart from one French company and two German companies, which functioned independently, in the early years foreign investors preferred to form partnerships with local firms. Few Austrian banks were willing to risk financing an oil-prospecting venture, and raising capital was a tedious process. Galicia had the reputation of being a particularly backward province, with little industry, mediocre agriculture, barely educated citizens, and widespread poverty.

In comparison with other regions of the empire (not to mention Western Europe), the extent of Galicia's backwardness was obvious during the oil industry's formative era. Newspapers often reported on how an oil well was sunk in Schodnica and nearby Boryslav. A square five feet by five feet was marked off, then a pit six and a half feet deep was dug, and the walls were shored with wooden poles. A windlass was installed above the pit, and a worker was lowered on a rope to the bottom, in order to deepen it. He dug with a pickax and sent the loosened earth up in a wooden bucket tied to the rope. When the laborer spotted paraffin welling up, or when he smelled the stench of gas, usually at a depth of between thirty and sixty-five feet, he was immediately hoisted out, lest he suffer harm. For several hours after that, the compressed gases usually bubbled out of the depths of the earth, followed by a strong flow of paraffin that filled the pit. Using the bucket and the windlass, men raised the paraffin out of the well and then poured it into a wooden tank that had been erected on the surface.

A good well would produce an average of two to three tons of paraffin a day. The work was hard and dangerous. The shoring tended to collapse, and one spark was enough to start a fire. Sometimes a strong gusher of oil erupted while a worker was in the pit. Workers often inhaled noxious gases and passed out. There were instances of workers being extricated only after they had died.

During the first years, almost no safety measures were taken. The producers acted according to their own interests, with no coordination or control, and the disorder was formidable. It was not commonly understood that oil was a flammable and dangerous substance. In Borislav, in September 1874, a worker lit a cigarette near an oil tank and a fire broke out. Hundreds of wooden drilling installations, sheds, and homes were destroyed, and at least ten workers were killed.[18]

The difficulties and the risks, however, never detracted from the tremendous enthusiasm of the landowners and the investors, who attacked the earth by storm, puncturing it with thousands of wells. In their mind's eye, they saw not bucket after bucket of paraffin, but a flood of guldens and florins (the currencies of the Austro-Hungarian Empire between 1754 and 1892; they were replaced by the krone in 1892, when the gold standard was introduced to the empire). Nevertheless, the politicians and the bankers of Vienna remained indifferent at first. The government made little effort to build an infrastructure for oil prospecting, production, and marketing, and the bankers displayed extreme caution, generally refusing to grant credit to the early oil entrepreneurs.

The Galician oil industry thus lagged behind its U.S. counterpart, in which John Davidson Rockefeller controlled most of the production and the refining. He set a uniform policy on his own, whereas in Galicia, dozens of investors, only a few of whom were experts, worked in complete disharmony. Rockefeller developed new technologies, but in Galicia they made do with primitive makeshift equipment that they devised on the spot. Rockefeller's company, Standard Oil of Ohio, was at least two decades ahead of the Galician industry. In Pennsylvania and Ontario, Canada, steam drills had been used to sink wells since 1865. The Galician oil producers apparently caught their first glimpse of a steam engine only in 1885, and they continued to have their wells dug with pickaxes. At least until the mid-1880s, paraffin was more profitable than fuel oil because no widespread use had yet been discovered for the latter, so the Galician producers had no motive to drill down to the depths where deposits of crude oil could be found.

The policy of Nafta Petroleum did not stand out in Galicia's business scene. It was based on experience the family had accumulated in its previous enterprises and during routine Austrian business transactions. Backenroth Brothers had one fundamental advantage, in that the family owned the lands, and Nafta Petroleum did not have to pay leasing fees or share the profits from the sale of crude oil. Apparently, the brothers feared that as Jews, it would be better for them to stay behind the scenes, so they delegated responsibility for all outside business dealings to their non-Jewish partners and tried to avoid taking positions in political disputes. This was also how they acted in a confrontation between the imperial administration and the Galician Diet (provincial parliament) concerning the regulation of the industry.[19]

During the mid-1870s, when Vienna realized the importance of Galicia's oil fields, the capital city began to take an interest. Viennese officials wanted to assume control of the fields by requisitioning them, but the Galician

Diet fought back firmly, to ensure that the oil rights remained in the hands of the landowners and those who had leased the land. Ultimately, the Diet triumphed, as a result of the extraordinarily strong coalition that had been formed between the Polish nobility and the Jews. At that time, the Polish-Jewish partnership administered Galicia's government and succeeded in voiding many of the empire's claims. A small fragment of the Ruthenian peasantry, the ones who leased their small plots of land to Jewish oil entrepreneurs, joined the Polish-Jewish coalition.

The Backenroth brothers stayed out of the confrontation, as they did in the dispute that broke out between the oil producers and the Ruthenian farmers, some of whom had been their neighbors for generations. The farmers were angry because thousands of oil wells had been drilled in agricultural land, with mounds of excavated earth piling up among puddles of filthy, malodorous paraffin that seeped into the soil and poisoned it. A few years later, however, when it was clear that the farmers had lost the battle, the brothers launched a quiet campaign to purchase land for oil prospecting. They collaborated with their neighbors by employing mainly local Jews and Ruthenians from Schodnica and the surrounding areas, and they generally refrained from recruiting outside workers.

Although the division of tasks between the partners worked well, and the company's affairs were conducted successfully and without crises, a careful examination of its functioning from the perspective of a century and a half later shows that the founding generation did not display remarkable innovativeness or creativity. The brothers followed conservative and cautious economic guidelines, and this was probably why the Backenroth Brothers company never flourished as a leader in any sector of entrepreneurial endeavor, neither in the location of oil fields, nor in production, refining, or marketing. Through the firm's entire history, it remained a medium-size company, one of dozens of similar enterprises that managed to acquire for itself only a tiny proportion of the paraffin and crude oil being extracted from Galician soil. Even though the Backenroths' previous occupations had been in finance and real estate and they were familiar with how the monetary market functioned, it appears that amassing substantial capital in order to gain control of a large slice of the market and achieve leadership in the industry was never at the top of their priorities.

The economic workings of the oil industry only gradually became clear to the brothers, and they learned by trial and error. From the very start, the oil producers' great disadvantage was their lack of control over demand. The market is subject to extreme fluctuations, due to the vagaries of nature or of human beings. Handling dangerous substances can cause disasters—fires, explosions, and so on—and competition between producers often creates a glut in the market, which drastically cuts prices and results in bankruptcies. On one hand, producing limited quantities may not meet market demand or might not cover expenses, and is liable to endanger the entire business. On the other hand, producing large amounts does not ensure success either, because of the expense of constructing infrastructure and storage facilities and because when prices fall, losses are incurred.

Beyond the difficult task of matching production to demand, complications often cropped up that demanded professional solutions. Within the Austro-Hungarian Empire, protective duties were imposed on the export of fuels from one district to another and even between the two major political partners, Austria and Hungary. It was complicated to achieve an equalization of duties. Transportation costs were enormous because infrastructure in Galicia, especially railroads, was undeveloped. And then there were the frauds, the forgeries, and dilution of the oil, schemes that were primarily carried out by local Mafia-like gangs using strong-arm tactics, but sometimes by the authorities themselves.

The Backenroths and their partners realized fairly late in the game a fundamental principle of the oil industry that Rockefeller had discerned early on: that control of the entire process, from the production stage to the marketing, to the end consumer, grants a high degree of protection against the whims of the market and speculative competitors, enables the management to carry out a financial turnover, and provides maximal profitability. This is why Rockefeller set out to gain domination of the complete cycle, from prospecting to drilling wells, to production, storage, transportation, refining, and all the way down to marketing and sales. His holding company, Standard Oil Trust, owned thirty refining, transportation, and marketing companies.

Another important discovery the Rockefellers made was that in a competitive market, profits from refining oil were greater than those from producing crude oil. Extraction involves heavy investment and is subject to risks. Refining is a straightforward operation that does not require much manpower and provides high marginal profits. Years later, the brothers also learned this lesson, and as they took control of the refining process, their profits soared.

But in the earlier stages, it was not Rockefeller who served as a role model for Avrumche. The American tycoon was distant from the Backenroths, both geographically and conceptually. Instead, a young Polish economist who arrived in Galicia from London was Avrumche's great source of inspiration. Stanislaw Szczepanowski (1846–1900) was a lanky man, whose narrow physique was always garbed in a black suit and a tie, and the tips of his mustache curled upward, in accordance with the dictates of male fashion of the era. He became famous throughout Galicia in the 1880s (and a few years later in Vienna as well) as a serious economic planner and a man of the world. He had acquired his experience as an economic researcher in Great Britain's India Office and was a great admirer of both the ancient Greeks and the modern British. Newspapers of the time called him a pioneer, a genius, and an idealist. His writings were closely studied in economics affairs ministries in both Lvov and Vienna.[20]

Szczepanowski had no prior experience in the oil industry, but nevertheless in 1880 he took out huge loans from banks, located a large oil-bearing tract in the district of Kolomyya (about seventy miles southwest of Schodnica) and, using a steam-powered drill, sank wells up to four hundred feet deep. Before his initiative, nobody in Galicia had dared to go as deep into the earth, but the outcome was extraordinary: during the 1880s, Szczepanowski's wells produced most of Galicia's crude oil, and local investors regarded him with admiration and envy. Avrumche met him several times in Schodnica and Drohobych and was impressed by his humility and his insights. Avrumche wondered at, but never managed to reproduce, the audacity shown by this man whose bushy black hair drooped over his eyes.[21]

In the terms of the time and the place, Avrumche was an excellent manager who radiated authority and self-confidence and made up his mind quickly. He remembered the smallest details and knew every employee by name. He could swiftly calculate profit and loss and was an outstanding negotiator. He was familiar with the land-leasing laws and the Mining Authority's inspection regulations. But there were gaps in Avrumche's skills and those of the Polish managers. As the industry became more specialized, it was apparent that Avrumche lacked a systematic education and knowledge of foreign languages, and although he knew the technical terminology, he did not always grasp the full extent of the chemical and geological processes that occurred in the refineries and in the depths of the earth. Eventually, professionals were hired and the management gaps were filled, but in the early period the company sustained losses because of the boss's shortcomings. Under the next generation of sons and sons-in-law, however, the company became more professional, with improved technology and sufficient capital.

All of this notwithstanding, in the eyes of his family and his employees, Avrumche was a leader who was head and shoulders above any other, a teacher and a ruler. Contradictions coexisted in his personality, as they do in many strong and decisive men. Some saw him as an extreme conservative, while others thought he was too advanced for his times. He wore traditional Hasidic garb and strictly observed the minor *mitzvoth*, as well as the major ones. He rode horses expertly and always carried a pistol. He knew a thing or two about the Talmud but lacked a secular education. Nevertheless, he held his own when negotiating with men of affairs from the Polish and the Hungarian aristocracy.

Avrumche seemed ambivalent about displaying his wealth. Within his own circles, he lived modestly. Once he traveled to Vienna to visit his daughter and his son-in-law, a wealthy businessman who, in order to honor his father-in-law, sent a black coach harnessed to six black horses to meet Avrumche at the station. The coach, according to a family tale, had a golden canopy. But Avrumche refused to ride in the fancy carriage and hired an ordinary hansom cab instead. On the roads of Galicia, he traveled in a simple peasant's wagon, although there was a carriage parked in the family yard. Yet in seeming contradiction to his day-to-day modesty, he broke with a significant, historical family tradition by abandoning the humble Hasidic court of Zhidachov and instead choosing to join the ostentatious court of the rabbi of Chortkov, the wealthiest in Galicia.

What was behind this preference? After all, the blessing that heralded the family's wealth had issued from the court of the rabbi of Zhidachov. Moreover, Avrumche's first wife, Haya Heller, had been a relative of the Admor Tzvi Hirsch of Zhidachov.[22] How, then, did Avrumche dare to leave the court that had benefited his family so greatly and go over to the competition, the court of the rabbi of Chortkov? Family members could not come up with a satisfactory explanation.[23]

Avrumche's father and his grandfather had objected to Hasidic activities. Shmuel Leib was like his father, Elimeilech. Neither of them took the trouble to visit the court of the tzaddik very often, and when they did deign to travel to Zhidachov, it was only because they had been urged to do so by their wives, Elimeilech's Tsiril and Shmuel Leib's Debora Schor. Avrumche, in contrast to his humbler forefathers, each of whom had stuck to their own paths, had certain characteristics common to politicians. Like his mother, Debora, he often took part in public affairs and knew how to use that to his advantage. This may well have been the reason for his preferring the rabbi of Chortkov over the rabbi of Zhidachov.

The court at Chortkov was totally different from the one at Zhidachov—indeed, its very opposite. The rabbis of Zhidachov espoused humility as a matter of principle, whereas those of Chortkov flaunted their wealth in luxurious surroundings. The Zhidachovers were poor; the Chortkovers, exceedingly rich. The rabbi of Zhidachov was mystical; the rabbi of Chortkov, down to earth. Zhidachovers were conservative, rigid, and devout in their beliefs; the Chortkovers were adaptable to changing times and ready to compromise. The Zhidachov synagogue was monastic, the one in Chortkov an ornate palace. Every summer and winter, thousands of Hasidim from all over Poland gathered to visit the "royal court" at Chortkov, to gape at the ostentatious building and the carved ceilings bedecked with colorful decorations and huge copper and porcelain chandeliers.

The heads of the Chortkov court were the descendants of Rabbi Dov Ber, the Maggid (preacher) of Mezhirech. The Maggid was the first student of the Baal Shem Tov, the founder of the Hasidic movement. Avrumche Backenroth's personal rabbi in his youth was David Moshe, the Admor of Chortkov (1828–1903), who was the son of Rabbi Israel Friedman of Rizhin and a direct descendant of the Maggid of Mezhirech. The Hasidic pedigree of the Chortkov court was infinitely superior to that of Zhidachov, and possibly this was the secret behind Avrumche's transferral of his loyalties. He had learned from his mother that descent was of the utmost importance, and this, combined with the Chortkov attitude toward wealth, may have swayed him. In the court of the rabbi of Zhidachov, Avrumche had no way to flaunt his wealth because the rabbi loathed such ostentation and extravagance, while instead preaching humility and spirituality. In contrast, in the Chortkov court Avrumche found a populist rabbi, one who acted like royalty, advocated "practical Hasidism," and aspired to be far more than a spiritual leader. In the eyes of his followers, the Admor of Chortkov was a king.

And indeed, Rabbi Israel Friedman of Rizhin (1798–1850), the father of David Moshe of Chortkov, had founded a dynasty with a tradition unmatched in any large Hasidic court until then, a tradition whereby the

Admor behaved like a king. Using the donations of his followers, Rabbi Israel built a magnificent court, and when he had to leave Rizhin, he settled at Sadigora in Bukovina, attracting tens of thousands of his followers to that city.[24] His son, David Moshe, Avrumche's rabbi, first settled in the city of Potok but was forced to leave it, and he relocated to the village of Chortkov, which lies about ninety-three miles southeast of Drohobych, near the border between Galicia and Romania. In Chortkov, David Moshe carried on his father's tradition. He, too, conducted a "royal court," and Avrumche belonged to his closest circle.

Rabbi Yisrael of Chortkov, the son of David Moshe, embellished the royal traditions even more, giving Judaism a very material expression that had no precedent in history. He proclaimed that the verse "And Yeshurun waxed fat and kicked" (Deuteronomy 32:15) applied only to the masses, for whom silver and gold are a stumbling block, whereas the tzaddik must lift himself above the common herd and conduct himself domineeringly. "The king must behave masterfully and condescendingly so that he will be the terror of the people, and therein lies the greatness of Israel," the rabbi of Chortkov was quoted as asserting. Such royal pretensions angered many in the Hasidic world. Renowned rabbis protested against the ostentation and the extravagance of the Chortkovers. The most outspoken of all was Rabbi Chaim Halberstam, the conservative Admor of Zanz, who proclaimed the excommunication of those who followed Rabbi David Moshe of Chortkov and his brother, Avraham Yaakov of Sadigora. In response, the Hasidim of these two courts declared their own excommunication of the Zanz Hasidim. The rabbi of Lvov, Yosef Shaul Nathanson, quickly intervened and published a proclamation of support for Halberstam. The *kulturkampf* between the two sides raged on until Rabbi Halberstam passed away in 1894 and tempers died down.

Avrumche Backenroth fought in the defense of his rabbi with all his soul, and not for nothing. In the royal pretensions of the Chortkov court, Avrumche's own personal truth found expression. He considered himself a representative of the Jewish aristocracy of Galicia. The social values that had suited his grandfather, the impecunious Elimeilech Backenroth, the tavern owner who had become impoverished in the economic crisis, never appealed to his grandson, who became a leader of his community precisely because of his wealth. Avrumche possessed acute political antennae and sensitivity about public relations. He identified the center of power in the

Hasidic community and thus became one of the frequenters of the "royal court" of Chortkov, a donor of funds to the "king," and a financer of some of his activities, as well as supporting several poor students of the Torah by paying their expenses. The rabbi's magnificent throne, covered in silver, was built with funds provided by Avrumche. (Today, this chair is located in the Chortkov synagogue in Tel Aviv.) Because of all of this munificence, the Admor bestowed honors and blessings on Avrumche, and from the time that his closeness with the rabbi became known, his stature in the community of Drohobych rose. Avrumche later became famous throughout eastern Galicia. There's no doubt that he helped the rabbi, and the rabbi helped him.

But because Avrumche was an honest man, and because he felt a heavy burden of responsibility toward the public, he interpreted his close relationship with the tzaddik as a duty that had been imposed upon him, and he related to his wealth as if it had been given to him to use for the public's well-being. Twice a week, poor women came to his kitchen to get food for their families, and every Sabbath eve a wonderful ritual took place outside his home. Dozens of impoverished people—widows, old folks, most of them Jews, but some Ukrainians, too—stood in line behind the kitchen door and received a gift of food: beef, poultry, oil, and potatoes. On festivals, he placed a huge table in the yard of his estate, and all of the needy were invited to come and eat their fill.

Haya and Avrumche Backenroth had six children; the youngest was Clara, who married Israel Moses Sobel. This young couple would be sent by Avrumche to the famed leatherworking center of Bolechow, not far from Schodnica, to run the family's oil refinery there. In Bolechow, one of the most interesting chapters in the annals of the Backenroths would occur, after the daughters of Clara and Israel Sobel got to know the oldest son of the Kahane family.

6

Ecological Disaster

It was nearly noon in Schodnica's Hasidic *kloiz* ("synagogue," in Yiddish), and the Torah reading was over. The *shaliah tzibur* (public representative) had begun the Musaf prayer when a frightened boy, about fifteen years old, burst into the synagogue.[1] He stood by the door panting for a few seconds, then shrieked, "Pogrom, pogrom!" It was Sunday, June 6, 1897, and Jews were celebrating the festival of Shavuoth, or Pentecost, the day that Moses received the Ten Commandments on Mount Sinai.

When the boy had caught his breath, he told the worshippers that hundreds of day laborers were rioting in the main street, beating up Jewish passersby, and smashing the chairs and the tables in Goldfischer's tavern. A group of congregants immediately left to find out what was happening, and Avrumche Backenroth whispered to one of the young men to go and call the police.

Usually, when Jews heard the shout "Pogrom!" their hearts froze in panic, but this time the worshippers did not become hysterical even though the situation seemed to warrant it. For several months, tension had been mounting between the hundreds of hired laborers and their employers. In May, the workers had gone on a one-day strike, in protest against the shortage of housing and the high cost of living. Just before the festival, the foremen, or *polustoki*, had reported that there was ferment among the workers and that only a spark was needed to start a conflagration. The *polustoki* were closely in touch with the situation. Every morning just before sunrise, they went to the "slave market" in the Drohobych town square and hired men who would be paid in cash after their day's work. Sometimes, they even arranged housing for the workers in Schodnica's shantytown.

Most of the day laborers were Ruthenian peasants who lived on the outskirts of town in wretched huts and in conditions of abject poverty. They were called the Mazurians, as many of them came from the broad plains of Mazur in the east.[2] They had been forced to seek work in the oil belt because it was impossible to make a living from their small plots of agricultural land.

At least two unskilled laborers were on duty on each shift every time a well was drilled. They stood at the top of the drilling tower, along with the trained derrickman, and, acting on the instructions of the shift supervisor, they pushed the drilling rod into the well and cleared away the mud that spilled out. Around 1880, the drill device was three to four feet long. It was screwed into a drilling rod on which a sinker and a jar were hung. The total weight of the tools that the unskilled laborers pushed down into the pit was around two thousand pounds. Their task was monotonous and difficult; their shifts were long, usually twelve hours; and their wages were meager. Most of them spent their spare time and their money in the taverns, all owned by Jews, and they bought their food from merchants, of whom most were Jewish. The workers voiced one constant complaint: that the Jews overcharged.

In the synagogue, a rumor went around that on the eve of the festival a socialist agitator had arrived in Schodnica from Lvov to stir up the workers. The agitator had lit the fuse, said one of the worshippers. But it turned out that the worshipper had not glimpsed any agitator, and like everyone else, he was merely repeating the rumors. In general, the oil entrepreneurs and the landowners in Schodnica did not distinguish between Marxists and socialists, and they placed the entire left wing within the revolutionary camp. They never concealed their suspicions that the socialist movement in Lvov was a dangerous hub of radical activity, whose only purpose was to destroy the oil industry.

The leaders of the socialists in Lvov were the Pole Ignacy Daszynski and his youthful Ruthenian protégé, Ivan Franko.[3] Austrian authorities suspected that both were engaged in subversive activities. They had been arrested several times by the police and charged with initiating illegal actions. Still, according to modern-day political definitions, we would refer to both men as moderate social democrats and opponents of the Marxist concept of the dictatorship of the proletariat (in July 1920, Lenin called Daszynski a "social-chauvinist").

Daszynski had grown up in Stanislav and Drohobych and was very familiar with the oil industry and the people who were active in it. It was said that he had learned to speak Yiddish from his Jewish neighbors. His political platform included three demands relating to the work conditions in the oil belt: an eight-hour workday, no night shift, and a ban on employing children younger than fourteen years old. In his speeches, he denounced the employers of the oil belt as "exploiters of the soil and of the simple workers." The oil barons, he repeatedly claimed, forced the workers to dig wells and endanger their lives in exchange for pennies.

Franko was also very well known in the oil belt, for he had been born in a village close to Boryslav. He was a left-winger and a nationalist and also a talented and prolific writer, poet, and commentator. He phrased his arguments in a delicate, literary style, but they were nevertheless exceedingly forceful. He and Daszynski organized a battalion of demonstrators in Lvov, composed declarations and petitions, and wrote poetry, articles, and short stories that often promoted workers' rights and sometimes Ruthenian independence.[4] His articles were hand-copied from the newspapers and hung on the walls of the workers' shacks in Boryslav and Schodnica, but as only a few workers were literate, an announcer was appointed to read them aloud during breaks.

The propaganda that Daszynski, Franko, and other socialist activists, among them Jews, disseminated among the workers was very skillfully phrased, but their message failed to take root. For more than twenty-five years, from 1860 to 1885, the daily laborers worked with almost no protest. Every few years, a strike was declared in the oil fields, but they all died down quickly. The Ruthenian and Polish workers had come to Schodnica to make a living, not to indulge in protests. In the hardscrabble conditions that were prevalent in Galicia, they were grateful to be employed. Moreover, most of them were devoid of class consciousness.

There had actually never been an Industrial Revolution in Galicia. The masses had never moved from the countryside to the cities because no genuine industry had arisen in the cities, and in the oil belt most of the employees had tenured jobs.[5] In Schodnica, some 70 percent were permanent workers, and in Boryslav, some 60 percent.

It is possible that this time, during Pentecost 1897, Jewish communists had joined the propaganda campaign being conducted by the socialists in the oil belt and had persuaded the workers to protest violently. Some of these communists had fled to Galicia from Russia and Germany, which in 1878 had outlawed the Socialist Party, and they were more adept at political agitation than were the local activists.

As was pointed out earlier, however, reports of day laborers rioting in the Jewish neighborhood never caused undue alarm in the synagogue because the number of young Jews in Schodnica was ten times greater than that of the day laborers, and the local police were professional and effective. The Jews were therefore not afraid. They recalled how a similar occurrence had ended in Boryslav three years earlier, in the summer of 1884. There, too, Ruthenian workers had accused Jewish food merchants of price gouging. A group of them staged a demonstration and shouted anti-Semitic slogans. The atmosphere heated up, and some of the protesters came to blows with passersby. Workers damaged some houses in the Jewish quarter. Although no one was badly hurt, that evening hundreds of young Jews paraded through the workers' shantytown and severely beat some of its residents. In particular, there was one small group of violent youngsters, known as the Borislawchicks, whose members enjoyed fighting it out with Ruthenians who were considered to be anti-Semites. After these events, the workers in Boryslav never tried to attack Jews again, and the Jews in the area felt that they had defended themselves well.

While the Jews in the synagogue were wondering how to respond to the rioting, they could hear the crowd of several dozen workers outside shouting slogans reminiscent of the mid-seventeenth century's Khmelnytsky's pogroms, such as "The Jews serve the *szlachta*" (the Polish nobility) and "The Jews exploit us on the Poles' behalf." Years later, Avrumche would tell his grandchildren that at the same time, not far from the synagogue, some frustrated workers broke into the home of a Jew, smashed the furniture, and threw it out of the window. Directly afterward, on a side street, the most serious assault took place. Some hooligans molested a woman who was carrying a baby and then pushed her. The woman tripped and fell and the baby slipped out of her grip, fell to the ground, and was killed.

By then, the police had arrived on the scene, and they reacted forcefully. An officer demanded that the demonstrators disperse, and when some of them continued to riot, the officer ordered his men to open fire. One protester was killed. Dozens were arrested. The official report of the investigation, which was published in Drohobych two months later, declared that young Poles who were looking for a fight were responsible for the disturbances. The prices of the goods sold by Jewish merchants were not unfair, the report said, and the wages paid to the day laborers in Schodnica were relatively high. It was possible that an agitator had been sent from Lvov, or perhaps the riot had broken out because of genuine distress. Jews doubted that the incident could be defined as a pogrom. The heads of the community quietly banished from the village some workers who were suspected of incitement and met with church leaders in Drohobych to see whether they would agree to intervene to help restrain the "anti-Semitic elements." This is what the Jewish newspapers called the politicians whom they thought were responsible for fanning the flames of hatred against Jews. Authorities also tried to reduce the levels of drunkenness among workers on weekends, but these attempts failed.

A few weeks later, peace and quiet prevailed once more. From an economic point of view, these were good years, and everyone, including most of the daily laborers, had an interest in seeing the drilling continue, the oil pumped out of the ground, and making a living.

Indeed, the last two decades of the nineteenth century were profitable ones for Schodnica. A new geological survey showed that under the ground in Boryslav and Schodnica, at a depth of 450 to 750 feet, lay a gigantic sea of oil. Soon, foreign investors poured resources into the oil fields. New wells were sunk and production boomed, as did the profits. It was the producers' golden age, as dozens of oil companies operated in Schodnica. The largest was a German firm—Gunter Schwarzburg Sonderhousen Company—that leased 3,350 acres and drilled five wells. The second largest was the Backenroth brothers' company, Nafta Petroleum Corporation, whose oilfields extended over 2,500 acres with four producing wells (and more than ten dry ones). Austrian and Polish companies also invested in drilling and refineries.[6] Two Polish cousins, Waclav Wolski and Kazimierz Odrzywolski, who had been trained by the entrepreneur Szczepanowski, sank money not only into oil production but also into advancing social goals and assisting weak segments of the community. They had set up an oil-prospecting company in Schodnica and a factory for engines and drilling machinery, and they helped to finance a school for the children of laborers, a local newspaper, and a Catholic church building.

Yet responsibility for the most significant technological leap forward lay with the Canadian oilman William MacGarvey, who was world famous as an expert and who brought the first machine drill to Galicia.[7] In 1884, he set up a partnership with the Austrian investor John Bergheim, and they called the company the Bergheim & MacGarvey Company, later named Galician-Carpathian Naphtha AG. The two men introduced the latest, most advanced innovation in the sphere of drilling: a wooden derrick seventy-five feet high that looked like a pyramid from a distance. The wooden tower was erected over a well. Its interior space was heated by steam and provided shelter for the drilling crew during the freezing Polish winter. The drilling machine was installed within the structure and was driven by steam. It could reach depths of five thousand feet. When oil was struck and had to be brought up to the surface, a pump was installed inside the rig, which sucked the black fluid out of the well and into pipes that led to a tank farm that had been erected nearby. Most of the time, though, there was no need for a pump because the natural pressure in the depths of the earth was strong enough to force a powerful gusher of oil up to the surface.

It is difficult to exaggerate the importance of the innovations that MacGarvey brought to Galicia. Production was streamlined, work conditions improved, and output expanded significantly. Instead of reaching an average daily depth of three feet by manual digging, the new technologies made it possible to drill between sixty and ninety feet a day and rapidly hit depths of thousands of feet. Consequently, the oil belt was soon studded with wooden pyramid-shaped derricks, dozens of them in Schodnica, standing close to the homes of the residents.

The adoption of modern technologies led to the oil producers joining forces for the first time in history and cooperating in investing a considerable portion of their revenues toward orderly physical and economic planning, based on geographical and geological surveys. Experts evaluated the Galician lands and deemed them especially blessed, saying that the enormous oil fields that lay beneath the surface would supply oil forever. (Thirty years later, when geology became a science, Galicians were forced to face reality as they learned how primitive and rudimentary these assessments had been. The committees of geologists, engineers, and chemists, which made the first field studies for the Viennese government and then for the oil producers' association, had not possessed genuine tools to conduct research in the early days of the oil industry. They had relied mainly on unfounded theories developed by German scientists.)

The oil companies planned their level of production based on data about current demand. They laid a network of pipelines and constructed giant tanks for storage. They broadened the railroad tracks to enable these to carry oil tankers and built new loading facilities at the railroad junction of Stanislav (today, it is in Ukraine and is called Ivano-Frankivs'k).[8] In addition, they constructed dozens of refineries. At the same time, safety regulations were instituted, and a special oil police force was set up.

MacGarvey's technological revolution and the regional infrastructure's development attracted more business corporations that had substantial means, among them the Galician Credit Bank and the Laender Bank of Vienna.[9] They purchased land and oil wells and pushed small and medium-size producers out of the oil market if they were unable to pay for the new technologies and professional personnel. At this stage of the game, many Jewish families left the industry. This led to large-scale dismissals of employees and a severe unemployment crisis. Schodnica managed to weather the technological revolution fairly well, however—chiefly because the Backenroth brothers' firm had remained a major player in the oil industry.

The result of reorganizing the oil economy was astounding. It is doubtful that any other area in fin de siècle Europe had created wealth as rapidly as the Drohobych-Boryslav-Schodnica triangle had.[10] But this remarkable success had an ugly side: environmental degradation, a widening gap between the rich and the poor, and increased corruption and crime.

Drohobych, which had a population of about twenty thousand in 1880, blossomed into a unique town, unlike the typical Galician city.[11] Three or four clean and well-lit European streets crossed the city, lined by mansions with magnificent facades, often in the classical Greek style. Other neighborhoods had villas much like those in Paris and Berlin. But hidden away some distance from these large residences were hundreds of ramshackle shanties that were home to the poor, most of whom were Ruthenians and Jews.

The city's new affluence seemed to happen overnight. From other locations in Galicia, people enviously watched the economic miracle taking place in Drohobych, but as time went by, the press reported more numerous incidents of corruption and crime in the city and its surroundings. Then Galicians began to wonder whether the community, with its rapid increase in wealth, was really a model to imitate. The cutthroat competition over who would sink more wells, who could pump more oil, who would get a higher price and sell more, and who would build a more ostentatious mansion; the unending stream of foreign workers coming and going, many of them drunken vagabonds; the greater numbers of homeless day laborers, who spent the icy winter nights in stairwells and the entrances of public buildings; the contrast between the laborers' shacks and the opulent residences of the wealthy; and the crimes of corruption involving businessmen, notable citizens, and community leaders—all of these gave Drohobych a bad name.

Boryslav, with its ten thousand inhabitants, did not gentrify, and it remained an environmental eyesore. A grayish malodorous slime covered the streets and the dirt tracks, which were lined with perforated pipes leaking oil. Debris from the three thousand or so excavations and wells had been dumped on every corner. More than two hundred companies were operating on the expansive plateau, which was crowded with oil derricks and tanks, wax and candle factories, and equipment depots. The stretch of the Tysmenytsia River that flowed through central Boryslav was thoroughly polluted, and the main streets near the river were always filthy.[12] No one would have dared to build luxury homes in Boryslav, not only because the extraction of oil was gradually causing the ground to sink, but because the town was fundamentally ugly and dirty. Many of the rich entrepreneurs preferred to build their residences in the nearby resorts of Zakopane and Krynica. The air in Boryslav was never clear; a cloud of smoke hung over the town, fed by a fire at one of the wells. Some of these fires were enormous, and one belched a pillar of smoke for five months.[13]

The press in Galicia, and sometimes in Vienna as well, devoted much space to accounts from Boryslav about economic activities, work conditions, and the volume of crime. Judging from reports in the Lvov newspaper *Kurjer Lwowsky* in the 1880s, crime in Boryslav and Drohobych soared to a shocking degree. There were reports of drunken brawls, robberies, and burglaries, as well as prostitution and soliciting, whereas in the past men requiring the services of ladies of the night would have had to travel to the big city, Lvov. Very seldom did newspapers focus on the environmental pollution that had changed the bucolic landscape into a scene that resembled a battlefield.[14]

In Schodnica, the era of opulence made a less visible mark. Perhaps the characteristic modesty of Schodnica's residents put a damper on the natural tendency of the nouveaux riches to show off their wealth in the vulgar and ostentatious manner displayed by affluent residents of Drohobych. In addition, Schodnica never looked as ugly as Boryslav because Schodnica's community leaders made efforts to preserve its rural nature. To a large extent, they succeeded, perhaps because the hilly topography and the trees and the vegetation hid the evidence of the expanding industrialization: oil derricks sprouting up between the houses, endless networks of pipelines, dozens of giant storage tanks, pits, and excavated debris. It was a common sight for workers to be drilling and pumping right next to homes, with children playing hide-and-seek around the oil barrels.[15]

The near-idyllic image of the village underwent a dramatic reversal in 1885, when a disastrous ecological accident polluted an extensive area and shocked the citizenry. The Austrian-Anglo Bank, known as Anglobank, had purchased a tract of land in the southern part of Schodnica, drilled wells, and begun to produce large quantities of crude oil—more than a hundred thousand tons a day.[16] A powerful gusher burst out of one of the wells, and the workers couldn't cap it. Tons of oil poured out onto the land.[17] The oil collected in a nearby pool, and streams of oil found their way to the valley of the Tysmenytsia River. Several dozen hectares of land were polluted, vegetation was destroyed, and workers who lived in the vicinity were forbidden to light fires, even inside their homes. Some oil flowed into the river, which provided drinking water for hundreds of farmers' families and also irrigated their fields. Plant life died on both banks, and in the river itself, the fish perished, and fishermen lost their livelihood.

The community leaders of Schodnica quickly rounded up the village residents for a cleanup operation. Hundreds of men, young and old, dug channels, drained the roads, excavated dozens of pits and buried oil sludge in them, and collected thousands of gallons of crude oil in drums and tins. But over wide areas, the oil had seeped through and contaminated the land so that even today one can see bald tracts where the soil absorbed large quantities of oil.

An ecological catastrophe on this scale could never have happened in an era when only paraffin pits were dug, but the surge of foreign entrepreneurs using modern technologies and drilling thousands of feet deep, combined with tremendously increased production, had created a new reality in the tranquil village.[18] Many small businesses were compelled to fold, and of the scores of Jewish oil pioneers who had excavated the first paraffin pits, only about ten remained.[19] By the time the disaster happened, most of the original producers had sold their land, wells, and rigs and abandoned the industry.

But not Avrumche. He had not only stayed in business, but had initiated a reorganization of the family firm in order to increase the volume of its economic activity and face the competition from his local counterparts as well as from U.S. oil, which was being sold cheaply in Europe. Production in the United States was still more efficient, however, and in the final years of the nineteenth century, Rockefeller's Standard Oil adopted a policy of flooding the European market with oil.[20] Rockefeller sent marketing teams to Austria and had fast bright-red carriages built for his agents to travel in. The agents gave out oil lamps free of charge in towns and villages and then marketed inexpensive oil to burn in the lamps.

Confronted with this cutthroat competition, the Backenroth brothers introduced three changes: they drilled more wells on the land they had acquired in Schodnica and Boryslav, they erected four refineries, and they began to specialize, assigning various spheres of business activity to separate subsidiary companies.[21] The brothers now controlled prospecting, drilling, production, transportation, refining, and marketing. Oil refined in Schodnica and Boryslav that was destined for export was loaded onto barges that plied the Tysmenytsia River, then floated along the Dniester River to the Black Sea. Oil that was refined in Krosno was carried on barges that navigated the San River, which flowed into the Vistula and from there to the Baltic Sea. Oil to be marketed in Poland and Austria was carried by railroad from Boryslav.

In Schodnica, the family's business was divided up among four companies: Backenroth, A.; Backenroth & Gaertner; Backenroth, M. & Leib, J.; and Backenroth, S. In Boryslav, the brothers operated within the framework of the first corporation in which they were partners, Nafta Petroleum. And a Backenroth & Horn partnership was registered in the village of Mraznica, near Boryslav. In addition to the oil wells and the refineries, the Backenroths owned sawmills and factories that manufactured wax, candles, and matchsticks, as well as warehouses and a fleet of trucks. The upshot of all this activity was that after 1890, the profit flowchart of the family business showed steep increases, peaking in the early twentieth century and then remaining stable for many years. By a conservative calculation, the annual profit of the companies owned by the Backenroth brothers at the end of the nineteenth century totaled about $1.5 million, which in today's currency amounts to $36 million.[22]

There were wealthier Jewish entrepreneurs in the oil belt, such as Foierstein, for example; Ephraim Schreier and Moshe Gartenberg, who were partners; Karol Katz, a manufacturer of drilling equipment; the businessman Lipa

Schutzman and one of the oil-refining pioneers, Binyamin Mermelstein, both men from Boryslav; and others.[23] But the Backenroths gained renown as philanthropists who had a social conscience and a sense of public responsibility. People stood in line to receive their help. Scores of Schodnica residents, Jews and Ukrainians, were employed by the brothers as clerks, engineers, geologists, economists, and accountants, as well as laborers, well drillers, plumbers, welders, carpenters, wagon drivers, and porters. The populace of Schodnica worshipped Avrumche and his family. "The Backenroths are aristocracy," they said in the village.

Toward the end of the century, the oil industry had become more advanced than other fields in the world economy. Although in most of Europe the production lines of the Industrial Revolution made it possible for farm workers to become factory hands without their having to undergo special training, in the realm of oil the situation was the other way around: men who had not acquired a scientific education or technical training had trouble finding jobs. The new technologies required skilled workers, while the demand for unskilled laborers dwindled. In the newspapers of Galicia and Vienna, employment ads ran alongside news reports of mass layoffs of manual laborers, particularly in Boryslav. Courses in the oil-related professions were offered in Lvov, and faculties of mine engineering were established at the university and the technical college in Kraków. In Boryslav as well, a trade school for mining and drilling was opened in 1896, and the Imperial Ministry of Mines initiated professional training in oil engineering, chemistry, and the skilled occupations associated with drilling. Those who completed their studies easily found employment at attractive salaries and under good working conditions. Large companies introduced health insurance and supplied housing for professional workers.

The excellent terms given to qualified employees further widened the gap between the educated and the ignorant classes. In the oil industry, almost everyone who never acquired a trade or a profession lost his ability to earn a living. The result was that thousands of Ruthenian and Jewish families found themselves relegated to the bottom rung of society's ladder, sometimes even becoming victims of starvation.

The mass dismissals in the oil belt swelled the flow of emigration from Galicia westward, but it was not the only cause. In the last twenty years of the century, this westward migration took place in two waves. The first was called "the Great Economic Migration," and it occurred in the 1880s when those leaving were mostly German farmers, the descendants of the families that had responded to the invitation of Polish kings and had settled in Galicia in the Middle Ages, at the same time as the Jews. Now it suited them to relocate to Imperial Germany, which was ruled by Emperor Wilhelm I of Prussia and his chancellor, Otto von Bismarck. Wilhelm I managed to shape modern Germany by uniting in 1871 the German principalities into a single political entity for the first time and then made it an industrialized power. Ruthenian peasants also emigrated to Germany because the soil of Galicia could no longer support them. Young Jews, attracted by the educational and cultural institutions of Berlin, left Galicia as well.

The second wave of emigration, a far more comprehensive one, began in the early 1890s and continued until mid-1914, when the Great War broke out. It led to a demographic change in Galicia that was perhaps the most significant in Europe in that period. This time, the destination was the New World. Most of the migrants settled in the United States, while smaller groups went to Canada and Brazil. The majority of Polish emigrants opted for New England and the Midwest, and Ukrainians generally chose Canada and Brazil, although a large number also went to the United States.[24] Most Jews chose the United States and settled primarily in New York City.

Between 1895 and 1900, some ten thousand unskilled Jewish workers were fired, including approximately seven thousand from Boryslav, and the emigration from the oil belt reached record levels. Certain Jewish community officials in Drohobych and Boryslav alleged that some of the foreign investors had decided to get rid of the Jews in the industry only because they were Jews and that non-Jews had not lost their jobs, but such contentions were baseless. Unskilled workers were dismissed, both Ruthenians and Jews, and at the same time professional Jewish workers were taken on. The first generation of oil entrepreneurs, most of whom were Jewish, had employed thousands of people in jobs that were not directly linked to production: as watchmen, wagon drivers, cleaners, personal assistants, water drawers, and cooks.

During the years when profits rapidly grew, there was a degree of concealed unemployment in the industry, but Jewish employers found it difficult to do away with it because they could not stand up to the pressure from the heads of the Jewish community, who took a stand in favor of simple working men. But the new generation of employers, most of whom were not Jewish, chose to cut costs in order to earn profits for their shareholders and better face the competition from U.S. companies that were flooding the markets with low-priced oil. So Jewish employers, too, among them the Backenroth brothers, were forced to fire unskilled Jewish workers, although they frequently offered to put them through training courses, sometimes at no cost to the workers. But not all of the workers were capable of undertaking such courses, as they lacked elementary education. In Schodnica, the crisis caused by the layoffs was not too severe because generally the men who were fired were immediately rehired for manual labor at new drilling sites. But in Boryslav, there was almost no new drilling going on, and the wave of dismissals was particularly painful.

The Jewish community in Drohobych rallied in support of the workers and turned to the Jews of the world for help.[25] Jewish assistance foundations in Galicia and Austria raised half a million Austrian gulden, but the money quickly ran out.[26]

A local Zionist club, Ahavat Zion ("the love of Zion"), appealed to the newly formed World Zionist Organization in 1899 and asked it to pay emigration expenses to the land of Israel for a hundred families of men from Boryslav and Schodnica who had been dismissed. Some of the families were to be settled in the Galilee, in the Jewish colony of Mahanayim, which had been founded by Galician Zionists a year earlier. The founder of the Zionist movement, Theodor Herzl, sent requests to Jewish organizations in Austria, Germany, and England to raise money to help the unemployed Jews of Boryslav, but not enough funds were raised, and the initiative fell through.[27] Yet substantial aid for the laid-off workers did come from the family of the German Jewish nobleman Baron Maurice von Hirsch, which in 1891 set up the Jewish Colonization Agency (ICA), financed agricultural studies for Galician Jewish youths, and sent more than five hundred of them to the United States.[28]

The dismissals in Boryslav thus boosted emigration to the United States. The rabbis tried to stem the flow but failed. Every third home in the poor Jewish quarters was emptied of its residents, classrooms in the Jewish school were closed, and synagogue buildings were sold off. The migrants packed their meager belongings and set off by train for the ports of Hamburg or Rotterdam to board ships bound for New York. Usually, the fares were paid in advance, sometimes by the companies that had fired the workers or by donations from local or American Jewish mutual assistance organizations. The migration from Galicia to the United States in the closing years of the nineteenth century was greater than that from the whole of Russia.

The wave of emigration shocked the Backenroths. Like most families of means, the Backenroth brothers never considered leaving Galicia. As businessmen, they were optimistic about the future, relying on their abilities and their faith in the economic system.

Indeed, at the beginning of the twentieth century, their future looked promising. More than seventeen hundred firms connected with the oil industry, operating in more than a hundred towns and villages, positioned Galicia in fourth place on the list of the world's oil producers, with a 4 percent share. Ninety percent of Galicia's oil production and refining was done in the oil belt, by large and medium-size companies that had adopted modern technologies and employed professional personnel of the highest level. The candle industry was also growing. The deposits of wax in the Boryslav area were the largest in the world, and the technologies for exploiting it had been streamlined. Most of the owners of the wax pits were Jews, and their investments continued to grow. Altogether, the momentum of economic development in Galicia was unprecedented: roads were built, railroads were extended and widened, and hotels, workers' housing, and schools were constructed.

But among all the roses there were also thorns. Galicia was not the only country that had been blessed with oil-rich soil; other parts of the world were producing even more. The world supply of oil was increasing, but the demand remained stable, and prices declined. Rockefeller's Standard Oil was able to reduce prices because of its efficiency, but in Galicia, the production, refining, and transportation costs were higher than those in the United States by roughly 20 percent. At the end of the first decade of the new century, most of the markets for Austrian oil in Europe, especially the German market, were pressing the producers to lower their prices and were threatening to switch to Standard Oil.

Salvation came from Detroit when, in 1908, Henry Ford began to sell his Model T automobile. Its four-cylinder internal combustion engine was fueled by gasoline. The demand for oil went up, and the Backenroths benefited. This was exactly what they had hoped for when they reorganized their companies and invested heavily in equipment and personnel. During the next four years, from 1910 to 1913, production lines went into operation at the Ford automobile plant in Highland Park, Michigan, and the demand for oil grew to vast proportions.

There were danger signs on the horizon, though, as geologists raised the possibility that the Galician wells would not supply oil forever, contrary to the predictions of "experts" in the 1860s and the 1880s. (What we now call the science of geology came into its own only after World War I.) The oil fields might be drying up, some researchers warned, but they could not provide definitive evidence for their forecasts.

In the meantime, Avrumche was not worried. He had his little notebook, in which he wrote down numbers in tiny handwriting. He remembered them all by heart: figures for production and refining, price comparisons, payrolls—data that today are processed by computers but were then calculated manually or mentally. In Schodnica, the future looked rosy.

7

A King Is Born

ONLY TWELVE MILES SEPARATED BOLECHOW AND SCHODNICA, but despite their proximity and the fact that both towns lay in the Carpathian foothills, there was no great similarity between them. While Schodnica's notoriety was derived from its oil tycoons and speculators' extravagant behavior, Bolechow gained a reputation for its prosperous leather-processing industry. Everything that was tarnished by the oil industry in Schodnica remained pristine and pure in Bolechow, not only the rivers and the air, but its inhabitants' souls. Oil was never discovered in Bolechow, so its fields were not excavated and drilled, and ugly derricks were not erected to mar the landscape. This was why the people of Bolechow were less wealthy but happier than the inhabitants of Schodnica.

There was thus no obvious connection between the oil entrepreneurs of Schodnica and the leather tanners of Bolechow, but those of us who are able to look back from the future may discern that from the time of the birth of Rachel and Yerahmiel Kahane's son, who became known by his nickname, Ullo, a fateful link was forged between the Kahanes in Bolechow and the Backenroths of Schodnica.[1] For as was mentioned earlier, in due course Ullo would marry the granddaughter of Avrumche Backenroth—Hanna Sobel, whom everyone called Nushka.

Rachel Kahane gave birth to Ullo in the bedroom of her home on a fine summer afternoon, June 29, 1911. It was an easy delivery. The baby slid right into the waiting hands of the Ruthenian midwife. Rachel had given birth four times before Ullo was born, but only two of the other babies had survived: the firstborn daughter, Leah, and her sister, Sara, known as Sonia.

Two others had died in infancy: Eva, who was born in 1905 and who succumbed to an illness at age two, and Haim, who was born in 1908 and died a year later of diphtheria.[2] It is no wonder, then, that three generations of the Kahane family looked forward to the birth of a male child the way that Jews long for the messiah to appear.

At the time of the birth, the father, Yerahmiel, was busy at his leather tannery across the river. Rachel's mother, Reisel, was looking after the two daughters in the yard of the house. Her husband, David, was napping in his room. All of a sudden, a cry was heard. At last. Grandma Reisel hugged Sonia and Leah tightly, spat three times on the ground to fend off the evil eye, and whispered in excitement, "*Mazel tov, mazel tov*, he is here." She had been certain that a male child would be born to make up for the loss of Haim. Sonia jumped up and down in glee. Leah wept. In the years to come, on each of Ullo's birthdays, Grandma Reisel would declare proudly, "Even the cocks in the yard crowed. King David was born."

Indeed, the setting was majestic. On that summer's day, the town of Bolechow looked like an idyllic landscape painting. The sky was blue and the air was clear. On the distant peaks of the mountain ridge, the last patches of snow sparkled in the sun's rays, and the broad Sukiel River flowed into the valley. The Carpathian slopes were covered in multiple shades of green: groves of tall light-green pines and of dark, low pines with spreading branches and, between them, chestnut trees with white blossoms, dark fir trees, white beeches, yellow-flowering lindens, and ancient oaks with pale green leaves, mushroom-shaped tops, and dark green ivy climbing up their huge trunks. Under the trees, the bushes were heavy with blueberries and bilberries. A blanket of strawberry plants covered the ground.

In the middle of this tableau stood the city hall, known locally by the German word *Magistrat*. It was topped by a square tower with a round clock on every side facing each of the four directions. The tower overlooked the marketplace, officially called the Ringplatz, which is German for "Bell Square," but it was known to everyone by its Polish name, the Rynek. The square was lined with houses, most of them wooden and painted red, like the Kahane family home. Other buildings were of gray stone, such as the graceful Orthodox church with its three domes and colorful fresco on the façade. Opposite the church loomed the Great Synagogue, with tall, narrow windows. Behind the houses, small huts of wood and clay were built around the lime pits that served as latrines. Some homes had red tile roofs and others,

Bolechow's city hall, which the townsfolk called the Magistrat.

flat roofs. Each residence had a big green yard with a water well, fruit trees, and rosebushes. Behind the homes was a stream, spanned by a bridge. In the streets, only some of which were paved with cobblestones, walked good people, hardworking and happy with their lot—leather producers, woodworkers, office clerks, teachers, housewives, schoolgirls, Hasidic Torah scholars, peasants, and merchants. They usually greeted one another with these words: "It's been a good year, and let's hope all the years to come will be as good."

After a hard winter, the people of Bolechow were enjoying the summer heat. The Polish clerks went home for an afternoon nap, the Ukrainian peasants harvested their crops, and in the leather tanneries and sawmills the Jewish craftsmen and merchants planned their summer vacations. Life was placid and serene, and no one was in a hurry. Everyone knew his or her place and felt a collective sense of security. It seemed as if the Austro-Hungarian

The great synagogue of Bolechow, which was very close to the Kahanes' home.

Empire, which stretched from the Alps to the Carpathians, was in good hands, those of the officials of the elderly Emperor Franz Josef, to whose title the Jews added, "May his glory be exalted." They believed that no one could be a more just ruler than the emperor.[3]

In the capital city of Vienna, dandified men with bushy sideburns waltzed beautiful women around the dance floors. In the salons of high society, there were earnest discussions about "the Balkan question" and the expansionist aims of "those wicked Russians." Tightly corseted matrons tsk-tsked in disapproval as, in distant regions, intense nationalists were already loading their rifles. In the south of the Austro-Hungarian Empire, the Italian minority was again insisting on being annexed as a part of Italy. In the east, the Russians encouraged the Slavs to rebel and the Czechs demanded independence. In Bosnia-Herzegovina, an uprising was being plotted. In three years' time, less one day, the heir apparent, Archduke Franz Ferdinand, would be assassinated in the Bosnian capital of Sarajevo, and all at once Europe would be thrust into chaos it had not experienced since the days of the Black Death.

Just three more years of tranquillity and happiness before war would spoil the beautiful world of the citizens of Bolechow.

Bolechow's church.

On that afternoon in Bolechow, when Rachel Kahane's bedroom had been tidied after the birth, her husband, Yerahmiel, entered to take a look at the baby. The Ukrainian maid scampered away to stand in a corner. The proud father stood over the wooden cradle, looked at his son in silence, and nodded his head with satisfaction. Then he kissed his wife. She was twenty-one years old, pale and lovely. He was twenty-four, tall and handsome, the father of three, and just setting out as a leather manufacturer.

"We'll name the child Israel Herz," Rachel said, but soon everyone was calling him Ullo. (It is not known why he was given this nickname; the story has been lost through the generations.)

Yerahmiel Kahane, Ullo's father, had married Rachel Graubart ("gray-beard," in German) two years into the twentieth century. He had been almost fifteen, an orderly and serious youth, and she was twelve. The groom had been born in Pechenizhin, near Kolomyya, and the bride in

Bolechow. Two years before the wedding, in 1900, an experienced *shadchan*, or matchmaker, had come from Pechenizhin to Bolechow on a mission for Yerahmiel's parents. Itche Kahane, the boy's father, was the owner of a brewery. David Graubart, Rachel's father, was a respected citizen of Bolechow, an ordained rabbi, a landowner, and a wealthy man.

The matchmaker sat with David Graubart and listed the virtues of Itche Kahane and of his son Rahmiel—dropping the first letters, as had the government officials who registered him as Rahmiel on his papers, although his given name was Yerahmiel. (Both names are Hebrew for "May God have mercy.")

"It is an educated family, respectable and not at all poor," the matchmaker told the girl's father. "Sarah Kahane has given her husband Itche four sons and daughters, Rahmiel being the last. His elder brother, Leibush, is the author of books. His two sisters, Esther and Carolina [known as Kreidel], married into good families and are living in Vienna. Carolina's husband is a lawyer, from the Ostersetzer family, Esther's married name is Scharf, and, of course, Rahmiel himself, who will soon be fifteen, is a lad full of talent, studying at the Polish gymnasium [high school], and he speaks German well. That is your son-in-law!"

But David Graubart would have none of the matchmaker's blandishments. "I'll find a scholar for my daughter," he said, and sneered, "If Itche Kahane of Pechenizhin decided not to send his son to study Torah in a yeshiva, that is his business, but I will have nothing to do with unbelievers, and his educated son Yerahmiel will have nothing to do with Graubart's daughter. Period."

The matchmaker did not give up and traveled back and forth from Pechenizhin to Bolechow several times until, at the end of the winter, a compromise was reached: before the wedding, Yerahmiel would give up his secular schooling and go to a yeshiva to study the Talmud. And that is what happened. Yerahmiel left the Polish school and studied for two years at a yeshiva far from home, in Lublin, and his bride-to-be, Rachel, waited for him in Bolechow.

David Graubart hired a private tutor for Rachel, a student from Vienna by the name of Ludringer, who had been born in Galicia and made a living teaching girls from good families. He was said to have been a respectable young man and an excellent teacher, but gossips had it that some virgins had lost their innocence while under his tutelage. At the Graubart home, however, the doors were always left open, and Rachel was already engaged to Yerahmiel. The student therefore earned his wages honestly, and Rachel studied diligently. Throughout her life, she loved to learn and often came up with surprising bits of knowledge. "She knows far more than one would think," her neighbors in Bolechow used to say.

As a child, Rachel had learned the Hebrew alphabet from the rebbetzin Sara Rivka, the wife of the rabbi of Bolechow. Rachel's only brother, Avraham, went to *heder*, the elementary Jewish school, where he was taught by the *melamed*, the rabbi's assistant, to read the Torah and the prayers. The rabbi lived in a little house in the synagogue's courtyard, and his wife crowded the ten girls whom she taught onto two wooden benches in a small chamber adjoining her kitchen. There, she provided them with their education. In the winter, cooking aromas filled the cold air. In the summer, it was hot and smelly. The rebbetzin taught the girls six mornings a week, while cooking and baking at the same time and paging through the *siddur* (prayer book), leaving grease stains on its pages. She kneaded the dough for challah, koshered freshly slaughtered chickens with salt, and stirred the dishes simmering on the stove.

Every now and then, Sara Rivka raised her arm, drew a Hebrew letter in the air, and told the girls, "Alef, like Abraham our father," or "Bet, like a *bayit* [house]," or "Gimmel, like a *gamal* [camel]." The rebbetzin's curriculum didn't include any stories, songs, walks in nature, or names of flowers or butterflies. The young girls spent their days reciting the Shema prayer and the blessing over food by heart and learning strange words like *totafot* (phylacteries), *tzitzis* (fringed garments), *yemot ha-mashiah* (the days of the messiah), and *Ha'Olam Haba* (the world to come).[4] The rebbetzin knew only one teaching method: by rote. In her monotonous voice, she read verses from the thick, worn prayer book: "Once again now, '*Shemo Yisroel ho-Shem Elokeinu ho-Shem Ehod*'" (Hear, Israel, the Lord is our God, the Lord is One)—and the little girls repeated the lines over and over.

"You are princesses," the rebbetzin taught the small girls, "and the beauty of a princess is internal. A princess never shows her face in public."

Sometimes the *melamed* took the boys to bathe in the river, which was forbidden to the girls. When they asked to go, Sara Rivka told them that the river was frozen over, and, in any case, girls didn't bathe in the open air.

"Do not be tempted, girls. There are dangers out there. Cover up your forearms and your calves, hide your hair, the Sitra-Achra is waiting for you patiently around the corner, waiting to tempt you." By using the alien kabbalistic term Sitra Achra (which means "the other side" in Aramaic), the rebbetzin warned the girls about their own evil inclination. They understood only a little of what she said, but the fear of the devil penetrated their minds.

Rachel Graubart didn't learn anything artistic from the rebbetzin, not even home crafts such as needlework. She learned only to memorize prayers and blessings and was told about superstitions and the customs of women. Nevertheless, Sara Rivka was Rachel's first teacher, and this first stage in her education was of prime importance. It was here that respect for the Creator, for the patriarchs and the matriarchs, and for her own conscience, while at the same time an awareness of the inferiority of her gender, were imprinted on her consciousness: "A woman's place is in the kitchen." "She does not learn more than she has to know."

As a child, Rachel had learned what to do, but even more, she learned what not to do. In the future, when her own children abandoned the *mitzvoth* of Judaism, she did not oppose them. Rachel Graubart, the daughter of Reisel and David and the granddaughter of Rabbi Graubart, grew up as an independent woman. She was not a feminist and was by no means a rebellious woman or a revolutionary. But she was a wise, quick-witted woman, who knew how to blend what she had inherited from her culture and what she learned in daily life.

When Rachel was six, she was registered at an elementary school, as required by the empire's compulsory education laws. For four years at that government school, she learned three languages (Polish, German, and some Ukrainian), history, geography, a little literature, and the basics of arithmetic. There was no Jewish school for girls in Bolechow, only one for boys. Therefore, most of the boys at the government school were Poles, and most of the girls Jewish, and they had nothing to do with one another. At the age of ten, Rachel had fulfilled her obligation to the empire, and after that, she stayed home and learned from the student Ludringer, while waiting for Yerahmiel to complete his stint in the yeshiva. Then he would return to consecrate her as his bride under the wedding canopy.

Ludringer recognized that she was a quick learner. During the year of her wedding to Yerahmiel, she read in German the *Buch der Lieder* (Book of Songs) by Heinrich Heine and knew some of his love poems by heart. She shared the excitement that Goethe's *Sorrows of Young Werther* generated in many young hearts. She followed the story of the friendship between

Goethe and Schiller with great interest. In her eyes, the Germans were the lords of creation, and Berlin and Vienna were the realms of the soul.

Rachel's father never interfered. He knew that the world did not stand still. David Graubart looked at the walls of the Jewish ghetto and saw that they were cracking, but he accepted it. He was a moderate man. He followed his daughter's growing up with equanimity, and he was pleased that she valued tradition as well as modern influences. In the morning, she intoned the Shaharit morning prayer in her room with great devotion, and in the afternoon she exchanged books in the Polish library. She avidly read Henryk Sienkiewicz's *Quo Vadis* and *The Deluge* and Adam Mickiewicz's epic poem *Pan Tadeusz* (Master Thaddeus) in Polish. At night in bed, she piously said the Shema and then read the first issues of the new German-language Zionist Jewish journal *Die Welt* (The World).[5] Her parents were proud of her. Although she did not agree with everything they had taught her, she was not defiant and kept her beliefs to herself.

Compromise was a way of life for her parents, as it had been for their parents and grandparents. "My way is the middle way," David Graubart used to declare solemnly to his family. He explained that taking the middle way was what Maimonides had preached. Rachel's father was a pragmatist. He always studied the world around him carefully and tried to adapt to reality. He did not go forward too rapidly, God forbid, or look for revolutions and troubles.

"Blessed is he who always fears," he taught his children. Take great care to preserve what there is, do not endanger anything, he told them, do not give up what has been achieved, don't run ahead, always be cautious, and don't be too daring. Like him, millions of Jews throughout the empire blessed the emperor, Franz Josef I, and wished him eternal life. They said to one another, "Just let it not get any worse." They remembered all too well the anti-Semitic mood that swept through the Austro-Hungarian Empire after the Napoleonic Wars.[6] "Just don't let it get worse," they pleaded. Whenever they took a great step forward, they took two little steps backward. And God heard their prayers. For more than three hundred years, Jews in Bolechow lived happily.

The first Jews of Bolechow, including the Graubart family, had left Ashkenaz at the end of the fourteenth century and came to settle in Poland about fifty years after the Backenroth family moved to Schodnica. Like the Backenroths, the Graubarts left Germany in a convoy of wagons, crossed

Bohemia from west to east in the direction of Ostrava (the administrative city of the Moravian-Silesian region; today it is in the Czech Republic), and turned north to Kraków. They crossed the San River, continued eastward for a few days into western Ukraine, and finally came to a halt at the foot of the Carpathian mountains on the lands of Nikolai Gidzinski, a Polish nobleman. In the beginning of the seventeenth century Gidzinski received permission from the king to set up the town of Bolechow. It was to be a private town, built on the nobleman's estate and run by Jewish immigrants from Germany. Until then, several hundred Ruthenian families had lived on Gidzinski's lands, dwelling in miserable shacks and cultivating the soil. The yields were small and the nobleman's income meager, which was why he had invited the Jews to settle on his estate. He wanted to improve it, streamline working methods, and increase his income.

By choosing the patronage of Gidzinski, the Graubarts secured an extremely fortunate future. In 1603, the polish nobleman wrote a charter for Bolechow's Jews and obtained the signature of King Zygmunt III on the document. It granted full and equal rights to the Jewish residents of the new town, including the right to vote for the town mayor. The king exempted them from public works and from the obligations imposed on the Ruthenian vassals, such as paving roads, constructing bridges, and supplying means of transportation. Gidzinski's charter assigned the Jews only one task: to guard the dam across the river against flooding. In regard to legal matters, the charter stipulated that Jews who were sued by Christians would be tried by the nobleman himself in the presence of the "elder of the Jews." Gidzinski guaranteed to build houses and shops for the Jews, to establish a synagogue with adjacent houses for the cantor and the beadle, and to assign a plot of land for a cemetery.

No wonder that the Jewish settlers, who were compelled to leave Germany, enthusiastically accepted Gidzinski's tempting offer. In early-seventeenth-century Europe, very few Jewish communities enjoyed full civil rights and such a high standard of living as the Polish nobleman offered. (The exceptions were the Jews of Holland and a few Jewish communities that lived in several regions in northern Germany. In most places, however, the Jews were deprived of rights, they paid special taxes, and their movements and professional occupations were restricted.)

The Graubart family settled in the middle of the new town, in the rectangle formed by the houses around the Rynek. A small house was built for the family on a one-hectare plot, with a fenced courtyard and garden. They earned their living by leasing the nobleman's lands, almost the same way the Backenroths had done in Schodnica. The head of the family leased agricultural land from the nobleman and rented it to the Ruthenian peasants in return for half the yield of their crops. In the autumn, he purchased the future crop, which was still in the field, from the peasants. When he sold the crop, soon after the harvest at the beginning of the following autumn, he paid the landowner the leasing fee that was due to him and kept the rest for himself. For almost three hundred years, the heads of the Graubart family leased land, and the last one to do so was Ullo's grandfather, David Graubart. His son-in-law Yerahmiel Kahane preferred another business—leather tanning.

The Jews of Bolechow were experts at making leather. Most of the producers, the merchants, and the workers were Jews, and their lives revolved around their own professional calendar, which was based on processing the hides. In the autumn and the winter they manufactured hides, in the spring they marketed them, and in the summer they rested and counted their profits—at least, that is what the leather producers boasted during the good years. The business forecast was made in the early spring. If, on Sundays, buyers from across the state were lining up outside the gates of their plants and warehouses, the Bolechow leather makers were pleased. But when money was scarce in Galicia, in the rest of Poland, and in neighboring Hungary, then the leather storerooms remained full of stock and the manufacturers were forced to borrow money or use up their savings, so that their plants would not stand idle during the following year.

But since Yerahmiel Kahane had arrived in Bolechow from his parents' home in Pechenizhin, the leather industry had thrived to an unprecedented degree, and the plant owners and the merchants raked in money, hand over fist.

The largest tannery in Bolechow had been founded in 1814, by Isroel Hauptmann.[7] At that time, by law, Jews were not allowed to be industrialists, and Hauptmann was forced to register his company under the name of a Christian. That discriminatory law was revoked in 1844, and the enterprise was registered as "The Emperor and Royal Privileged Leather Factory, Isroel Hauptmann and Co." By the end of the nineteenth century, dozens of leather-processing factories had been set up in the town, and its reputation spread far and wide, as far as Kraków and even Vienna.[8]

At an 1878 industrial fair in Leipzig, hides processed in Bolechow received a first prize, and in the wake of that success, the local industry was represented at an international shoe exhibition in Paris. One Jew from Drohobych reported from the French capital to his friend in Bolechow that Bolechow's leather had been well received at the show. He said, "There was very high praise for the processed hides in different colors, precious in appearance, size and quality, and they are from the workshops of my in-laws and my friends, the well known gentlemen, the pleasant and godfearing brothers, Yisrael Leib and Rabbi Eli Neta Hauptmann, May his Light shine, from the town of Bolechow, who are known under the name of 'Isroel Hauptmann and Company' and they have already been honored at the gate of the exhibition in Vienna and after that in the city of Kraków."[9]

From the beginning of Jewish settlement, there were close business contacts between Jewish merchants and Christian buyers and sellers. Town documents reveal that the Christians had complete trust in the Jewish merchants. The relations between the Jewish community and the Christian community were tranquil and honest. The oath of office taken by the mayor of Bolechow, composed in 1660, states as follows: "I swear to live in peace with all citizens of the town, both Roman Catholics, Greek Catholics and Jews, with the rich and the poor, to guard the rights of all three peoples and to defend them." And indeed, life in Bolechow was conducted in a spirit of peace and cooperation. Jews enjoyed equal rights and freedom of economic, cultural, and religious activities. They were able to establish the infrastructure of an active and lively community. This delicate balance between the religions was maintained in Bolechow for almost 350 years.

That calmness and positive spirit helped Yerahmiel Kahane to establish his business. Step by step, he learned the trade of leather processing, a complicated and difficult endeavor, some of it performed by expert professionals and some by manual laborers.

After the *shohatim,* or ritual slaughterers, had completed their kosher dispatch of the cows or bulls—all called "oxen" by the locals—and the carcasses had been brought to the meat wholesalers, the skinners were called in to do their job.[10] Since dawn, their apprentices had been sharpening their long knives, rubbing the blades on a round flint stone dozens of times and testing the knives' edges on their own filthy fingernails. When the tools of their trade were ready, each skilled skinner took up a position close to the belly of a dead beast and made one long, fine cut from the neck to the rump and four similar cuts along the length of the legs. This accomplished, they called in the apprentices, who stripped the hide from the flesh using brute force.

This removal of the hide from the "ox" was the first stage. Now the process of tanning would begin at the tanneries. First, the hides were salted to kill worms and parasites. Then the hair was removed, by placing the hides in barrels full of limewater, which seeped through the upper layer of skin, burned the roots of the hair, and melted the fat. After a few days, the limewater was rinsed off, and each hide was stretched over a wooden board. Using a long dull knife, the apprentices then carefully shaved off the remaining fine fuzz.

Skinning was a skill that was handed down from father to son, but soaking the hides in limewater was just plain hard work. Mostly, it was done by simple laborers, but sometimes schoolboys came and asked to work with the lime barrels. After a few hours of the lime burning their skin and the stench permeating their bodies, however, they gave up and left, never to return.

When the crude preliminary processes were over, the tanning began: softening the hides by using chemical materials and the bark of trees and plants containing the bitter substance called tannin. The bark was purchased from the large sawmill owned by a Jew named Griffel. There, the bark had been stripped from the huge trunks of firs, cypresses, pines, oaks, and sumac trees, which were known as tanners' trees.

The trees had been cut down in the Carpathian forests and brought to the sawmill on cast-iron coaches that looked like long, flat open wagons.[11] Men pushed the wagons loaded with logs down narrow-gauge metal tracks that were laid along the mountain slopes. The wagons swiftly rolled downhill powered by the force of gravity, passed through the forest with a whistling sound that could be heard clearly in Bolechow, and drew to a stop on a narrow flat area on the bank of the Sukiel River. In the sawmill yard, the bark was stripped off the logs and piled up, and the tanners decided how much to take, according to the number of hides they were going to process.

Tanning was a complex process. Right after the large square of hide was removed from the lime mixture, it was folded into a kind of pocket that looked like an inflated skin water bag and was filled with bark, nutgalls (a small nut-shaped protrusion on trees produced by the gall wasp), alum (a stone that was used to stanch blood after shaving and that contains potassium sulfate and potassium aluminate), oil, and softening plants. Innovators among the leather makers used to soften the hides in a shorter process, with manufactured and pure chemical substances: chrome salts and aluminum, which is extracted from potassium aluminate. Most of the Bolechow tanners employed the traditional methods, though, in order to preserve the original shades and smells of the leather, just as their ancient predecessors had done in the Near East. In the winter they soaked the hides in pits dug into the earth, in alternating layers of hides, bark, nutgalls, and nettles, and then poured water over them and left the solution to seep into the skins and soften them. At the end of the winter, the hides were removed from the pits tenderized, flexible, and soft to the touch. This natural method suited Bolechow because the town was surrounded by forests with plenty of nutgalls and bark, which were rich in softening substances.[12]

Next, the softened leather was passed on to the expert cutters, known in Yiddish as *garberim,* who were considered the elite workers of the industry. They cut the sheets of leather into lengths and straightened the edges with sharp knives. These strips were known in the trade as *panta* and were of the densest skin, sturdy and waterproof, which would serve for the uppers of shoes. Or they cut *gilda*—crude, simple, thick strips that were used to make harnesses, leather bags, or soldiers' boots. The medium strips were used for shoes and belts, the thin ones for whips for carriage drivers and women's handbags, and the very thinnest ones for evening shoes for Viennese society matrons. But most of these products were not made in Bolechow, where only the processing was done. There were only two factories for leather products in Bolechow at that time, one belonging to Chaim Frisch and the other to the Landes brothers. They made boot soles for the Polish army and boxing gloves, but, even so, the preliminary stages of the leather-making industry in Bolechow supplied many people with good livelihoods: industrialists and processors, cutters and skinners, hair removers, and those employed in the small allied factories that produced hide glue, soap, and brushes made of the hair that was removed from the hides.

After Yerahmiel learned the tanning trade, his father-in-law, David Graubart, gave him a plot of land adjacent to a canal. Yerahmiel built a shack there and hung out his shingle with the name of the enterprise: "Sukiel," after the river. He hired workers, bought hides that had been stripped from the "oxen," filled pits with lime, collected bark, and hired some *garberim,* expert cutters, at high rates of pay.

One thing led to another, and by the end of the first decade of the twentieth century, Yerahmiel was doing well. In 1907, Rachel gave birth to Leah.

Sonia was three. And in less than four years' time, Ullo was born. Another year passed, and there were already two buildings of the Kahane leather works standing next to the canal.

Yerahmiel was now a success, and his business flourished. This was demonstrated every year during the sale season, at the end of spring and during early summer, when every Sunday the leather buyers of Poland and Hungary made their way to Bolechow by train. In the morning they walked along Linden Avenue in the Bahnhofstrasse, passed the courthouse and the home of Dr. Blumenthal, crossed the bridge over the Sukiel, and reached the warehouse district. Here they greeted the salesmen and chatted politely with them, checked the prices, touched the goods with their fingers and smelled them, bargained a little, and assessed the market. The leather buyers mentally figured out what they would sell to the leather goods manufacturers and what they would hold on to, in the hope that prices would rise. Then they paid for their purchases and headed for the tavern. In the afternoon, the sellers packed the leather strips into huge bales, tied them up with strong cords, and then hired a porter. Before the last train was due to leave, they called the buyer out of the tavern and loaded the bales onto the backs of the porters, most of whom were students earning some pocket money. In a few years' time, when Ullo was a youth, he, too, would come to his father's storerooms to earn a few zlotys as a "Sunday porter."

This was the spectacle seen by passersby in the streets of Bolechow, on Sundays before sunset: dozens of teenage porters carrying giant bales of leather strips on their backs, trudging down the main street from the water canal to the train station. Following them were the merchants, some clad in three-piece suits and gleaming leather shoes, others dressed casually. Toward evening, the train's whistle blew as it pulled away into the hills, and the town took on a relaxed ambience. The manufacturers counted their banknotes, the young porters counted their coins, and elderly couples strolled along the river bank.

Year after year, the buyers poured into Bolechow, and Yerahmiel Kahane expanded his business. His wife, Rachel, did the bookkeeping. At the end of each year, his sales kept increasing. Yerahmiel put most of the profits back into his business and saved the rest for bleaker days. He was a realistic man, like his father-in-law—mild, responsible, and even-tempered. Things went well. Grandma Reisel ran the shared household, supervising the two maids, the cleaner, and the cook, and pampered her grandchildren. Sonia, the elder, was a joyful, plump girl. Leah was slender, smart, serious, and a worrier. Ullo, the chubby infant, was king, always chortling and endlessly spoiled. His life was shaped during the calm years of his childhood.

One summery Sabbath eve, David Graubart walked with his son-in-law Yerahmiel to pray at the synagogue of the bourgeoisie. The date was June 26, 1914. In two days' time, on Sunday, the empire's crown prince, Archduke Ferdinand, would be murdered in Sarajevo. In a month, Austria would attack Serbia. Then Russia would advance on Austria, Germany would invade Belgium in order to attack France, and England would retaliate against Germany to defend Belgium. Later, the Ruthenians would fight the Poles in Lvov and Jews would be murdered in a pogrom. Galicia would pass from hand to hand.

But all that lay ahead. After the service, David Graubart told his son-in-law, "If the future will be like the present, we have no reason to worry," and Yerahmiel Kahane agreed wholeheartedly.

PART TWO

Disillusionment

8

For God, Emperor, and Homeland

IN THE RINGPLATZ, BOLECHOW'S TOWN SQUARE, the weekly Monday market was drawing to a close. A cloud of dust rose into the sky as scores of Ruthenian farmers folded up their stalls, loaded their unsold wares onto the wagons, and began to return home. Some tardy buyers were still roaming between the wagons, snapping up onions here and potatoes there and trying to fill their shopping baskets before the square emptied out. A light wind rustled the tops of the venerable chestnut trees, and the evening was neither hot nor cold, precisely the way it should be on this green and tranquil mountain plateau on a clear early summer's evening. In the distance, just beyond the line of houses, farmers were using scythes to harvest the last rows of oats. Their fields were bordered by forests, stretching out to the horizon. A lone Jew, a short man wearing a hat, hurried across the big bridge. Children played in the river underneath. The breeze carried their joyful yells and laughter up to the bridge.

Suddenly, the tranquillity was shattered. Shouts rang out. Who was shouting on such a wonderful evening? The sun's last rays lit up the figure of the man on the bridge. It was Hendel, David Graubart's clerk, who was known as *der Ruthiner Man* (German for "the Ruthenian man"). He represented Graubart in his dealings with the Ruthenian peasants who leased his land. Hendel spoke their language, and he heard everything that went on among them. He mediated disputes that broke out among them, and when their children were ill, he called in the local physician, Yaakov Blumenthal, to take care of them.

Hendel wore an old-fashioned three-piece European suit and a European hat. He ran from the bridge into the Rynek, the main street, shouting, "Cossacks, Cossacks." He stopped in the square, took off his hat, and fanned himself with it. His hair fell over his forehead, his face was red, and sweat ran down his cheeks.

"Cossacks, Cossacks! Danger, danger!" he yelled hysterically and strode swiftly forward. "They're coming, they're coming! The Cossacks are coming!"

By "Cossacks," he meant Ruthenians, and, as was mentioned earlier, in that part of the world the shout "Cossacks!" had been fixed in the collective memory of the Jews since the middle of the seventeenth century, during the days of the Khmelnytsky pogroms. It was enough to make the blood freeze in their veins.

Hendel stopped in the southern stretch of the Rynek, near the entrance to the Kahane home, but went on shouting, "Jews, danger! Jews, danger!" Inside his home, old man Graubart heard the shouts and gestured to his son-in-law Yerahmiel to go out. Rachel and her mother stood at the window.

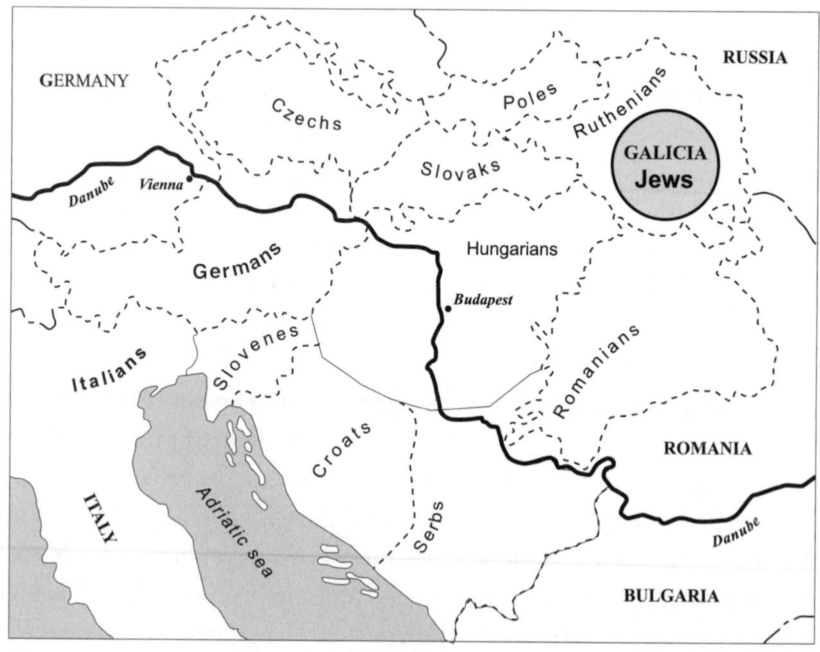

The myriad people of the Austro-Hungarian Empire, 1914.

Now, there was silence and everyone on the square was frozen in shock. The last peddlers and shoppers in the marketplace looked at Hendel in astonishment and then scanned the large square. Cossacks? Where were the Cossacks? No, nothing unusual was happening.

What was wrong with the man? No one was following him. "The Ruthenian man" had obviously gone crazy.

Yerahmiel walked quickly down the dirt path to the garden gate and stopped where Hendel was standing. He gazed into Hendel's frantic face, gripped him by the shoulder and embraced him, then said quietly, "Come, let's go inside."

The crowd remained quiet, but within a minute or two, the scene came to life again. People began to carry on with their business. Inside, Hendel washed his face in the kitchen and calmed down. Graubart looked worried, with deep furrows on his brow.

With a wry smile, Hendel said, "Nothing has happened to me. It's just that war has broken out."

That was exactly how the town of Bolechow heard about the beginning of the Great War on August 3, 1914.[1] Ullo was only three at the time, and everything that he remembered in later years was from the stories he heard afterward. When he grew older, he laughed out loud to hear how Hendel, his grandfather's clerk, had brought news of the war to Bolechow. Of course, there had been no raid by the Cossacks on that day. Hendel had panicked when he saw a group of Ukrainian youths dressed in their worn rags, looking for trouble. They had bullied him on the bridge, chasing him and swearing at him in Ruthenian. Shortly before that, at the railway station, Hendel had met a friend who had just arrived from Lvov. The friend said that war had broken out. Somehow, this news had conflated with the battle cries of the Ukrainian kids, and a pogrom was born in his mind. Only inside the Kahane home did his composure return, and he finally calmed down.

On that day, while everything was clear to the Germans, the Poles, and the Ukrainians, only the Jews were taken by surprise. The war caught them unprepared. Years later, when they were reminiscing, the Jews of Bolechow enjoyed speaking about their naiveté, and Ullo Kahane asked, "And if they had known that war was going to break out, what would they have done, stopped it?"

So far, it had been a year of plenty—business was good, profits were high, and everyone in the family was healthy. No disasters, no epidemics, no wars, and no pogroms. Nevertheless, doubts had crept into their hearts because certain rumormongers insisted on spoiling things by saying that something bad was going to happen. But the elderly Jews of Bolechow, educated by experience, had decided among themselves that there really was nothing new happening, and if in the eastern reaches of the empire some signs of dissatisfaction had been observed, as the correspondents of the Yiddish newspaper *Haynt* (Today) and the Polish *Nowy Dziennik* (New Daily) had cautiously reported, why not, with all due respect, let the officials in Vienna take care of it? Why should the whole world bother with their affairs?

After all, everyone knew that the impertinent Serbs could not endanger the stability of the empire. Knowledgeable sources in Bolechow said that as soon as the kaiser intervened, the east would immediately calm down. For sixty-six years, Franz Josef had ruled in Vienna. Every year, every month, if not every day, someone somewhere in the vast empire was sure to be dissatisfied, but, nevertheless, the kaiser was still sitting on his throne in the Burg, his palace in the First Quarter.[2] The Jews definitely relied on their kaiser. Once they had even prepared to welcome him when it seemed that he might pay a visit to Bolechow. He had come very close to stopping there but in fact had only passed by quickly.

The imperial near-visit took place on an autumn night in 1902. The kaiser's train was on its way from the capital, Vienna, to eastern Galicia. The Jews waited at the railway station, lining the tracks and carrying a Torah scroll and the traditional welcoming bread and salt, in case the emperor decided to stop and take a break from his journey. Franz Josef was on his way to observe military maneuvers being staged by his army. He had a million troops under his command, and it was said that these were the biggest maneuvers ever held anywhere in the world. The Poles never bothered to come to the station. Franz Josef was not one of them. The Ukrainians expressed their contempt for the Austrian kaiser by spitting and cursing him, and they, too, stayed away from the station. The diligent Germans were fast asleep in the town's well-kept "Deutsche Colony." True, the Austrian ruler spoke German, but their king was called Wilhelm.[3]

Of all the kaiser's subjects in Bolechow, only the Jews felt the need to come out and thank their benefactor. There was no King of the Jews in the Diaspora, and according to custom and religious law, the ruler of the land where they lived was their ruler, and they owed him loyalty. This was especially true in the case of the elderly Franz Josef, who took such good care of their well-being. This was also how the Jews had acted some one hundred years earlier, when Napoleon Bonaparte had passed through Galicia on his way to conquer Russia. They had lined the highways and sung him songs of praise.

Most of the royal families of Europe had special trains with coaches especially built for them, but the Austro-Hungarian imperial train was particularly famous for its up-to-date technology and luxuries.[4] People used to say that at exactly five in the morning, wherever the train was, it would slow down to a walking pace because that was when the kaiser shaved.

People often commented that Franz Josef hated bodyguards. "Let me walk around alone. Nobody wants to harm me," he was quoted as saying. This was certainly true of his Jewish subjects. Moreover, the Jews felt a special need to show respect for the emperor, and this is why the leaders of the Bolechow community put on their festive clothing and stood and waited at the local railway station in the middle of a cold night. As the train approached, the *gabbai* told the people to remove their hats in honor of the emperor, and that's what they did. The Hasidim, who stood in a separate group, hesitated for a moment, but they, too, were moved by the momentous occasion. They took off their fur *shtreimels* and waved them enthusiastically.

The same thing happened throughout Galicia that night, in towns and villages along the railroad. As the imperial coach rolled by, hearts skipped a beat: perhaps the kaiser would stop his train and meet his loyal citizens. But the train sped through the Bolechow station toward the district capital of Stryj, as the clickety-clack of the wheels faded slowly and the lights gradually dimmed until they disappeared in the distance. The Jews sighed in disappointment. Still, they consoled themselves, if our kaiser passed this way, it's a sign that everything will be fine.

By the time the war broke out, twelve years had passed. The emperor had grown older, his advisers and officials in Vienna had plotted his foreign policy along a bumpy road, and the empire was on the wane. On the eastern border, relations with Russia had suffered a fatal blow when Austria backed the Ottoman Empire in the Crimean War (1853–1856); thus, the czar had supported any element that threatened to undermine Austro-Hungarian rule.[5] In the west, the unification of Germany under Otto von Bismarck in 1871 had shaken the standing of the Austro-Hungarian Empire in Europe. Mistakes had been made inside the empire as well. Its bureaucracy

Refugees and Austrian soldiers in Stryj's train station immediately after World War I broke out in 1914.

had granted powers to the two stronger minorities, the Germans and the Hungarians, at the expense of the Slavs, who had been discriminated against from the start. This caused resentment among the Slavs, which grew into the secessionists declaring a rebellion.[6] At the same time, a series of family tragedies took the lives of the kaiser's legal heirs, one by one, and Franz Josef hated the surviving crown prince, Franz Ferdinand (1863–1914), the son of his younger brother, so much that the emperor stayed away from his wedding.[7] After Franz Ferdinand was assassinated by an anarchist in Sarajevo, the kaiser didn't bother to attend his funeral.

The murder in Sarajevo set in motion the chain of events that led to the outbreak of World War I. First, the Austro-Hungarian Empire presented Serbia with an ultimatum in the form of a list of tough demands. Serbia actually gave in, but Vienna, using a number of secondary clauses rejected by the Serbians as a pretext, declared war. Immediately, the network of defense treaties between the states of Europe was activated, with one country after another jumping into the war.[8]

In Bolechow, rumors abounded. "The kaiser's dead," citizens whispered among themselves. "The czar's army is coming." "People are starving in Vienna." "There's a civil war going on in Kiev." Two days after the war began, life changed radically. Soldiers took over the Magistrat building in the Rynek, near the home of the Graubarts and the Kahanes. That evening, the postman knocked on doors and delivered mobilization orders. The schools closed down. In the evenings, families shut themselves up in their homes and discussed their future. Those who had amassed fortunes went to their secret caches and counted their money. Mothers made bundles of clothing. Wagons were prepared for the road. As yet, no one had threatened them, and no army was approaching, but the Jews were getting ready.

Everything that had been stable and sacred in the Galicia of July 1914 became unstable and worthless in August. Neighbors eyed one another with suspicion in the streets. What is that Pole plotting? What do they want, those Ruthenians? All at once, the Polish officials stood taller. Their dream was about to come true. They could already see on the distant horizon how the fragments of dismembered Poland would once more reunite in an independent state, and they could sing Dombrowski's march, "Poland Is Not Yet Lost."

Rachel Kahane despised them. "The Pole is an anti-Semite," she said, "bowing and scraping before the rulers, but when he sings his anthem, he downs another vodka and becomes a patriot, and from that moment on his deeds are not controlled by reason."

From the Jewish point of view, however, the concrete danger lay in the Ruthenians' political aspirations. They also yearned for self-determination. The Jews spoke of the tension and the edginess in their neighborhoods. They also observed the rising pressure in the German neighborhood. For years, the generals in Germany had wanted to expand eastward, and now they would endeavor to take advantage of this great opportunity.

People could see, therefore, in their mind's eye, a "new order"—their own particular new order—and only the Jews trembled with anxiety. They feared that they would be the first to pay the price. The way they saw it, Franz Josef's empire had been a safe haven for almost seventy years, a land of tranquillity. In neighboring Russia, there were pogroms, revolutions, and riots, but in Austro-Hungary, order reigned. In Russia, there was popular, brutal, and savage anti-Semitism; in the kaiser's empire, the authorities permitted only a certain degree of intellectual anti-Semitism. Some people wrote and spoke anti-Semitic ideas, but only a very few actually practiced them. The kaiser protected his Jews, and Yerahmiel Kahane used to say, "Our kaiser, may his glory rise, is the love of our hearts. May his glory rise!" Jewish merchants from Poland who came to buy hides in Bolechow mockingly called Kahane "His Eminence's Jew." In Reisel Graubart's living room, a portrait of Franz Josef hung on the eastern wall, alongside a portrait of Theodore Herzl.[9] For his whole life, Ullo remembered the emperor's portrait and could describe it in detail: an old man, very solemn, with a small, round face, a white mustache, and white hair, dressed, of course, in a uniform with a stiff collar and rows and rows of medals and ribbons on his chest.

A few weeks into the war, the fighting divisions were moving eastward to the front, while the refugees moved westward. Rich refugees are not the same as poor refugees. The rich man flees in a carriage with some of his possessions and lots of gold coins. The poor man hastily takes a bundle of belongings on his back and starts walking. Then he begins throwing his possessions onto the fire to keep warm, until he has nothing left but the shirt on his back.

Yerahmiel Kahane was a rich refugee. First, he had planned his flight. Before he emptied his safe, collected his debts, locked up his leather tannery, and paid his Polish neighbor to look after his property until his return, he sat with his father and his mother-in-law and analyzed the situation.

There was no doubt, Kahane told his in-laws, that the front line would be established right there, in Galicia. And he was right. One didn't have to be a graduate from a military staff college to see where the fighting would take place. The Russians had always aimed to expand their Ukrainian territory and gain control of the Slavic regions, and the Germans and the Austrians would therefore be forced to defend themselves precisely in Galicia. Then the Russians would be weakened by their effort, and the Germans would put their efficient war machine into action and invade Russia. The Germans longed to occupy vast areas of Russian eastern Ukraine, the breadbasket of Eastern Europe. This was the plan, and this was what would happen, Yerahmiel told his in-laws. The Germans would wear down the Russians, the Russians would wear down the Germans, and the Poles and the Ruthenians would sit and wait for their opportunity. The smell of smoke was in their nostrils, and they could feel the greatness of the times down to the tips of their fingers. In Kraków, Jozef Pilsudski was recruiting troops and marshaling legions.[10] Many Jews were joining his forces.

"The Poles and the Ukrainians are sharpening their knives," said Kahane.

"This is why we are with the Germans," said Graubart.

"If so, we'll go to Vienna," the two decided.

The empire was on the move. Millions of civilians traveled from the edges toward the center, looking for shelter, and at the same time millions of soldiers moved from the center outward, toward the front. Galicia was deemed a perilous area. The border with Russia was close. In eastern Prussia, on Russia's border, huge battles were raging. In Tannenberg, the German military leaders Paul von Hindenburg and Erich Ludendorf defeated the Russian invaders.[11] In the south, beyond the Carpathian forests, Romania was sitting on the fence, but the Russians were about to attack. Just east of Galicia, Jewish inhabitants fled Bukovina, which is situated in the northernmost part of the northeastern Carpathian Mountains and which was in danger of being occupied by Russia. Jews also fled from Romania and Hungary, from the Sudetenland (south of Galicia), and from Galicia.[12] Hundreds of thousands of Jews and Germans moved in trains, in wagons, and on foot from the east westward and southward, everyone running away from the Russians, fleeing the fire, and scrambling for shelter under the kaiser's wings. In the end, they all gathered in the empire's capital. Vienna would be their city of refuge for several weeks, at the most several months—that is what they believed. They never suspected that the war would continue for years because, after all, everyone knew that no modern war lasted for more than a month or two.

Yerahmiel Kahane, too, was sure that he would soon be returning home with his family. In his eyes, the Austro-Hungarian Empire was incapable of losing. For any other force to overcome a million Austrian soldiers and another million German troops was impossible. To beat them? To crumble the empire? The Russians were unable to do anything right, and the British did not even have conscription.

In Bolechow, Polish patriots whispered behind Yerahmiel and Rachel Kahane's backs that they were "Deutsch" (German). In Vienna, there were rumors that they were "Juden." Nonetheless, the couple quickly settled in the capital. Every third refugee in Vienna was Jewish, and most of them came from Galicia. Yerahmiel rented a four-room apartment in the First

Quarter, behind St. Stephen's Cathedral, in an alley at the end of Judengasse (Jews' Lane, where in ancient times Jews were allowed to settle in Vienna). In the Kahanes' apartment, there were three bedrooms linked to one another by a long corridor, at the end of which lay a spacious parlor. The Graubarts slept in the front room, Yerahmiel and Rachel in the back room, and the three children in the middle one. In the parlor, they placed a cluster of armchairs and a dining table. The windows of the parlor overlooked a backyard, which contained the garbage bins. The big yard was devoid of trees and greenery. The stone house was gray and old, with the plaster peeling off its walls. Uninviting as it was, few refugees in that area lived in such comfort.

In the mornings, Rachel Kahane took the food-rationing coupons and lined up at the stores. Most of the day, the stores were closed because there was nothing to sell. Rachel carried a padded stool with her and sat down and waited in line until the store opened. Sometimes she waited an hour; other times, six. Everyone in the line made sure that no one pushed ahead of the others, and each person knew his or her exact place. People often saved places for others. Sometimes Rachel sat and waited in the same line; at other times she left and waited in another line, then went back to the first. Rachel spoke excellent German, and the gentlemen and the ladies who stood with her in the queues treated her with respect.

At the outset of the war, human beings had not yet become beasts. Vienna was crowded and cold and was short of food and coal for heating, but, nonetheless, the Viennese and the new refugees were polite and cheerful. People generally felt that the war was far away, and as for those who were called to arms, may God have mercy on their souls. Whoever stayed in the city deserved to live, as long as this was possible.

Yerahmiel and Rachel went to the opera and the theater several times. One wintry weekend, they hired a carriage and traveled to Baden, the town that had hot springs at the edge of the Wienerwald, the Vienna Woods, which was an hour's ride from the center of the city. They lodged for one night at the Herzog Hof, a hotel near the park, and during the day they toured the area. Some of the wealthy families of Galicia, among them several from Bolechow, had decided to settle in Baden until the storm passed. Rachel was reminded of the oil town of Drohobych. The magnificent facades of Baden's palaces, with the pillars and the cornices designed in the classical Greek style, resembled the homes of the newly rich of Drohobych, and the smell of sulfur emanating from the Baden springs was reminiscent of the odor of oil that filled the air there.

But Drohobych lacked the romantic atmosphere of Baden. Drohobych didn't have a magnificent statue of Wolfgang Amadeus Mozart.[13] Tales about Beethoven had not been woven in Drohobych, with the great composer roaming the parks in rags, writing the score of his Ninth Symphony. And in Drohobych, there was no glorious park full of rose beds. The notion that King Fredrick III and the Hapsburg emperors had strolled down the avenues of Baden filled Rachel with exhilaration, but Yerahmiel was less poetic. He refused to take a dip in the famous Roman Well, and the Biedermeier-style furniture in the hotel seemed vulgar to him. Yerahmiel preferred the big city.

"Baden's good for loafers; it's in Vienna that we'll make money," his children quoted him as saying, many years later.

In the big city, life continued as if the war was on another planet. There was no real unemployment. Anyone who tried could find work right away, and people with the know-how and the ability to adapt to the new situation made fortunes. There were two million people in Vienna, and every day, every hour, more refugees poured in. The people needed food, houses, and clothing, and nimble entrepreneurs found ample scope for their talents.

Yerahmiel undoubtedly had entrepreneurial talents. From the minute that he succeeded in rescuing his family from danger and settling them in Vienna, his mind was preoccupied with leather. There is no army without boots and no boots without leather and no leather without tanned hides, and who knew more than Yerahmiel about the efficient tanning of ox hides and making them into strong soles for boots that could stand up to the Russian winter or the trench warfare of the Somme Valley?[14] Kahane, the industrialist, had several advantages. He spoke German fluently, and he knew the business inside out. He was young and energetic, and he carried with him a small fortune in gold coins, diamonds, and jewelry. Of course, he was a great supporter of the kaiser and was convinced that his empire would win the war.

Yerahmiel had a long face, a broad forehead, and eyes sunk deep in their sockets. He was six feet tall and wore a European suit and hat; his beard was short and neatly combed. He was a modern Jew, not a black-coated Hasid. Although he was fluent in Yiddish, he preferred to speak German. The Austrian officials liked this quiet, polite Jew, but they were helpless. The chaos of war triumphed over the efficiency of the bureaucrats.

In the winter of 1915, Kahane and Graubart scurried back and forth between the ministries. In the morning, they were at the Ministry of War to see the officials in charge of supplies, and in the afternoon, they presented their requests to similar officials at the Interior Ministry. They spent one morning at the Industry Ministry and the other at the Commerce Ministry. The imperial ministries were all located in one district, in the First Quarter, between the kaiser's Burg and the Danube Canal. The officials tried hard to be helpful, but the war had confused everything. Those who knew where the oxen were slaughtered did not know where their skins were shipped to, and those who knew where the skins were kept did not know whether they had been earmarked for shoe production.

Meanwhile, "the four-week war" had already been going on for six months with no clear-cut victory, neither in the east nor in the west. Although, in the Battle of the Marne, the Germans were halted before they managed to enter Paris, both sides had been forced to build fortifications facing each other and to fight a trench war, one that would continue for four years.[15] In Prussia, the Russians invaded Germany and were dealt a tremendous blow. Turkey joined Austria and struck at the Russians in the Caucasus. The British landed in Gallipoli and failed. Movement on the battlefields came to a standstill, and the gay Viennese summer gave way to the frost of autumn. Then came a winter that saw a frozen city, with no more marching bands or parades in the streets. Here and there, propaganda officials still sounded the battle slogan that Yerahmiel Kahane relished: "For God, Emperor, and homeland." Yet the enthusiasm of August 1914 had died down. Only a year earlier, Yerahmiel had enjoyed watching battalions of troops marching down the streets, singing songs of victory to the music of military bands, as girls and boys ran after the soldiers and tossed flowers at them and a trumpeter played the anthem.

A long line formed at the entrance to the offices of the Jewish community in the First Quarter. Youngsters pushed and shoved with their elbows, straining to reach the door. A woman sat behind a table taking down names. Yerahmiel stopped. What was the clamor all about?

"They're recruiting for the Jewish Battalion," explained one young man. A rumor had spread throughout the city that the authorities intended to send Jewish fighters to the eastern front, and many were quick to volunteer. Jewish publicists wrote ardent articles calling on the youths to go to war to take vengeance against the Russians for the pogroms and the Beilis Trial, which had taken place in Kiev in 1913 and was followed by Jews all over the world. The defendant was a Ukrainian Jew from Kiev, Menahem Mendel Beilis, accused of ritually murdering a thirteen-year-old Ukrainian boy. Although the trial ended with Beilis's acquittal, Jews considered the affair to be extremely humiliating.[16]

But in Vienna, the Jewish Battalion was formed on paper only, and the Jewish youngsters had to wait their turn to enlist in existing units. More and more casualties were suffered on the front, and new recruits replenished the ranks.

Now the imperial war council ordered the conscription of men from the ages of seventeen to fifty. Some Jews bribed members of medical boards and avoided the army permanently. Yerahmiel was twenty-eight, and under the law he had to be drafted. But a medical board ruled that his heart was weak and gave him an exemption. Upon his release from duty, Yerahmiel increased his efforts to obtain hides.

"If the officials find me a good source of skins suitable for tanning, I will return to Bolechow and open my factory under the auspices of the authorities," Yerahmiel decided. Yet the officials could not tell him when and where the supply of hides would be renewed.

In the mornings, Grandma Reisel went for walks through the alleys of the old city with the two little ones: Leah, nicknamed Lidka, and Ullo. Sara, whom everyone called Sonia, was at school. Seven times, Reisel circled the famous church at the Stephansplatz square but never dared to enter it. Reisel wore long, dark dresses with the hems reaching her ankles. A tall woman, with flowing hair gathered by an array of hairpins, she wore boots made of delicate, shiny black leather. She loved to adorn herself with jewelry. At home, she wore rings and bracelets of silver and gold, ruby brooches, ivory earrings, and diamond necklaces—but out on the street there were dangers. Muggers snatched purses and jewelry.

Lidka was seven years old, a serious and smart girl. She was busy "educating" Ullo, who was three years younger. They played hopscotch in the alleys of the old city, marking squares on the pavement with chalk. It was difficult to keep the game going without interruption because of the crowds and the traffic. The public square in front of the church was bustling. Carriages unloaded their passengers. Riders fed their horses hay from enormous straw baskets. Priests went in and out of the cathedral doors. A dark-colored Opel automobile stopped with a screech. A uniformed chauffeur opened the door for a wealthy *frau*, who strode in and made her way to the confessional.

On every corner, refugees huddled in groups and exchanged information. Everyone advised, recommended, and gossiped. A wholesale market of information was available, in a variety of languages: Slovak, Romanian, Hungarian, Russian, Italian, and Yiddish, which sounded something like the German of the Viennese. Romanians gathered on one corner, refugees from Lvov on another, and Bukovinians behind the church. Sudetens sat in Café Herz without ordering anything. Along the main street that led to the church, elderly people pleaded for alms. "Petition writers" put up wooden stalls and folding chairs and offered to fill in official forms for a fee. Children rummaged for food in garbage bins. On the sidewalks, men and women offered furniture and jewelry for sale. They exchanged property for food because money had lost its value.

Gold coins had disappeared altogether, and one-krone and five-kroner silver coins were rarely seen. Even nickel and copper coins had almost vanished; instead people's pockets were filled with odd-looking banknotes and food coupons: coupons for bread and meat, for fat, and for milk. Clerks handed out dozens of food coupons of all kinds, but the food itself was nowhere to be found. Real hunger gripped the town. Along the Danube, scores of carriages stood idle, and the stench of horse manure filled the air. Not even a second went by after a horse had deposited its droppings before its owner leaped to pick them up in order to dry them and sell them for heating fuel.

Next to an embankment on the river, weeping girls kissed their young lovers good-bye. The soldiers were going to war. The young people's eyes no longer sparkled with joy, and happiness faded from their hearts. The certainty of victory had dissipated. At the train station, soldiers bound for the front looked sad. On both the eastern and the western front, fighting was at a standstill. While in the west both sides bombarded each other with mustard gas shells, in the Old City of Vienna, Lidka and Ullo watched the tragic consequences of war. A long convoy of ambulances packed with stretchers had arrived from the front, and male nurses, whose white uniforms were splattered with blood, carried the injured into the Saint Maria Hospital. Perplexed, the two children saw the orderlies unload stretchers carrying soldiers with burn injuries who were coughing and groaning, their faces twisted, their bodies covered with bloody bandages. The children could not turn their eyes away from the wounded men.

Grandma Reisel saw the soldiers and was appalled. "Move, move, move away immediately," she ordered, but the children were glued to the spot. All of a sudden, Lidka shrieked and Ullo's mouth gaped in astonishment as a wounded man fell from his stretcher. One of the orderlies carrying him had stumbled on a stone, slipped, and tumbled down. He lost his grip on the stretcher, and it crashed to the ground. The wounded man slid off it, and the gray blanket dropped away. The man had no legs.

The children looked at the bandaged red stumps, and Ullo mumbled, "He has no legs, he has no legs." Grandma Reisel covered the boy's eyes and turned him away. (Years later, after finishing her medical studies at the University of Prague, Leah reminded her brother of the horrors they had witnessed in Vienna, in front of the Saint Maria Hospital. Ullo remembered nothing. Leah said, "We saw two things. An amputee in Vienna and typhus in Azerbaijan." Typhus plagued Russia mercilessly during World War II, and Leah, as a physician in Azerbaijan, devotedly took care of the victims. But as a seven-year-old girl seeing the amputee in Vienna, she had been helpless, and the legless soldier had visited her in her dreams ever since. Ullo, though, never remembered a thing.)

Hunger and deprivation in the city grew, food lines got longer, and overcrowding worsened as more refugees poured in. Yerahmiel wondered whether his kaiser still had a chance of winning the war and whether it would be better to take the children back to Bolechow. Supplies were not reaching Vienna regularly, and in Bolechow people grew vegetables next to their houses, and wild fruit, strawberries, and cherries grew in the woods. The children were both cause and effect of parents' decisions. "If it's better for the children . . ." was a phrase frequently repeated by Yerahmiel and Rachel. They protected their offspring to the very best of their ability. Sometimes they went without food so that the children would have enough. When famine is prevalent, even people who have money for food cannot obtain what simply doesn't exist.

At the end of 1916, Kaiser Franz Josef passed away, but the Kahanes and the Graubarts did not have a chance to mourn him suitably, as they were once again immersed in the leather-tanning business. In view of the army's need for boots and with hides plentiful in Hungary, the Ministry of War had ordered the factories in Bolechow to reopen immediately and begin tanning leather. The officials in Vienna revoked Kahane's "medical exemption" and issued him an "industrial exemption." Yerahmiel and his father-in-law and mother-in-law returned to Bolechow and hired workers. The factory operated at full steam, and the army paid with gold coins. A month later, at the end of the winter, Yerahmiel had his family come back home.

The war had passed over Bolechow. The church, the synagogue, and the wooden houses stood as always on the square, and the Sukiel flowed through the town exactly as it had before the war. Residents who had not been drafted continued to ply their trades. Graubart sent a letter to his clerk, Hendel, the man who had first brought news of the war to Bolechow: "Come back from Vienna. Galicia is quiet. The eastern front is far. The Poles sing their anthem and the Ruthenians sharpen their knives, but the delicate balance has not collapsed."

History does not reveal its secrets in advance. It plays with the fate of millions of innocent people. Most of them believe that what once was is what will be. Only a select few, the wisest of the wise, fathom the essence of events as they take place. Many years would pass, a decade or two or three, until the Jews of Galicia would realize that precisely at that time, the good old order and values had begun to collapse, and new wild weeds were sprouting out of the ruins. Few of them were clever enough to see how, near the time that World War I was drawing to an end, a chapter in Jewish history was also ending and a new one beginning—a ghastly, horrible chapter.

Right then, however, Galicia was still Austrian and Bolechow was still calm, as during its peaceful past. An acrid odor again wafted out of the tanning factory, and Yerahmiel was happy once more. Rachel dusted the furniture. Sonia dreamed of going back to the big city of Vienna. She would be the first to leave Bolechow. Lidka held the hand of her five-year-old brother and led him to the *heder*, the Hebrew school. That moment would be what Ullo later recalled nostalgically as the beginning of his childhood in Bolechow.

9

Crime and Punishment

EARLY IN AUGUST 1914, at the opening battle of the war, Avrumche Backenroth's beloved oldest son, Arie, was taken prisoner by the Russians. He had been recruited into the Austrian army and was sent to the ancient city of Przemysl. This city had been turned into a fortress, around which the Austro-Hungarian forces had deployed for a defensive battle against an anticipated attack by the czar's army. Russia entered the war with the largest army in the world, standing at 1,400,000 soldiers. For its chief commander, Czar Nicholas II (1868–1918), the conquest of Galicia was a primary goal.[1] The territory of "Congress Poland" had been in Russian hands since 1832, when Congress Kingdom of Poland was incorporated into Russia.[2] Now the czar aspired to annex another sizable chunk of Slavic land, together with its population, to Mother Russia.

In late August, in a successful lightning campaign, 300,000 Russian troops surrounded Przemysl.[3] They broke through the Austro-Hungarian lines and advanced rapidly southward toward the Carpathian Mountains and westward, toward Kraków. At the beginning of the battle for Przemysl, Arie Backenroth's unit had been sent from the fortifications to man positions near the city of Krosno (southeast of Przemysl), but due to the Russians' numerical superiority, the unit was forced to surrender and all of the men were taken prisoner. Arie was transported to Siberia and incarcerated in a POW camp in the town of Spasskoy, where a year later, in the midsummer of 1915, he was murdered in cold blood.

One morning, the camp commandant ordered the prisoners to line up, as if for a parade, and then indicated that they were free to make an escape. As the prisoners made a mad dash for the gates, the Russian officers opened fire at their backs. Arie was killed, and a distant relative, who was also a prisoner, buried him in Spasskoy and notified the Red Cross, requesting that it inform the family in Schodnica.[4]

Arie's wife, Sara-Ethel, received a postcard of notification from the Red Cross but refused to believe that her husband was dead. "Daddy isn't dead! This story isn't true, and the postcard is a forgery," she told her four children and immediately set out for the Red Cross office in Drohobych, where she demanded proof that Arie had been killed. The evidence turned up two months later, in the form of official confirmation from the Red Cross in Siberia, borne out by the added testimony of the relative who had buried Arie. The relative proved his family ties with the deceased by relating that when Arie had left home to report for duty, his stepmother had handed him a shirt through the window.[5] Now that they accepted that the report was true, the family began to sit *shivah* (seven, in Hebrew), the seven-day period of mourning for the deceased. Out of concern for the health of Arie's father, Avrumche, however, they didn't tell him anything.

August 1914. At the beginning of World War I, Russian Cossacks conquered the Austrian fortifications around Przemysl, where Avrumche's son Arie was positioned.

How, then, would Arie's sons say the mourner's prayer, Kaddish, for their father three times a day for eleven months, without their grandfather finding out?[6] A scheme was devised. Avrumche prayed regularly at the Hasidic *kloiz* ("synagogue," in Yiddish) near the Backenroth home in Schodnica. Not far from there, near the area where the foreign workers lived, was another synagogue, frequented by the poor Jews. So that Avrumche would not find out that his oldest grandson, Shmuel Yitzhak, was saying Kaddish for his father, the grandson was forced to pray twice. First he went to the synagogue of the poor and said the mourner's prayer in the early dawn *minyan*, the quorum of ten adult Jewish males that was required for communal worship.[7] Later, he hurried to the regular morning *minyan* at the *kloiz* to pray again so that his grandfather would see him there as usual and not realize that something was wrong. On Sabbaths, Shmuel Yitzhak was accompanied by his younger brother, David Moses, known to everyone by the nickname Moye. Once when Avrumche met his two grandsons walking to the poor people's synagogue at an early morning hour, he thought that they were out for a stroll and urged them to come and pray at the *kloiz*.

The entire family was in on the scheme.[8] They all hid the tragic news from Avrumche. But the truth of the matter was that Avrumche was also pretending. The family hid the truth from him, but he knew the truth (presumably he sensed that something awful had happened to his son) and hid his knowledge of it from them. And while they knew that he knew, they pretended that he didn't, and he knew they knew that he knew, but he made believe that he didn't know they knew. If this weren't such a tragic matter, we would surely laugh.

Such family play-acting is an ancient Jewish way of ignoring the ills of fate, of circumventing Satan, of cloaking the harsh truth in ambiguity, or even of deluding themselves that the incident never happened at all. Ostensibly, the white lie was intended to spare the health of the weak—the sick, the elderly, children—and it certainly was in no way duplicity, for it was meant to do good to those who were being deceived. But nonetheless, in this case, the lie grew and became more tangled.

After the end of the war, it was clear to everyone that Avrumche was not only mourning his oldest son but blaming himself for his son's death. He was certain that God had taken away his son as punishment for a terrible sin that he had committed during the High Holy Days. Could it be that the observant and levelheaded Avrumche would reach the point of blasphemy?

When the Russian army broke through the Austro-Hungarian defenses in the area of Przemysl and advanced toward the Carpathian Mountains, panic spread through the Jewish community. Many fled south, to Vienna, including some of the Backenroths, but Avrumche refused to go too far from Schodnica. He wanted to keep an eye on the oil wells and the refineries, to make sure they would not be destroyed. If need be, he would find temporary shelter for his family nearby, at the family's refinery in the desolate village of Lisko, close to the city of Sanok and not far from the San River.

That is what Avrumche planned, and he nervously kept track of the Russian advance. When September came, and the High Holy Days were approaching, a decision had to be made about where to spend them. After discussions and consultations, it was agreed that the whole Backenroth family, its old and young, would harness their wagons and carriages, load suitcases and trunks packed with festive garb and silverware, as well as food and ritual utensils, and move west to Lisko.

On the morning of September 7, two weeks before Rosh Hashanah, the Jewish New Year, the Backenroths set out. On the way they met Jews from Sanok, who told them how the city had been conquered. Russian troops had pillaged shops and homes, and the city's economy was paralyzed. Many Jewish families lost all of their property and had to flee the city.[9]

The next day, when the Backenroths arrived at the refinery in Lisko, they set about preparing for the holiday, under the women's supervision. The first day of Rosh Hashanah (September 21) was celebrated in the proper manner.[10] On the second morning of the holiday, however, a great fear overcame Avrumche. In his mind's eye, he saw the Russian occupiers wildly attacking the oil installations, blowing up the tanks and the wells, puncturing the pipes, and wrecking his life's work. He immediately consulted his sons and sons-in-law who were there with him and announced his decision: "We are returning at once to Schodnica." It was a fateful step because it was still a holy day when travel is forbidden, and the family was very observant, but no one protested.[11] Perhaps if Avrumche's beloved daughter Clara, and her husband, Israel Moses Sobel, had been with them, they would have managed to persuade Avrumche to put off the departure until the day after the holiday. But Clara and Israel Moses had found refuge in Vienna when the fighting first broke out, and now there was no one to warn the head of the family against sinning. In Lisko, the great panic that took hold of Avrumche infected everyone, and they packed their belongings again, loaded them onto the wagons and the carriages, and on the second day of the holiday, they took the highway eastward.

"We rode on wagons into the battle zone," Moye, Avrumche's grandson, recalled almost sixty years afterward. "On the roads, battalions of Cossack troops, the finest of the czar's units, were marching, and in their hands they carried bayoneted rifles. They did not harm us." Moye rode on a wagon with his mother and three brothers. His father, Arie, was in the army, and no one knew yet that he had been captured by the Russians.

"On the way we saw many Muscophiles hanging from trees," Moye added. Muscophiles were people who lived in Galicia and were loyal to the czar.[12] The ones Moye saw had been suspected of spying and were caught and hanged by the retreating Austrians.

The journey back to Schodnica passed without incident, and on Tuesday evening, September 22, the Backenroths returned home, precisely when the Russian conquerors began to sabotage the oil infrastructure in Schodnica and its surroundings. They burned oil derricks and tanks of crude oil.[13] They had not touched Backenroth property yet, and because Avrumche had managed to return in time, he was able to negotiate with them. He shouted and screamed, threatened, paid off those who had to be paid, and at the end of the day rescued his property from the soldiers.

Had his decision to return to Schodnica in the middle of the holiday been the right one? Avrumche justified it by declaring that the deed was a matter of life or death (*pikuah nefesh*, in Hebrew), and his family supported him. The strict among the ultra-Orthodox, however, would not have seen eye to eye with him.[14] Yet his property was saved.

In the coming months, the Germans and the Austrians grew stronger and launched a counterattack. In May 1915, they broke through the Russian defense lines and drove the Russians out of Galicia. The war machines of Germany and Austria were in dire need of fuel, so the Austrian kaiser sent officers to the Galician oil fields to prod the producers to step up their output.[15] When the officers came to Boryslav and Schodnica, they saw that much of the production gear was damaged, but the Backenroths' was intact and working. Later, they made inquiries and found that Avrumche had stood up alone against the Russians to protect his wells. When the Austrian officers reported this to the kaiser, he decided to honor Avrumche at a special ball. A messenger traveled from Vienna to Schodnica, carrying an invitation sealed in a silken envelope: "The Kaiser Franz Josef I of the House of Hapsburg will honor Herr Avrumche Backenroth at a special ball at the Belvedere Palace in Vienna, the capital city."

Although two of Avrumche's married daughters, Gittel Turkel and Clara Sobel, had found refuge in Vienna at the beginning of the war, and although they were both young and beautiful, Avrumche decided that his niece Papche Backenroth would accompany him to the palace. Her father, Isaac Backenroth, was no less talented and remarkable a man than Avrumche was. In Galicia, Isaac resided with his children in the village of Chizna, and the Ukrainians called them *kharbias*, or landowners. They had an expansive estate near the city of Sanok. They leased its surrounding lands to Ukrainian peasants in return for part of their crops, and in the spring they sold visitors licenses to pick berries, apples, and plums. Peasants who had finished reaping and harvesting the crops on their own lands came to the estate, picked fruit, and sold it at the marketplace. Isaac Backenroth and his sons made most of their wealth from real estate dealings, and part of it came from the family's oil consortium.

Isaac and his sons were not as observant as Avrumche and his sons were. The boys had been the first members of the family to leave the religious ghetto and to study at a private, secular high school. Nevertheless, they were very close to Avrumche's sons and grandsons and often met with them. So profound was the friendship between them that Avrumche preferred that Papche, the daughter of his assimilated brother, go with him to the ball in the kaiser's palace—or perhaps he decided to take her precisely because she was not strictly observant.

Papche's Viennese salon was famous among the aristocracy of Vienna. Oscar Kokoschka showed her his paintings, and the composer Alban Berg played the piano in her home.[16] Karl Seitz, who served as the mayor of the capital after the war, was among her friends.[17] Robert Stricker, who was later elected to parliament, consulted with Papche about the fate of tens of thousands of Jewish refugees who had fled to Vienna at the outset of the war.[18]

When the great day came, at the entrance to the ballroom of the Belvedere Palace, the announcer called out, "The Guests of Honor, Papche and Avraham Backenroth." Avrumche's appearance aroused excitement. On his head he wore a *shtreimel*, the festive Hasidic hat made of mink or fox tails, and under it, a black silk *yarmulke*. His body was wrapped in a *razhivalka*, a black robe of precious satin, with a black woolen sash around his waist. On his feet were rugged leather boots, and his long legs were encased in white stockings. Avrumche was tall, over six feet. A short red beard sprouted from his chin, and spiraling earlocks dangled beside his cheeks. One of the ministers of the Austrian government approached Avrumche, greeted him, and then proceeded to closely examine his apparel.

"Herr Backenroth," the minister asked, "what is the price of a coat like this?"

Avrumche answered that the price was such and such.

"And how much does this hat cost?" the minister queried.

Avrumche answered politely and named the price.

Then the minister asked, "If this is how the rich among you dress, what do the poor wear?"

Avrumche replied, in German, "Herr Minister, bei uns, arme Leute kleiden wie Sie" (Our poor people dress like you, in ordinary suits).

Standing on the dais with the kaiser, Avrumche was thrilled as he watched the guests waltz. At the end of the first dance, dozens of Viennese women in evening gowns approached the dais and curtsied before the kaiser. The ball was very much to Avrumche's liking, and when he returned to the home of his daughter Gittel Turkel, he spoke ardently, "This country is so wonderful that it is worth sending the boys to fight for it." At just about the same time, his oldest son was murdered in captivity in Siberia.

One Saturday afternoon some months later, at Avrumche's house in Schodnica, Avrumche's grandson Moye saw that his grandfather was crying as he paced to and fro in his room and quietly hummed the tune of the hymn "Yadid Nefesh" ("Beloved of the Soul," in Hebrew).[19]

"Usually, he would sing it with great pleasure in a rippling voice," Moye recalled, "but this time he sang sorrowfully, he sang and groaned until tears began falling from his eyes, and then he burst into bitter weeping. The other members of the household heard him crying, and although he said nothing, they all knew he was weeping for his son, my father."

In the coming years, Avrumche said several times, "At the ball I tempted the devil," and his daughter-in-law, Arie's widow, Sarah-Ethel, made up her mind to spare him more grief. She moved to live with her sons in Lvov. "It is better that he does not see his son's children every day," she explained to Moye.

10

The *Drasha* Speech

On a rainy Thursday morning, November 28, 1918, Yerahmiel Kahane stood at the entrance to the ancient Jewish cemetery of Lvov, his heart pounding. He was surrounded by people wailing and weeping. Forty thousand mourners heard the master of ceremonies call upon Rabbi Aryeh Leib Braude to eulogize the dead—seventy-two Jews who had been murdered in a pogrom. The rabbi climbed onto the makeshift platform facing the crowd and broke into bitter tears. He was incapable of speaking. Everyone cried with him. Then Rabbi Dr. Guttmann was asked to deliver a eulogy on behalf of the Lvov Jewish community, but he was seized by a fit of trembling and collapsed.

The Jews called Lvov by its German name, Lemberg, and a Jew from the city is called a Lemberger.[1] The first Jews settled there soon after 1340. Some of them became merchants whose labors were blessed, and they resided in magnificent homes in the city center. The poor built homes of straw and clay in a neighborhood known as Kraków, on the outskirts of Lvov, where the merchants' caravans were organized before they set out westward. The Jewish traders were so successful, both within the city and outside of it, that in the late fifteenth century, a delegation of Christian merchants came to complain to the king, Jan I Olbracht of the Jagiellon Dynasty.[2] The Christians claimed that their livelihood was threatened because the Jews were taking over commerce in the city. The king ordered that the Jews be restricted to trading in only two commodities: cattle—no more than a thousand head a year—and cloth.[3]

But Poland at the time was enjoying a period of economic plenty, and it turned out that the restrictions imposed by Jan on Jewish commerce only detracted from Lvov's wealth. Thus, ten years later, in 1503, his successor, King Alexander (1461–1506), annulled them and granted the Jews full freedom to trade at markets and fairs. Four years after that, King Zygmunt I (1467–1548) extended their trading privileges further, and so it continued with the kings of Poland, as they in turn extended and restricted the rights of Jews to engage in commerce. One king embraced them and the next persecuted them, one loosened the grip and another tightened it, until the reign of Wladyslaw IV (1595–1648). On March 17, 1633, he issued a privilege giving Jews the right to live in the Kraków neighborhood on the outskirts of Lvov, in exchange for "a fair rental," and to engage in any occupation, apart from the higher ranks of the civil service or university professorships and without belonging to the craft guilds.[4] Twenty-five years later, on August 29, 1658, at the request of Yaacobi Lewkowitz, the manager of synagogue affairs and a community activist, King Jan II Casimir (1609–1672) re-endorsed the residential and trading privileges.[5] Since then, Jews had lived in Lvov and its suburbs, setting up their own guilds and prospering in commerce, industry, and banking.

Yerahmiel traveled often to the capital of East Galicia. Every few months, he spent some time there with his family, going to the theater or the opera. Since October 1918, however, he had kept away from the city, first because of the tense atmosphere that prevailed between Poles and Ruthenians and then because of the reports of civil war raging there. Very little accurate news came out of Lvov about the confrontation, and the people of Bolechow had to make do mainly with rumors. Initially, there was a message that the Ruthenians had won a crushing victory. Then people said that the Poles had driven the Ruthenians out of Lvov. But the conflict and the rumors continued, and when terrible reports were whispered from mouth to ear about a pogrom that the Poles had perpetrated against the Jews on the evening of November 24, nobody believed them.

More than seventy-five thousand Jews lived in Lvov, about 35 percent of the population.[6] Most of them were small retail shopkeepers or craftsmen. Some were bankers; others were big wholesalers who traded with Hungary, Russia, and western lands. There were also a large number of Jews in the free professions. A third of the doctors in the city and half of the lawyers were Jews. In the ancient University of Lvov (where Ullo Kahane would study economics in a few years' time), more than a third of the students were Jewish. The community included a group of ultra-Orthodox (most of them Hasidim, the others Mitnagdim), whose everyday language was Yiddish. There was a strong Zionist movement, including right-wing members of Betar and Marxist Zionists belonging to the Hashomer Hatzair movement.[7] Socialist and communist Jews were of some influence, but the assimilated bourgeois group was the strongest, and it controlled the community's institutions. On the margins were small groups such as the Reform community, which worshipped at its "temple"; a number of supporters of the socialist Bund party; and even groups of Karaites and Shabbateans.[8]

Each Jewish group and sect had its adherents in Lvov, and they all mourned on that rainy morning with a shared sense of danger. It seemed that every able-bodied Jew had made his way to the funeral of the Jews killed in the pogrom. The roads were crowded. The wagons of the farmers, the carriages of the wealthy, a few automobiles, and masses of pedestrians—men, women, and children—flowed toward the Jewish cemetery. In the nearby streets, a tense quiet prevailed. Those on foot walked rapidly, in silence. Their faces were downcast, and the only sound was the clatter of their heels on the paving stones, like the echo of a great clock ticking.

In the funeral hall, the bodies were laid out on the floor in rows, wrapped in prayer shawls. The surging crowds pushed Yerahmiel Kahane forward. He was filled with rage at Marshal Pilsudski's Polish Legions, whose troops had carried out the massacre, and at the Polish civilians who applauded them as they slaughtered the Jews. Some of Lvov's citizens, among them students, teachers, a police commissar, and a court official, as well as several women, had joined in the pogrom, murdering Jews and setting their homes on fire.[9]

Yerahmiel couldn't remember ever having such emotions before. He felt tremendous anger at the blind wickedness and at the fact that the murdered souls were trapped by the circumstances. His face flushed and his hands trembled. Why did they kill these unoffending people? Why had they left more than four hundred wounded, widows, and orphans who would continue to suffer all their lives? What did these innocent Jews have to do with the war between the nationalist Poles and Ruthenians? Some of the names of the victims were familiar to him: Hermann Bardach and Henryk Lewin. Two members of the Goldberg family, Joseph and Julius, had been murdered. Salomon Katz had been killed with his son. And why had they burned down the ghetto and the ancient synagogue and all of its treasures?

As the funeral procession made its way from the prayer hall toward the open graves, people still streamed through the cemetery gate. The mourners opened a narrow corridor for the long line of stretchers, each of which was carried by four men. Yerahmiel felt a dull pain in his chest, and his whole body shook. Close to the exit from the hall, he had a dizzy spell and had to lean his head against the wall. As he usually did, he tried to analyze what had happened in a logical manner, but the spectacle he visualized was like a punch in the face and disrupted his ability to think reasonably. One thought flashed across his mind: Rachel is right. There is no solution in Europe for the Jews. In a panic, he stepped out of the hall into the open air and tried to organize his thoughts. Could this pogrom be construed as an extraordinary, one-time event, a by-product of the stormy conflict between the Poles and the Ruthenians? Or had a new era begun, in which the Jews' very existence was in peril? Two days earlier, when two Ruthenian peasants had attacked him in the yard of his home, he had belittled the importance of the incident and had pushed away the thought that the Jews were in danger, but perhaps he was wrong.

It had happened on Tuesday. Yerahmiel was strolling in his garden in the twilight, deep in thought. Two tall, yellow-haired youths were walking on the dirt path along the fence. Yerahmiel did not know them. They both wore cloth coats and rubber boots and apparently had been working to clean up one of the neighborhood yards or perhaps as porters in the nearby market. Suddenly, they stopped and looked at Yerahmiel.

"Hey, Zhid," one of them called out mockingly. "How much money have you got?"

"Have you got gold, Moshek?" the other one chimed in.

Of all the anti-Semitic epithets, none made Yerahmiel's blood boil more than "Moshek," an insulting corruption of the name of the greatest of the prophets. But he restrained himself. He waved the two hooligans away with a dismissive gesture and muttered the equivalent of "Drop dead."

The two looked at each other. The Jew had dared to be snippy. The youths vaulted over the low fence separating the yard from the path and walked toward Yerahmiel, one to the left and the other to the right. Rachel was watching from the window. Yerahmiel took a few steps back. The Ruthenians advanced, and the one on the left took out a knife. Yerahmiel froze in his tracks.

Rachel cried out, "Run, Yerahmiel, run!" The two grabbed him by his coat. "Let them take the coat!" Rachel yelled. Ullo's head appeared in the window next to her. Yerahmiel quickly slipped his arms out of the coat sleeves and fled in the direction of the house.

Rachel shouted, "Help, help, Jews, help!" The two Ruthenians stood watching and laughing. One of them checked the pockets of the coat, and when he saw that they were empty, he dropped it on the ground. He signaled to his friend and the two ran off.

Yerahmiel entered the house and chuckled, "Thieves, just a couple of miserable thieves." But Rachel warned that they would have to watch out now because their lives were in danger, and Reisel, her mother, nodded in agreement. That evening, Rachel read her husband a satirical sketch from the Yiddish newspaper *Haynt.*[10] The headline said, "Rules for Jews, or How to Live in Poland." The writer urged his readers to obey twelve commandments: "Do not live in a city where there are demonstrations. Do not let the evil impulse make you ride a tram. Do not go to meetings. Do not visit the theater. Do not walk in the street. Do not stay home. Do not engage in commerce. Do not work. Do not be idle. Do not eat and do not sleep. Do not live and do not die." Any Jew who adopted these rules, the writer concluded, "is assured that he will live out his life in comfort and in happiness, and enjoy equal rights without regard for religion or nationality."

Although Yerahmiel's presence at the funeral had not been officially required because he was not a functionary in the Bolechow community, he felt a deep sense of identification with the victims' relatives. That morning he felt a powerful wish to be among the mourners. He traveled on the train from Bolechow with the official delegation of the Jewish community, and as they sat in their compartment, he thought of the satirical sketch in the *Haynt* and of the two young Ruthenians who had tried to rob him. No, he said to himself. Ukrainian thieves, wretchedly poor, were one thing, and a pogrom carried out by Polish soldiers against Jews was another thing entirely. The pogrom had not been spontaneous. It had been planned in advance, there was no doubt about that. Every evening during recent weeks, Rachel had taken the trouble to read to him inflammatory articles from a new Polish newspaper, *Pobudka* (Wake Up), which was first published in November and was the organ of Pilsudski's Polish Legions.

Rachel subscribed to several newspapers and periodicals, among them the daily *Haynt* and the weekly *Der Yud* ("The Jew," in Yiddish). Every day they were brought straight from the train station to her home by the paper delivery man, a Jew who was known in Bolechow as Gabai'le (Yiddish for "little public servant"). Gabai'le was an educated eccentric, and no one knew his real name. He looked like a Jesuit friar. He was short and slight, with the long, narrow face of an ascetic and a sparse beard dangling from his chin. Summer and winter, on his rounds to the homes of newspaper subscribers, he wore shabby leather boots and an old leather satchel strapped on his chest. Taciturn and mournful, he was the complete opposite of the cheerful mailman Igrenski. Sometimes his clients asked Gabai'le why he carried the world's troubles around with him on his shoulders.

Gabai'le had a strange custom. He would never enter his customers' homes but instead stood at the gate, handed the paper to them at arm's length, and recited the main headline in a whisper. He had two kinds of client, favorites and ordinary ones. The favorites, Rachel Kahane among them, paid their subscription and delivery fees a month in advance, and Gabai'le respectfully brought the papers to their homes. The ordinary clients had to make their own way to his house, near the bridge, and pay cash for their papers. On Saturdays, he gave his customers credit, so that they would not have to carry money on the Sabbath. For some families, his visits were eagerly awaited. As the local representative for the Reuters, PAT, and JTA news agencies, Gabai'le always had up-to-date information.[11] During the war, he traced the front lines on a map in his home and reported the latest troop movements to his customers.

Beginning in early November, Gabai'le found some copies of the new *Pobudka* in the package of newspapers that arrived every day on the train from Lvov, and he gave them out free of charge to regular customers. Five days before the pogrom in Lvov, on November 17, he placed the paper in Rachel's hand and whispered, "They are planning a pogrom in Lvov. See what's inside." That evening, Rachel read to Yerahmiel an astonishing item from the new paper: "Jews in Lvov shoot at Poles and pillage their property." Yerahmiel kept the clipping, and it was in his pocket on the train to the funeral. He took it out and read it again. It was headlined "The Neutrals" and it said,

> In our military circles there have been complaints that Jews have been firing from the windows of their homes at our patrols. Travelers from Lvov say that the attitude of the Jews toward the Poles is in no way

> compatible with their declaration of neutrality. We are publishing here for the first time the testimony of an eyewitness: "I know with certainty that in the Jewish neighborhood Zolkiewska, in Cebulnagasse, there is a complete armory ready for use by the Jews. Moreover, I affirm that almost every Jew in the city carries arms, which they claim are for self-defense but are actually for use against the Polish army and Polish civilians. As proof of my testimony, I declare that I myself saw, on November 10, at 11 o'clock, a gang of armed Jews leaving the synagogue and storming toward the citadel and opening fire. On their return, the Jews said, 'We have done what was necessary.' In addition, I myself saw a Jew shooting civilians with a pistol in the Krakauerplatz. I have also learned that many places of business owned by Christians have been looted by Jews."

Yerahmiel showed the clipping to the members of the community leadership he was traveling with, and they were stunned. The item was pure invention. Now they had no doubt that the Polish Legion's organ had signaled to its readers that the Jews should be attacked.[12] There was a consensus in the coach that the Jewish leadership's vigorous efforts to stay out of the conflict by demonstrating neutrality had failed, despite the fact that the Jewish militia had received strict orders to remain in position within the Jewish quarter and to refrain from any action that could be seen as aggressive. Each of the militia men wore an armband emblazoned with the Jewish star.

Discussion in the compartment centered on the political turnabout made by the founder of the Polish Legions, Marshal Jozef Pilsudski. How was it possible, Yerahmiel asked, that Pilsudski, who was considered a stalwart liberal who

A postcard with Field Marshal Jozef Pilsudski's photograph was found in one of Hella Backenroth-Horn's photograph albums.

opposed any form of anti-Semitism and who had willingly recruited Jews to his legion, had joined with the Endeks, as the nationalistic anti-Semitic members of the National Democratic Party headed by Roman Dmowski were known? No one in the carriage had an answer for him.

In 1914, when World War I broke out, the gap between the two Polish organizations had indeed appeared to be unbridgeable. Pilsudski's legions fought alongside the Germans, while many of the Endeks had enlisted in the army of the Russian czar. In 1918, when the war appeared to be drawing to a close, and the Poles' dream to regain their independence was getting closer to realization, Pilsudski left the Socialist Party and joined with the nationalist right wing in formulating a plan for an independent Poland that included Galicia. The Endeks abandoned the czar's army immediately after the communists seized power in Russia, and Pilsudski agreed to take them into his legion without probing the political past of each individual. Some of the officers who joined the legion were known to be inveterate anti-Semites.

The tension between Poles and Ruthenians had already been felt in Galicia in early October, several weeks before the last emperor of the Austrians, Karl I, agreed to the Allies' proposal for a cease-fire.[13] There had always been a wall of hatred between the Poles and the Ruthenians, but under the umbrella of the Austro-Hungarian Empire, both sides had managed to live with each other. Which is to say, many of them carried sharpened knives in their pockets and cursed one another behind their backs, but in public they spoke politely and smiled falsely at one another. The space between the Ruthenian peasantry, most of whom were illiterate and ignorant, and the Polish landlords, officials, and teachers was filled by the Jewish merchants, wholesalers, craftsmen, doctors, and lawyers. Each minority went its own way and in its heart felt contempt for the others. Until now, to their good fortune, they had all been the subjects of a foreign ruler and thus a delicate balance had been maintained. But now that the Austro-Hungarian Empire had fallen apart, the Hapsburg Dynasty had, once and for all, left the stage of history.[14] As anticipated, the old sores had reopened and the struggle for Galicia's future was renewed. During Hapsburg rule, Jews had faced no official discrimination because most of them were ardent supporters of the multinational state and the monarchy. Now many of them feared that the rise of ardent nationalism on both sides, Polish and Ruthenian, would break up the delicate political balance in Galicia.

That is exactly what happened. With the demise of the empire, the establishment of the new Poland was declared and a provisional government was set up in Warsaw. The officials of the local administration in Galicia, most of whom were Poles, announced their support for that government and transferred the province into its hands. The Poles flew their white-and-red flags, and the Ruthenians' fury flared up.

"We will never agree to the Polish minority establishing fait accompli in our territory," their leaders declared and immediately went into action. On November 1, at three o'clock in the morning, the Ruthenians took over the headquarters of the military governor of Lvov. The next day, the Ukrainian National Council proclaimed that Galicia was under its control and declared an independent "West Ukraine."[15] The Poles called this declaration of independence "a *putsch*" and demanded that it be rescinded. The Ukrainians refused and tried to enlist the Jews on their side. The Ukrainian National Council announced that it recognized the Jews as a "national minority with equal rights" and invited their representatives to take part in its meetings. But the Jews turned down the invitation, for fear of the Polish reaction. They preferred to sit on the fence and announced their neutrality, while at the same time organizing a militia for self-defense.

Armed conflict broke out the next day. The first to open fire in the streets of Lvov were the Ukrainians. The Poles returned the attack. Legionnaires of Pilsudski's forces occupied the building that housed the Henryk Sienkiewicz School and fired in all directions from its windows. In response, the Ukrainians tossed burning bottles of kerosene from the cover of fences and barricades, and innocent civilians were hurt. For several days, the fighting spread, with neither side being able to claim victory. Life in the city came to a standstill. Then the Poles took the initiative. They suspected that the Jews were aiding the Ukrainians and sent legionnaires to disarm the Jewish militia. The Jewish commanders did not allow them to do so, and it is possible that this resistance led to the pogrom.

On the morning of November 10, the Jews attempted to turn the clock back and sent a delegation to negotiate with the headquarters of the Polish Legions. The Jewish delegation included three men who had fought with the legions against the Russians during World War I: Lieutenant Isidore Fuchs, Second Lieutenant Anshel Reiss, and Dr. Alexandrowitsch, a warrant officer. On the Polish side of the talks were the commanding officer of the legion, Captain Czeslav Montashinski, and his chief of staff, Captain

Bronislav Lepinski. The Jews repeated their declaration of neutrality, and the Poles accepted the declaration and promised to respect the special status of the Jewish militia. At the end of the meeting, the Poles affirmed that the armed Jewish militia would be permitted to maintain order and security in Jewish districts of the city and would not intervene in the battles.

The panic in the Jewish community subsided, although the fighting continued. The Ukrainians had numerical superiority, but the Poles had more weapons. They continued to advance steadily into the western part of the city, pushing the Ukrainians eastward. The Poles broke into the Zrodlana neighborhood and conquered the railway station and the Szpitalnagasse. The Ukrainians responded with heavy fire. A war of attrition continued for three weeks, with dozens of civilian casualties every day. Toward the decisive stage, the battle zone was in the Old City, very close to the Jewish quarter. The Ukrainians courageously held on to their positions, and the final battle may well have gone their way had they not agreed to a three-day cease-fire.

On November 21, the Polish Legion took advantage of the cease-fire to bring in reinforcements and arms from Kraków, as a result of which the Ukrainians were forced to withdraw. Early on the morning of November 22, the Ukrainian forces retreated eastward out of the city, and the Republic of Western Ukraine was dead. By noon, Polish Legionnaires had occupied the center of the city and the Jewish quarter. Crowds of Poles poured into the streets to celebrate their victory and wave their flags. Thus was eastern Galicia annexed to independent Poland. The next day, with the celebrations at their height, legionnaires and Polish civilians began to slaughter Jews and torch their homes.[16]

At the Lvov railway station, Yerahmiel recalled that when rumors of the pogrom had spread in Bolechow and Rachel had said that everything had happened that she had expected, he thought that she was exaggerating. "Facts!" he said to her. "It is impossible to reach conclusions without facts!"

Now, in view of the spectacle that confronted him, he realized that he had belittled her. In the coming years, he repeatedly described to his children the shock that had overcome him in the cemetery, when he suddenly grasped that for a long time, he had avoided confronting the truth. He recalled the fears that had crossed his mind since returning with his family from Vienna, but how could he anticipate that three kings, the Austrian, the German, and the Russian, would topple from their thrones? Who had imagined that the map of Europe would be redrawn, with a united and independent Poland and a communist Russia, and that Galicia would become part of Poland? The unbelievable events of the last few years flashed before his eyes. Had he not seen that the bureaucracy in Vienna was rotten, that the kaiser's army was weak, and that the empire was sinking? Of course he had seen it, but he had managed to mentally suppress the significance of the facts and the events. Deep in his consciousness, he understood that the golden age of the Austro-Hungarian Empire had come to an end. He knew for certain that the annexation of Galicia to independent Poland would bring bundles of troubles in its wake for the Jews. But who could have believed that all this would have turned out the way that it did? Why had he not added one to one and arrived at two? After all, from the minute the United States had joined the Allies, the fate of Germany and its Austro-Hungarian ally had been sealed.[17]

And when it was clear that the Central Powers would lose the war, the Jews' situation in Galicia had become perilous. Nothing could be more paradoxical: it was precisely the end of the war that increased the danger. But it was nonetheless the truth. By night, slogans had appeared on the walls in downtown Lvov: "Boycott Jewish shops." In the newspaper *Gazeta Polska,* Roman Dmowski called on the Polish citizenry to *Swoj do Swego po Swoje* (Your own, to your own, for your own), or patronize Poles and not the foreign Jews.[18] Dmowski's supporters, the Endeks, printed this motto on flyers that were distributed in front of churches. Polish nationalists disseminated the slogan "On the banks of the Vistula, there is no room for two nationalities." In every town and village, Poles voiced the buzzword *Ojczyzna*, or "motherland," that terrified Jews and made them hide away in their homes. As long as the nationalists were victimizing Jews far away from Galicia, in the Warsaw area, in Kielce, and in some villages near Lublin, the Galicians were not overly anxious, but now the nationalists were killing Jews right on their doorstep, in Lvov.

Because Yerahmiel was familiar with Lvov's history, he was astonished that a pogrom had taken place there. At the time of the Ruthenian rebellion led by Bogdan Khmelnytsky in the mid-seventeenth century, Poles had protected their Jewish neighbors with their own bodies. When the Cossacks attacked Lvov in 1648 and the Russians in 1655, at the height of those two assaults, the Polish townsfolk had refused to hand over the Jews to the assailants, who had made do with ransoms.[19] Now, however, feelings of hatred toward the Jews, which had been suppressed in the Poles' subconsciousness during the days of the empire, burst out and exploded into violence, Yerahmiel said to himself, It was as if the Poles had waited for 150 years for that historical moment when the new Poland would arise, only so that they could make the Jews scapegoats for the century and a half that Poland was ruled by foreigners.

At the end of the funeral procession, rabbis bore wooden boxes that looked something like small coffins, each carrying torn and burned fragments of parchment. They were what remained of the Torah scrolls that had been taken out of the Holy Ark of the synagogue, after it had been set alight by forty Polish Legionnaires at ten o'clock in the morning on November 23. By Jewish law, desecrated Torah scrolls must be buried in the earth in a religious ceremony, as if they were deceased people. The burned sheets of parchment, on which scribes had handwritten the Torah in Hebrew lettering, were buried close to the victims of the massacre. As clods of earth were shoveled onto the bodies, Jews stood around their graves and wailed in mourning. In the eyes of Orthodox Jews, burning a Torah scroll is sacrilege, and hardly any sin is more serious. Violating the Holy Ark is no less than a violation against the Deity itself. Near Yerahmiel stood a group of black-clad ultra-Orthodox Jews, who ripped their coats in mourning. Women scratched their cheeks. Yerahmiel, too, felt pain over the desecrated scriptures, but to him the sanctity of life was much greater than the sanctity of the scrolls. He left the cemetery and walked to the train station.

On the train ride back to Bolechow, Yerahmiel was alone in the compartment. Drizzling rain smeared the windows and blurred the scenery. Disjointed scenes from the dramatic experiences that he had undergone in the cemetery conflated in his mind with events of recent days. He recalled a fire that had broken out in the Rynek on Saturday night.

The Jews had already completed the Havdala service marking the end of the Sabbath, but the sacred spirit of the Day of Rest seemed reluctant to depart the town.[20] It was a moment of grace, of tranquility, Yerahmiel remembered, but suddenly the calm was broken by shouts in Yiddish from the square, "*Es brent, es brent, gevalt!*" (It's burning, help!). The wooden house next door to the Kahanes' home was on fire. Flames burst from the windows and threatened to spread to adjoining houses. Yerahmiel picked Ullo up and carried him outside. Rachel urged Leah and Sonia to hurry up and leave the house, then followed them out.

To extinguish the fire, men were already filling buckets of water at the Ring Stock, the canal that ran between the houses and the road. The canal was about a foot and a half deep and wide and was lined at the bottom and on the sides with wooden boards. It ran from the bank of the Sukiel River, where a wooden gate had been installed, along the main street to the Rynek. Whenever a fire alarm was sounded, one of the children would run and open the gate so that the canal would fill up with water. This is what happened on that Saturday night. The men rolled up their sleeves and stood in a line along the Ring Stock. They bent over to dip the buckets into the water, then straightened up again like robots, and women and children also formed a line and passed the full buckets from one to another until they reached the burning house. The blaze illuminated the square with a theatrical effect, creating a haphazard interplay of light and shadows. More people emerged from the side streets to join the dozens of men, women, and children fighting the blaze. They filled the buckets, passed them along, and hurled the water at the flames. On this occasion, the fire was especially powerful. Great flames leaped from all the windows and smoke poured out of the roof. One woman didn't stop screaming *"Es brent, es brent!"* and the children's sobbing could be heard in the darkness.

Rachel gathered her children and held them close in her arms to calm them. Sonia was laughing; she enjoyed the excitement. Leah, as usual for her, was serious and logical, looking around for the family, Grandma, and Grandpa. Looking back on that night, Yerahmiel remembered that Ullo had been quiet. The boy was at his best at times of crisis, in control of his feelings and levelheaded. He had just turned seven, and the next day he was scheduled to make a ceremonial address (*drasha,* in Hebrew) before the congregation to mark the occasion.

Known as the *drasha-shpruch* (in Yiddish, "sermon speech"), this was an ancient tradition preserved for centuries in the autonomous Jewish congregation, the *kehilla,* and was meant to recall, and in a way also to imitate, the Giving of the Torah at Mount Sinai.[21] A child who had just finished learning the letters of the Hebrew alphabet and reading and understanding the Book of Genesis would be dressed in his best suit and tie, with a gold watch hanging from a chain at his waist (which his father loaned to him for the occasion), and would be presented before the congregation to be tested.

Ullo Kahane delivered his *drasha-shpruch* on Sunday afternoon. He watched from the window as all of his friends, the students of Shloime

Hashwar, along with the *melamed*, or teacher, at the *heder*, walked in pairs around the square, passed the house that had burned down, and quietly drew near to his home. The acrid smell of burned wood was still hanging in the air. In the parlor, dozens of relatives, friends, and neighbors had gathered, as well as Ullo's *heder* classmates. There were also two of the town's Jewish dignitaries, Rabbi Perlov, the spiritual leader of the Hasidim, and the doctor, Yaakov Blumenthal, who was a leader of the assimilated Jews. They nodded to each other once but never exchanged a word.

Ullo's father, Yerahmiel, was popular with everyone. He was no Hasid, but neither did he identify with the "Mosheks"—the contemptuous epithet that the Poles used to refer to an assimilated Jew. Nonetheless, the leaders of both of those communities came to his house on the occasion of his son's *drasha.* This was unusual. As thoroughly as the elderly rummaged through their memories, they could not recall a single previous instance when the Hasidic rabbi and the assimilated doctor had ever spent time together under the same roof. In a few years' time, Ullo would join the Zionists of the town, and the doctor would look askance at him, although the rabbi's daughter would cast longing gazes in his direction. But today, Ullo was facing his family and the townsfolk in his first public trial. The *heder* children were crowded onto two wooden benches that had been brought from the synagogue, and the adults sat on padded chairs or armchairs.

Everything was ready. Hashwar, the *melamed*, was seated at the head of the table, and the examinee stood facing him. The boy tried to answer, and the audience enjoyed the performance.

"Come closer, little boy," said the teacher in Polish.

"I am not little. I'm a big boy, seven years old," replied Ullo.

"Indeed, you are a big boy, Yisrael Herz," said the *melamed.* "So tell us, what have you learned so far?"

"Humash [the Pentateuch]," said the boy.

"What does Humash mean?"

"Five."

"Five? What do you mean? Five candies?" The teacher chuckled, to the crowd's laughter.

"No," replied Ullo without faltering. "The five books of the Holy Torah."

The adults nodded in agreement.

"And what are the names of those five holy books?"

Ullo raised his hand and counted off on his fingers, in Hebrew now: "Bereshit, Shemot, Vayikra, Bamidbar, Devarim [the Hebrew names of the books of the Pentateuch: Genesis, Exodus, Leviticus, Numbers, and Deuteronomy]. Five."

"And which one are you studying now?"

"I am learning the second one. The first one, in which the world is created, I have already finished, and the second one is called Shemot."

"And what does Shemot mean, Yisrael Herz? What does it mean?" asked the *melamed.*

"Names," said Ullo, and he calmly recited the first verse of the book of Exodus: "And these are the names of the children of Israel who came to Egypt."

"And how many came to Egypt?" the teacher asked with a smile.

The audience waited for Ullo to answer. The boy thought. He would never reply without first weighing his answer well. Yerahmiel and Rachel knew that their son knew the answer. On the eve of the Sabbath, they had read the first chapter of Exodus with him twice.

"Seventy. Seventy souls," the boy said proudly.

The audience breathed out in relief, and some clapped their hands.

"And Joseph?" the *melamed* pressed him. "Where was Joseph?"

"Joseph was in Egypt," Ullo replied at once.

"And what was Joseph doing there?"

"He was the adviser of Pharaoh. Joseph was the king's deputy."

"A nice answer," the teacher complimented his pupil and smiled with pleasure. "Tell me, Yisrael Herz Kahane, please tell me, how old was Joseph at that time?" Hashwar was sure that the boy would get confused because the story of Joseph's appointment to the post of deputy to Pharaoh is told in the book of Genesis, and Ullo had prepared for today by learning the first chapter of Exodus.

But Ullo surprised him. "Joseph was thirty when Pharaoh made him his adviser."

It was for this reason that the Kahanes read the weekly Torah portion every Friday night in their home and explained the difficult verses. Rachel wiped away a tear, thinking, I hope that I will be able to bring him to his *huppah* [marriage canopy] like this. Rabbi Perlov was enthusiastic. He shook the boy's hand and blessed him as the whole audience listened in. Ullo then read the first chapter of Exodus out loud, and everyone was suitably impressed.

The formal ceremony was over. Now Rachel and the *melamed* stood at the door, holding a basket full of small bags of sweets, as the children lined up whispering excitedly to one another in Yiddish, "*A beitel, a beitel*" (A bag, a bag). As they politely said good-bye, each one received his candy before dashing off into the square to play, while the adults partook of festive refreshments. Yerahmiel Kahane opened a bottle of vodka, not the Ukrainian Ludka Horauka, but the real thing: Smirnov, brought from Moscow before the revolution. Everyone chatted. The rabbi took a pinch of snuff, and the tension eased. Ullo passed his test.

When evening came and the guests went home, Rachel cleared away the dishes.

As the train drew into the station, Yerahmiel mulled over the terrible fire at his neighbor's house and the joyous *drasha* ceremony of his son. He got off the train and walked home. It was drizzling, and a wind was blowing. He passed by brightly lit windows of his neighbors' houses. After the tumultuous morning in Lvov, it seemed to Yerahmiel that Bolechow belonged to another world. He mused about the difference between himself and Rachel. With her intuition, she had sensed the dangers, while he had demanded proof, facts, in order to be convinced that there was no solution to the "Jewish problem" in the Diaspora. If on that autumn evening he had told her, "Come, my dear wife, let's pack up and move to Palestine," Rachel would have agreed at once. But Yerahmiel never proposed a move, neither to Palestine nor to the United States, and Rachel never took the initiative herself. She followed him, for better or for worse, despite the fact that she was the first to understand the significance of the newspaper headlines.

In the following day's *Haynt*, they read of a demonstration by thousands of Jews in Madison Square Garden in New York to protest the pogrom in Lvov. The Lvov community council sent a telegram to U.S. president Woodrow Wilson, asking for protection. As a result, at the peace conference that convened at Versailles, Wilson insisted that Poland's independence be made conditional on the granting of rights to its Jewish population.[22]

But in a few days' time, the Jews forgot about the pogrom and Wilson's promise, as Jews are wont to do. Life must go on. Yerahmiel, too, went back to business as normal. From the point of view of the leather tanner from Bolechow, things were not bad at all. For years to come, armies of troops and refugees would continue to tramp across Polish territory.[23] The white czarists would withdraw, and the red legions would advance. Germans would evacuate, and Poles would take their place. Prisoners would trudge all the way home from Germany to Russia. Polish Legionnaires would chase down Ukrainians. Bolsheviks and Poles would storm one another again and again, taking turns at advancing and retreating. It would be another six years before Galicia calmed down. Until then, troops and officers in formations of all sizes would march Galicia's length and breadth over and over, as would prisoners and refugees. The soles of their boots would wear out, and the demand for processed leather would steadily increase. Yerahmiel would recruit more workers, and his factory would operate two shifts a day. At the end of each year, he would read the bottom line on his balance sheet and inform the family that profits were up.

Others, however, learned practical lessons from the pogrom. Many in Bolechow put their houses up for sale and prepared to depart for the United States. The following year, the first group of pioneers from Bolechow would leave for Palestine. To the disappointment of Rachel and Yerahmiel, Sonia would fall in love with Nunio Krauthammer, the son of neighbors. Lidka would reveal musical talent, and Ullo would be registered at the Homburg Jewish elementary school.[24] Life returned to its routines, and the eye of the storm moved farther away from Bolechow.

11

Pilgrimage to Jerusalem

DURING THE POGROM CARRIED out by the Polish Legion in Lvov, the family of Sara-Ethel Backenroth came within a hairbreadth of being killed. Sara-Ethel was in mourning for her husband, Arie, Avrumche's eldest son, who had been murdered in a Russian prisoner of war camp. As was mentioned earlier, she had moved from Schodnica to Lvov to make things easier for her father-in-law, who was not formally told that the Russians had killed his son. She explained that it would be better for Avrumche not to face his son's children every day. Sara-Ethel's son Moye described what he saw of the pogrom in detail in his diary.[1]

On the morning of November 23, 1918, the residents of the Jewish Quarter awoke to the sound of military preparations—whistles, shouted orders, the revving of engines. "Strangely, in the background, there was also a harmonica playing," Moye related. The Jews peered through their windows, but few dared to go out onto the street. Later, they learned that trucks and armored cars of the Polish Legion had been deployed throughout the quarter and had blocked the exits to other parts of the city.[2] The operation's headquarters was set up close to the State Theater, and the officers began to send out units according to a prearranged plan. About an hour after that, shots were heard in the neighborhood. Machine guns mounted on trucks had been placed at the exits from the quarter, and from time to time, they fired bursts down the main streets so that no one would go outside. One of the guns was positioned on Zolkiewska Street, where Moye's family lived.[3]

A neighbor told Moye's mother that the Polish maneuvers were connected to the civil war. Perhaps Ukrainian units, which had withdrawn the day before, had reentered the city and the Poles were preparing to fight them, the neighbor said. No one imagined that the Polish Legion's movements were intended to harm the Jews. Nonetheless, Sara-Ethel prepared her four sons for the possibility that soldiers would come to their door.

"Tell them your parents are out," she said, and she donned the clothing of a peasant woman, intending to pose as a Polish servant.

"A few minutes later," Moye recalled, "we heard loud knocking on the door. The four of us were in the living room, and Mother was washing dishes in the kitchen. My older brother, Shmuel Yitzhak, opened the door and two soldiers came in." One was carrying a rifle and the other a pistol.

"Where are your parents?" one of them barked, and the frightened boys said that they were not home. The soldiers demanded to know where the money was hidden, but the children remained silent.

One of the soldiers said, "Let's shoot them now. We've got to shoot them right now." He ordered them to stand against the wall and fired a shot over their heads.

Their mother burst into the room, fell at the soldiers' feet, and begged for their lives. "Please leave the children," she implored. "They are orphans, their father was killed in the war." Sara-Ethel offered the men money, and they took a few banknotes and left. Just then, as the firing continued outside, Moye fell down, lost consciousness, and became feverish. His mother carried him down to the cellar and called a doctor. When he awoke, he wrote in his diary that he had had a wonderful dream.

"It was an epiphany, a true epiphany. I was in a distant land and I saw a prophetic vision," he related. A strong sun was radiating a shining light, and around him there were young people singing songs in Hebrew. "I heard battle songs, songs of the Jewish Legion," he wrote, and added, "In my dream, the redemption of the Jewish nation in its country was realized."

Now, for a twelve-year-old boy to have a dream after a traumatic experience is not remarkable, but when that boy announces in all seriousness that he intends to make the dream come true, and when he begins to take practical steps, organizes groups of young Jews, raises the necessary funds, and sets out with eight hundred young people on the journey to the land of Israel, people can only look on in wonder.

Moye Backenroth's life story was hardly normal.[4] For one thing, as a small child he mistakenly believed that his aunt Clara, his father's sister, was his mother. Once she had smacked him for getting his clothes dirty. If she is allowed to hit me, he thought with a child's logic, she must be closer to me than the others. "My mother never hit me," he said.

Moye had what it takes to be a preacher: a rich imagination, broad general knowledge, and the power of persuasion, qualities that infused his naive and romantic soul. From a young age, he conjured up strange visions, some of which he made happen in reality. He dabbled in various crafts, devised inventions, wrote essays, bought and sold various goods, and wrote letters to world leaders.

"I am just 12 years old," he wrote in his diary, " and I don't know what I am. Austrian? Polish? Ukrainian? For whom did my father die in the war? All the nations rise up to fight for their liberty, why are the Jews asleep?" And indeed, the pogrom aroused an enormous emotional storm among the Jews of Lvov: fear, rage, and a deep concern about the future.

Against this background, in the early winter of 1918, the charismatic boy, who looked older than his age, combed the city for organized Jewish youths, visited Jewish schools and the offices of Jewish political parties, talked to members of the young people's movements, and gathered around himself a group that he inspired with his Zionist speeches. Out of a profound conviction and guileless faith that nothing would stand in his way, Moye described the epiphany he had experienced and explained that fate had destined him "to uproot the Diaspora by setting up a Jewish Legion that would settle in the land of Israel."

He took the idea for the legion from the Polish Legions that were set up by Marshal Pilsudski before World War I to help Poland attain independence—the same legions whose soldiers had slaughtered Jews in Lvov. Moye was also influenced by ideas currently fermenting in the debate within the Zionist movement in Eastern Europe.[5] He had no trouble in getting young people to discuss his plans seriously. Many of them admitted that the sand dunes of the land of Israel appealed to them, and that the danger of contracting malaria was ten times less repellent than the persecution in Europe. So far, though, few had been ready to take on the role of pioneer and travel to that remote region, which the British army had just taken from the Turks. Although only a year earlier British foreign secretary Arthur Balfour had declared that the British government "viewed with favour" the establishment of a Jewish national home in Palestine, this had not led to a mass migration of Jews to Israel.[6] Most of them found the idea of traveling to the United States more appealing, Moye recalled sixty years later. The gates of the United States were still open to immigrants from Europe, and thousands of Lvov Jews hastened to sell their property, board trains for the ports of Hamburg or Bremen in Germany, and embark on ships bound for New York.[7] Nevertheless, Moye managed to arouse interest in his proposal for a Jewish legion. Among those he attracted were yeshiva students, high school graduates, and workers. In one diary entry, he listed some of the youngsters who had joined his group of "legionnaires": a Hebrew teacher, a shoemaker, a peddler, a glazier, a high school graduate, and a dentist.

Moye made all of his savings, five thousand Austrian kroner, available for the mission.[8] He also asked his rich grandfather Avrumche for money to help finance his project. Avrumche was astonished, while some family members criticized Moye and others were mockingly dismissive. His mother was desperate. "In her youth she had lost her husband, and now she was about to lose her son," Moye wrote in his diary. "In their eyes I am insane."

How could it be otherwise? A twelve-year-old boy demands money from his grandfather to pay for a group of hundreds of young people to journey to the land of Israel. His mother wept and threatened, and his grandfather warned, "The plan is crazy!" But despite it all, Moye was determined. "All of the pleas and the threats have not changed my mind," he wrote.

Moye's vision was the last thing that Avrumche Backenroth was worried about. From his point of view as a businessman, 1918 was the worst year of the war. In the summer, inflation was rampant and basic foodstuffs were in short supply.[9] Consequently, working-class families suffered. In October, strikes broke out in the oil fields, and relations between the workers and the employers deteriorated. The producers, Backenroth among them, were compelled to raise wages. At the same time, incitement against the Poles grew. Ukrainian nationalists threatened to harm those working in the oil fields, and many skilled workers were forced to leave Galicia with their families. The result was that oil output dropped, and the production companies were on the verge of bankruptcy.[10]

In early November, military conflict broke out between the Poles and the Ukrainians over control of eastern Galicia. Both sides were well armed, and it would have taken only one spark to ignite the whole oil belt and destroy the industry. The producers launched a mediation effort and convened delegations from both sides in Drohobych. The Polish interests were represented by the lawyer Stanislaw Victor Szczepanowski, the son of the oil entrepreneur Stanislaw Szczepanowski, who had chalked up great successes early in his business career but then became entangled in financial scandals and went bankrupt.

In Avrumche's eyes, Szczepanowski senior had been a Polish patriot and an exemplary businessman. Yet Avrumche detested Szczepanowski's son, who was close to Roman Dmowski, the head of the National Democratic Party. Avrumche believed that Szczepanowski Jr. was an extreme nationalist and an anti-Semite.

The Ukrainian side was represented by the trade union leader Semen Vityk, who achieved notoriety in the oil belt for the strikes that he organized. The mediators were Jewish businessmen, directors of international production companies, and some of the leaders of the Socialist Party, whose aim was to save the workers' jobs. On November 9, the talks reached an impasse, and Poles tried to take over the oil belt by force, but they were blocked by the Ukrainians. The confrontation was indecisive, and the oil field infrastructure remained intact. Another attempt was therefore made to reach a compromise, but to no avail. Nevertheless, the producers did manage to persuade both sides to refrain from hostilities, in order to avoid destroying the goose that laid the golden eggs. Control of the oil fields would ensure a certain degree of economic independence for the side that held them.[11]

Meanwhile, the battle for the regional capital, Lvov, had begun, and this would determine the fate of the whole of eastern Galicia. As mentioned earlier, the Polish Legion had reinforced its forces in Lvov on November 21, and the Ukrainians had been compelled to withdraw. The Poles took the city by force and then deployed their units in the oil belt without having to fight because the Ukrainians retreated. From the Backenroths' point of view, this was the desirable outcome, as the threat that Ukraine would nationalize the oil fields had been hanging in the air.

In January 1919, when the Paris Peace Conference opened, the Ukrainian delegation was convinced that it would be able to use diplomatic means to reverse the reality that had been established on the battlefield. The Ukrainians relied on the political vision of U.S. president Woodrow Wilson, who had pledged self-determination to every nation. Of his famous Fourteen Points, the last two clearly supported Ukrainian national aspirations.[12] But the State Department was wary of the close link between the Ukrainians and the Bolsheviks, so the Americans eventually decided in favor of the Poles.

In behind-the-scenes talks at the peace conference, the issue of who controlled the oil fields was of prime importance. France and Britain aimed to support the foreign companies that had invested in the infrastructure of the Galician oil industry. To do this, an international committee was named to study ways of "protecting the interests of the powers," and it gave blanket support to the Polish position. Apprehension about Ukraine nationalizing the oil industry was apparently the main reason for the committee favoring Poland, especially since Poland had promised to protect foreign interests. The Ukrainians never used one important argument that might have helped them: since 1910, there had been signs that the wells were drying up, and as a result the link between the oil industry and the government that controlled the territory was not all that important. But presumably, even if the Ukrainians had proved to the powers that the oil was running out, it is doubtful that the oil fields would have been given to them. The Poles had been scattering promises all over the place, while the Ukrainians, in their innocence, simply expected the powers to compensate them for the fact that they had been maltreated for centuries. Ultimately, it transpired that Wilson's vision, as formulated in his Fourteen Points, not only failed to withstand British and French interests, but it was even ignored in Washington's official position.

Hard at work in Paris was the nationalist Polish leader Roman Dmowski, who tried to persuade the powers that they needed a strong Poland that could resist the expansionist aspirations of Germany. This view was also received with understanding, while the basic contentions of the Ukrainians were rejected: that the Ruthenians were the majority in Galicia, that it had been their land since ancient times, and that throughout history they had been given a raw deal.[13] At the end of the bargaining, in the spring of 1919, the Allied Powers divided Galicia between Poland and Ukraine. The Lvov district was annexed to Poland, and Ukraine was given control of the oil belt. Ukraine agreed at once. Poland rejected the compromise and occupied the oil fields by force. The Ukrainians did not have enough power to eject them, and the powers gave the Polish conquest de facto recognition. This was the final death blow to Ukraine's declaration of independence.[14] The powers preferred to weaken Bolshevik Russia and Germany and therefore handed eastern Galicia and the oil belt to Poland.

In the middle of April 1919, when all the branches of the Backenroth family had once again gathered in Schodnica to celebrate the Passover festival, it was clear that Ukraine had lost the struggle and that the oil fields would be given to Poland. Avrumche's mood had improved, and thirteen-year-old

Moye's plan to actualize the revelation that he had experienced and lead a legion of youths to Jerusalem was on the agenda again.

This first Passover after the war was celebrated in magnificent style. The Backenroths gathered from all over: from Vienna, Chernovitz, Bucharest, Kraków, Lvov, and Bolechow. Everyone was excited. The harsh memories melted away with the winter snows that became streams of water flowing through green meadows. Even the memory of the pogrom in Lvov had dimmed, as had the images of the last year of war. The oil-pumping grasshoppers were working around the clock again, the refineries produced at full capacity, and new locomotives pulled trains of oil tanks westward, into the new Poland.[15] After the war, the global demand for petroleum grew. The Ford plant in Detroit was producing Model Ts in three shifts, and Igor Sikorski was building four-engine airplanes.[16] That year, for the first time, a plane had crossed the Atlantic in one hop. Optimism was in the air, and Jews forgot their past troubles quickly.

On the eve of the festival, poor people from the neighborhood again gathered near the Backenroth home, and Avrumche himself gave each a food package. This was a clear sign that times were good again, Moye wrote in his diary. Thrilled by his grandfather's generosity, he listed the contents of each package: a bag of potatoes, 4.5 pounds of meat, five *funts* of raisins, ten eggs, and 18 ounces of margarine.[17]

Moye counted the guests at the *seder* (the ceremonial dinner), the boys and the girls, the sons and the daughters-in-law, the grandchildren and the cousins. Altogether, no fewer than 104 relatives took part in the festive meal, and there were also other guests from Drohobych and Schodnica, including some solitary Jews and some poor ones, it being a *mitzvah* to host such people. They were all seated in the vast dining room, under a huge chandelier. In the center was a round table for Avrumche and his sons and daughters and their spouses and children. The other families were each seated at one of ten rectangular tables. Moye was enthralled by the sight. There were dozens of candles and a Haggadah for each participant, and on every table sat a solid-silver seder plate.[18] The women of the family wore evening gowns adorned with sparkling diamonds and pearls, and the men were clad in white. Avrumche read the Haggadah, and the children asked the Four Questions.[19]

Seventy years later, Naftali Backenroth-Bronicki, who would experience many thrilling events in the years to come, said this about the seder in

1919: "I have never in my life been as excited as I was before I asked the Four Questions at Avrumche's seder in Schodnica."

Thirteen-year-old Moye stole the *afikoman*, and when his grandfather asked him to return it so that he would be able to end the seder, as is customary, Moye replied, "I will give it back if you do what I have asked you to do"—meaning, pay for the journey to Palestine.[20] Avrumche bargained with his grandson.

"You're a soldier, Moye, a legionnaire," he coaxed the boy. "Soldiers don't steal."

Moye was persuaded, and he handed his grandfather the *afikoman*. In the early morning hours, after the seder was over, Moye was certain that although his grandfather had not yet agreed to give him the money for the journey, his vision was about to come true.

"I believed that this was to be my last seder at grandfather's house," he wrote in his diary. And he was right. His pleadings bore fruit. Shortly afterward, his mother's opposition softened and Avrumche, too, was convinced and gave him 20,000 kroner, roughly the equivalent of $20,000 today, to pay for the journey. Moye had a legionnaire's uniform made for himself, and he readied his group for departure. Thirty-six boys and girls boarded the train at Lvov and traveled south, toward the Czech border. At the city of Munkach in Czechoslovakia, anti-Zionist ultra-Orthodox Jews greeted them with curses and refused to accommodate them.[21] The youths spread out among the neighboring villages, described their mission, and recruited more pioneers. In Bratislava, the capital of Slovakia, a heated argument broke out between the young Zionists and a group of yeshiva students. Moye described it in his diary: "They told us that the messiah had not yet come and there was still time before the redemption of the Jews. The arguments turned into fistfights, but there were already a hundred of us."

In Vienna, the group attracted a lot of attention. They were put up in an army barracks that was made available to them, and relatives came to try to persuade Moye to go home. Another sharp dispute ensued, but Moye never gave in. The disagreement ended when the British consul granted the group visas to Palestine.

"Eight hundred people set out from Vienna," Moye wrote. "We are going to Jerusalem. Certainly, the railway terminal in Vienna has never seen such a departure." They traveled to Trieste by train, and there they boarded a ship and set sail for Jaffa. "We were taken ashore by Arabs in boats. English officials took our passports and sent us to a canteen. They inoculated us, and everyone who went out fell on the ground and kissed it. We had reached the Promised Land. There were crowds standing on the shore, and tears flowed from our eyes."

Moye was fourteen. He had achieved his dream of reaching Jerusalem, to save the Jews from the disgrace of exile and to rebuild the ancient motherland. But reality was a lot less romantic than he had imagined and the life in Palestine a lot harder. Two groups were opposed to pioneering Zionists: the Jews who had resided in Palestine for many generations and generally lived off donations from Jews abroad, and the Arabs, who constituted the majority of the population.

"We, the pioneers, are not liked by the Jews of the Old *Yishuv*, who see us as desecrating the sanctity of the Land.[22] The Arabs call for a holy war against us," was how Moye summed up the situation. He would stay in Palestine for five years, come down with malaria, take part in the Zionist workers' struggle to get the Jewish farmers to employ them, experience hunger, and study at the British Civil Service and Law School.[23] Then, at the age of eighteen, he traveled to England and registered as a student at Oxford University. Later, he returned to Galicia.

Three years after Moye went to Palestine, his cousin Leopold Weiss, a journalist, arrived in Jerusalem. The two lived in the city at the same time, but no one knows whether they ever met. Both of them documented their stays—Moye in his diary, Leopold in articles that he sent to his paper in Berlin. Moye never mentioned Leopold in his diary, and Leopold never mentioned Moye in his articles. Their depictions of Jerusalem in the 1920s are very similar, although their motives and their political positions were diametrically opposed. And if Moye's behavior seems unusual, it is nothing compared to the life of Leopold Weiss, soon to become known by a new name: Muhammad Asad.

PART THREE

Redemption

12

The Road to Mecca

LIKE MANY YOUNG PEOPLE WHO were born in the early twentieth century and grew up during World War I, Leopold Weiss was searching for direction in a world with no moral compass, a world whose values systems had collapsed. No war in the past had changed the face of Europe so dramatically. Four empires had vanished as if they had never existed, and four imperial dynasties were deposed from their hitherto omnipotent status.[1] The aristocracy was pushed aside, from center stage to the margins. The simple fighting men who returned from the battlefields struggled to fill the power vacuum that the aristocrats had left. Many ex-soldiers were suffering from what was then called shell shock and is now known as posttraumatic stress disorder. Even so, they were evidently determined to oust the rulers who had brought about the disasters of the war and to take responsibility for a world where peace would reign. Against this background, revolutionary forces gained strength: on one hand, the socialists and the communists, who preached international working-class solidarity and pacifism; and on the other hand, the radical nationalists who boosted the growth of fascism and Nazism.

After the war, an oppressive cloud hung over Europe. Sociologists spoke of the entire continent suffering from a collective trauma, and the term "lost generation" was used to describe those who were born around the beginning of the twentieth century and who came of age during or immediately after the war.[2] In Great Britain, at reunions of servicemen and at memorial services in military graveyards, people read the poem "Anthem for Doomed Youth" by Wilfred Owen, which begins, "What passing bells for these who

A Backenroth Becomes Asad

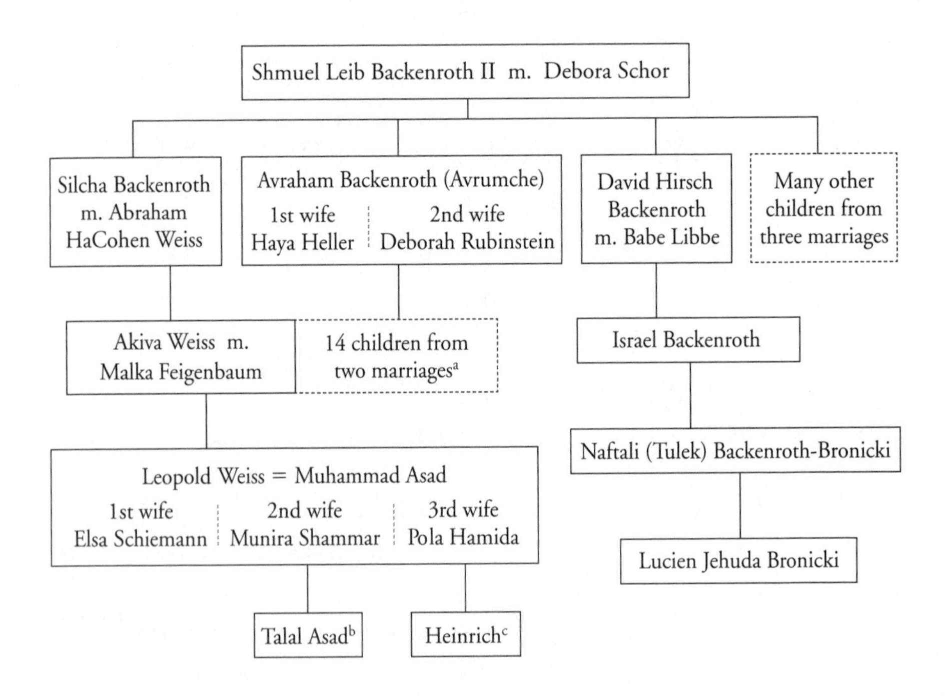

[a] Haya Heller bore Avrumche one son and three daughters. His firstborn, Arie, was drafted into the Austrian army, captured by the Russians, and murdered in Siberia (see chapter 9). Gittel married Yaakov Tirkel, nephew of the renowned rabbi of Chavin. Tirkel was a brilliant student and studied under Meir Ark, who was considered one of the sages of his time. Miriam Yuta was married three times. Her first husband was the rabbi of Czernovitz, Ben Zion Katz, the grandson of the Gaon (brilliant scholar) Zvi Katz. Her second husband, Chaim Rabinovitz, was the head of the Bucharest religious court. Her third husband, Avraham Yaakov Derbremidiger, was the head of the Galatz religious tribunal. Clara, the youngest daughter of Avrumche by his first marriage, wed Israel Moses Sobel, who was considered a prodigy in childhood. Haya Heller died young, in 1894, and a year later Avrumche took a second wife, Deborah Rubinstein. His second marriage lasted thirty-nine years until his death and produced ten sons and daughters. Most of the children of the second marriage were murdered by the Nazis.

[b] Anthropology professor at City University of New York. He was born in Saudi Arabia in 1931 and was brought up in a missionary boarding school in Pakistan. His PhD is from Oxford University in England. He is an expert on the Kababish tribe in north Sudan. His recent writings focused on secularism and modernity tendencies in Islam.

[c] Elsa Schiemann's son from her first marriage was adopted by Asad. After Elsa's sudden death in Saudi Arabia, her parents in Germany took custody of Heinrich.

Leopold-Muhammad Weiss-Asad.

die as cattle? Only the monstrous anger of the guns."[3] Antiwar literature was read avidly. *The Good Soldier Svejk*, a satirical novel by the Czech writer Jaroslav Hasek, was translated into sixty languages and became an immediate best-seller, as did Hemingway's *A Farewell to Arms* and Erich Maria Remarque's *All Quiet on the Western Front.*[4]

The process of internalizing the nightmarish ordeals of the war and attempting to define and understand its lessons aroused extreme reactions among many people. Some rejected society's conventions or became nihilistic, cynical, or full of contempt for the old values of ethical behavior, propriety, and civil discipline. Others succumbed to escapism, a denial of reality, or obsession with the occult, or they even prepared for the approaching end of the world.

It is easy to understand how the young Leopold Weiss absorbed and assimilated the ideological postwar chaos because throughout his life he wrote about contemporary affairs: political, social, and religious. His opinions and thoughts are a matter of written record, for anyone who is interested. But nevertheless, it is doubtful that the perplexity that is evident in his early writings sprang from his generation's ideological-social crisis. It is more likely that the characteristics of his personality sealed his fate and destined him for a radical form of youthful rebellion. Just like Johann Wolfgang von Goethe's Young Werther, Weiss felt as if the world's burdens were on his shoulders, and he aspired to discover the key to perfect spiritual contentment. His soul, like Werther's, was fragile and twisted, and both of them resolved their distress in drastic, but very different, ways. Werther committed suicide. Weiss chose another path of escape.

Leopold Weiss was born in Lvov on July 12, 1900, and at his circumcision ceremony he was given the Hebrew name Aryeh, meaning "lion." In official state documents, he was registered as Leopold. In childhood, he was known as Leibale, and when he grew older, his friends called him Poldi.

Leopold was the grandson of Avrumche Backenroth's sister Silcha, who married Benjamin HaCohen Weiss, the chief rabbi of Chernivtsi, which was the capital of the Bukovina district.[5] Their son Akiva married Malka, the daughter of the banker Menahem Mendel Feigenbaum of Lvov, and Leopold was the middle of their three boys.

Akiva Weiss studied law, joined his father-in-law's financial business, and did very well. "If I were asked to describe my father, I would say he was handsome and slim, of average height, dark complexioned with gloomy, sensitive eyes. He was not in harmony with his surroundings," Leopold wrote of Akiva. Leopold portrayed him as an unyielding, stubborn man with a stormy soul. In his youth, Akiva was attracted to the study of physics, and he hoped to devote his life to science. This dream never came to fruition, however, because Akiva's father, despite also being keenly interested in mathematics and astronomy, wanted Akiva to be a rabbi like his forefathers and refused to allow his son to study science. It took a great effort on Akiva's part to persuade his father to let him attend university. "I still remember my grandfather—a righteous man with delicate hands and a sensitive face framed in a long white beard," Leopold wrote of the chief rabbi Benjamin HaCohen Weiss.

In addition to having scientific interests, the rabbi was an excellent chess player. On the long winter evenings he often hosted the Greek Orthodox archbishop, another outstanding chess master. The two played chess and had deep conversations in German, developing metaphysical ideas and interpreting them according to their respective faiths. Why did a progressive man like Rabbi Weiss dismiss his son's wish to study science? The answer lies in events that had occurred six generations earlier. "A mythical story . . . a skeleton in the family cupboard," is how Leopold described it.

It is the tale of a young member of the family who abandoned his wife, and when he was located many years afterward, it turned out that he had become a Christian. This act cast a severe blemish on the family. In the closed and Orthodox Jewish society of the time, being baptized in a church was considered an unforgivable treason. The relatives of converts would observe a week of mourning for them, as if they had passed away. Upstanding families would refuse to allow their sons and daughters to marry into converts' families.

Because of the shame and in order to keep the secret from strangers, the Weiss family spoke of the apostate in whispers. When one of the relatives summoned up the courage to break the news of the terrible treason to his children, he made them swear that they would not mention the affair to outsiders. Thus, the tale of the convert was passed from mouth to ear, from generation to generation. Fathers told their sons so that they would learn the lesson and beware of falling into temptation. In Leopold's case, however, the effect may well have been the reverse. There is no explicit evidence in his writings that he decided to emulate the convert in order to take revenge on his father, but he does tell the tale with a great deal of irony, almost spite, at the family's expense.

The convert (whose name is not known) was born in the middle of the eighteenth century and was apparently a prodigy because he was ordained as a rabbi at a very young age. At around the same time, he was married to a girl who had been found by a matchmaker and whom he did not love. A rabbi's wages then were not enough to support a family, and the young groom went into business. He chose to deal in furs, and every year he traveled to buy goods at the great fair in Leipzig. Soon after he turned twenty-five, he traveled to Leipzig as usual, but instead of trading in furs, he sold his horse and carriage, shaved off his beard and sidelocks, and vanished into thin air. His wife became an *agunah*—"a chained woman" whose husband had abandoned her without giving her a divorce.[6]

Many years went by before the man was traced to London. It turned out that he had worked as a manual laborer for years, studying at night.

A wealthy Christian discerned that he had a remarkable mind and paid for him to go to Oxford University. He studied astronomy, and after graduating, he converted to Christianity and got a teaching position. Only then did he send his wife a bill of divorce, and he himself married a Christian Englishwoman. Before he died, he was granted a nobleman's title.

"This terrible example," wrote Leopold Weiss, "persuaded my grandfather to adopt a totally negative stand towards my father's desire to study 'Christian' sciences. My grandfather had been required to become a rabbi and so should his son. My father, however, was not willing to give up his dreams so easily. By day he studied Talmud and at night, clandestinely, he studied on his own, without a teacher, the entire high school curriculum."

At the age of twenty-two, Akiva Weiss passed his high school graduation exams with top grades and then, with his mother's help, persuaded his father to allow him to enroll at the university. He wanted to study physics, but his father preferred that he study law, and that is what he did. "This unfulfilled aspiration of my father," Weiss wrote, "was reflected in the amount of time he spent reading scientific material, and apparently also in his reserved, strange and extremely harsh attitude towards his middle son, myself." Thus, the son blamed his father for the painful dispute that developed between them.

Like most of the wealthy Jews of Galicia, when World War I broke out, the Weiss family left Lvov and moved to Vienna, where Leopold went to high school. He was a tall, robust, and independent lad. Toward the end of 1914, he left home and of his own accord joined the Austrian army. His father found him in one of the induction camps and took him home. Forced to go back to school, Leopold felt humiliated. His distress grew as his father demanded that he devote his efforts to the study of science, although he was drawn to the humanities. To his father's dismay, he spent his time reading Sienkiewicz and Jules Verne and avidly followed the adventures of the Indians of James Fenimore Cooper and Karl May. He paid little regard to his science lessons and neglected Greek and Latin grammar, which angered his father. "My father is disappointed with me," he wrote in his diary.

The well-off assimilated Jewish families of Europe used to engage private tutors to supplement their children's education, and Leopold was required to take lessons at home in piano and Judaism. He enjoyed classical music and learned to play the piano well. His achievements at religious studies were also impressive, ostensibly at least. His Hebrew and Judaism teachers managed to arouse his curiosity, and he studied the Bible and the Talmud seriously. It soon became clear, however, that the results of his studies were calamitous: the deeper he delved into Jewish wisdom, the more he was disappointed by it. Apparently, this was no reason for a family crisis because his parents were not observant. Leopold had the impression that they did not believe in the existence of God. "My parents pay lip service to religion," was how he put it in his diary, a harsh indictment of their hypocrisy.

Despite his reservations, Leopold did well at his Judaic studies. He read and spoke Hebrew fluently and reached a high level of proficiency in Aramaic, as well as in his studies of the Bible, the Mishna, and the Gemara.[7] He could distinguish between the Babylonian Talmud and the Jerusalem Talmud.[8] On one hand, he enjoyed these studies and spoke proudly of his achievements. On the other hand, he rebelled against his father for forcing him to study, and he formed an extremely negative attitude toward Judaism.

"Despite all the religious wisdom, or perhaps because of it, I rapidly developed an arrogant attitude towards most of the values of the Jewish faith," he wrote later. "It seemed to me that the God of the Old Testament and the Talmud was endlessly preoccupied with religious ritual, by means of which His believers were supposed to express their faith in Him. It seems to me that this God chose, strangely enough, to be involved in the fate of one particular people, the Hebrews. The very style of the Old Testament, presented as the history of the sons of Abraham, depicts God not as the founder and arbiter of all Creation, but as a tribal god, Who created the world according to the needs of the chosen people."

Leopold's unequivocal conclusion was that the effect of his Torah studies was the opposite of what his father had intended. "Instead of bringing me closer, it distanced me," he wrote in his diary, and he set out to seek a spiritual purpose for his life. His father demanded that he learn a practical, lucrative profession—law, for instance—but he was drawn to the humanities and registered as a student of the history of art and philosophy at the University of Vienna. Modern Europe made him miserable.

"Materialism repels me," he declared and rejected the social revolution advocated by his leftist friends. "There is a sense of bitterness and of insecurity in the air. . . . Everything seems to be flowing in an amorphous stream, and the spiritual restlessness of the young cannot find a prop." Leopold summed up the situation: "The old European order has fallen into ruins and nothing has grown up in its place. Spiritual values have been lost and people have no faith in gods"—and here he stated his unequivocal conclusion—"and without them society is doomed to live in a state of chaos."

The despondent youth saw only one way out: to find his faith and his god elsewhere. For a brief time, he thought that he had discovered them. In a Vienna bookshop he came across a German translation of *Tao Te Ching*, which means "The way and its power" in Chinese.[9] It is an ancient guide to a full life, composed in verses and maxims, whose format and formulations reminded him of the biblical books of Ecclesiastes and Proverbs. It was written by Lao Tzu, a philosopher who lived in Hunan province in the beginning of the sixth century BCE and was among the founders of Taoism. The followers of this faith and philosophy believe in the rule of a supreme reason, which is in fact a condition of no-rule or of near anarchy. The doctrine asserts that there is no need for institutions of state, social laws, or cultural rules. The fundamental belief underlying Taoism is that human beings are naturally good (as Jean-Jacques Rousseau postulated hundreds of years after Lao Tzu). The evil inclination is aroused precisely by the laws and the rules that society lays down for itself. Leopold learned from the Taoist writings that contrary to natural reason, which fosters peace and tranquillity, social order promotes hatred, aggression, and ambition. This is why the Taoists do not believe in placing politicians at the head of society, but rather in having philosophers or sages as leaders. The main role of the sage is opposite that of the ordinary ruler. He has to refrain from action or at least to restrict it to a minimum, in order to avoid interfering with the functioning of natural reason.

Leopold Weiss was enchanted by Lao Tzu's verses, and the spiritual message riveted him. "Herein lies the truth, I know," Leopold wrote. "From that moment and for several years, Lao Tzu became for me the window through which I looked out to realms as clear as glass." Leopold was so taken by Taoist philosophy because it is utterly devoid of materialism. Nevertheless, he understood that the solution that it offered was not suitable for Europe. "Preaching and intellectual self fulfillment alone," he wrote, "cannot revolutionize the spiritual faith of European society. A new faith of the heart is required now . . . . Where will I find such faith?"

Leopold grew up in an era when material wealth had become the supreme goal of Western man. People in his family and in the society around him were busily amassing property, but within Leopold's soul was an opposite inclination, an instinctive desire for pristine purity. It found expression in an aspiration to return to the roots of faith and in his attempts to decipher the essence of primeval divine insight. He wrote, "The average European, whether a democrat or communist, a factory worker or an intellectual, worships, so it seems, one religion: the religion of materialistic advancement—the temples of this religion are the giant factories, cinemas, chemical laboratories, dance halls, electrical power stations; its priests are bankers, engineers, politicians, movie stars, statisticians, factory owners, test-pilots, commissars."

The rift between Leopold and his father grew deeper, and at the age of twenty-one, Leopold decided to leave home for good. His mother had died, and his father had lost most of his fortune. After a short sojourn in Prague, Leopold settled in Berlin. His money soon ran out, and he made his living from a series of odd jobs. He attached himself to a group of impecunious intellectuals who idled their time away at the fashionable Romanische Café on the Kurfurstendamm.[10] He spent days and nights lingering over cups of coffee in the company of famous artists and writers, drinking in their words and aspiring to become a journalist. He befriended a series of liberated women and slept in a different bed every night.

His father wrote him an angry letter from Vienna: "I imagine that one day you will be found dead in a ditch at the roadside." To it, Leopold responded arrogantly, "I will end up not in a ditch but at the top."

And at least from his own point of view, Leopold Weiss did make it to the top. His journey there began on the day he set out for Jerusalem. In the spring of 1922, he was surprised to receive a letter from his uncle Dorian Isidor Feigenbaum, who lived in the Holy City.[11] Uncle Dorian, his mother's younger brother, was a bachelor and a psychiatrist, one of the first students of Sigmund Freud. In the early 1920s, after specializing in psychoanalysis in Vienna and Berlin, he was asked to come to Jerusalem to head the Ezrat Nashim hospital (*Ezrat Nashim* means "women's aid" in Hebrew).[12] It had been the first psychiatric hospital in the Middle East when it was founded by a philanthropist in 1895. Uncle Dorian lived in a spacious Arab building in the Mamilla neighborhood, facing the Jaffa Gate in the Old City wall.

"Why don't you come and spend a few months here with me?" the uncle wrote to his nephew. "I will pay for your return trip. You will be free to return to Berlin whenever you choose, and while you are staying here, in this wonderful stone Arab house, which is cool in summer, we will spend some time together."

There are disagreements over how the idea of inviting Leopold to Jerusalem was born. According to Leopold's version, his uncle was miserable and needed company: "He was lonely, felt set apart from the society around him, which offered him nothing apart from a job and a salary, because he was not a Zionist. He was not particularly sympathetic towards Zionist aims, nor was he particularly attracted towards the Arabs." But according to a member of the Feigenbaum family, it was Leopold's father's idea. In early 1922, Dr. Dorian Feigenbaum received an urgent letter from his brother-in-law in Vienna. "My son is in great trouble," wrote Akiva Weiss. "He is living in the gutters of Berlin and I beg you to try to bring him back to the straight and narrow path, otherwise I shall go mad!" Feigenbaum obliged. He would invite his nephew to visit him in Jerusalem and try to save the youth's soul.

Yet the upshot was entirely different from what Akiva Weiss had hoped for. According to Weiss Senior, instead of redeeming his son's battered soul, Leopold's journey to Jerusalem caused irreparable damage. From Leopold's point of view, however, the visit was nothing short of a miracle. "The trip to Jerusalem," he wrote, "was a turning point in my life."

Had Leopold been affected by a case of "Jerusalem syndrome," a phenomenon that afflicts several tourists in the Holy City every year?[13] Although much has been written about the syndrome, it is difficult to define its symptoms precisely because they differ from case to case. But in broad outline, it can be described as a psychological metamorphosis caused by a profound religious or spiritual experience. It affects mainly educated tourists from the West. In most cases, it takes the form of a brief spell of confusion that causes normal men and women to perform bizarre but harmless acts such as walking around naked in public, or people may be overcome by a sense of sanctity or start to prophesy aloud in crowded places and perform similar acts. In other cases, however, the acts are extreme and even dangerous, such as self-inflicted wounds or suicide.

Whether Leopold Weiss was a victim of the syndrome or not, he underwent a fundamental psychological transformation. It's as if he were a plant whose seeds had been sown when he was still in Vienna and his roots were stuck in Berlin while his flowers blossomed in Jerusalem. His delicate soul had been prepared for the upheaval, and what happened to him in Jerusalem was only the catalyst.

In retrospect, it is clear that what happened was only to be expected. The writing was on the wall: Leopold Weiss came to Jerusalem to fall in love with the Arabs and to become estranged from his own people. From the balcony of Feigenbaum's home, Leopold watched the Arabs of Jerusalem walking through the Jaffa Gate garbed in their robes and white *keffiyeh* headdresses. To Leopold, one Bedouin who walked along the street resembled King David. When Leopold roamed the Judean Desert, he came across Arab peasants and imagined that they were the true Hebrews, the Israelites of the Scriptures, the sons of Abraham who had come from the land of Haran.

Leopold did a lot of hiking, with a knapsack and a walking stick, through the paths of picturesque Galilee. He lodged in the ancient villages. Later on, he traveled north to Syria and Lebanon and south to Egypt, becoming familiar with the Bedouin tribes and other Arabian peoples. Soon, he could chat with them in their language. After all, when he was young, he had thoroughly learned Hebrew and Aramaic, the sister tongues of Arabic. He enjoyed the Arabs' hospitality. He slept in their homes, ate their bread, and wore their clothing. He dispatched excerpts from his diary to the editors of the daily newspaper *Frankfurter Zeitung*, who enthused over his talents as a writer and appointed him their correspondent in the Middle East. From day to day, his feelings of identification with the Arabs grew stronger, while at the same time his criticism of the Zionists sharpened. "What are they seeking in Palestine, these corrupt Europeans?" he asked himself quietly, but soon he was addressing the question to his friends and his readers as well.

Leopold had a quick and sharp pen, and the perceptive pieces he wrote on his Middle Eastern journeys are still considered classics of journalism in Germany. His work carried him all over the region, and he filed dispatches from Palestine, Syria, Lebanon, Egypt, and Saudi Arabia. He described what he saw without distorting facts and figures, but his personal preference between the sides of the budding dispute over Palestine was clear: the Arabs were the sons of the land and its owners, and the Jews were outsiders. Leopold wrote, "In 1922 five Arabs are living in Palestine for every Jew." He reported the factual situation, and the Jews were outraged. Zionist propaganda was based on the claim that the Jews were returning to settle an empty land. Some Zionist leaders in Jerusalem accused him of incitement.

A meeting with Menahem Ussishkin (1863–1941), the chairman of the Zionist Executive, convinced Weiss that the Zionists were knowingly ignoring the existence of an Arab majority in Palestine. In retrospect, historical research has shown that Weiss's conclusion was correct. The majority of Zionist leaders simply turned a blind eye to the Arab presence in Palestine. Those who never denied the reality asserted that the interests of the two groups were identical: the Jewish immigrants from Europe, most of whom were liberals and socialists, and the Arab agricultural laborers, who were exploited by the landowning *effendis*.

After the meeting with Ussishkin, Weiss wrote that the Zionist leaders were afflicted with blindness and that "there is nothing wrong with the Arab decision to rebel against the idea of a [Jewish] national home in their midst. On the contrary, I immediately realized that this idea was being forced on the Arabs, and that they were defending themselves against it, and rightly so." When this appeared in a Frankfurt newspaper, German Zionists were furious at "this Jewish journalist from Lvov who hates his people," as he was described in the Zionist weekly the *Judische Rundschau*, published in Germany.

But a meeting with Chaim Weizmann (1874–1952), the leader of the Zionist movement, left Weiss confused. On one hand, Weizmann's personality made a strong impression on Weiss. He described Weizmann as a man "with boundless energy and tremendous spiritual force," a compliment that must have been difficult for Weiss to concede. But Weizmann's political views seemed totally erroneous to Weiss. When he asked Weizmann how he intended to turn Palestine into a Jewish national home in the face of the Arab majority's opposition, the reply was brief: "We hope that shortly the Arabs will no longer be a majority." Weiss explained why he thought that the Jews didn't belong in Palestine, but Weizmann smiled and changed the subject. Weiss was disappointed by the encounter. "Weizmann had no answer to my arguments," he observed. He reiterated to his readers his view that Zionism was no more than a passing episode and added, "A people that has suffered so much at the hand of persecutors in the course of a long and unhappy exile . . . is acting cruelly towards another people, who are in no way to blame for the troubles of the Jews."

It may well be that Weiss's host, his uncle Dorian, reinforced his nephew's negative feelings about Zionism. During the time that Weiss was in Jerusalem, the psychiatrist's career had run into obstacles, mainly because of his failed attempt to get Jerusalem's Jewish elites to swallow his psychoanalytical doctrines. Conservative circles attacked him openly, asking, "How is it that the honorable psychiatrist exposes doctors, nurses, and teachers to this experimental therapeutic system, the benefits of which have not been proved?" Some described the methods he had brought from Europe as dangerous. In at least one case, in April 1923, a series of lectures that he gave to doctors and teachers on the interpretation of dreams and the nature of the subconscious was stopped in the middle because he aroused so much controversy. In 1924, the board of the hospital that he was running, Ezrat Nashim, terminated his contract, and he was forced to emigrate to New York.[14] Two family members heard from their parents that the blunt attacks that Dorian's nephew and guest had made against Zionism in the German press hindered Dorian from gaining support in Jerusalem.

On one of Weiss's visits to Cairo, he met Jacob de Hahn, a man of similarly unusual opinions.[15] De Hahn was a talented poet, an author, a polemicist, and the son of an assimilated Dutch Jewish family who had found religion and become ultra-Orthodox. In his youth, de Hahn had been a socialist and a Zionist, and later his religious faith took him to the Mizrahi movement.[16] This moderate religious Zionist movement was founded in 1902 and aimed at keeping religious values in the society and the state and providing for the needs of the modern Orthodox public.

In 1922, Jacob de Hahn arrived in Jerusalem as the correspondent for two Dutch newspapers. Before long, his viewpoints had become radicalized, and he found himself deeply mired in political intrigue. He joined an ultra-Orthodox circle, published articles condemning Zionism, and became a spokesman for the Agudath Israel movement ("Israel's fraternity," in Hebrew)—the most significant theologically conservative movement in Judaism. It represented the majority of Haredi (ultra-Orthodox) Jews and formally rejected secular Zionism. At that time, Zionism was predominantly an antireligious movement, expressing socialist and Jewish-nationalist views.

Both journalists shared opinions and interests. On one hand, de Hahn's extreme anti-Zionism attracted the young journalist Weiss. On the other hand, de Hahn admired Weiss's witty writings. "How do you manage to convey in a half-sentence an almost mystical significance to things that are apparently so commonplace?" de Hahn asked. Both agreed that Zionism was an imperialistic, transient movement, doomed to lose its battle with the Arabs. This, incidentally, was not the only prophecy made by the two that never came true. Most of their forecasts about Zionism and the Jewish people proved incorrect. But Leopold did make some accurate predictions. He foresaw that the British Empire would collapse and that Britain would lose all of its possessions in the Middle East.

De Hahn's anti-Zionism attracted the attention of Arab leaders throughout the Middle East, and he was able to forge strong ties with some of the most influential among them. When the rabbis of the Jewish community in Jerusalem sent a political delegation to Hussein bin Ali, the king of the Hejaz, de Hahn joined the party as its spokesman.[17] In the summer of 1923, de Hahn helped Weiss by securing him an interview with Hussein's son, the emir Abdallah.[18] The emir was the founder of the Kingdom of Transjordan (which was part of the British Mandate over Palestine and since 1949 has been called the Hashemite Kingdom of Jordan). The connection with de Hahn later helped Weiss to be received by the Saudi royal court and to realize his personal ambition of deepening his connections with Arab leaders.[19]

Early in 1926, Weiss returned to Berlin, triumphant. His articles had been popular, he planned to write a book, and his sweetheart Elsa Schiemann, a German painter whom he had met before going to Jerusalem, was ready to marry him. He described her as "probably the finest representative of the pure 'Nordic' type I have ever encountered." Her hair was fair and her eyes were blue. When they married, she was forty-five, a widow, and the mother of a small child. Weiss was twenty-seven.

In September 1926, an everyday trip on the Berlin tram led Leopold to reflect profoundly on the contrast between the spiritual depth he had found among the Muslims of the Middle East and the emptiness and the pointlessness that he saw in the faces of the Berliners traveling with him and his wife in the first-class section of the train. He observed the passenger sitting opposite him, a well-dressed man immersed in thought.

"When I looked at his face, I did not seem to be looking at a happy face. He appeared to be worried: and not merely worried but acutely unhappy, with eyes staring vacantly ahead and the corners of his mouth drawn in as if in pain, but not in bodily pain. Not wanting to be rude, I turned my eyes away and saw next to him a lady of some elegance. She also had a strangely unhappy expression on her face, as if contemplating or experiencing something that caused her pain. And then I began to look around at all the other faces in the compartment—faces belonging without exception to well-dressed, well-fed people: and in almost every one of them I could discern an expression of hidden suffering, so hidden that the owner of the face seemed to be quite unaware of it. . . . The impression was so strong that I mentioned it to Elsa; and she too began to look around with the careful eyes of a painter accustomed to studying human features. Then she turned to me, astonished, and said: 'You are right. They all look as though they were suffering torments of hell.' "

Pondering the reason for these people's suffering, Weiss concluded that it was because of the vacuous nature of their lives. They had no faith and no purpose, he mused, apart from the desire to improve their standard of living, to obtain more amenities, belongings, appliances, or perhaps more power. When he arrived home with Elsa, his eyes set upon the Koran lying on his desk. Later, he wrote,

"Mechanically, I picked the book up to put it away, but just as I was about to close it, my eyes fell on the open page before me, and I read:

> You are obsessed by greed for more and more
> Until you go down to your graves.
> Nay, but you will come to know!
> And once again: Nay, but you will come to know!
> Nay, if you but knew it with the knowledge of certainty,
> You would indeed see the hell you are in.
> In time, indeed, you shall see it with the eye of certainty:
> And on that Day you will be asked what you have done with the boon of life.

"For a moment I was speechless. I think that the book shook in my hands. Then I handed it to Elsa. 'Read this. Is it not an answer to what we saw in the train?' "

Weiss was convinced that he must become a Muslim, and his new wife decided that she, too, would convert. He assumed an Arabic name, Muhammad Asad—*asad* means "lion," as do Leopold and his Hebrew name, Aryeh—and he went to the mufti of Berlin to utter the oath: "There is no God but Allah, and Muhammad is the messenger of Allah." Years later, Weiss wrote, "I did not convert to Islam merely because I had lived for many years among Muslims. I came to Islam on the mission of the Prophet."

Throughout the rest of his life, he endeavored to explain that his joining Islam was not the result of a whim but sprang from a deep conviction that Islam was superior to the other religions. He was certain that Christians and Jews had the common purpose of besmirching Islam and belittling its achievements. From the start, Islam's status was inferior in the eyes of Westerners, the descendants of Greco-Roman culture. This prejudice had crystallized during the period of the Crusades after the first Christian millennium, when European civilization was taking shape. As Weiss had been so greatly influenced by Freud and his disciples, he used the tools of psychoanalysis to interpret social phenomena. Just as the Freudians saw the origins of patterns of a person's behavior in his or her infancy, Leopold sought the causes of the Europeans' collective behavior in the period when the tribes of the continent merged into a single political entity. "A nation is a collection of individuals," he asserted, and rewrote history to suit his arguments.

His reasoning went like this. The Crusades got under way during the infancy of the current Western civilization, at a time when its values were taking shape. The First Crusade set out in 1096. In Clermont, France, Pope Urban II delivered his historic address calling on the faithful to take up arms and do battle with the "infamous race" that had conquered the Holy Land. Here, in the wars of the crusaders against the Muslims, lay the key to understanding the West's contemptuous view of Islam. These campaigns were the first collective experience that a unified Europe ever underwent. For the first time in their history, the tribes of Europe surmounted their cultural and political barriers and undertook a common mission, and after they carried it out, Western civilization was born. This was the origin of Christian unity in Europe, and since then, it had maintained its primacy in the world.

The clearest expression of unified European identity, in Weiss's opinion, was the hatred for Islam, Christianity's absolute antithesis. He blamed the crusaders for "poisoning the soul of Europeans against Islam" because, on their return from the wars, the crusaders presented Europe with a false interpretation of Islam's ideas and principles. This is why Westerners consider the prophecy of Islam to be anti-Christian and the precepts of the Islamic religion to be immoral and pathological. The crusaders were therefore responsible for the West's erroneous view of Islam, which was created at the beginning of the first millennium and has been unchanged since then. This image of fanaticism and brutality, instead of purity of heart and innocence, made the prophet Muhammad into a barbaric leader in Christian eyes, although he had commanded his followers to respect other faiths. Weiss found evidence of how the Crusades sowed the seeds of hatred for Islam in the Christians' mythical hymn of victory over the Muslims, which was composed in France after the Crusades. It became an unofficial European anthem, the epic poem *The Song of Roland*.[20]

"It is not surprising," Weiss wrote, "that this anti-Muslim anthem was considered the first work of united European literature." Before *The Song of Roland*, literary expression was confined to tribe and place, but since the Crusades, the conflict with Islam had superseded intra-European rivalries. The shadow of the wars of the Crusades had prevailed in the West until that very day, Weiss concluded in his analysis, long after the religious concepts that they were based on had vanished from the world.

How had Weiss used this historical analysis of the Crusades to arrive at his fateful decision to become a Muslim? He assumed the role of a religious reformer who had given up Judaism and Christianity (although the conception of God in the latter religion was in his opinion superior to that of Judaism) and finally discovered truth and justice in Islam, which was perfection in his eyes. For one thing, it provided solutions to problems in every aspect of life: physical, mental, spiritual, and sexual. Second, like Lao Tzu, the Chinese philosopher whom Weiss admired, Islam also positions human society under divine consciousness. Islam, in Weiss's view, overrode nationality, selfish interests, class, sectors, and factions and established a theocracy of godliness, whose basis was in democratic relations between human beings. The Christians failed because they were incapable of subjecting society to their credo's primary moral virtues. Islam triumphed over Christianity, while Judaism remained far behind and was inferior, in Weiss's eyes.

Weiss informed his father that he had converted, but the letter he sent to Vienna was never acknowledged. His sister wrote to him that his father had erased Weiss from his consciousness and related to his son as if he were dead. "I sent him another letter," Weiss said, "assuring him that my acceptance of Islam did not change anything in my attitude toward him or my love for him; that, on the contrary, Islam enjoined upon me to love and honor my parents above all other people." His father never replied to the second letter, either.

In January 1926, Muhammad Asad took his wife and her son and traveled with them to Mecca, in order to be purified, to circumambulate the Kaaba, and to earn the title *haj*, as is recommended in Islam. The journey, which he portrayed as the most important one in his life, was marred by a tragedy. Nine days after they arrived in Mecca, Elsa died after contracting a mysterious disease (apparently, food poisoning) and was buried in a pilgrims' cemetery. Asad sank into a depression. Friends from the Saudi royal family offered him a twelve-year-old Bedouin girl for a wife, but his European sensibilities prevented him from accepting. He preferred instead to marry Munira, the adult daughter of Husayn al-Shammari, the Shammar tribe's chieftain from the Najd region.[21] The marriage ceremony was held in Medina in the year 1930, and less than a year later his only son, Talal, was born. On a visit to Amman, Asad had seen the son of Emir Abdallah, Talal, riding a wild horse, and Asad was so impressed that he named his son after him.

In Medina, Asad spent most of his time studying Islam. During a visit to the library of the largest mosque in the country, he accidentally encountered Prince Faisal, who invited Asad to the palace to have coffee with his father, Ibn Saud.[22] On one of his visits to the palace, an extraordinary event took place. The king and his entourage and guests were sitting in the reception room and conversing when the crown prince turned to Asad and said to him, "Somebody expressed doubts today about you, Muhammad. He claimed that he is not sure that you are not an English spy, disguised as a Muslim. But do not worry. I told him that you are a faithful Muslim."

Asad bowed to the prince and thanked him. The prince then said that he had dreamed of seeing Asad standing in the gallery of a mosque and reading aloud the oath from the Koran, "Allah is great and there is no other but Allah." The king now intervened in the conversation and explained that such things do actually happen sometimes, when God appears in a dream and announces what will happen and interprets for the dreamer things that have happened. "Has nothing like this ever happened to you, Muhammad?" he asked Asad, who replied without hesitating, "Of course, undoubtedly, your majesty, something like that happened many years ago before I decided to become a Muslim, even before I had set foot on the soil of a Muslim country. It happened when I was nineteen, in my father's house in Vienna. I had a dream."

On that night in Vienna, Leopold had had a long dream, replete with Freudian symbols, prophecies, and revelations, and at its end "a dazzling white light, not like the rising sun, but rather a cold ray of light, which kept growing." He described this dream in detail, and King Saud was amazed. He cried out excitedly, "Blessed be the name of Allah. You know, Muhammad, that dream was a sign. Allah has destined you for Islam!" King Saud immediately invited Asad into his circle of advisers and sent him on missions to neighboring countries.[23] Thus, the Austrian Jewish convert rode on camels across the length and breadth of the Middle East, from Yemen to Turkey.

Asad lived in Saudi Arabia for six years, learned perfect Arabic, and deepened his roots in Islam. He wore a *keffiyeh* on his head and grew a goatee, as was the local custom. While this was happening, his relatives in Galicia anxiously witnessed Poland's enslavement to a chauvinistic and anti-Semitic world outlook. The Paris Agreement, which had redrawn the map of Europe, had borne a poisonous fruit. Muhammad-Leopold, who had predicted what was happening in Europe, had managed to get away from the Judeo-Christian civilization that he so despised. It is true that in the early 1930s, the eye of the storm that would soon cruelly menace his relatives was distant from his body and his soul, but he, too, would have to surmount a formidable obstacle in the near future, although of an entirely different nature.

13
A Love Story

To HIS RELATIVES IN GALICIA, Weiss-Asad's Middle East experiences seemed remote and eccentric. During family gatherings, secular relatives considered his conversion to Islam an amusing incident, even comical, and not in any way an act of betrayal, while religious relatives felt exactly the opposite. When Leopold's name was mentioned, they spat to the side to express their disgust for their cousin, whom they viewed as the worst among those who desecrate God's name.[1] Nevertheless, even the relatives who were observant Jews didn't put Leopold's fate high on their daily agendas, for they were obliged to focus on their own businesses.

As the civil wars waned in the early 1920s, the future of Galicia's Jewish community seemed relatively promising. The Bolsheviks retreated northeastward toward Kiev, and the Ukrainians pulled back to the Dnieper in the southeast. Western Galicia became part of Poland, and its Jews looked to the capital city, Warsaw, with some trepidation but also with hope. At the Paris Peace Conference, the Polish government had undertaken to protect the rights of minorities, and the 1921 constitution guaranteed equality for all. The Jews of Galicia hoped that a commonality of interests would grow between themselves and the Poles. The Poles had no alternative, the Jewish leaders believed: if they wanted to attain economic prosperity, if they hoped that Poland would develop and emulate Germany and France, they would have to let the Jews share in the government and the economy. And indeed, in the early 1920s, Bolechow's leather industry was growing. Old factories—those of the Landes brothers and Frisch and Kahane—had expanded, and new workshops were opened, among them those belonging to Roth, Gottesman, Adler, Rothfeld, and Feder.

The physician Yaakov Blumenthal, who was known as a Polophile, walked around Bolechow full of self-importance, as if he had single-handedly won the Polish war of independence. At his Sabbath morning meetings with Yerahmiel Kahane in the large garden of the Friedman family home, they sprawled on sofas and cushions under the fruit trees enjoying the finest foods and beverages. The doctor painted the future in rosy shades: "Poland will be democratic, like England and Czechoslovakia, and all of its patriotic citizens will be equal before the law."

Yerahmiel sniggered. Only a few of Galicia's Jews felt a connection with the Poles' romantic nationalism. When Poland had lost its independence, they felt no deep pain, and when it regained its independence, they felt no joy. "I have no sense of patriotism," Yerahmiel said. "I do not celebrate the memorial day of the battle of Grunwald, when the Teutons were beaten back five hundred years ago, and I have no Polish heroes from the civil war, and you, Dr. Blumenthal, don't forget that they killed dozens of Jews in the Lvov pogrom."[2]

Rachel Kahane chimed in, "I have no great love for Chopin, but I play Brahms's waltzes with great pleasure."[3]

"Of course," Blumenthal replied, "your heroes are Theodor Herzl, and Hazanovitz, and that strange Russian Trumpeldor, who was killed in the Galilee.[4] But we are here, Yerahmiel Kahane! Here we live and here we'll die, and the same goes for our children after us, and if we don't learn to be Poles, we won't live at all."

The doctor wondered why Yerahmiel had agreed to be the head of the committee of the Zionists' Jewish National Fund. "There's no need at all to collect money for the *halutzim*, the pioneers, in Palestine," Blumenthal said. "It's better for us to raise funds for our own community."

Rachel objected, "You, dear doctor, equate Poland with Czechoslovakia, and Pilsudski with Thomas Masaryk, but you are wrong.[5] The Czechs are like the Germans, members of a cultured and decent nation, and the Poles are like the Russians, anti-Semites and barbarians. Masaryk is a democrat, and Pilsudski, whom you admire so much, is a dictator. If Masaryk's democracy endures, the Jews will prosper, but if Pilsudski becomes president, we will suffer."

The argument grew sharp, as usual, and voices were raised. Rachel stood up and quoted from Masaryk's famous speech: "How can the suppressed nations deny the Jews that which they demand for themselves?"

Even the doctor applauded her and said, "Yerahmiel, you are hiding a skillful politician in your home." Rachel blushed.

During World War I, after the Kahane family had returned from Vienna, Rachel busied herself with domestic matters. She rebuilt the family nest in Bolechow, leaving the day-to-day care of the children to her mother, Reisel. That was the custom among many of Galicia's Jews—three generations or sometimes four lived together, with the children being looked after by their experienced grandmothers.

In the morning, Grandma Reisel rose early, lit the fire in the cooking stove, and then awakened the children. All three slept in one large, chilly room. Reisel tiptoed from one bed to another, bent over each little face, and whispered the prayer, "I gratefully thank Thee . . . , I gratefully thank Thee . . ."[6]

The children woke up smiling. With their eyes still half closed, they sat up in bed, shivering with cold, and recited, "I gratefully thank Thee, O living and eternal King, for You have returned my soul within me with compassion. Abundant is Your faithfulness!" Then Reisel helped them to get dressed.

During the years that Ullo studied in preschool, the *heder*, he wore a skullcap on his head, and the *tzitzit*, or four-fringed garment, under his shirt, in the ultra-Orthodox way. But from the day that he began first grade, instead of the *tzitzit* he found a sailor suit and a scarf next to his bed when he woke up. The change that he underwent on that day was both external and internal. All at once, he stopped donning his religious garb, the yarmulke and the fringes, and after that he saw himself as secular. Grandma Reisel objected strenuously, but Rachel was adamant. "In the Graubart home, heads are covered," said the mother in Yiddish, and her daughter replied in Polish, "And at the Kahanes, the world is changing."

Reisel came to terms with this. Generations come and go, and the world does not stand still.

Reisel always laid out a magnificent breakfast: scrambled eggs, several cheeses, sour cream, fruit and vegetables, *pierogi*—dumplings filled with cheese that she prepared herself—and, of course, fresh black farm bread.[7] The children were happy. Their grandmother saw that they had enough to eat, wrapped their lunch sandwiches in greased paper, and sent them off to school. Before they left, she buttoned their overcoats and gave them lots of advice. Take care, she told them. Be careful all the time. Walk slowly in the snow. Don't make any sudden movements. Keep away from the Ukrainian hooligans who look for

Jews to beat up, and come home directly after school. She repeated this speech every morning, a cluster of commandments, "do this" and "don't do that," to see them through the entire day.

Sonia, the oldest, knew it all by heart. She imitated her grandma's way of speaking and added all kinds of orders of her own: "And don't run and don't shout and don't be cheeky." Everyone always laughed.

Then Reisel would draw herself up to her full height and in a stentorian voice remind the *belfer*, the helper of the *melamed*, the teacher, that it was his duty to carry Ullo, "my only grandson," on his back, "right into the classroom to his place next to the fireplace, so that he won't have to walk in the snow, and his feet won't get cold, perish the thought."

The *belfer* was short and thin, a bag of bones. He begged to be let off. Ullo's father is a tanner, he whined, and the boy's boots are of the finest thick leather, fur lined, and there was no chance that even a drop of dampness could seep in. "Really," he whined, "there is no danger to the boy's health."

But Reisel was adamant. She pulled Ullo's hat down over his ears and scolded the *belfer*: "You get good money, and this is a very special child. He must be cared for."

Rachel could only sigh. Either way, the child was growing up. When Ullo was an infant, Dr. Blumenthal had told the family that Ullo had weak lungs and recommended that they take him to the nearby resort town of Morschin to get fresh air, as if the air in Bolechow was polluted. But his lungs became stronger, and soon his face was covered with the wisps of a beard. He grew taller and the lines of his face took shape: fine, delicate features, long, narrow, and smooth; brown eyes; and a high forehead. He was careful about his appearance. Each morning he spent many minutes meticulously combing his hair and polishing his shoes.

Rachel used to say that Ullo was a wonderful child because he had no "bees in his bonnet" and he was pleasant and good-natured, without a drop of malice or spite. He inherited his looks from his father, his nature from her. Like her, he knew how to observe the world patiently, to pick up whatever was necessary or useful and discard what was worthless. He did everything in proportion, never excessively, and most important, he was content with his lot. Both of my daughters, Rachel mused, have complex characters, but Ullo is simple and straightforward.

Leah, who was a little older than Ullo and was nicknamed Lidka, had taken a particularly difficult path in life. She always struggled over her place and status in the world. She was achievement-oriented, determined to stand out and to go far. The older sister, Sarah, whom everyone called Sonia, was anxious to start her own family, and she got involved with a medical student, which caused her parents many a sleepless night. Was she genuinely engaged to be married to him, or was his pledge to come back to Bolechow and become her husband merely the whim of a callow youth who had fallen in love for the first time in his life and, when he had to leave the town, made a promise simply because he did not want to hurt the girl?

The tale of Sonia's love for the student Nunio Krauthammer is reminiscent of a cheap novel, the kind that is usually read only by housemaids and shop girls. Both Sonia and Nunio grew up in Bolechow. She was a pretty, plump girl, and he promised to marry her, but then he left, traveling to Strasbourg to study medicine. After that, they wrote to each other. Every weekend, they sat down, put pen to paper, and summed up in a few pages what they had done and had thought about during the previous week, then mailed the letters to each other. For six years, Sonia waited at home for Nunio to finish his studies, to come back to Bolechow and make her his wife.

Town gossips said that Dr. Raifaizen, the lawyer, was in love with Sonia. This confirmed socialist was planning to get an Argentinean visa and take Sonia Kahane with him to South America, people whispered behind her back. Although he was at least ten years older than she was, his appearance was captivating: tall and lean, with a well-trimmed beard. In the winter he donned his ski outfit and took to the Carpathian slopes. Once he broke his leg, and Sonia cooked him soup. But the knowledgeable lawyer, who didn't call her Sonia but always Miss Sarah, never proposed to her, and if he had, it is unlikely that she would have accepted. She remained faithful to Nunio Krauthammer and gave her family much grief.

Foremost among those who opposed the match with Nunio was Grandma Reisel, who had inherited from her parents both pedigree and wealth. In the sixteenth century, Nikolai Gidzinski, the Polish nobleman who founded Bolechow, had granted farmland to her family so that they would settle on his land. As soon as Grandma Reisel found out that her granddaughter was attracted to Krauthammer, Reisel declared war on the man. At first she tried persuasion, sending her husband to talk to their daughter in order to get her to nip the romance in the bud. But David Graubart's conversation with Rachel produced nothing. Then Reisel herself went to try to convince her son-in-law of Nunio's unsuitability.

"The Krauthammers are small-time wagon owners," she said to Yerahmiel. "Compared to them, we are aristocrats. And there are unpleasant stories going around town as to their honesty." Yerahmiel understood her anguish, but he hesitated to throw his weight behind her campaign, while Rachel was wary of tightening the rope around her daughter, lest she lose her completely.

When Reisel's efforts at persuasion failed, she tried a new ploy: temptation. She invited Sonia to her room and showed her a present she had been given as part of her dowry, a precious gem-studded head scarf, known in Yiddish as a *schtechel-tichel.* Made of damask silk, this rare object was adorned with diamonds, emeralds, rubies, and pearls. Jews had always preferred keeping their wealth in the form of precious stones because in times of danger and flight, they could be stashed in small bundles, hidden on the body, and smuggled across borders. If a pogrom broke out, they could snatch up the *schtechel-tichel* and escape. If their assailants put a knife to their throats, they could buy their lives with the scarf, and if they made good their escape, with God's help, they could hide it again until the next pogrom. Rachel's *schtechel-tichel* was hundreds of years old, and although its exact worth had never been determined, the Jews of Bolechow knew that the Graubarts gave their daughters valuable dowries.

When Sonia saw the scarf in Reisel's room, she was amazed. Her grandmother didn't normally show off her wealth to the children. Reisel was sure that Sonia would not be able to resist the temptation. "If you give up Krauthammer, I'll give you the scarf as a present," she said. "It will be all yours. I will not divide it up among my grandchildren, as I had intended to do."

Sonia thought for a moment, and then said, "There's no need, Grandma. I will take Nunio as my husband, and even so the scarf will be mine. After all, you can't take it with you to your grave."

While Nunio was away studying in Strasbourg, Reisel passed away, and a few months later so did her husband, David. Sonia took over her grandmother's tasks in running the household, and she served the family wholeheartedly. She especially pampered little Ullo, immediately fulfilling his every wish and satisfying any whim that occurred to him. He liked his milk lukewarm, without a layer of skin on it; he liked his eggs medium, not too soft and not too hard; and he liked his black peasant bread sliced very thin and spread with a fine layer of fat. When he didn't want to eat, Sonia gave him a zloty for every bread roll that he consumed. Throughout her life, she looked into his eyes with concern and submission. She faithfully took care of him and was always there to serve him. (And when he was able, he reciprocated generously, looking after her affairs and even traveling to Paris to bring her stray beloved Nunio back to her. After Ullo grew up, Sonia still fussed over him to the extent that some of their friends whispered to him that she was overdoing it, but he never voiced any complaints out loud against her. At most, he might make a joke that had a hint of criticism, which was understood only by those in the know. Total loyalty prevailed between the three siblings, and if any of them had a complaint about the others, it was dealt with in privacy.)

Ullo went to Bolechow's Jewish elementary school, which was run by the community. It served as a cultural center and had a large library that was open to all the residents of the town. The Jewish school was a modern institution, with classes based on the official Polish curriculum and additional lessons in Judaism. Three languages were taught: Polish, German, and Ukrainian. Students said their prayers with covered heads. In the afternoons and the evenings at the school, scores of young and old people took courses in Jewish history, Scripture, Hebrew, and theater.

The main building was surrounded by a large courtyard, about three-quarters of an acre in size. In it were beds of flowers and vegetables that the students took care of. The children stood up when the teachers entered the classrooms and called them "sir" or "madam," but during recess, the staff and the students chatted informally. Many teachers were role models for their pupils and were very involved in the Jewish community. Two Zionist educators, Dogilewsky and Hendel, ran the school and also served as officials in the community. No one knew Principal Dogilewsky's first name. He had become a Zionist after World War I, and people forgave him for the years when he had been a "Polophile." In Bolechow, the Jews did not like the Poles and even less the "Mosheks," as they called the Jews who assimilated into Polish culture and abandoned their Jewish heritage. Hendel was the secretary of the community and taught Hebrew in first grade. He made his living from a shoe store that he owned.

People remember three things about the Jewish school in Bolechow: Dogilewsky, the principal, whom everyone admired; the fact that teachers and children alike spoke Hebrew; and the long, supple cane that was used to punish misbehaving students.

Worse than the actual pain was the humiliation of being punished. The student was stretched over the seat of a little chair, buttocks in the air, like a lamb about to be slaughtered. He or she had to listen to the teacher's scolding between the strokes and, worst of all, the other students' laughter. The children's soft rumps could take the lashes without their feeling too much pain because the teachers tried not to hit them very hard, but nevertheless their hearts beat wildly in terror. From the victims' point of view, the posture was terrifying: they faced downward with only the concrete floor visible to their tearful eyes, their posteriors were raised, and the other children happily counted the strokes aloud: "One, two, three, four . . ."

The cane made life easier for the teachers, and although (or perhaps because) corporal punishment had been used since ancient times, educators and parents never tried to abolish it. They quoted this biblical verse to critics: "He who spares the rod spoils the child" (Proverbs 13:24). Every now and then, the practice was denounced within the community, but Dogilewsky insisted on using corporal punishment. Then came Ullo's good friend Munia Mehring, however, who rebelled in the fourth grade.

It began as a routine matter but developed into a near revolution. Dogilewsky had told his students to learn a poem in Polish by heart. Mehring preferred to play with his friends and came to class unprepared. Dogilewsky asked him to stand up and recite the poem. Mehring confessed that he had not learned it. Dogilewsky told him to bend over the caning chair, but Mehring refused. "You won't humiliate me," he said to the teacher and sat down.

There was silence in the classroom. Once more Principal Dogilewsky called Mehring to come up and take his punishment, but again Mehring refused. The principal went red in the face and ordered, "Go home immediately and come with your father tomorrow."

Mehring went home, and the next day he came to school with his older brother, a university student. The brother and Dogilewsky went into the principal's office and closed the door. Dogilewsky insisted that the child be punished. The brother spoke about the canings and human dignity. Dogilewsky said that children were not entitled to the same dignity as adults, and Munia Mehring's brother replied, "God created both of them in His image." Dogilewsky made a speech about the importance of discipline in education, and the big brother countered that discipline should be taught by example, to which the principal could only agree. The conversation went on and on, and the children sat and waited in suspense until Mehring's brother came out. They all began to cheer because Dogilewsky had given in.

The punishment was canceled, and Mehring was allowed to return to class, on the condition that he learn the poem by heart.

"Did you see how I guarded my dignity?" Munia boasted, and Ullo admired his courage.

In the school's graduation photograph, Ullo stood upright in the top row of students, visibly excited and smiling at the camera. He wore a blue sailor suit, with a red scarf around his neck and hanging down on his chest. Of everyone in the class, only Mehring was taller than he was. Their friend Isser Hausman, the brother of Hanina, the teacher, was short and stood between them, with his head reaching to their shoulders. The music teacher, visualizing notes, remarked out loud, "Look, two crotchets and a quaver standing on the stage."

After the photograph was taken, Dogilewsky told Rachel and Yerahmiel Kahane that Ullo was a talented boy, "a realist, with an orderly and precise mind." After the principal's praise, the teacher Hendel chimed in, "He writes beautifully in Polish. He's a born humanist."

Everyone smiled in embarrassment. Hendel was not entirely at home with the ins and outs of Polish grammar and was therefore not allowed to teach in the higher grades. Rachel said that if the boy was so clever, he should continue his studies at a private high school in the city, and Yerahmiel agreed at once. The local high school across the river in Bolechow was considered inferior, and the children of the poor went there. Smart children from well-off families had to compete for places at private schools in the large cities of Stryj and Lvov. Most of these children were Jews or Poles. Few Ukrainians went to schools for the elite. Although Munia Mehring was at least as talented as Ullo was, he remained in Bolechow. His father was a watchmaker and could not afford to send his son to school in Stryj.

Mehring was an outstanding teenager, and Ullo's sister Lidka was attracted to him. She admired his self-confidence and his determination, but Mehring was interested in the Christian girls. He suggested to Lidka that they be friends and was impressed by her desire for knowledge. She was a serious girl, with a sharp tongue.

"I'll be a pianist or a doctor," she predicted.

"You'd better become a pianist," her mother advised her. "The life of a Polish doctor is like slavery."

Her parents never doubted that Lidka and Ullo were meant to study. To help the children pass the entrance exams to good schools, they hired two teachers, Dogilewsky himself and Moshe Hanina Hausman, the educated brother of their friend Isser, to tutor them privately in Latin, mathematics, physics, and chemistry. Lidka was diligent and thorough, and she had to spend time digesting and assimilating the material, while Ullo was like a butterfly, hovering for a second over a blossom, sipping its nectar, and flitting away.

Ullo was preoccupied with the affairs of the local branch of the Zionist-Marxist youth movement Hashomer Hatzair and did not always do his homework. Lidka never skipped a single line, though. Once, out of jealousy, she even stirred up a hornet's nest because her brother spent so much time with his friends. On that occasion she went to Dogilewsky's house and told him that Ullo had not done his homework. The teacher was angry and the next day demanded an explanation from Ullo. The boy shamefully mumbled a weak excuse, and later at home he repeatedly struck his sister until she fell to the ground. How could she dare to breach the code of loyalty and inform on him? Full of indignation, Lidka told Dogilewsky that Ullo had beaten her up. The teacher in turn lost his temper and gave Ullo a resounding slap in the face. For her entire life Lidka remembered how Ullo had beaten her, and he remembered the slap from the teacher.

At the end of the year, both of the Kahane children passed their exams. Ullo enrolled at the private high school in Stryj, half an hour's train ride away. Yerahmiel planned for Lidka to stay home until she got married, but the girl had other ideas.

"I'm going to school in Lvov," she announced to her parents.

Yerahmiel was on the verge of squelching the notion, but Rachel quickly nodded in agreement, and Yerahmiel remained silent.

Rachel knew full well that Lidka would have gotten her way, and she enrolled her daughter at a Polish high school for girls in Lvov. Lidka was fifteen. She stayed in the home of the sister of a well-known educator, Professor Moshe Shor, the founder of the first Jewish teachers' seminary. Yerahmiel paid a lot of money for her education—40 zloty a month for tuition (equal to a purchasing power of approximately $190 in the beginning of 2008) and another 40 zlotys a month for room and board—but Lidka's achievements justified every cent.[8] The Jewish principal, Mrs. Karp, never stopped praising the short, independent-minded girl from Bolechow, who was always the first to raise her hand in class.

Lidka's older sister, Sonia, was never interested in acquiring an education. At age ten, after four years of elementary school, she declared, "I can't concentrate, I want to get married and leave this place."

She wasn't among the worst students in her class, but nevertheless, after the graduation ceremony, Dogilewsky told Yerahmiel, "You don't need to be brainy to get rich."

This angered Yerahmiel, and he told Rachel, "Prophecy has been given to fools." Dogilewsky was right, though. Bolechow was too small for Sonia, who said, "I want to live in a big city." She missed the years her family had spent in Vienna during the war. But instead of going there, she remained a prisoner in her parents' home, waiting for her beloved Nunio Krauthammer, who dallied for years over his studies in Strasbourg and then in Geneva. Sonia pampered Ullo and took care of the household, supervising the two maids and the cow, the chickens, and the geese in the yard. She displayed great talent in the kitchen and cooked delicious dishes.

Now a high school student, Ullo was happy to exchange the rural quiet of Bolechow for the bustle and noise of the big city. There, cars were already on the roads, even one red Packard, model 1912, that belonged to a Jewish millionaire. In Bolechow, a steamroller would smooth out a stretch of dirt, and that was considered a road. There were no sidewalks. In the winter, people wore crude rubber boots. Stryj, in contrast, was an important road-and-railway junction. Hundreds of people bustled around on its paved streets and sidewalks: businessmen, clerks, officers, soldiers, messenger boys, nurses in uniform, street sweepers, and policemen. About half of the population was Jewish. There were sixteen lawyers, fifteen of whom were Jews. In the 1920s, during the days of prosperity, wealthy Jews made money from manufacturing and commerce. Some of them supplied equipment and food to the army; others were factory owners or contractors.[9] They were known in Galicia by the Yiddish words *kugel fressers*, "greedy people."[10]

Due to its proximity to the town of Zidichov, home of the Hasidic court of the Eichenstein dynasty, Stryj had many Hasidim in residence. On weekdays, they wore modern European clothing: tailored suits, with silken waistcoats known as *kamizelkas* under the jackets, and special fob pockets for their round golden watches. On the Sabbath, they donned the garb of the Orthodox Hasid, the *razhivalka*, or black robe of precious satin, and the *shtreimel*, the fur hat made of mink or fox tails. The simple folk of Stryj were small shopkeepers, publicans, peddlers, waggoners, or salary-earning clerks. But they, too, were well dressed, and although Stryj was only twenty miles from Bolechow, the city was like Paris in Ullo's eyes.

Ullo's classmates were the offspring of merchants, landlords, lawyers, doctors, and contractors. Most of them were Orthodox and observed the *mitzvoth*, or precepts of the Torah, but they nevertheless wanted to find a compromise between religion and modern life and thus sent their sons to the high school. On the Sabbath, both parents walked to the synagogue, the father wearing a *shtreimel* and the mother a wig on her shaven head.[11] At the same time, their sons were hard at work in their classrooms.

In the springtime, after school and before they got on the train to Bolechow, Ullo and his friend Gustav Reisman often sat on a park bench and listened to the music of a brass band. There was a grove of trees in the middle of Stryj, with a carefully kept garden. A stream ran through the park, a small tributary of the mighty Dnieper, and formed a pond in its center that was inhabited by two white swans. A wooden bandstand stood nearby, and in the springtime, a band played folk songs, marches, and light classical works. The citizenry strolled along the main avenue, lined with low-rise buildings whose facades formed a magnificent long backdrop. Some were built in the old rural style, red and gray oblongs, with molded cornices over the windows. Next to them were buildings in the ancient Greek style, with marble pillars, and others had classical German architecture, all straight lines. To seventeen-year-old Ullo, the striking row of facades on Stryj's main street symbolized wealth and stability. He already knew that he wanted to attend university, and he fluctuated between economics and law as his choice. His parents encouraged him. Yerahmiel said that if the economic boom of the 1920s lasted into the next decade, he would have no problem sending his son to the university in Lvov. But the worldwide economic downturn would soon dash his hopes, although Yerahmiel still managed to put Ullo and Lidka through college.

The first signs of the Great Depression were noticeable in Bolechow's business sector in the early winter of 1929. Trade declined sharply, as did prices and profits. In the collective memory of the town's inhabitants, the dramatic change in the economy was linked to the death of Dovidl *der meshuggeneh*, Bolechow's village idiot. The two events happened at the same time. Dovidl had been sleeping on the stone steps in the synagogue, which were warmed by the embers of a fireplace situated underneath them.

One morning the *shamash* (beadle), shook Dovidl's legs and shouted into his ear, "Dovidl, wake up!" as he always did just before the Shaharit prayers. But Dovidl didn't move. The beadle yelled again, "Get up, you idiot, the worshippers will soon be here!"

Dovidl's body was warm because of the fireplace, but his legs were stiff. To be absolutely certain that he was dead, the beadle placed a feather next to his nostrils, but it didn't quiver. The beadle called in the undertakers. There wasn't enough money in the community chest to pay for a tombstone, so Dovidl's name was inscribed in black paint on a simple board. This was attached to an iron pole stuck into the pile of earth that was his grave. He had been the butt of much mockery—an old, diminutive, retarded, mumbling Jew. The tip of his tongue lolled between his lips. Every day, summer and winter, he roamed the streets, and the children chased him and threw stones at him. "Dovidl the *meshuggeneh*, go away," they yelled in chorus, and he skipped between the stones and ran to hide in the public bathhouse.

Once a week, on Mondays, when the Ukrainian peasants held a market in the Rynek, Dovidl was a guest in Rachel's kitchen. The Ukrainian servant seated him at the table and gave him a glass of milk and a slice of dry sponge cake, which was left over from the Sabbath. Every Monday afternoon, when Dovidl came in through the back door, the Kahane children would run out the front door and disappear.

After Dovidl died, some Hasidim who claimed familiarity with the doctrines of kabbalah found meaning in his death. They said that because he had died in the synagogue, the coming year would be a hard one for the Jews of Bolechow. The sharp-witted physician Dr. Blumenthal, who related to Orthodox Jews and especially to the kabbalists with open contempt, said that Dovidl's death proved one thing: that although he was crazy, he wasn't stupid. "He did himself a great favor by dying in the wintertime," said Blumenthal. "If he had waited for the summer, he would have died of hunger, not old age. This is the beginning of the end." That was the doctor's prognosis, and he did not know how right he was. The fool's death was the first sign of the end of the gay 1920s.

The optimistic spirit of the age was displaced by despair during Ullo's final years of school in Stryj. In December 1929, the New York Stock Exchange collapsed, and the world's economy snowballed downhill to a crisis (in some countries the economic downturn began as early as 1928).

Throughout Europe during the coming two-year period, banks would fail, factories would close down, and millions of workers would lose their jobs.

In Poland, the economic crisis aroused yet another wave of chauvinism. In Stryj, on Fridays, Poles from the government school came to pick fights with the Jewish high school students, and blows were frequently exchanged between Poles and Jews. Bands of Endeks, members of Roman Dmowski's National Party, marched through the streets in brown uniforms looking for Jews to beat up, as they shouted, "Zhid, Zhid, go to Palestine." Ullo and his schoolmates had to travel in groups, carrying wooden clubs for self-defense.

At the height of the tension, a Polish teacher asked a student named Taras to give an example of a natural disaster. Taras said, "The economic disaster is a natural disaster."

The students laughed, and the teacher scolded the Ukrainian boy: "Be aware, Mr. Taras, that natural disasters take place in nature. The economic crisis is man-made. Here is an example, Taras. When the Dnieper overflows its banks, that is a natural disaster."

The Ukrainian student pointed at the map and said loudly and in anger, "No, sir. We call this river the Dniepro."

The Polish teacher bristled and, raising his voice, declared, "In Poland, we say Dnieper."

"No," Taras said defiantly, "in Ukraine, we say Dniepro."

"Get out of the classroom," was the teacher's response—his solution to the dispute.

Ullo's friend Gustav Reisman passed him a note: "He's a proud Ukrainian, this Taras Small-head."

Ullo smiled. Taras was the only Ukrainian in the class. His surname was Holova, which means "head" in Ukrainian, and the Jewish boys called him Taras Small-head. Ullo liked Taras, who tried his best to get good grades "like the Jews," but Reisman had nothing but contempt for him, calling him "the grandson of Bogdan Khmelnytsky." Reisman was a member of the Betar movement, a youth organization that espoused Jewish nationalist ideology. He came from a poor family and was an excellent student. Reisman and Ullo were the only boys from Bolechow in the class.

Meanwhile, the economic crisis struck Bolechow with great force. Within a few months, many businessmen were on the verge of bankruptcy. The two hardest-hit industries were leather and lumber. Because the livelihood of most of the townspeople depended on these industries, poverty and hunger spread through the town. The leather trade suffered the most. In the families of unemployed Jews, three children would use the same pair of shoes, one after the other. Poles stopped buying shoes altogether, and the Ukrainians went barefoot. Smokers quit buying cigarettes and rolled their own instead. A packet of cigarette papers cost four grosz, a hundredth of a zloty, and some people asked the vendor to sell them a quarter of a packet. The vendor would take out precisely ten papers, counting them carefully as if he had gold in his hands, so that the buyer would get exactly his due, and then would collect one grosz.

Yerahmiel Kahane was close to despair. On Sundays, the trains were empty. Few buyers came to buy his goods. Those who did come bargained stubbornly, and often he had to sell sheets of leather at a loss. Yerahmiel tried to cut expenses and dismissed workers, then stopped buying rawhide. On the eve of Passover, he traveled to Lvov to sell gold coins.

The Kahane children never bothered to ask how their father made his money, how many workers he employed, and what the state of his business was. They never dreamed that he was using up his savings. In their eyes, the family's prosperity was a given. The parents never spoke about the impact of the crisis in the children's presence or hinted at the possibility of bankruptcy. Revealing their financial straits might jeopardize their efforts to find a suitable groom for Sonia, and the neighbors would have shaken their heads at the Kahanes in pity. But, of course, their friends and neighbors were aware of the situation and whispered behind Yerahmiel's back that he was suffering from depression. His lips were tightly pursed all the time, and he never smiled. He walked with a stoop, and his eyes were downcast in shame. Few guests came to the house. In the evenings he and Rachel shut themselves in their room and pored over their ledgers. While he was still a young man, Yerahmiel aged and his health gradually declined. Hunger was not the menace, but rather his fall from status in his own eyes. In the 1920s he had accumulated enough assets to support his family for many years, but he lost his joy in living. Even the fact that many others suffered in the same way was no consolation to him.

The great sawmills belonging to Kimmel and Grippel, which employed hundreds of Jewish clerks, economists, lumber experts, and two thousand laborers, most of them Ukrainians, were on the verge of collapse. In the winter, the Danzig port authorities returned shipments of processed wood, with the words "Danzig port warehouses are full" stamped on the bills of consignment. German industrial firms stopped buying timber. The market had simply died. The same went for the leather industry. Hides could not be sold, and production ceased. A score of small factories, including Yerahmiel Kahane's, faced closure, and there was no solution in sight.

Some of Yerahmiel's close friends joined together to help the victims of the crisis. The condition of the Ukrainian workers and the Jewish tradesmen was particularly difficult. Dr. Ben-Zion Schindler, the Jewish mayor, went to the homes of the wealthy citizens who had not been hit and collected contributions to assist the unemployed. At the beginning of the winter of 1931, Schindler set up a soup kitchen, handed out coal for heating, and provided each child with a glass of milk every day, all paid for out of the municipal treasury. Yerahmiel's friend the lawyer Dr. Raifaizen gave free advice to people who faced bankruptcy. Dr. Blumenthal, the physician, made a note of each infant who died, and the list grew long.

Lidka was a student. The Polish authorities refused to let Jews enroll in medical schools in Galicia, so she took the entrance examination for the German university in Prague and passed with flying colors. She rented a room in an apartment in the Old City of Prague not far from the Jewish cemetery. She told her friends that her father was a clerk. "Everyone around me was a communist, and I was ashamed of my father's occupation and of the bourgeois origins of my family," she recalled years later. "Grandfather was a landowner. He leased farmland to poor Ukrainian peasants. Father was a leather manufacturer, who employed wretched laborers. Among my communist friends in the medical faculty the words *bourgeois* and *factory owner* were dirty words, and to avoid unpleasantness, I told them my father was a clerk."

Despite the crisis, Yerahmiel continued to send his daughter a monthly allowance of 70 zlotys (equal to the buying power of approximately $385 in the beginning of 2008) to cover her tuition and living expenses, and she took advantage of the money, although she was embarrassed about its source. When her parents heard that she was associating with communists, they were shocked. Yerahmiel blamed Rachel and reminded her that when Lidka had graduated from high school in Lvov, he had doubted whether it was a good idea to send her to study in Prague. He would have preferred that she find a husband and start a family. At first, Rachel had urged Lidka to take advantage of her musical talents and become a pianist. "Medicine isn't a suitable occupation for a women," she advised her daughter, but in the end she gave in and persuaded Yerahmiel to agree, too. Twice a year, at festival times, Lidka came back to Bolechow from Prague, gave her father the money that she had not spent, and hurried off to see her sweetheart, Abraham Feder, the son of neighbors in Bolechow, who was studying economics in Lvov.

On the surface, the family went on with life as always. Leah attended the university in Prague and Ullo was at school in Stryj. Every morning, Yerahmiel walked to his silent factory and came home depressed at noon. Rachel took care of her husband, trying to encourage and console him but not succeeding. Sonia ran the household and looked after the livestock in the yard. Now, because of the crisis, all of the food that they produced was important—the fruit that grew on the trees in the yard, every duck, every fattened goose, and every egg helped them to overcome the shortages. Sonia turned twenty-five, and the wagging tongues of Bolechow gave her the title of "old maid." She was short and naturally plump, and because she was depressed she put on weight. She neglected her appearance to the extent that visitors sometimes mistook her for the Ukrainian servant. This woman lived in the cellar and received her wages in produce. The servant was grateful for this and was willing to do any type of work, but even so, her mistress was impatient and intolerant with her.

Sonia's mood was determined by the letters she received from Nunio. When he wrote of the wonders of Geneva and how happy he was there, she became sad. A week later, when he ended his letter with a declaration of love for her, she was as happy as could be. One moment she was laughing aloud, and the next minute tears poured down her cheeks. During the day, she disciplined herself by doing hard labor in the house and the yard. At night she read books and wrote letters to Nunio. Yerahmiel and Rachel observed her every day and sighed to themselves, wondering why she was so loyal to the simple fellow who had gone off to study medicine in Switzerland. When would this *dybbuk* that had possessed her leave? they asked each other.

Nunio was specializing at a hospital in Geneva, and in another few months he would have his professional diploma and be qualified to practice his profession. During the years at university, he had made a living out of buying gold coins, pearls, and jewelry from Polish immigrants and selling them to American tourists whom he met on the shores of the lake. Once or twice a month, he carried little cloth bags hidden on his body that contained the valuables he'd purchased from the Poles, who passed his address from one to another. His profits were modest, but so were his needs—rent and food, with a little left over to be saved. Some of the money that he saved he sent to his family in Bolechow. Once he put a fifty-franc note in a letter to Sonia, who was offended and sent it back to him in Switzerland.

As the end of Nunio's specialization period drew near, Sonia's anxiety increased. Her mental state could only have deepened her father's depression. Yerahmiel and Rachel had no idea what would happen at the end of the year, and even Sonia herself couldn't manage to extract from Nunio precisely what his intentions were. "I have options," he wrote. "It looks like I'll be working in Paris."

Sonia excitedly conjured up images of the broad boulevards of Paris but soon sobered up and became doubtful. Could she permit herself to dream of walking down a Parisian avenue, on the arm of Nunio the doctor, with the Eiffel Tower in the background? She had never visited France, but she tried to fill in the gap with her memories of Vienna during World War I. Since Nunio had completed his studies in Strasbourg three years earlier, he had not come back to Bolechow. All that she knew of his doings and feelings was what she could glean from his letters. In the last few months he had tried to persuade her to join him in Geneva, but she insisted on getting him back to Bolechow. "I do not want to leave home at this difficult time," she wrote. For his part, he showed an interest in the tiny details of her life. "You say that you have bathed in the river and have already been into the cold water several times. I am not happy to hear this. I don't think that your climate is more suitable for bathing than ours, and I have so far not dared to go into the waters of the Rhône and I haven't even bathed in the lake. 'You must wait, my flower, it is early yet, it is still dark as night, the cold still reigns.'"

To judge from his letters, Nunio remained faithful to Sonia, but their love, even if it was true love, appeared to be dying on the vine. "Everything that I have done, everything that I do, I do for you," he wrote but immediately smothered such outbursts of love with highly detailed accounts of his studies, his cramped daily routine, and many descriptions of scenery. "My apartment is a few steps away from the hospital, so that I will not have to run and lose time, and when I go out the fresh air is pleasant. Everyone knows that Switzerland is very pretty and that Geneva is a charming city, many believe that it is the most beautiful city in the world. Like a fortress, it is surrounded by high mountains, with eternal snows shining on them. The magnificent Mont Blanc towers high over the city, very close by, indeed, walking distance, and a cool wind blows from it, caresses my face, like an angel's hand. How can I describe beauty that cannot be described in words."

As the weeks and months went by, however, Sonia became tired of such descriptions and asked for a resolution, something definite. Nunio never satisfied her demand. Perhaps he did not precisely understand, or maybe he was evading the issue. "On the lake there are steamships and rowboats, and on the shore there are bands that play Wagner, Mozart and Beethoven, and over the lake there are gardens and roads, boulevards and villas, fountains and statues, whose beauty is beyond any human conception. The city is built in the finest taste; after all I have seen something of the world, and I must confess that this is a true Garden of Eden, a precious Garden of Eden, the most precious in the world. The Americans and the English come here, Turks and Negroes, with millions in foreign currency in their pockets. There are not many Poles here. At the university there are students from Congress Poland, Wolyn and Podolia, but none from Galicia. Only me! And what does that mean? Nothing? I dissect the cadavers at the mortuary, work until late at night and get up again early in the morning and miss you endlessly. I hug you and kiss your beloved lips."[12] But Sonia was not sure that these declarations of love were sincere.

In her distress, she discovered God. Since her girlhood, she had drifted away from religion, like all of her young friends, but during the last year she had returned to the faith, apparently under the influence of Nunio. His family was observant, and he donned phylacteries every morning in Strasbourg. In faith, Sonia found consolation for her sorrow. She prayed that Nunio would come back to Bolechow and make her his wife. Rachel observed her from the window and slowly shook her head. She regretted that her oldest daughter was wasting the best years of her life. The child is destroying herself, she thought. Why does she stick to him? Why him?

At last, close to noon, Sonia saw the mailman from a distance, beginning his Rynek round at the farthest corner of the square. Before he came much closer, she ran up to him and held out her hand. The mailman was not surprised. The package of letters in his hand had been sorted according to family names and arranged in the order of the houses on his route. The houses on the Rynek were not numbered. The name of the family was the address. Strangers had to ask, "Where is the Graubart house?" for example, and the locals would point in the direction and say, "Over there, the third house in the row, opposite the Magistrat."

The mailman's fingers flicked through the pile of letters in his satchel. He knew exactly what to look for. Among the gossips of Bolechow, the romance between Sonia Kahane and Nunio Krauthammer was no secret. Everyone knew that Nunio had made a promise but showed no signs of keeping it, and the evil tongues said that he had never intended to keep it. The neighbors pitied Kahane's daughter, who had been a lively girl and had become a bundle of nerves. "She's wasting her best years," they whispered. "Look at the happy girl who has turned into an embittered widow."

The mailman took out a brown envelope, bearing Swiss stamps. "My Sun," the letter began. Sonia read it avidly. She leaned against the fence in the corner of the yard, and Rachel, as usual, watched her from the window. "I received your lovely letter and it made me very happy." Sonia smiled. Her sweetheart's handwriting was very handsome. He wrote in small letters, tiny and regular. His lines were as straight as a ruler. But his language was evasive, noncommittal. Did intrigue hide behind those straight lines? Was this a cheater writing in such a neat script? Sonia was not sure. In recent weeks, Nunio had changed his tune. No, he would not be returning from Geneva to Bolechow. His plan was to go to work in Paris. He was evading her, and she was going out of her mind. In her last letter, she hinted that she doubted the sincerity of his intentions toward her, and here he was telling her that the letter had made him happy, the bastard. And yet, now he had changed course again: "You wrote things that upset me, and I have a lot of packing still to do, together with Schulem, my brother, and to take care of all kinds of matters, complications, to decide, to consult . . ."

"I'm getting in your way," Sonia said to herself. "I want to get married, and you get upset." Her eyes rapidly scanned the lines. "In brief, I want to report that last week I took out a new passport because the old one had expired and then I got a visa, and perhaps I'll leave for Paris. God willing [written in Hebrew initials] I'll leave this evening and travel through Basel."

"He's fooling with me," she muttered, "simply fooling." Her eyes grew moist. "He's drifting away, and in the end I'll be by myself."

"Please, my dearest, don't meddle in other people's affairs. So what if Boma's wife makes mistakes when she writes? And so what if Bronia reads other people's letters?[13] At least, don't tell me about it. It irritates me." He was still avoiding the issue and not committing himself, she thought. He was being evasive and twisting and turning and not replying to my questions. All this about Boma's wife and Bronia, what did it matter? But no, after all, he was coming to the point: "In your letter you write that between the lines you have understood. 'Now I understand everything about your studies.' That is exactly what you said. I don't understand you. What has happened? My imagination isn't all that fertile. First you say that I misled you, and then you say that you understand. No, I didn't mean to mislead you and I never did mislead you, but you never believed in me and if that's the way it is, take it the way that you want to."

Sonia was disappointed. Was Nunio really angry with her? And even so, he wasn't headed for Bolechow, and why didn't he say when he was coming and when we'll get married? But Nunio skipped over such issues. "Regards to Epstein and Heller, and thank them for their regards. Write more, and don't make me sad, I beg you, if you love me. Now I'll go back to my beloved cadavers. What's happening with your politics over there? Have the 'pulcha' been beating each other up? I hug you and kiss your beloved mouth, Yours, Nunio. P.S. I kiss the hands of your beloved parents and send warm regards to the beloved Ullo." (*Pulcha* was a derogatory nickname for the Poles that was used by Ukrainians and Jews.) Sonia folded the letter and wept quietly. Rachel watched from afar, with pain in her heart.

A short time later, in the summer of 1937, the Kahanes dispatched their son, Ullo, to Paris to clear up the Krauthammer business. The two young men met at the Gare du Nord railroad station. Ullo wasted no time and went straight on the attack. "You promised, and now you've got to keep your promise," he told Nunio. "If you don't marry Sonia, you'll never be able to come back to Bolechow."

Nunio had never intended to return to Bolechow, but nevertheless, standing face-to-face with Ullo, he surrendered. Two months later, Sonia traveled to Paris and was reunited with her beloved. The couple settled down in Lyon. Nunio gave up medicine. His French was fluent, and she could stammer a few words in a heavy Polish accent. Their neighbors knew that he was a qualified doctor, but no patients called on them. Ever since he had graduated in Geneva, he had preferred trading in precious metals to being a doctor. Sonia enjoyed the good life and encouraged him. For the rest of her days, she would be grateful to Ullo for saving her from abandonment and for making her husband, Nunio, keep his promise.

14

Deceptive Fate

The Jews of Poland watched the Nazi rise to power in Germany with curiosity and concern, but most of them found good reasons to assume that the persecution of the Jews was an internal German matter. Hitler's political credo contained two salient programs: the removal of the Jews and the conquest of *lebensraum*, "living space," for the Germans in the east.[1] The juxtaposition of these two goals should have made Polish Jews flee for their lives, but for the most part they assumed that Hitler's plans, as laid out in his book *Mein Kampf* and in his speeches, were mere fantasies. They never imagined that the German people would allow him to carry them out.

Apprehension increased in March 1938, when Hitler annexed Austria in the Anschluss, and then again in October of that year, when the Nazis seized the Sudetenland region of Czechoslovakia. Yet even then, the masses of Polish Jewry never translated their misgivings into action. Not even the Kristallnacht pogrom of November 9–10 led them to draw the obvious conclusion.[2] A handful of Jewish leaders and community activists warned that it would be advisable to seek refuge outside of Europe, but, by and large, these admonitions were met with indifference. The prevalent view among Poland's Jews was that Hitler wanted to expel the Jews from Germany. It was inconceivable that Germany would execute a plan to destroy all of Europe's Jews.

Poland's Jews grasped the gravity of the danger facing them only at the end of August 1939, when the foreign ministers of Nazi Germany and the Soviet Union, Joachim von Ribbentrop and Vyacheslav Molotov, signed a treaty in Moscow that bore their name: the Molotov-Ribbentrop Pact.[3]

This ten-year nonaggression treaty between the German Third Reich and the Soviet Union included a secret protocol stipulating that the two countries would share Poland. Only when the news about the German-Soviet alliance became known did Poland's Jews realize that Stalin had granted Hitler a free hand to carry out his aggressive plans. But although they now shook off their apathy and in some communities even panicked, the awakening came too late. The gates of the United States were closed. Emigrating from Europe to Palestine was still possible, but it took a long time to get an entry visa from the British Mandatory authorities. Flight eastward into the Soviet Union was also possible, but as long as Germany hadn't invaded Poland, most Jews feared that it would be a case of jumping out of the frying pan into the fire, from Nazi menace to Soviet oppression.

The Backenroths of Schodnica were no different from their fellow Jews, and they, too, became aware of the danger too late. The dilemma was stark because in their eyes the communist threat was no less than the Nazi threat. It was clear to everyone that if the Soviets annexed Galicia, they would nationalize private property and persecute the capitalists. The business elite was repelled by communism as strongly as the Orthodox leadership was. Rachel Kahane called the Russians "barbarians" and prayed that the Germans, whom she thought of as "civilized," would come. After some of the secret clauses of the Molotov-Ribbentrop Pact were made public, Yerahmiel Kahane asked his son, Ullo, "Why did they divide Poland up this way? Why not the opposite, the west to the Russians and the east to the Germans?"

Unlike during World War I, the Jews couldn't escape to Vienna because the Nazis were already there. But eighteen-year-old Stella Backenroth (later Wieseltier) was lucky, or so she thought early on.[4] Her father, Leib, who managed the family's oil business, decided to smuggle his family into Romania to join their relatives, the Panzer family, in Bucharest. The idea was to get as far southward as possible from Galicia, in the direction of Palestine. A friend of Leib's from Romania, a man called Roth, and his son were in Schodnica at the time and were ready to help. The plan was for everyone to travel together to the town of Zlaszicki, where the passport and visa office was located, and to apply for the necessary papers. But whether they got them or not, they would find a way to cross the border into Romania and there would board a ship bound for Palestine.

The German army invaded Poland on September 1, 1939, and in a blitzkrieg campaign conquered the western part of the country and laid siege to Warsaw. Under the terms of the Molotov-Ribbentrop Pact, the Soviets moved into eastern Poland on September 17 and occupied Galicia. The next day, the president of Poland and the army commander fled to Romania. The Jewish New Year, Rosh Hashanah, fell on September 14 and 15, between the two invasions. Some of the Backenroths severely underestimated the perilous situation, and out of religious considerations, they put off their departure from Poland until after the High Holy Days. In fact, none of the Backenroths who had planned to leave Poland, and would have been able to do so, escaped in time because their need to observe Rosh Hashanah and Yom Kippur (which falls a week later) was greater than their desire to leave Poland as fast as possible.

Leib Backenroth and his friend Roth had planned the trip to Romania, but Stella's brother, Zygus, who was observant, asked his parents to delay the departure until after the holidays. Stella's mother also wanted to stay in Schodnica for the festivals, so that Stella was the only one from her entire family who left. On her way to the frontier, in the city of Chortkov, she met her uncle Moye, Moshe Backenroth-Heller. This was the same Moye who as a twelve-year-old boy in the early 1920s had almost been murdered in the Lvov pogrom and, after a vision that came to him in a dream, had led a legion of young Jews to Palestine. Moye had a Palestinian passport. His two younger brothers, Uri and Pinhas, were traveling with him on their way to Romania, but they, too, had delayed their journey because of the holiday.

Stella crossed the border alone and traveled to Bucharest. Her relatives welcomed her with open arms, but she wasn't sure that she had made the right decision. Her link with her family had been severed, and she was worried about their fate. Would she ever see them again, or had she left them forever? She was so worried that she stopped thinking rationally and decided to return to Poland. Her cousin Hella Sobel-Horn, who had gone to Palestine after her beloved Mondak, wrote Stella an urgent letter from Haifa, warning her in these words: "Don't dare to go back to Poland, Stella. Leave right away for Eretz Yisrael" (the land of Israel). Moye, whom she met again in Bucharest, had her name added to his passport. He promised to take her across the borders and to accompany her until she arrived in Palestine. But Stella's heart was heavy. Was it right to save herself while her family was endangered? She asked her relatives to take her back to Schodnica, and Moye replied, "I am not worried about you, but how will I explain to your father after the war that I could have saved you but didn't do it? I will not travel to Palestine without you."

By now, the Red Army had invaded Romania, and Stella was overcome by confusion. Which way to turn? Should she continue on to Palestine or go back to Galicia? Her relatives pleaded with her to save herself, and when she told them that she was determined to rejoin her family in Poland, they tore their hair out. But she left Bucharest on a train to Czernowitz, and there, too, friends warned her not to go back and to leave Europe immediately. Stella, however, was not able to abandon her family. Her conscience tormented her.

In a café in central Czernowitz a friend introduced Stella to two Soviet journalists who had come with the Red Army; one of them was an educated Jew, the son of a rabbi. He had studied in Switzerland and then returned to the Soviet Union. Stella told him of her dilemma, and he was ready to help. "I have a daughter your age in Russia," he said. "I don't know where she is and I would like to believe that if she were in trouble, good people would help her." The journalist organized an official pass for her to return to occupied Poland. She would join a convoy of Soviet reporters headed for Lvov. Before they set out from Czernowitz for the border, the journalist made his colleagues swear to take care of her. "Her blood is on your head if this young lady doesn't get home safely," he warned.

The Soviets were gentlemen, and Stella reached Schodnica. Her family and neighbors moaned when they saw her and called her a perfect idiot. "People are ready to pay fortunes to get out of Poland," they said to her, "and you, in your stupidity, came back."

In retrospect, Stella was not sorry. "Of course, I could have been in a safer place when the war started, in Palestine or America," she said forty years later, on a stormy winter night at her home in Brighton Beach, New York. "But I was young and foolish, and I wanted to go home. I never had the courage to go on wandering the world on my own. I felt that my family's fate was my fate and that whatever happens to them must happen to me, and today I swear to you, after everything I went through, that I am convinced that my choice was the right one. Then I was happy to come home, and today I am happy that I decided to go back. If I had gone my own way when the war began, if I escaped to America or Palestine, I would always have felt terrible pangs of conscience toward my family."

Fate sometimes plays tricks. While Stella was making her way back to Poland, the High Holy Days had ended, and her family set off in the opposite direction. When they arrived in Czernowitz, the communists arrested her father, Leib, and imprisoned him as a capitalist. Polish friends intervened on his behalf and signed a petition for his release. It worked, and he returned to Schodnica with his wife and son. If he had stayed in prison, he probably would have been sent with his family to Siberia, as was done later with his relatives, the Sobel family from Bolechow. And if he had been sent to Siberia, he might have survived the war, but when he returned home with his wife and his son, their fate was sealed. The Soviets were already ruling in Galicia, and later he had no opportunity to leave Poland.

On the very day that Stella Backenroth reached Schodnica, an event of an entirely different kind occurred not far away. Nikita Sergeyevitch Khrushchev, the first secretary of the Ukrainian Communist Party, who was known as an excellent organizer and an ardent Stalinist, toured the villages west of the district capital of Stryj.[5] Stalin had ordered Khrushchev to carry out two policies: to nationalize the oil fields and to double agricultural production. The Soviet Union needed fuel and grain, and it was up to Khrushchev to see that Ukraine delivered the goods.

Khrushchev's guide on the tour was the young Jewish agronomist Naftali Backenroth, Stella's cousin. He had graduated from the University of Nancy in France ten years earlier and had won a prize for his plan to excavate a canal to link the Mediterranean and the Dead Sea. At age twenty-three, he had become a lecturer at the Ecole Polytechnique, the most prestigious academy for engineering and science in France. In 1930, Naftali's father, Israel, died, and Naftali was summoned back to Schodnica to run the drilling operations of the family oil business, Nafta Ltd.[6] Naftali's grandfather David Hirsh Backenroth was the brother of the legendary Avrumche, who had expanded the business and consolidated it. When Avrumche had grown old, parts of the partnership had been divided among the brothers.

Naftali's childhood nickname, Tulek, stuck with him. He was tall, sturdy, and forceful, with quick reflexes. He had blue eyes and a fair mustache. "Tulek looks like a goy and behaves like a goy," quipped his cousin Hella Sobel, and Stella Backenroth agreed wholeheartedly. They all lived close together in Drohobych. More than once, Naftali's cousins called him to deal with Ukrainian youths who threatened to harm them. Naftali excelled at his studies, and he was always thinking up inventions and taking things apart and putting them together again.

The wedding of Naftali's sister Sabina, 1928. The bride sits fourth from the left. Naftali stands at the far left, and his sister Junia stands beside him (second from the left). His father, Israel Backenroth, sits third from the right. Naftali's brother, the student Leib, stands at the far right. Naftali's two sisters were murdered by the Nazis, and his brother, Leib, committed suicide.

In September 1939, Naftali was building a mobile drilling machine and supervising a drill at a new site, but his work was halted by the Soviet takeover of Galicia. The occupation authorities seized the family's oil business. Naftali was forced to go back to agriculture and then was asked to join the entourage of the party boss. When Khrushchev asked questions, Naftali replied, and received orders. "No matter what ways and means are used, agricultural production must be doubled by next summer," Khrushchev commanded. Naftali made a positive impression on the leader, and he was appointed district agronomist.

To carry out the party's plan, Naftali recruited a group of Jewish engineers, some of them communist friends who had helped him get the job. He named another good friend, Josephson, a lawyer, as legal adviser to the agricultural administration, but the occupation authorities refused to approve the appointment, although Josephson was a good communist. Someone complained about him, he was called in for questioning, and soon afterward he was executed. That was the way the Soviets did things. If someone was

Naftali Backenroth-Bronicki (second from the right) at the gate of one of the Backenroths' oil installations in Climovka, Galicia, about 1938.

suspected of acting against them, they never dug too deeply; in many cases they simply eliminated the person, without a trial.

Although Naftali was not a communist, they trusted him completely, perhaps because he never showed them reverence or simply because there were no other experienced agronomists around. Whatever the reason, Nikita Khrushchev placed his confidence in the young Jew, the son of prosperous businessmen. This was highly unusual—members of the bourgeoisie like Naftali were rarely trusted by the communists. On the contrary, since the Soviet invasion, the communists had tried to wipe out all traces of the free economy in Galicia, replacing it with a collectivized system. Most of the bourgeoisie were condemned and boycotted, including Naftali's relatives from Bolechow, Israel Moses and Clara Sobel, and their neighbors Yerahmiel and Rachel

Naftali Backenroth-Bronicki and his son, Lucien, in Schodnica, about 1938.

Kahane, Ullo's parents. Like most of the manufacturers and the businessmen, they had a restrictive "paragraph" registered against them, and their ID cards were stamped with the words "Dangerous bourgeois" in red letters. In Yerahmiel Kahane's documents he was described as "an important industrialist," and his leather factory was nationalized.

The complexity of the new political situation was the main topic of a postcard mailed from Bolechow to Lyon, France, on October 10, 1939, soon after the Soviets established themselves in Galicia. In it, Ullo Kahane informed his sister Sonia and her husband, the physician Nunio Krauthammer, that so far the situation was under control: "My dear ones, we are trying to keep in touch. Write to us via Romania. Please write two copies and send them to the two addresses that I am appending. They are the addresses of the Feder relatives in Romania and, if you can, please use international stamps.[7]

Everything is alright with us. None of us was conscripted to the Soviet army. Neither is any of the Krauthammers in the service. Bolechow was completely unharmed by the occupation. We are all healthy and we are all here, also Lidka and her husband, Feder. It's good that the storm has passed over us and now a new order is beginning here. Write back. Big kisses, Ullo." His parents added their wishes in a few lines at the end. The father, Yerahmiel, wrote, "My dear children, we find ourselves with God's help, in a good situation. Waiting for good news from you, kisses, Father." And his wife, Rachel, wrote in tiny letters, "As you know, dear Lidka and dear Feder are with us, and Ullo is also with us, and we are feeling good, kisses, Mother." And Lidka also added a line: "Everything is fine with us. I've even found work as a doctor. Waiting to hear from you, warm kisses, Lidka."

Although Sonia never told her parents that her husband wasn't practicing medicine, her family in Bolechow knew everything about his doings. They read between the lines of the letters from Lyon, and every now and again they questioned acquaintances who had visited the couple in France. Sonia, too, knew how to decipher the letters she received from Bolechow. She easily separated the wheat from the chaff, discerned the unmentioned difficult events, and grasped what lay behind the calming sentences. Everything was fine in Bolechow, they wrote on the postcard. This was highly suspicious. How could that be in a town that had been taken over by the communists? Obviously, private property had been confiscated, and her father had been left without a livelihood, but, on the other hand, Lidka and her husband were working. Feder was a communist and Ullo, too, was close to the left, so that item was probably true and they were certainly giving some of their earnings to the parents. Things were not good, that was clear, but neither were they too terrible.

Sonia quickly wrote back via Romania, as Ullo had told her to. She put some dollar bills into the envelopes, but the letters never arrived.

15
The Wedding

In the tense summer of 1940, there were fewer than ten guests at the wedding in Stanislav, all of whom were close friends of the bride, Nushka Sobel, and the groom, Ullo Kahane.[1] Their parents and most family members were absent. Only two relatives had come: Ullo's sister Lidka and her husband, the economist Abraham Feder. The ceremony was very brief and businesslike, lasting less than five minutes. When it was over, Ullo waved a hand and said, "A wedding is like a funeral, only with music. But we don't even have music." Everyone laughed. They each sipped a glass of sweet wine and said, "*L'chayim*, Ullo. *L'chayim*, Nushka" (To life). And that was it. Without musicians, bridal dress, bouquets, or canapés, Nushka and Ullo were legally and religiously joined together in a wartime wedding.

Why weren't they wed in Bolechow, their hometown, and why weren't their parents present? To answer, we must go back seven years.

There had been a number of bad omens during the summer of 1933. Everyone saw them, but few dared to predict the outcome. In Berlin, the Nazi thug Adolf Hitler had come to power several months earlier, but most Polish Jews perceived the event as a domestic German affair. In Poland, nationalism and anti-Semitism were rampant and Poland's Jews felt apprehensive, but most of them were in no hurry to flee—because the free countries were closed to them, and because their leadership was divided and hesitant. There were so many political factions among the Jews, and so many false solutions were offered by their leaders, that most of them were confused to the point of paralysis. So Poland's Jews continued their lives as usual,

The 1933–1934 high school class of Nushka Sobel-Kahane (first row, second from the left).

working and studying, marrying and bringing children into the world, and vacationing in the summer.

One day, Ullo Kahane, now a tall, handsome student dressed in a white shirt and a dark, formal suit, visited the Sobel home in Bolechow for the first time. Ullo's home in the Rynek (marketplace) was on the western bank of the Sukiel River. The Sobel home was east of the river, on the edge of the town closest to the diesel generator that produced the region's electricity and was managed by Bernhard Lew. It was about half an hour's walk from the Rynek to the large house in the courtyard of the Backenroth refinery, which belonged to Backenroth Brothers Limited and was managed by Israel Moses Sobel, whose wife was Clara (née Backenroth), Avrumche's daughter. The Sobels were Orthodox Hasidic Jews, followers of the rabbi of Zhidachov, and they had set up a small synagogue and a *mikveh* (ritual bath) alongside the family house.

Not far from the Sobel refinery was the leather-processing factory owned by Yerahmiel Kahane, Ullo's father, but Ullo had never wanted to visit the industrial area. He was not interested in his father's leather factory or in the Backenroth refinery. He would soon get his law degree from Lvov University, and he made the thirty-minute walk to the Sobel home to earn pocket money. The Sobels' oldest daughter, Hella, would soon take her

The gate to Nafta's refinery in Bolechow. The woman at the right is Clara Backenroth-Sobel. The photograph was taken during the 1920s.

high school graduation exams, and although she was clever and her grades outstanding, her parents decided to hire Ullo to tutor her in languages and mathematics. The high school examinations in Poland were known to be very difficult.

But the tutor soon became a suitor, whose courtship in the Sobel home in Bolechow recalls the biblical story of Jacob's love for Rachel (as related in Genesis 29). Jacob labored for seven years to win Rachel, the younger daughter of Laban, but in the end had to be content with Leah, the older daughter. For Ullo, the order was reversed. He fell in love with the older sister, Hella. She was his first love, but years later he married the younger one, Nushka.

Hella Sobel-Horn.

From the first, Ullo was enchanted by Hella's beauty, which turned men's heads whenever she went by. At their first lesson, moreover, he realized how talented she was. Before the summer was over, he had fallen head over heels in love. He found her beautiful and clever, original and independent, firm-minded and decisive. He had never before met a young Jewish girl who knew with such confidence exactly where she was going. At the age of eighteen, Hella had clearly defined secular liberal views with a socialist tinge. Ullo also held left-wing views, but, unlike her, he was not obliged to rebel against religion since his parents were progressive and the path of higher education was naturally open to him. By choosing to go to university, Hella had courageously and unconventionally defied her Orthodox parents, who believed that secular education for women was wrong.

Hella did not really need a private tutor since she was well versed in the curriculum, and Ullo did not have to exert himself. They spent most of their time in soulful conversations, expressing deep emotions to each other. Hella's cousin Stella Backenroth-Wieseltier was the first witness to the love story. "A romantic relationship," is how she tactfully described the connection between the tutor and his pupil.

The relationship did not last long, however. From the outset, there was a considerable discrepancy between their emotions. Ullo tried to envelop Hella in his love. He wanted to own her entirely and demanded total fidelity, and she, though a passionate woman, hesitated to commit herself to the first man she had ever loved. At home, Ullo had been nurtured by females who worshipped him as if the world revolved around him. Consequently, as Stella noted, he had need of an adoring woman, who would agree to surrender her autonomy and accept his guidance. Hella had no need of a mentor. She supplied her own solutions, tended toward introspection, and gazed at the

Linking Backenroth to Kahane

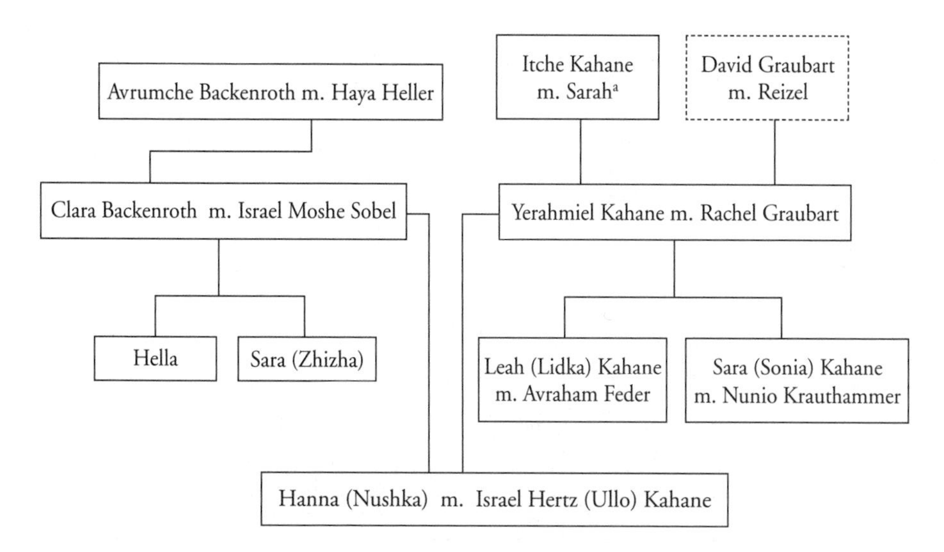

[a]Sara Kahane gave birth to four children. The other three were Leibush, who was an author; Esther, who married in Vienna into the Scharf family; and Carolina, known as Kreidel, who married a Viennese lawyer, Ostersetzer.

world, as it were, from on high—remote from the crowd and even somewhat arrogant. Ullo clung to her fiercely at first, but he did not really know her deeply. He was convinced that he had found the love of his life. After a short time, he came to his senses when he began to perceive her remoteness and reserve. Then she went away to the university at Lvov, and the connection between them was severed.

Stella Wieseltier vividly remembered all of these events. "I loved Hella so much and I was attached to Nushka with all my heart and soul," she said with great emotion many years later. "The two sisters were completely different. Hella was beautiful, sophisticated, intellectual; Nushka was charming with two dimples, lighthearted and funny." The third Sobel sister, Sara, nicknamed Zhizha, was still a baby then.

The Sobel sisters used to spend most of their summer vacations at the home of Stella's father, Shmuel Leib (nicknamed Leibele) Backenroth, in the village of Schodnica. He managed the Backenroths' oil business and for

Backenroth-Bronicki Family Tree

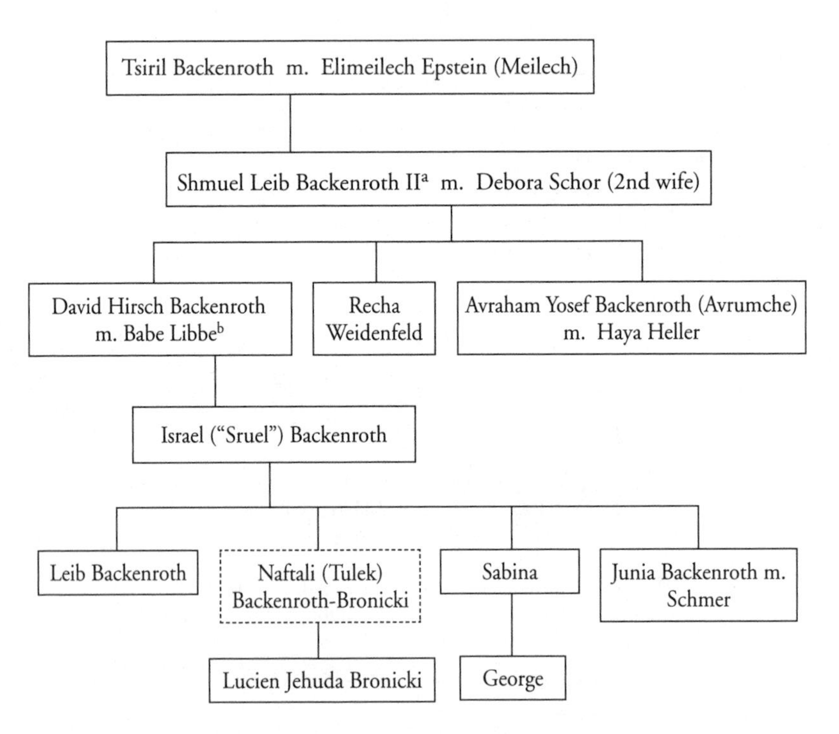

[a] Shmuel Leib's first wife was Silke Kupermann (or Kuperberg), and after she died he married Debora Schor. When Debora died, it is possible that Shmuel married for a third time. His wives gave birth to at least ten children.

[b] David Hirsch Backenroth and his wife, Babe, had at least ten children. Israel Backenroth had nine brothers and sisters: Melech Backenroth, Pearle Loew, Hanna Weintraub, Sirel Thorne, Sara Barsam, Sara Wickler, Silka Wickler, Isaiah (Schie) Backenroth, and Wolf Backenroth.

many years served as the mayor of Schodnica. He became deeply involved in Zionism and donated money to pioneers who immigrated to Palestine. He was not an Orthodox Jew, and thus he was clean-shaven and had no side locks. He wore a European hat, but without the large black *kippah* under it, as worn by Orthodox Jews. His home was open and liberal but still traditional—"progressive," but not assimilated, and certainly much less religiously observant than the Sobel home in Bolechow. The secular and the religious could coexist then because fundamentalist extremism was not in fashion among Polish Jews during the first half of the twentieth century. Many rabbis preached moderation and mutual respect. The code of religious conduct was flexible, and the zeitgeist was characterized by the Maimonidean concept of the "middle path" and by the ideal of "Torah and seemliness" (*Torah ve-derekh eretz*, in Hebrew), which meant that decency and genuine ethics had preceded the Torah's directives.

"In my young days I brought boys home, and my father welcomed them," said Stella, "although generally speaking, religious parents did not approve of friendships between the sexes." Nonetheless, Hella and Nushka Sobel were permitted to hang out with their less observant cousin, Stella, at places of entertainment. "We went with them to cafés in Schodnica, Drohobych, and Strij, and there we met young men. We grew up in homes where the services of a matchmaker were not required. Our parents invested great efforts in our education; they enrolled us in libraries and sent us out to enjoy ourselves. They were not afraid that we would be corrupted. We read *Uncle Tom's Cabin* in Polish and Emile Zola in French. I spoke German with my mother. My parents read secular books and in Lvov they went to the opera."

Stella waxed even more enthusiastic, and the words tumbled out, as she remembered that her father took them to see Josephine Baker at the Lvov opera house. "It was in 1935. No, no, I think it was in 1936, and Josephine Baker was a sensation. Hella was with us and so was Clara, her mother. My father went especially to Bolechow and brought them to Lvov." A Jewish theater troupe from Warsaw sometimes came to Schodnica. Together, the girls saw *Tevya the Milkman* and *The Dybbuk*, with the actor Maurice Schwartz, who was later prominent in the Yiddish theater in New York. They often went to the cinema and to cafés for the cocktail hour. In the afternoons there was an orchestra, and boys and girls danced together. "Nushka was an excellent dancer, and Hella danced as well. Three times a week we went out dancing, the tango and the foxtrot, and the boys held the girls in their arms."

The young members of the Backenroth family, who came of age during the 1920s, enjoyed a happy childhood and adolescence. Their parents employed nursemaids, servants, gardeners, and chauffeurs. The parents spent their vacations at spas in Germany, Austria, and Czechoslovakia. One summer night, Stella's father woke the girls at three in the morning and took them down to the river to fish for trout. One of their aunts, Erna Turkel, had a school for acrobats in Vienna, and in the summer she vacationed in Schodnica. She usually rose at six, awakened the girls, took them all out to the fields, and ordered them to practice gymnastic exercises. Hella exercised willingly; Nushka preferred to sleep. In the winter they skated on the ice, and in the summer they played tennis and went out hunting with the adults. "Nushka hated hunting, but Hella loved to hunt," said Stella.

Those were happy years, but in December 1929, when Wall Street crashed and an economic crisis spread across the globe, the mood changed. Places like Schodnica, where the oil industry provided most of the jobs, were only marginally affected by the crisis. But in the leather-tanning town of Bolechow, the economic downturn struck with great force. In the summer of 1930, most of the businesspeople faced bankruptcy, among them the Kahanes.

In the 1920s, Aunt Erna Turkel, who had a school for acrobats in Vienna, came to Schodnica on winter vacations and taught the Backenroth youngsters skiing on the Carpathian Mountains' icy slopes. (The man behind Erna was not identified.)

In the wake of the Depression, anti-Jewish discrimination intensified in Poland, and a wave of ultranationalism swept through the country. Ostensibly, the strongman of Poland, the dictator Marshal Jozef Pilsudski, was a friend of the Jews, and community leaders considered him a last resort and a savior. "Does Pilsudski not appreciate the Jews' contribution to Polish society?" they asked. "Doesn't he remember the valor of his Jewish comrades in arms in the War of Independence?" The marshal did remember, and he condemned the anti-Semites; in exchange, the Jews supported his compromise proposal, according to which Polish independence must be closely guarded, and in order to preserve it, majority and minority must coexist. Pilsudski's motto was *Idea Pan'stwowa*—"the compromise concept"—but most of the Poles (among them, more than a few of Pilsudski's comrades and supporters) backed the ultranationalists.

Some Backenroths had planned to leave Poland for the United States, but, as related earlier, only a few (from the Heller and the Turkel branches) managed to obtain visas. Getting a visa had become more difficult because U.S. immigration quotas were constantly being lowered. Others planned to migrate to Palestine, but they put off their departure until it was too late. Some were attracted by communist ideology, but for most Jews, the looming catastrophe was only a theoretical possibility, and they did nothing about it.[2]

Hella Sobel was among the few who grasped the implications of political developments. At seventeen, to the consternation of her Orthodox parents, she rebelled against religion, left her studies at the Orthodox Bet-Yaakov seminary in Kraków, and enrolled at Lvov University. There, she joined a secular group of Jewish students who persuaded her to migrate to Palestine.

Abandoning the religious lifestyle was a protracted and anguished intellectual ordeal for Hella because of her parents' religious observance and because of her upbringing. Drawing on her inner reserves, she put herself through a process of feminist self-persuasion, rather than being influenced by external events, organizations, or politics. She did not revel in her rebellion but was driven by a need to protest against women's inferior role in Orthodox Jewish society. At an early age she had told her sister Nushka, "Jewish women live without a purpose. Their lives are empty. I refuse to live like that."

Hella Sobel's class at the orthodox Bet-Yaakov seminary in Kraków, about 1934. Hella, in a white sweater, sits third from the right in the first row.

In Orthodox families, the girls were given only an elementary education at a basic level because, according to religious law and tradition, women were meant to marry at an early age, to bear many children, and to raise them to follow the exact same path as their parents. This was what Israel Moses and Clara Sobel had planned for their oldest daughter, but her teachers advised them to allow her to study. Consequently, when she completed elementary school, her parents agreed to enroll her at the Jewish high school in Stryj. This obliged them to compromise their principles because the school was both secular and Zionist in orientation. There were no classes on the Sabbath, but the boys went bareheaded and the classes were of mixed gender.

Hella's parents later tried to amend their error. When Hella graduated from the school at Stryj, they insisted that she enroll at the Bet-Yaakov seminary in Kraków, which combined teacher training with Jewish studies. Had she completed her studies at the seminary, it is reasonable to assume that she would have married a yeshiva student from an Orthodox family and become a virtuous housewife and perhaps a teacher at the seminary. She refused to follow the traditional path for women, however, and left the seminary after only one year. The truth is that from the outset, she had no desire to follow

Israel Moses and Clara Sobel in the port of Haifa. At the end of 1938, the Sobels accompanied their daughter Hella by ship to Palestine, where she married Mondek Horn. The Sobels returned to Poland in February 1939.

the Orthodox path and agreed to try it only out of respect for her parents. Her younger sister, Zhizha, believed that Hella came to a tacit agreement with her parents: if the experiment failed after one year, they would permit her to enroll at the university.

Hella's parents apparently hoped that the Bet-Yaakov indoctrination would set her on the Orthodox path, as had happened to many young girls, but Hella was made of different stuff. She was repelled by Bet-Yaakov and disappointed with the other pupils; in particular she disliked their hypocrisy. She immediately discerned that many of the young women were insincere in their professed devotion to faith. They were far more interested in hairstyles, fashion, and gossip than in education and religious faith. Thus, when Hella informed her parents that she had decided to leave, they did not resist, although they knew only too well that she had now crossed the Rubicon and was adopting a totally different lifestyle from their own. Stella remembered that Hella confessed to her that "She was no longer observant, but the emotional cost was great. She suffered from guilt feelings."

Hella was caught up in tragic circumstances: on one hand, her pain was strong and genuine. On the other hand, she was not able to change her inner convictions. In the Sobel family, solidarity and interdependence between the generations were firmly upheld, and the commandment "Honor thy father and thy mother" was not taken as lip service but as an exhortation to the younger generation to maintain continuity, not to deviate from the path of their parents. This defining awareness passed subconsciously from generation to generation, and its purpose and effect were to guarantee Jewish survival. How does a community ensure the continuity of its religious or communal singularity? How does it guarantee survival? According to Orthodox Jewry, there is only one way—by the observance of religious laws. They believe that the Jewish moral code, the Torah and the *halakha*, distinguishes Jews from other peoples and ensures future survival. To abandon it is to assimilate. In Jewish tradition, assimilation means betrayal of the community and affiliation with the gentile world. This is an extreme step and is known as *shmad*, "annihilation" (from the Hebrew word *hashmada*—"destruction"). In other words, assimilation leads to destruction, and people who assimilate bring death on themselves, not symbolically but in actual fact. Thus, for religious parents nothing is more important than religious continuity, and they make every effort to raise their children in such a fashion that they will never abandon the path of faith.

The younger generation's rebellion against tradition is a new phenomenon in Jewish society. Until secular enlightenment broke down the walls of the closed and confined Jewish ghetto, until Jewish society opened up to alien influences, Jews were marked by exemplary religious discipline. The elders determined the path and ensured that the young kept to it. The independent Jewish educational system was unique: hermetically sealed against innovation and external influence, highly unpluralistic and undemocratic. Since the Middle Ages, other Jewish community institutions had been run in a democratic fashion, in contrast to the situation in most non-Jewish societies at the time, but the educational system was always well structured and well supervised at all stages, from infancy to adulthood.

All of this was true until the mid-eighteenth century, when the ghetto walls tumbled in Germany and a new era arrived: the Age of Enlightenment. In less than a century, masses of German Jews had abandoned tradition, religion, and the community and made every effort to assimilate into the German people. Assimilation became a mass phenomenon. Hundreds of thousands of Jews ceased to live according to religious injunctions, and tens of thousands converted to Christianity. A similar process subsequently occurred in most of the Austro-Hungarian Empire and even in Galicia. In Eastern Europe, Orthodox Jewry, both Hasidim and their opponents, the Mitnagdim, battled fiercely against the Enlightenment and succeeded in holding it back until the beginning of the twentieth century. But by World War I, the traditional structure of the community, the *kahal*, had been greatly weakened.[3]

The assimilation process had been very rapid because many young Jews could not withstand the lure of exposure to secular culture. They were expected to make a sacrifice that they were unable to make. Anyone who wished to move from the yeshiva to the world of secular culture was forced to choose between loyalty to religion and the secular way of life, out of fear that observing all the religious directives would reduce their capabilities to compete in the free market for professional and economical success. In this respect, most young Polish Jews had no alternative. Those who attended high school were obliged to study on the Sabbath, and once they transgressed in this way, the entire structure of their religious faith collapsed. According to the Orthodox Jewish outlook, the Sabbath was the primary line of defense. When the first line fell, all of the other religious injunctions were inevitably invalidated. Almost everyone who studied at a university during those years was forced to compromise, particularly with regard to Sabbath observance and sometimes *kashruth* (eating only kosher food according to the Jewish dietary laws) as well. Choosing secular studies was their main way of achieving a compromise with religion.

Indeed, between the wars, profound processes of secularization and Polonization occurred in Polish Jewry, particularly among the middle class and the rich, but these changes did not cause the disintegration of Jewish society. The reverse occurred. Counter to all expectations and despite the widespread assimilation, Jewish identification did not weaken. In fact, it was reinforced, due to the upsurge of anti-Semitism, which prevented Jews, even those who had assimilated, from becoming part of Polish society. An absurd situation ensued: The religious leaders warned that those who abandoned their Jewish faith would end up converting and claimed that the Jewish people were in danger of *shmad.* On the other hand, the leaders of the assimilation movement advocated abandoning religion and endeavored to persuade Jews to integrate into Polish society even at the price of forfeiting their singular traits. And, in fact, most Jews chose assimilation. They cast off traditional values but at the same time hesitated to renounce their religious identity entirely, for reasons connected to anti-Semitism. It makes a fascinating study. If the Jews had not lived under the threat of extreme anti-Semitism in the 1930s, it is unlikely that the process of assimilation in Eastern Europe could have been checked. Once anti-Semitic activity was stepped up, however, most Jews chose to preserve their ethnic identity. Polish anti-Semitism, which sought to undermine Jewish ethnic and religious cohesion, reinforced it instead.[4]

Hella's parents, Israel Moses and Clara, cautiously considered the situation. They feared that their relations with their daughter might deteriorate to a point of no return. If they confronted her, if they threatened her with boycott or banishment, they would lose her forever. From their point of view, this was unthinkable, but they also felt that it was unlikely that they would succeed in persuading her by reasoning. How does one change the mind of a young person who is firmly resolved to abandon religious observance? They had never faced such a dilemma. True enough, among the younger generation, many of Avrumche Backenroth's grandchildren no longer strictly observed many of the prescribed 613 religious injunctions. At most, they maintained traditions, but the Sobels were different. They had always set themselves two rules that must not be violated: keeping the Sabbath and eating kosher.[5] To have a daughter who did not observe the Sabbath and the kosher laws implied a shameful failure of education on the part of the parents. But now they knew that the battle was lost. They had raised their daughters to be independent, and Hella's independence was about to win the day. Israel Moses and Clara decided to give in. Their love for Hella prevailed over their conservatism.

"My parents were deeply distressed," said Hella's younger sister, Zhizha, "but they knew that they could not oppose her." Later, when Israel Moses and Clara discovered that their second daughter, Nushka, was also no longer observant, it caused them great pain. They never stayed at their two secular daughters' homes because their kitchens were not kosher. Clara told Zhizha, the only daughter who was observant, "How terrible it is that I can't go and visit them because I can't eat in their homes." But nonetheless, said the younger sister, love prevailed over contention. "If Hella had not been allowed to go to university, she would have been unhappy, and they wanted her to be happy. They knew she was talented and clever and could never just sit at home."

Hella's life choices were not exceptional. In the 1920s and 1930s, rebellion against religion and tradition characterized the younger generation of Polish Jews more than any other social phenomenon. This rebellion undermined the social structure of the middle class and caused rifts in many Jewish families. Parents severed their ties with their own children. Fathers and sons were separated forever. In some cases, children of Orthodox parents became active communists, while others immigrated to Palestine. There were cases where parents sat *shiva* (observed the seven days of mourning) for their secular children, as if they had died. And there are stories of parents who fettered their daughters, actually tied them up, to prevent them from leaving home to study at a university or to marry secular Jews. Thus, the Enlightenment movement found its way into the Sobel home. Hella returned from Kraków and then left Bolechow for Lvov University. Her parents financed her studies and paid all of her expenses.

Hella was prevented from majoring in medicine because the university restricted Jewish students' access to the most sought-after courses. In fact, Lvov University was the first in Poland to implement the *numerus clausus* regulation at its medical school in 1921 and then at its veterinary medicine school. It was a rule whereby Jewish students were admitted to universities only in proportion to the number of Jews in the country.[6] The university proposed that Hella study law. She was ready to compromise by studying biology, but that course of study was closed to Jews. Hence, she was obliged to renounce her ambition and enrolled in the school of agriculture. (Lidka, Ullo's sister, as mentioned earlier, was compelled to study medicine in Prague because she was rejected by Lvov University.)

In Lvov, Hella initially lived with a female relative and later she rented an apartment and became independent. Now, for the first time, she encountered Polish nationalism and anti-Semitism. In Bolechow and Schodnica, there had been no real manifestations of anti-Semitism. In these small towns the Jewish community was strong and influential and was able to suppress signs of anti-Semitism as soon as they were recognized. Even in the district capital, Stryj, Hella had never personally experienced anti-Semitism. In Lvov, things were different. The anti-Semites were well entrenched at the university.

The years of Hella's university studies (1935–1937) were difficult times for Jewish students. Since the establishment of the new Poland at the end of World War I, student organizations had become bastions of nationalism, controlled by the young guard of the Endecja—the right-wing nationalist political movement. At the universities, extremist circles enjoyed complete freedom to conduct their anti-Semitic and nationalist activities because the government had a policy of not intervening in academic life, the police abstained from entering universities' premises, and particularly because most of the faculty and the non-Jewish students were indifferent to the Jews' well-being. Anti-Semites were free to engage in incitement and acts of terror against Jewish students. The Endeks were so violent that the authorities were sometimes obliged to close the universities for brief periods, until calm was restored.

From time to time, the Endeks proclaimed a "Jewless day," during which Jewish students were ostracized, humiliated, and beaten. When the nationalists realized that the authorities were not going to react, they extended the boycott and proclaimed a "Jewless week." In October 1937, the university heads acceded to Endek demands and announced the introduction of "reforms" in the seating arrangements in lecture halls. They instituted "seating ghettos for Jews," forbidding Jewish students to sit in most parts of the lecture halls and confining them to one corner. At Lvov University, Jewish students were forbidden to sit on the left-hand side of the lecture halls. But they rejected the ludicrous regulation, and in protest they stood along the walls throughout the lectures. This gave the university authorities a pretext for accusing them of provocation and refusing to protect them from the increasing violence. Hella found the prolonged standing very arduous, and her sister Zhizha recalled that she bought special boots to make it easier. At Warsaw University, some professors threw Jewish students out of their classes if they refused to sit in the designated "ghettos" and insisted on standing.

Fifty years later, Stella's husband, Mark Wieseltier, described how in 1937, at the University of Lvov, anti-Semites murdered his friend Zellermeier. A gang of thirty Endeks, wearing caps that bore fascist insignia, attacked Zellermeier in a university corridor and hit him on the head with a spiked club. He tried to escape to the rector's office but fell dead before he got there.

Throughout Poland, the persecution of Jews grew in intensity, and nationalism became increasingly extreme. There was a consensus regarding the legitimacy of anti-Semitic policy, to the point that a kind of apartheid was enforced against the Jews. The wave of anti-Semitism bolstered two movements among Jewish youngsters: communism and Zionism. The communists favored fighting the fanatical nationalism of the Endeks, whereas the Zionists

Hella Sobel-Horn and her husband, Israel Moshe Horn, known as Mondek.

offered a solution outside of Poland. Hella was drawn to both movements and eventually chose the Zionist path. In Lvov, at the Zionist club, she met her cousin Israel Moshe Horn, known as Mondek, who was nothing like Ullo Kahane, and the two entered into a relationship. Mondek was a dreamy poet, an ardent Zionist who yearned to become a pioneer in Palestine. He soon left Poland for Palestine, and his parents followed. Hella spent another year at Lvov University, and when she was accepted by Hebrew University in Jerusalem, she decided to follow him. Acceptance by the university enabled her to obtain a student entry certificate from the British Mandatatory authorities in Palestine. At the end of 1938, her parents accompanied her by ship to Palestine.

Two months later, the young couple wed in Jerusalem and immediately afterward, in February 1939, the parents returned to Poland. Her two sisters, Nushka and Zhizha, did not accompany them to Palestine. "I'm not sure that my parents accepted her move to Palestine willingly," Zhizha said. "Europe was on the brink of a grave crisis, but at home we didn't talk much, and after their return, my parents said only that life in Palestine was very hard and took comfort in the fact that Mondek's father, Yehiel Horn, had taken money with him. The couple were both students, and my father said, 'They're managing there not too badly.'"

Shortly before Hella left for Palestine, she played matchmaker for Ullo and her sister. In the role of tutor, Ullo returned to the Sobel home in Bolechow, five years older and more experienced. His new pupil, Nushka, worshipped him from the start. The division of roles between them was clear: he was the guide and the mentor, sometimes the surrogate father, and she was the protégée. He talked and she listened. He set the agenda, and she took care of his comfort. Soon they were deeply in love and complemented each other perfectly. Ullo came to the Sobel home almost every day to tutor Nushka in order to improve her *matura* (high school graduation) grades. Nushka intended to continue her studies, although she had not yet decided what subject to pursue. But they spent more time planning their joint future than studying.

Nushka had followed in Hella's footsteps. In her heart she had already abandoned religion, although outwardly she had not changed her lifestyle. Unlike her older sister, she was not attracted to politics and was neither a Zionist nor a leftist. Her aspirations were purely bourgeois. Above all, she wanted a family, a profession, and a comfortable life. She was happy to discover that Ullo's plans did not clash with these aspirations. He, too, was uninterested in political activity, and although he still had leftist tendencies, he was careful not to be associated with the communists. With regard to Zionism, he could now be defined as a sympathizer and an observer. His boyish desire to set up a Jewish home in Palestine had been relegated to the sidelines. Ullo planned to combine a career as a lawyer in private practice with that of an academic. He was apprenticed to a lawyer, Nunio Kahane, a relative who lived in Stryj, and he intended to return to the university to get a PhD in economics. Thus, the couple's modest aspirations harmonized, and their love blossomed. But their path was not to be smooth. Nushka's mother, Clara, took note of the deepening bond between her daughter and Ullo Kahane and resolved to put an end to the relationship.

In the fall of 1937, Nushka was suddenly invited to Vienna to stay with her rich aunt Gittel Turkel. Nushka parted tearfully from Ullo but left in good spirits. For an eighteen-year-old from Bolechow, Vienna was the center of the world. The echoes of war were remote. Vienna beckoned and Ullo could wait. Nushka spent seven months with her aunt in the suburb of Scheinbrun. Every week she sent Ullo a postcard telling him how much she was enjoying every moment. She often explored the alleyways of the Old City and rode the train to the spa town of Baden. On Sundays she took the boat along the Danube to the Prater Gardens and strolled in the Wienerwald Woods. She attended the opera and the Burgtheater, the Austrian national theater. Political tension in Austria was increasing and anti-Semitism was at its height, but Nushka noticed nothing. She enjoyed the big city and felt relaxed.

In mid-March 1938, Hitler annexed Austria. The next night Israel Moses Sobel telephoned his daughter and ordered her to return to Bolechow at once. Her parents met her at Lvov station, and as she entered the house, her sister Zhizha asked her whether she had seen Hitler with her own eyes. Nushka laughed. A few minutes later, Ullo appeared. How had he known Nushka was back when she had returned unexpectedly? She was so glad to see him that she stretched out her arms and they embraced for a long moment. Her mother turned pale. Seven months in Vienna had not dampened their love.

After Nushka's return, she and Ullo met daily, mostly at the Kahane home in the Rynek, planning their future and declaring their love for each other. Nushka wanted to pursue a profession. For several months she hesitated between choosing a teacher's seminary or nursing school, but before she could decide, in August 1939, Germany and the Soviet Union signed the Molotov-Ribbentrop treaty, which called for the division of Poland. All at once, Ullo's and Nushka's plans were disrupted. The Red Army crossed the Polish border along its entire length, from Latvia to Romania, and took over Galicia. The Polish army surrendered without a fight. Sixty-eight thousand Polish officers and troops were taken prisoner, and Prime Minister Molotov delivered a speech in the Supreme Soviet welcoming the annihilation of the "monster born of the Versailles treaty"—namely, free Poland.[7] The Soviet press published numerous descriptions of the "enthusiastic and emotional response of the Ukrainians as they welcomed the Soviet army." In Eastern Poland some twelve million people had now been annexed to the Soviet Union—three million White Russians, six million Ukrainians and Poles, and about a million Jews who had not escaped Galicia in time.

In Bolechow, due to the change of regime, a strange incident forced Ullo to find refuge in another town. A young Bolechow man, Berele Rubinstein, wanted Ullo to help him to establish a new political club for young Jewish communist sympathizers, but Ullo refused to commit himself. It was a straightforward dispute that turned into an open fight between the two. When the Soviets moved in, Rubinstein went to the colonel in charge of the provisional military government and told him that Ullo Kahane was an enemy of communism. The authorities immediately ostracized Ullo and cut off the electricity to his father's factory. Several weeks after the occupation, Ullo learned that the communists had issued a public warning against employing him. He could no longer make a living in Bolechow, even in the factory that would soon be confiscated from his father.

Ullo was forced to leave immediately for Stanislav, about two hours' journey by train southeast of Bolechow. The Soviet authorities in Stanislav knew nothing about Ullo Kahane and Berele Rubinstein, and Ullo found work there as an economic planner in the new Soviet administration. Nushka followed him, arousing her parents' ire. In the annals of the Sobel family, there had never been a daughter who left home and moved in with a man before marriage. Nonetheless, her parents didn't fight her since they had troubles of their own, much more complicated and urgent. The communists were about to banish them to Siberia.

Zhizha Sobel (right) with a friend in Bolechow, 1939.

In hindsight, it is obvious that Ullo's move to Stanislav saved his and Nushka's lives. Ullo's parents could also have been saved. He suggested that they join him and rent an apartment near the place where he and Nushka lived, but his mother refused. "Are you crazy, Ullo? Why should I pay rent? We have a home of our own in Bolechow," she cried, and Ullo did not insist. After the war, he bitterly regretted not being more assertive.

Immediately after Ullo left Bolechow, the communists confiscated Yerahmiel Kahane's leather factory and appointed one of his workers, an ardent communist, as manager. "A proletarian instead of the bourgeoisie" was the occupiers' slogan. The next day the Soviets brought in seven senior workers of their own, including a technical manager and an accountant. Their wages were paid by the Soviet government, but there was no work for them because raw materials were unobtainable. A few days later, several of Yerahmiel's veteran workers left the factories to work on a natural gas pipeline in the adjacent small town of Tashov. Many years earlier, gas had been discovered at Tashov, but the Poles did not know how to exploit it. Now the Soviets were recruiting workers to lay a pipeline that would bring gas to Moscow.

Skilled workers had no problem in finding work with the Soviets, but most merchants and members of the free professions were unemployed. Some businessmen who were left without a livelihood joined the labor brigades in the forests as lumberjacks. Making life even harder was the fact that the Polish currency, the zloty, had been taken out of circulation and replaced by the Soviet ruble. All grocery stores had been nationalized, and there was a shortage of food. Bread was rationed, and the black market flourished. Anyone caught profiteering was declared an enemy of the revolution and imprisoned.

Several weeks after occupying Bolechow, the communists confiscated the Polish passports of Rachel and Yerahmiel Kahane. These were replaced by provisional Soviet identity cards, stamped "Bourgeoisie," which marked the Kahanes as enemies of the revolution. Rachel and Yerahmiel sensed that banishment to Siberia was imminent. Twice a week, Yerahmiel was required to present himself at the district office, in the home of a Jew named Gross. The new mayor, the communist Moshe Hoyftman, requisitioned half of the Kahane home for two Soviet officers. Then the family of a Soviet officer also began to live there. Yerahmiel and Rachel were ordered to vacate two rooms and to feed the officer, his wife, and two children. All at once, the Kahanes lost most of their assets, as well as their identities.

Thus, by the time Ullo and Nushka announced their intention to marry, the Soviets had already consolidated their grip on Bolechow, and the district governor refused to permit Rachel and Yerahmiel to leave town. They were unable to attend their son's wedding. Nushka's parents, Clara and Israel Moses Sobel, on the other hand, decided for themselves not to attend the ceremony. They did not consider Ullo Kahane a worthy son-in-law. He was a violator of the Sabbath and the son of common leather traders, who had now lost all they possessed. The Sobels might have resigned themselves to the family's lowly origins and could even have decided that the family's assets were not that important, but not observing the Sabbath was a cardinal sin to them. Consequently, they boycotted their daughter's wedding. The Sobels were part of the old world and did not realize, or perhaps refused to understand, that the issue at stake at that point in history was much more critical than their son-in-law's religious transgressions. Their very survival now hung in the balance. In a few weeks' time, Stalin would order the Jews to be driven from their homes by force. Stunned and in despair, they would be marched to the railway station, loaded like cattle onto freight trains, and exiled to Siberia.

Banishment to Siberia was considered a death sentence, but war has a logic of its own. In retrospect, it is evident that the banishment actually saved the Sobels' lives. Stalin murdered many Jews in the Soviet Union, but numerous Jews in Poland and Ukraine owed him their lives because they were in the USSR when the Nazis systematically liquidated Polish Jewry.

None of these events were reflected in Rachel Kahane's weekly letters to her daughter Sonia. It was her habit to soften the sharp corners and make no mention of troubles. At most, she permitted herself to drop hints. But Sonia was no fool. After the war, she said to her brother, "Although you revealed nothing, I knew it all."

The following letter written by Rachel to Sonia and her husband, Nunio Krauthammer, was sent from Bolechow to Lyon, where Sonia and Nunio were living, on June 4, 1940, ten days after the wedding. It was a masterpiece of historical revision.

> My beloved children, we are happy to inform you that our dear son, your loyal brother, was married, at a good hour, on Sunday, May 25. His wife is the daughter of Israel Moses Sobel of Bolechow and she is

> exactly what we wanted, from an intelligent Jewish family and a good home. She has all the good qualities, she is educated and intelligent, a high-school graduate, a good housekeeper and has good taste. She loves Ullo very much and he loves her. Everything, therefore, thanks be to God, is as we wished and the Holy One blessed be He will ensure that they, like us, will enjoy constant happiness. The wedding took place in Stanislav. We were there with the bride's parents and with our beloved Lidka and her husband, and nobody else came because we informed nobody. We very much wanted Ullo to marry because their relationship has lasted a long time. I wept a lot, my children, and as for you, my child Sonia, what a pity you were not able to be there. I regret that you were unable to be with us and hope we will soon rejoice together. It is very quiet here and we are staying put. The dear children live in Stanislav. In Western Ukraine everyone has work and many are employed in manual labor. Father is making money from his previous occupation and is trying to find employment. Buma and Yaakobovitz have work in the forestry office and our son-in-law Feder is managing a bank and making good money. If everything is pleasant and calm at Herz's, I would be very happy if we could meet there. Endless kisses, your loving mother.

There are many subtle hints and inexactitudes, to put it mildly, in Rachel's letter—one might even say "white lies." Why distress a daughter who was far away? Why inform her of the boycott of the wedding? In good time she would learn the facts. Why write that the communists were persecuting her father and humiliating him daily? The heaviest hint that clarified the situation for Sonia came at the end of the letter, in the reference to Herz. Sonia knew that Herz Graubart, a relative, was living in Haifa in Palestine, and she understood that if her mother was indicating that she would prefer to be in Palestine, things must be very difficult in Bolechow.

A little more than two months later, when the Germans conquered France, Sonia and Nunio would again pack their suitcases, hide gold and jewelry on their bodies, and escape to Portugal. Their last station in Europe was in the capital city of Lisbon, where Nunio managed to buy entry visas to Brazil.

On August 25, 1940, Ullo wrote to Sonia in Lisbon:

> I am writing to my dear ones, even though I believe that my voice will not reach you, since you are so far away. An ocean separates us. Truly, the brain cannot grasp how people who are so closely linked can be separated suddenly and forced to live so far apart. Is Brazil your final destination? What are your financial means? What is your forecast for the future? I urge you to write everything, exactly! Commonsense tells me to rejoice and dance at your success in leaving this hell behind, and I must express my admiration for your sharp instincts, Nunio. Despite the difficulties you succeeded in carrying out your plan. And you, my Sonia, dear little sister, weren't you afraid to set out on such a journey? Poor little one, trouble has made you a courageous woman but I know, my dearest, that you are afraid to enter a dark room alone. I can report to you that I and my wife are happy and prefer not to look at the world around us. Here, of course, there are few changes compared to the changes in your lives. Please write a lot and often. I embrace you tenderly; there is even no need to stretch out hands across the ocean. Kisses, Ullo.

Sonia and Nunio Krauthammer were among the last Jews to be able to leave Europe. They set sail for Cuba and then arrived at their final destination, Brazil.

16

The Communist Train

ONE EVENT WAS DEEPLY ENGRAVED in Ullo Kahane's memory and often came back to him: a waking nightmare that resurfaced again and again and would never go away. Throughout his life, the scene cropped up in his mind but never in his sleep. At first, it terrified him. His skin crawled, he broke out in a cold sweat, and his mouth became dry. At the end, though, he felt calm and contented, like a baby after feeding.

In the scene, Ullo is at the large railroad junction in Stanislav, the district capital. There are twenty freight trains standing on parallel tracks. The locomotives face east. Ullo races past the first train, stopping for an instant at the door of every coach. He ducks his head inside and scans the compartment, calling out his wife's name, "Nu-shka, Nu-shka!" and then the name of his sister, "Lid-ka, Lid-ka!" He runs along shouting their names, and his voice mingles with hubbub as crowds of Poles push and shove to get on one of the trains or to see off their loved ones who are escaping to the Soviet Union. In the distance, Ullo hears the roar of explosions. Mushroom-shaped smoke clouds hang in the sky. German artillery is firing and German planes bomb the city every few minutes. The Hungarian army is attacking from one flank, and the German army is advancing rapidly from the other.[1] In a short while, perhaps only a matter of minutes, their tanks will sweep into the railway junction.

There's no time, thinks Ullo. His muscles grow taut and his legs run even faster. He passes one train, then another and another, without finding his dear ones. Here's the last track, the last train, a long string of coaches, this is his train. Ullo dashes alongside it, pleading desperately, "Nu-shka, Nu-shka," at each boxcar that he passes. His heart is pounding. He can't believe that now, at this critical moment, he and his wife will part ways forever.

"Nu-shka, Nu-shka!" He wants to stop the world until he can find his beloved. Hundreds of people are milling around, all with their own concerns. No one pays any attention to his plight, just as he is indifferent to theirs and ignores the masses of people swirling around him. Nothing is important to him now but finding Nushka. He takes another look at his surroundings. Near the boxcar doors, groups of people bid emotional farewells to their departing relatives. But they are calm compared to him. His Nushka is missing. Why hadn't he brought her to the station himself? He should have come with her last night and found a place on one of the trains, but instead he foolishly carried on with the task his communist bosses had given him. He is enveloped by sorrow, his heart is full of pain.

Before Ullo's eyes, soundless images pass in slow motion, like a silent movie: A porter loading huge crates, a Polish officer dragging a horse onto a coach. An old woman kissing her son good-bye, hugging and kissing him, refusing to let him go. A crying child holds tightly to an older man's trouser leg and is pulled behind him into a cloud of dust. A youth roughly shoves children into a coach. The locomotive is fired up and ready to set off; in a second the whistle will blow. Is it moving? Not yet. There's still a glimmer of hope, a few coaches he hasn't reached. Perhaps . . . perhaps . . . His shirt is stained with sweat, saliva foams on his lips, his voice is hoarse. One coach, another one, here's the last one, what's that? Whose bubbling laugh is that?

"Nushka, is it you?"

"I was like a lunatic." That's what Ullo said later, when describing that summer morning as the Germans advanced on Stanislav. For the previous few months, he had been working as an inspector of building materials for the Soviet administration. A few days earlier, a representative of the governor had informed him that all of the industrial plants in the region were to be dismantled and shipped by train to the Soviet Union.

"You will be in charge of one of the trains," his boss told him, but Ullo did not know whether he was meant to travel east on that train. He had not yet clarified the point, first, because plans were being made for youngsters to go into the forests and set up an underground to fight the Nazis and, second, because Nushka had said she didn't want to go to the Soviet Union. "I don't want to live with the communists," she told her new husband, and he hesitated. Perhaps a miracle would happen and the Germans would be stopped in their tracks. But that morning, there had been a drastic change in the situation, and a decision had to be made. Shells were falling near the railway junction.

"Nushka knew that I was in charge of shipping equipment from the industrial plants to Russia, but she did not know whether I was also supposed to travel east. We had agreed between us that if the Germans came, we would try to save ourselves until things calmed down, but during the previous night I had thought a little about what could be expected, and I summoned the Russian captain whom the governor had put at my disposal and instructed him to take a truck and pick up my family, Nushka and Lidka—and, of course, her husband, Feder—and all of the relations and the friends whom he would find there with them, and to take them to the station. The Russian captain hesitated because at that very moment Stanislav was being heavily bombarded. And indeed, not a minute had gone by before the truck was hit by a shell and destroyed. The captain never went, and I was busy. All night long, I organized the loading of the equipment.

"In the morning the Germans were closer, and the trains were ready to move out. And so, without any logical reason, I began to look for Nushka in the trains. Why should she have been there at all? There's no logic in it, but driven by a sixth sense, I began jumping from train to train, looking into the coaches, until I got to the train that I was in charge of. I moved quickly from coach to coach, calling out their names, Nushka, Lidka, and from the very last coach I heard that familiar laugh, and when I went in, I saw them sitting there and laughing, not at all excited, as if there wasn't a war going on outside, and everything was normal. They were just sitting there, in my train, and the whistle blew, and the train began moving, and we traveled farther and farther away into Ukraine. Something like that happens, perhaps, only once in two hundred years."

The train chugged eastward, toward the Ukrainian plains, with the Germans trying every few minutes to hit it with bombs from the air. Ullo and Nushka embraced. His sweat mingled with tears of excitement. A miracle had happened. He had found his beloved Nushka, and she was laughing. She had never doubted for a moment that he would show up. Amazingly, even Ullo's sister, Lidka, a physician, was smiling. She was an inveterate worrier, always seeing the glass as half empty, but this morning she, too, was contented. Lidka was a great admirer of Stalin, and the very thought of living in the Soviet Union filled her with joy.

But Lidka's husband, Abraham Feder, the economist, didn't understand why they were cheerful. "The war is chasing us, and they are happy," he said. He tried to draw Ullo into a political discussion: "You see, at last Hitler has fallen into the Russian trap, just like Napoleon."

But Ullo shut him up quickly. "Cut out the politics now, Feder," he snapped. "The main thing is that we got out in time." Feder was their senior by ten years, and the weight of the world rested heavily on his shoulders. He had a Jewish sense of humor, bitter and sarcastic, whereas Ullo was an expert at telling jokes about neurotic Jews like Feder. ("Two Jews are about to be shot. Suddenly, the order comes to hang them instead. One says to the other, 'Cheer up! They're running out of bullets.'")

At every station, crowds of people were waiting, but Ullo's train steamed onward. Nushka asked about their destination, and Ullo's deputy, a Jewish communist called Diekman, said they were heading north to Kharkov (located in northeast Ukraine) and then on to Moscow. Ullo was sunk in thought. Nushka believed that it was preferable to stay in Ukrainian territory.

"I keep telling you, Ullo, we mustn't link up with the communists," she said, but Ullo still hesitated. He hugged Nushka and caressed her. Strangely, it was the image of Rabbi Shlomo Perlov's beautiful daughter that came to his mind at that moment. He remembered how Munia Mehring had boasted to him as they stood at the edge of the wide courtyard, watching the daughter's marriage celebration: "If I'd really wanted to, I could have had her as well."

Ullo had blushed. "Don't exaggerate, Munia," he said. "She is the daughter of the rabbi." Munia waved a hand dismissively, and Ullo asked, "Really? Do you really think you could have? It's impossible that she's not a virgin!"

Munia laughed and said, "They are all easy to get, particularly the saintly ones."

The wedding of the rabbi's daughter had been the last big festivity held in Bolechow. For an entire week, people had eaten and drunk and sung and danced to the music of a *klezmer* band.[2] All of the town's Jews had been invited, along with hundreds of Hasidim who streamed in from near and far, from Lvov, Brody, Warsaw, and Kraków. On a large sandy plot adjoining the rabbi's house an imposing marquee had been set up, and inside it were row upon row of wooden trestle tables all covered with white sheets. Waiters carrying huge trays scurried between the tables. A mustached waiter beckoned to the two secular youths and showed them to a table loaded with delicacies: pickled herring, smoked salmon, gefilte fish, chopped liver, chicken, stuffed ducks, roast goose, strings of *kishke* sausage, potatoes roasted in goose fat, *tzimmes*, bottles of Russian vodka, French cognac, sweet wines, and *slivovice*, plum brandy brought especially from Prague.[3]

The men and the women danced separately, each gender in a different part of the marquee, with the young couple in between. The groom barely brushed against the beautiful girl whose innocence Munia Mehring doubted. Her face was veiled, and the hem of her long white dress trailed on the sandy ground. Her father, the Admor, sat on a padded armchair at the head of the largest table and watched the dancing. Then his *gabbai* (the person who assists in running the Admor's court) banged loudly on the tabletop with his fist, and people called out in Yiddish and German, "*Ruhig sein, ganz shtill! Ruhe!*"—"Be quiet! Silence!"

Everyone immediately hushed up, and the rabbi began to sing quietly. He stared into space, and the hundreds of guests, Hasidim and secular, followed the movements of his lips as if mesmerized. Gradually, his voice rose. Everyone in Bolechow knew the Perlov *niggun*, or tune, which was full of sadness. In the Middle Ages, it was sung in Ashkenaz. When the Jews were expelled from the principalities, they had hummed the melancholy air while trudging eastward. They kept on singing it after they settled in the foothills of the Carpathians. They had been living there, in Bolechow, for three hundred years now, each family under its own grapevine and fig tree, and on that clear, warm summer night, they were overcome by a feeling of oneness. The rabbi sang the tune alone, and until he signaled to everyone to join in, they were all silent. Not even a child's laughter broke the silence.

Then Perlov raised his massive frame and stood up. The crowd of wedding guests, who had been eagerly waiting for the sign, began to sing the wordless, ululating melody along with him, "Yah yah yah yah yah yah yah." Ullo and Mehring looked on, entranced. They would soon turn eighteen, and the Hasidic world of their forebears seemed to them like a foreign, peculiar, folkloric performance. But these two smartly dressed, handsome, strapping Jewish youths, Munia the communist and Ullo the Zionist, sat there riveted by the ancient Jewish ritual, although they no longer were a part of it.

The huge figure of Rabbi Perlov reminded Mehring of a childhood prank he'd once played. "Do you remember that trick with the lighted candles in the river?" he asked, and, of course, Ullo remembered. They had been six or seven years old when they prepared a little surprise for the pious Jews who were taking part in the Tashlikh procession along the bank of the Sukiel River.[4] It was the first day of Rosh Hashanah, the Jewish New Year, and the worshippers were preparing to cast their sins into water and thereby cleanse themselves.

The rabbi walked at the head of the group, followed by his flock, all singing the prayer "And You shall cast their sins into the sea." The weak mid-September sun was setting, and the air was cool. On the bridge, a few secular Jews stood and watched the procession. Two Ruthenian women crossed themselves. At the edge of the Deutsche Colony, some Germans observed the proceedings from their yards. In that moment of grace, it seemed that even if two angels had appeared and hovered in the skies above them, no one would have been surprised.

Rabbi Perlov was a man of impressive bulk, tall and broad. From a distance, one could not make out his facial features but could see only a gigantic *shtreimel*, a long black beard, and a heavyweight wrestler's broad shoulders draped in a long white silken robe that reached almost to the ground. He took small steps forward, and his body swayed as he walked. Although the Hasidic movement did not have many followers in Bolechow because most of the Jews were educated and progressive (in their own eyes, at least), everyone nevertheless respected the rabbi. Even the communists and the atheists greeted him with a bow of the head. Bolechow honored the leader of the Hasidim, and anyone who said a bad word about him in public or cracked a joke about him was soon put in his place. Rabbi Perlov was considered a great Torah scholar, by virtue of his book of commentary on the Psalms. Hasidim made pilgrimages to his court from afar. Sometimes even secular Jews asked for his help. When, for example, a disagreement arose over a commercial or financial deal or a quarrel occurred over a partnership or a debt, people didn't hesitate to turn to the Admor, to make him the arbitrator.

But at the Tashlikh ceremony, it was not permitted to even think about such matters. The rabbi's mind was elsewhere as he danced along ahead of his Hasidim, who were clad in their festive white kaftans, *shtreimels*, and white stockings up to their knees. Those watching from above, on the bridge, could see some black spots among the sea of brown fur. These were the simple woolen caps worn by the Hasidim who had come from Warsaw and Lublin to celebrate the High Holy Days in the rabbi's court.

Following the group of men who led the procession came their wives, keeping an appropriate distance and carrying prayer books. They wore long, dark dresses and kerchiefs tightly wrapped around their shaven heads and tied at the napes of their necks. After the masses of Hasidim, the less Orthodox citizens walked in couples. The men had donned regular European suits and fedora hats and the women long, colorful floral dresses, in keeping with the latest Viennese fashions, and hats of all colors and shapes, fur and felt, straw and silk. Ullo's grandparents, Reisel and David Graubart, and his parents, Rachel and Yerahmiel Kahane, were in this group.

It was a gorgeous autumn day. The congregation's attention was riveted on the red ball of the sun setting slowly over a clear horizon. At Rabbi Perlov's signal, the procession drew to a halt. Everyone turned to face the water and chanted loudly in unison, "I called upon the Lord in distress. The Lord has answered me and set me in a large place." The silence after this chant was broken only by a gull's shriek and the beating wings of a frightened swan. Everyone whispered the verses from the Psalms and the Book of Micah, shook their clothing, and turned their pockets inside out, some with sacred fervor and others symbolically going through the motions. Then they cried aloud, "Thou wilt show faithfulness to Jacob, and loving kindness to Abraham, as Thou hast sworn unto our fathers from the days of old."

At that moment, Ullo Kahane and a cluster of children were leaning over the water, right at a bend in the river. The boy was tense. This was the first time that he was taking part in a Tashlikh trick. He waited for a signal from Mehring, who was on the bridge watching the procession. Just as Rabbi Perlov's feet came close to the water line and the believers began to empty their pockets, Mehring was supposed to give his friends the signal. Ullo waited, with his body stretched out over the water, ready for action. He held a ball of straw with an unlit candle in it. Alongside him, also leaning over the water and holding candles stuffed into straw balls, were dozens of other boys and girls, the children of the middle-class and working-class Jews. The children of the Hasidim wouldn't dream of playing a trick like this on a High Holy Day.

At last, Mehring gave the signal by flashing a piece of glass to reflect the sun's dying rays. Thirteen-year-old Mottel was the first to strike a match and light the candle in his bundle of straw. After him, all of the other children did the same and launched the little bundles onto the water. All of the floating candles moved slowly to the center of the river, and then the current pulled them toward the worshippers. The flames looked like little stars. The river seemed to be ablaze with them, just as the congregation wailed from the river banks, "He will take us back in love; He will cover up our iniquities. And You will cast all their sins into the depths of the sea."

It was a pretty sight, but the Hasidim were shocked. Jewish law forbids the lighting of fire on Rosh Hashanah, except for heating food. Clearly, whoever had lit the candles and set them floating on the river had committed a grave offense. But tolerance was the rule among Bolechow's Jews. Each group respected the customs of the others, and the secular children were permitted to carry on playing while their elders stood before the Creator. No one was punished.

Ullo had fond memories of the prank and of Mehring, who had instigated it. As the eastward-bound train carrying him and his wife rattled on, he mused aloud, "Nushka, I wonder where Munia is now."

Nushka was sure that Mehring could take care of himself. He was a real survivor.

True," said Ullo, "he's strong and he's got a brain."

The two had met for the last time a few weeks earlier, when Munia had come home on vacation from the university in Czestochowa, the city of the Black Madonna. Ullo adored him. Every time they met, they argued passionately and shouted wildly at each other, sometimes cursing and even exchanging blows and kicks. But after each fight, when they were worn out, they fell into each other's arms. They were like brothers. They were both talented, sharp, precise, and outstanding in math and physics. They read a lot and were highly articulate in Polish. Mehring was an excellent soccer player. Ullo preferred tennis. They were very different in character and physique, but they complemented each other. Mehring was stout and blunt, sometimes to the point of rudeness, as well as impatient and quick to anger, but he was devilishly smart. Ullo was tall and gentle, always moderate and tolerant. Mehring was a hard-bitten man of principles, Ullo more of a pampered softy. Mehring was like a magnet to women, attracting and repelling them at the same time. He spoke openly of his love affairs.

"I prefer Christian girls. I enjoy myself with gentile women, but I live with Jewish ones," he once said to Ullo, who looked at him and blushed.

"When it comes to women, you don't behave like a Jew," Ullo once told him.

"And you are the epitome of normalcy," Mehring laughed back at him. Everybody liked Ullo, girls and boys, and he liked them all.

"All of Ullo's shortcomings were my virtues, and all of my shortcomings were his virtues," Mehring summed it up almost fifty years later.

On the Sabbath, Bolechow's younger set often gathered in the manicured public gardens and argued under the chestnut trees that surrounded the statues of the writer Adam Mickiewicz and the poet Juliusz Slowacki.[5] The youths stood in groups, munching sweets and sipping soft drinks that they had bought at Landau's kiosk. Three of them set the tone: Ullo, Mehring, and Gustav Reisman. In contrast to Mehring the communist and Ullo the Zionist and socialist who sympathized with the communists, Reisman was a right-winger and a member of Betar, the Revisionist Zionist youth movement. When Reisman and Mehring argued, the sparks flew. Sometimes they came to blows, and Ullo could barely separate them.

Reisman was adamant in his belief that all of the gentiles were no good. "Poles, Ukrainians, they're all the same," he said.

Mehring could not disagree more. "The Jews are no better than anyone else," he countered. He liked quoting passages from the *Communist Manifesto* by Marx and Engels, and he declared, "Communism is best because it's not racist. All men are equal."

He loaned Ullo a book by Lenin, *One Step Forward, Two Steps Back*, but Ullo was not convinced.[6] Mehring quoted from the writings of Bucharin and Radek, and Ullo said there was nothing new in them.[7] Then Ullo repeated the sayings of his own favorite thinker, the prophet Amos: "Thus saith the Lord: For three transgressions of Israel and for four I will not turn away the punishment thereof: because they sold the righteous for silver and the poor for a pair of shoes" (Amos 2:6).

Mehring was amazed: "In the twentieth century you quote the Bible to me?"

And Ullo retorted, "Thousands of years ago, a simple herdsman from Tekoa in Judaea summed up your whole communist doctrine in one simple sentence, and you come to me with Marx and Lenin."

All three boys dreamed big dreams, but none of them were yet ready to make these come true. They rebelled against their parents' faith, yet at the same time remained loyal to their families. Their talk was boastful, but they lived for the moment. They were practical—studies, exams, and careers were what really mattered. When they tired of arguing, they bathed naked in the river, played chess, or kicked a ball around. They rode their bikes to the resort town of Morshan and then took a train to Strij to see a movie. In Bolechow, there were movie shows only twice a week. Mehring told them about the nights he spent with Christian girls. They stood around chatting for hours, laughing and scuffling like fighting cocks: Zionism against communism, Revisionism against socialism.

"The Zionists are wrong," Mehring argued. "The land of Israel cannot solve the Jewish problem."

"Ullo thought that the existence of the Jewish nation must be protected. He thought that was the most important thing," said Mehring five decades later. "I argued that that was not so important. It was more important that people should have food to eat. I was argumentative, and he tended to shy away from confrontation, but I used to tease him." Mehring always started off with his opening argument: "Look. Ullo, in Poland there are three and a half million Jews, and fifteen million in all of Europe. Most of them, you'll agree with me, will stay here. So it's better to try to solve their problem here, in the place you call the Diaspora."

Ullo knew his friends' arguments and reasoning by heart, so he merely nodded indulgently.

"Theoretically," Mehring continued, "Communism is capable of solving the Jewish problem because it is not racist. It relates to all human beings equally and fairly."

Mehring called his theory "the communist model." In his first year at the University of Czestochowa, he began a relationship with the daughter of the head of the local Jewish community, a wealthy Orthodox mover and shaker, who was also a member of the city council. The young communist told his girlfriend's father about his beliefs, and the man was shocked. "I asked him," Mehring recounted to Ullo, "why he wanted all his wealth. After all, come the revolution, the communists would take it all away. The communists will make sure you do your work and you will be paid according to your needs and no more. Why do you need more than you consume?"

"Watch out that you don't lose his daughter," Ullo laughed, and he expounded upon the "Palestine model" that he had developed. The fundamental goal must be to preserve the integrity of the Jewish people, he said. "Mehring, where can the wholeness of the nation be preserved? No, don't answer me. Let me tell you. Only in the motherland can the nation be preserved, and our motherland is Palestine."

"In theory, you are great," came the rejoinder. "But let's see you become a pioneer in Palestine."

At this point, Ullo usually squirmed because Mehring had touched on a sore point. A few months previously, on August 23, 1929, in the Palestinian city of Hebron in the Judean hills, Arabs had attacked their Jewish neighbors, slaughtering fifty-nine of them and driving the others out of the City of the Patriarchs. In a single day, the ancient community of Jews in Hebron was wiped out. The Polish press reported extensively on the massacre, and Ullo, influenced by his friends in Hashomer Hatzair, resolved to realize the aims of the movement. He would go to Eretz Israel to join its pioneers. But the moment he revealed his goal to his parents, he sensed that he had presented them with a difficult dilemma. He suddenly understood that his mother's Zionist ideals were merely ideals, and her vision was only a dream. Rachel and Yerahmiel shut themselves up in their bedroom, discussed Ullo's plan from all angles, and arrived at a compromise proposal: "First of all, graduate high school, and then go to university and learn a profession; then you can go to Palestine and be a pioneer." Ullo accepted the judgment. If the Hebron massacre had happened a year later, perhaps he would have done what his heart told him to do, but this time he had to give in. His dream of being a *halutz* (pioneer) was put on hold, and his life was destined to take a different course.

Mehring claimed that he knew from the start that Ullo's parents wouldn't agree to part with their only son and that without their blessing, he would never dare to set out for Palestine. Mehring's father, the watchmaker, was also a supporter of the Zionist movement, but the boy knew full well that there was a great gap between ideals and practice. "They were playing mind games, paying lip service," Mehring asserted many years later, "but it was all talk, because none of them actually took steps to make their dream real and put their ideals into practice, and once they understood that this lethargy was fateful, it was too late."

The train crossed the Dnieper and soon left Galicia far behind. Ullo said he was sure that Mehring would escape from the Nazis, and Nushka nodded in agreement. "So will Gustav Reisman find a way," Lidka said. Gustav was studying engineering, and he had gone to Paris, leaving his family in Bolechow. Feder looked worried, and Ullo asked him why he wasn't relieved.

"We're out of there," Feder replied, "but perhaps we are getting into an even bigger mess. Do you think the Russians know that the Germans have invaded them? If they are digging in now to resist the Nazis, it certainly can't be seen from where we are."

It was true, on both sides of the railway tracks peace and quiet reigned, and there was no sign of military activity. Soon after they had left Stanislav and chugged off across the Ukrainian prairie, the boom of German artillery and the menacing shriek of the Luftwaffe's Stuka dive bombers could no longer be heard.

Tranquillity also prevailed inside their freight car, and the passengers seemed more like a serene group of travelers than refugees from the war. Outside, a breeze played in the treetops, the sun was setting, and everyone sank into thoughts about the loved ones who had been left behind. Ullo and Lidka thought about their parents in Bolechow, and Nushka wondered about her family, whom the communists had sent to Siberia. Exactly one year had passed since then. The Sobel family, along with thousands of Poles who had been declared "enemies of communism"—most of them middle-class Jews—had been forcibly transferred to labor camps in Siberia.

The journey from Galicia to Siberia had taken approximately four months. The refugees were transported in cattle cars. The train made slow progress, moving ahead for a day or two, then stopping and waiting for five days in the middle of nowhere, as it crossed Ukraine and the entire breadth of the Soviet Union, from west to east, across the Urals. The train carried just enough food and water to keep its passengers alive; they were exhausted and fearful, bleary-eyed, depressed, filthy, and far from sure that they would survive. From the district capital of Novosibirsk in western Siberia, they traveled on a spur of the Trans-Siberian Railway to the last stop, at Tomsk. Here the communist guards loaded the deportees onto wagons drawn by mules, and they moved slowly northward on unpaved roads through snow-covered forests. They finally arrived at the outskirts of a small town called Asino, fifty miles north of Tomsk, where the average annual temperature is around 34 degrees Fahrenheit. They stopped at a site where only the foundations of a long hut had been built.

"This is where you'll live," said the guards. "Those who build themselves a room will have a roof over their heads. Those who don't will sleep in the open, in the snow." Until then, the passengers had not been told where they were going.

Most of the younger men were given work cutting down trees, and Israel Moses Sobel, who wasn't fit for physical labor, spent the whole day guarding their coats at the edge of the forest. After a few days, he found permanent employment; the camp commander was looking for a bookkeeper to manage the camp's accounts and keep an eye on revenues and expenditures. Sobel was handed an abacus of wooden beads and given a chance to try out for the job. Until then, it had taken the camp management six days to prepare the monthly balance sheet, but Sobel did it in one day, and he was immediately named camp bookkeeper. He was given a place in the camp office, together with some of the other more educated exiles—the lawyers and the economists, who had come with him from Poland. Sobel soon won the confidence of the Soviets and served as an intermediary between them and the inmates and as an adviser to his fellow exiles.

Living conditions were tough. Each family had one room. There were five souls in the Sobels' room. Three beds took up the whole floor space. The daughter Zhizha slept in the same bed as her parents, and two cousins slept separately. Everyone worked, young and old, and with what they earned, they bought their meager rations and crude washing soap. If Israel Moses had been forced to work in the forest, he never would have survived. Many woodcutters died of exhaustion. Other inmates succumbed to diseases. The lavatories were holes dug in the frozen ground. There were no baths. Once a week, they heated water over a coal fire and washed from a bucket. Most of the time, everyone was filthy, hungry, and exhausted.

Thinking about them, Nushka heaved a sigh. Would she ever see her parents and her little sister again? The train continued its journey as Ullo remembered their last visit to his parents' home in Bolechow. It was on Thursday, June 26, 1941, exactly a week before the Germans occupied the town. Ullo, Nushka, Lidka, and Feder walked ten minutes from the train station to the Kahane home in the center of the Rynek. The communists were still running the town, and Yerahmiel was gloomy, but Rachel was optimistic. "A miracle will still happen," she told her children. Four days before the Germans moved in, on June 30, Ullo spoke to his parents on the phone for the last time. Years would pass before he knew about the ordeals and the suffering that they were forced to undergo.

The communists' train sped northeastward, leaving the Germans far behind. Ullo began to take stock. Nushka was with him, as were Lidka and Feder. Nushka's parents were in Siberia. His parents had remained in

Bolechow. May they survive the war, he prayed. Only his sister Sonia was unaccounted for.

"What do you think?" he asked Lidka. They had not had any news from Sonia for months.

"Don't you worry, Ullo," said Lidka, "Sonia will manage. You don't need a special education to understand the world. All you need is healthy instincts and common sense."

Ullo agreed. Sonia had excellent instincts, and she always managed to get what she wanted.

The train raced through Kiev without stopping. Ullo was still wondering: "I had twelve, or perhaps fourteen coaches, and the communists said they would tell me where to take the train when we reach Russia. But, of course, when we got moving there was chaos, shells were falling, and they didn't give me any more information. I had to decide for myself. What to do? My assistant Diekman wanted to go north, and I thought he was right, it was better to turn north. But Nushka insisted that it was better to get away from Russia. She said, 'Let's go south and get closer to the Middle East.'"

In the end, they reached an agreement. Diekman would take the train north, and Ullo would take his group south. "I still have the papers of the train that saved our lives," related Ullo fifty years later. "I have kept them with me all my life."

The train stopped at Kharkov, on Ukraine's eastern border. The expanded Kahane family disembarked, and Diekman continued to Moscow. In Kharkov, Ullo's group took a southbound train to the remote town of Armavir, between the Black Sea and the Caspian Sea. They rented a small house there and found jobs. They spent four peaceful months in Armavir, during the early stage of the German offensive against the Soviet Union, from the end of June until November 1941.

But then they had to move on because the Germans marched deeper into the Soviet Union, and, as Feder said, Hitler had given his army special orders to pursue Ullo and his travel party.

17

Judenrat

THE RED ARMY RETREATED EASTWARD, and with it went the secretary general of the Ukrainian Communist Party, Nikita Khrushchev.[1] Had the agronomist Naftali Backenroth chosen to leave, there can be no doubt that Khrushchev would have helped him and his family, but Naftali preferred to stay in Drohobych, where the family property was. It soon became clear to him that compared to the Nazis, the communists were like innocent lambs. But Naftali's spirits never fell. He had confidence in himself. Just as he had survived the Soviet occupation, he would manage under the Germans.

In the morning hours of June 30, 1941, as the Wehrmacht's combat troops marched toward Drohobych's center, the Ukrainians came out in droves to celebrate in the public squares. They pelted the Germans with flowers. Most of the Poles and the Jews, however, secluded themselves in their homes.

For the next three years, Galicia's Jews would belong to a new political entity that the Germans called Generalgouvernement—"General Government of the occupied Polish lands." In September 1939, upon the Germans' occupying Poland, the General Government was established and divided into four districts: Warsaw, Radom, Kraków, and Lublin. Immediately after the Germans invaded the Soviet Union, East Galicia was incorporated into the General Government and became its fifth district. The Nazis intended the General Government to supply the Third Reich with an abundance of Slavic slaves and to be a site where the mass extermination of European Jewry could be implemented. The SS (Schutzstaffeln—the special police force of the Nazi party) took charge of administering the liquidation

A Nazi stamp that was issued in 1941 to mark the occupation of Galicia's oil strip.

of Jews and at the beginning went to extensive lengths to segregate them from the gentile population. *Einsatzgruppen*, or special task forces, were sent to Galicia to kill large numbers of Jews, mainly old people, women, and children, who could not be used as laborers. The special German task forces used simple weapons—pistols, rifles, grenades, and machine guns. Their victims were taken to the forests and forced to strip off their clothes and then dig their own graves. In a few months the SS would seek more efficient facilities for the extermination process.

In Drohobych, the Nazis enforced the anti-Jewish decrees gradually. At first, Jews were made to wear armbands and were restricted from moving freely on selected streets. The Germans confiscated Jewish public and privately owned buildings. Occasionally, Jewish businesses and stores in Polish and Ukrainian neighborhoods were looted. Hooligans often beat up Jewish passersby. Because these incidents happened during the transition period between the communists' and the Nazis' rule, most Jews were caught off guard. They did not realize that the German occupation was not an ordinary occupation and that an extremely dangerous era had begun.

Just as the Germans had imposed their authority in each Polish town that they occupied in the summer of 1941, they did over the Jews of Drohobych through a Jewish council, or Judenrat. Although it would seemingly be advantageous for a persecuted community to have its own authorized representatives to negotiate with the subjugator, the Nazis made cunning and cynical use of the institution of the Judenrat to entrap the Jews in a tragic, inescapable fate. Tens of thousands of Jews were living in Drohobych and its environs.[2] Most of them were connected to the oil industry, and despite the nationalization of property carried out by the Soviets, the Jews' economic situation was good.[3] If the Jews had been given a chance to buy their lives with money, as had sometimes happened in the past, when they had paid ransoms to their persecutors, the Jews of the oil belt would have been able to afford it. But the Germans wanted more than the Jews' wealth; their main goal was to kill all the Jews, and the Judenrat served as an instrument to carry this out. Moreover, the heads of the German security services were very adept at exploiting the weak points of the Jewish community in order to expedite their liquidation.

The community of the Drohobych district had its share of these weaknesses, divided as it was into different factions that were linked by complex relationships. A raft of corruption incidents that occurred during the get-rich-quick period of the oil boom now burdened these relationships, creating a situation where there was less solidarity between members of the Jewish community than existed in other locations. Since the middle of the eighteenth century, the opportunity to quickly acquire a fortune had drawn entrepreneurs and investors to the oil belt, and they subsequently energized and fomented economic activity in that region. They also stirred up Jewish political life. The newly rich, some of them from local families and others recent arrivals, introduced a lifestyle that Galicia had never seen before. They built mansions, imported furnishings and foodstuffs from Paris, threw parties, and raised the ire of the more traditional and modest social circles in the community—most of whom were Orthodox and the others, members of the intelligentsia, Zionists, and socialists, who were disgusted by the ostentation and the extravagance. Over time, relations between these disparate groups had become very tense, and the ensuing confrontations only intensified the stench that emanated from the oil wells.

The German governor of the district gave a Ukrainian veterinarian the task of picking the members of the Judenrat, and he approached Naftali Backenroth, who asked not to be co-opted. Other people agreed to be members, however. The Ukrainian appointed Dr. Rosenblatt to head the committee and Dr. Ruhrberg as his deputy; both of them were respected members of the community.[4] The others were also old-timers, educated and well-off, including Doctors Gerstenfeld, Margulies, and Schmer, the latter a physician who was married to Naftali's sister Junya. Before the war, Schmer had been a popular figure in Drohobych. He was known to have refused payment from poor patients and to have given them food.

Naftali Backenroth understood the trap that the Judenrat represented for the Jews, and he demanded that the heads of the community refuse to join. He was not alone in this. In most Jewish communities, the Judenrat was a topic of sharp controversy and had its supporters and its opponents. In every city and town, some people rebelled against the Judenrat system and acted against it in various ways, without much real success. But Naftali was different.

Before the German security police and the Gestapo moved in, the German military took over and immediately demanded that the Drohobych Judenrat provide workers to gather the equipment the Soviets had left behind when they fled. Because Naftali knew German, one member of the Judenrat council asked him to be in charge of that ad hoc group of workers, and he agreed. Right after that, the German captain who was in charge of the hospital recruited Naftali to work in the laboratories. The officer was pleased with his industriousness and offered him sugar rations and cigarettes, but Naftali refused to take them.

Three days later, on July 4, the German security squads arrived. One member of the Gestapo was an Austrian-born SS man, the noncommissioned officer (NCO) Felix Landau, who was chosen to oversee the Jewish labor assignments and who became a central figure in establishing brutally insane relations with the terrified and confused Jewish community.[5] For his headquarters, Landau confiscated Villa Himmel, where the Jewish Home for the Aged had been housed.

The first thing the Security Police did was to reopen the prison, which was empty because the communists had murdered the inmates before retreating. After taking over in Drohobych in September 1939, the Soviets had rounded up "dangerous elements," which was what they called members of the bourgeoisie and politicians who had a right-wing outlook. Two Zionist leaders, Doctors Nacht and Edelsberg, were among the thirty-six Ukrainians and Jews who were imprisoned. In June 1941, as the communists were about to withdraw, they shot all of the prisoners and buried their bodies in the Jewish cemetery.[6] As soon as the Soviets were gone, local Ukrainians hurried to open the graves and exhume the bodies of their compatriots for reburial in

The deportation of Jews from Drohobych, probably at the end of 1941 (this rare picture is undated, and the photographer is unidentified).

their own cemetery. Some Ukrainian leaders accused the Jews of cooperating with the security apparatus of the Soviet occupation, with the Soviet secret police—the NKVD—and with the militia that the communists had set up, and these leaders vowed to take revenge. And indeed, as the Ukrainians who had been executed by the communists in Drohobych were being reburied, Ukrainians were attacking Jews in nearby Schodnica, where a pogrom was underway.

On the eve of the German occupation, some of the Backenroths who lived in Drohobych had moved to Schodnica so that the family could be together and feel more secure, Naftali said fifty years later. "Our relatives in Schodnica had always said to one another, 'Nothing terrible can happen to us because our family is strong and it's a small place and everybody knows everybody else.' But the Ukrainians in the village had been waiting for their chance. We knew them well. Some of them earned their living in our factories, and others sold us their crops. There was one Pole there, a pig butcher. As soon as the Germans came, he organized the first pogrom in Schodnica, and they killed about three hundred Jewish men."

Leon Thorne was a Backenroth relative who had moved to Schodnica. He kept one of the most important diaries written during the Nazi occupation.[7] He wrote it as if he had used his own blood as ink. He feared that at the end of the war, no Jews would be left alive, and he wanted to leave a written testimony behind. The pogrom began on July 4, 1941, he wrote, and on the day after it was over, half of the town's Jewish men lay dead in the forest.

Stella Backenroth-Wieseltier was another eyewitness. She related how the Ukrainian neighbors from Schodnica and from nearby villages, many of them previous employees of the Backenroths, gathered the town's Jews, and in order to humiliate them forced the young women to scrub the paving stones of the main road with toothbrushes. Then the Ukrainians marched the men to the Bronica Forest in small groups, where they shot or stabbed the men to death. Stella's father, Shmuel Leib, was saved by a miracle. While he was being dragged by the mob along with other men to the mass murder site, a Ukrainian neighbor pulled him out of the group of victims and sent him back home. Stella was taken to the forest the next day and ordered to help bury the dead.

On the Friday of the Ukrainian-initiated pogrom, Naftali Backenroth was in Drohobych. A messenger came from Schodnica and told him what was happening. He rushed to complain to the German captain he was working for at the hospital, and the pogrom was halted. The German soldiers did not actively participate in this first massacre.

Immediately afterward, the Gestapo unit in Stryj ordered the Drohobych Judenrat to provide twelve Jews to work as laborers.[8] Stryj is located less than twelve miles from Drohobych, to the southeast. "The Judenrat members were panic-stricken," recalled Naftali, "because rumor had it that the twelve were sure to be killed, but nevertheless I decided to act."

Naftali went to the captain again and asked him to have the order rescinded, but the German urged him to persuade the Judenrat to send the workers to the Gestapo in order to avoid a violent reaction. Naftali thereupon went to the Judenrat's Arbeitsamt, or employment office, on Sobieski Street and volunteered to head the work group.[9] He selected twelve men and women, and they reported to the Gestapo headquarters in Stryj. They were ordered to unload equipment and to clean up. They did the job quickly, and the Gestapo officers were pleased. They ordered the Judenrat to send the same group the following day.

Naftali used the first few days at work in the Gestapo offices in Stryj and Drohobych to scout the territory. He told his fellow workers to observe the Germans, to read the messages lying on their desks, and to remember every detail. He instructed the women working as chambermaids and cleaners to listen closely to the Germans' conversations. He then collected all of the information and analyzed it. He learned the structure of the local German military and Nazi organizations and details about the relationships among the commanders.

To maintain a satisfactory standard of living, the Germans required various types of service personnel. The Gestapo needed chambermaids, janitors, cleaners, gardeners, and handymen. The army needed technicians and engineers to operate and maintain the oil wells and the refining facilities. Naftali came to an important conclusion: he had to gather a serious group of skilled and diligent workers and tradesmen, independent from the Judenrat, and to supply the Germans with whatever services they wanted, at the highest possible level, thereby making his workers indispensable and possibly saving their lives and the lives of their families.

In the meantime, the Judenrat's employment office sent another group of fifty Jews to work for the Gestapo, most of them old, and not one who understood German. Naftali used the opposite tactic and recruited youthful, energetic laborers to his working group, which now numbered ten young men, to do cleaning and repair assignments for the Gestapo office in Stryj.

On July 11, a group of forty Jewish and Ukrainian women and men from the intelligentsia were arrested. The next day twenty-three of them were brought to Bronica Forest, forced to dig their own graves, and shot. NCO Felix Landau was one of the executioners. He kept a diary of his daily activities during his service in Galicia, and he copied some passages and sent them to his sweetheart, Gertrude. Here is how Landau described the murder of the twenty-three victims in his elementary German:

> We had to find a suitable spot to shoot and bury them. After a few minutes we found a place. Those intended to die were gathered with shovels to dig their own graves. Two of them were weeping. The others certainly have inconceivable courage. Strange, I am completely unaffected. No mercy, nothing. That's the way it is and then everything is over. The two women arranged themselves at one end of the grave ready to be shot first. As the women walked to the grave they were completely self-controlled. They turned backwards. Six of us had to shoot them. The task was assigned thus: three [would shoot] at the heart, three at the head. I took the heart. The shots were fired and the brains whizzed through the air. Two [hits] in the head are too much.

The public interpreted the execution of twenty-three civilians from the intelligentsia, many of them communists, as the customary punishment that the two warring factions—Nazis and communists—typically inflicted on each other. The execution was not perceived as a clear warning that the next targets of the Germans' merciless slaughter would be Polish civilians and Jews.

Nevertheless, an incident that occurred in Drohobych on July 22 opened the eyes of many unsuspecting Jews: members of the Gestapo beat up some of the Jews whom the Judenrat sent to do the routine daily chores at the Gestapo headquarters, and twenty-two of the workers walked out in protest. The Gestapo's officer on duty, Hauptscharführer (sergeant major) Felix Landau, was boiling with anger. He demanded a list of the absentee workers from the Judenrat, which tried to evade handing it over. In response, the Gestapo picked up ten Jews in the street, took them to Bronica Forest, and murdered them.[10] Later, Landau ordered that another twenty-two be killed, the number of laborers who had left work in protest. Landau himself burst into the Judenrat office leading a group of Gestapo men, and they shot twenty Jews with their pistols.[11]

Naftali was shocked at the Nazis' inhumanity but was also angry with the Judenrat. After the war, he told a Jewish inquiry committee (which was researching the Nazi occupation's activities) that he went to the Judenrat members and accused them of being responsible for the pogrom.[12] "I told them, 'The Germans are out to harm us and kill us, and we must try not to provoke them to kill more Jews than they intend to. Our people must not be allowed to get out of working. It won't happen with my people because they are hard workers, exactly as they have to be, and everything works the way it should.' That's what I told the Judenrat heads, and I volunteered to take responsibility for all the work that the Gestapo demanded from the Jews." The Judenrat agreed, and Naftali selected 240 workers and brought them to Landau's headquarters in the Villa Himmel. Then Naftali told Landau, "Now I am in charge of the group. You'll give me the list of tasks and the instructions, and I'll divide the work between these people. If anything goes wrong, I'll be responsible."

Felix Landau's life story was similar to those of many lower-ranking German and Austrian members of the Nazi security services, who grew up in simple neighborhoods among fragile families. His mother was an Austrian singer, who made her living working as a domestic servant in the home of a Jewish doctor in Vienna by the name of Landau. She became pregnant by him, and in 1910 their illegitimate son Felix was born. In the early 1930s, Felix worked as a trainee in a bank, and in his spare time he helped the leader of the Christian Social Party, Engelbert Dollfuss, who awarded Landau a decoration in recognition of his loyal service to the party. Later he joined the Austrian army and became active in the Nazi Party.

In 1932, Dollfuss was elected chancellor of Austria but was assassinated by Nazis two years later because he outlawed the Nazi Party and refused to support its plans for Austria to be annexed to Germany.[13] His former aide, Landau, helped to plan the assassination and was arrested and sentenced to three years in prison. In 1938, following the Anschluss, Landau enlisted in the Gestapo.

Naftali gradually learned much about the personality of this tough, stalwart Nazi and what made him tick, and he used this knowledge to improve the living conditions of the work teams that he had set up. Landau and Naftali often met on work matters, but they also discussed personal affairs. Landau kept his father's Jewish ethnicity secret from everyone except from Naftali, and when Landau's mother came to visit her son in Drohobych, Landau introduced her to Naftali. Years later, Naftali said that in order to save his relatives and neighbors, he was ready to negotiate with Satan.

Landau's superior was Captain Nicolaus Tolle, a Gestapo officer who was stationed in Stryj. Tolle was a Teutonic type who had previously served in the French department of the German espionage service, the Abwehr, where his chief task had been to keep an eye on German officers and officials and to test their loyalty. Officer Tolle despised the NCO Landau but needed him because of his familiarity with the territory. Leon Thorne wrote in his diary that the Judenrat member Dr. Ruhrberg gave money to Tolle and his servant so that they would show the Jews pity. According to Thorne, the attempts to save Jews by bribing Germans were carried out through a special section of the Judenrat that was set up for this purpose. It was headed by three men: Dr. Samuel Rothenberg, Nahum Petranker, and Moses Kartin. They offered the Germans cash, valuables, and scarce foodstuffs, but their efforts were in vain. The Germans took the bribes but continued to treat the Jews harshly and to kill them whenever they saw fit.

Naftali was careful not to get involved in bribery, preferring to take advantage of the complex relations within the Gestapo command. Thanks to the information channeled to him by his people, Naftali managed to instigate quarrels among the Germans and to confuse them. He understood, however, that spying on the Germans would be of only limited value, and he doubted that Landau would provide his work teams with a life belt. The Germans had received orders from above to liquidate the Jews, and the most that could be done was to postpone their fate for a short while. Naftali could only pray for salvation, but his fears came to pass sooner than he expected. On November 22, 1941, the first systematic mass execution took place, when 350 unemployed Drohobych Jews were killed in Bronica Forest.

"It was then that the mayor of Stryj, a Ukrainian named Kostinsky, came to me with a tall and pleasant German in civilian clothes; it was immediately clear to me that he was an aristocrat. He wanted to talk to me. I said, 'Go and get permission from the Gestapo. I am prohibited from talking during work hours.' That's what I said, but he ignored it and introduced himself. 'My name is Helmrich, and I am in charge of agriculture in this region.' We talked. He was very affable. I told him how I had organized the agriculture during the Russian occupation, and he proposed that I join his agricultural administration. 'You surely cannot want to stay with these murderers,' Helmrich said to me, meaning the Gestapo. It was now clear to me that this was a special man whom I was talking to, but I nevertheless didn't made it easy for him. 'Now I am a forced laborer of yours,' I said. 'The Russians never forced me to work. You are forcing me. I do not want to work with you and to be considered a collaborator.' Then Helmrich said, in precisely these words: 'But Mr. Backenroth, I want to be your friend. I have no interest in forcing you.'"

Eberhard Helmrich began to help Naftali and became his friend and confidant. Before the war, Helmrich had lived with his wife, Donata Hardt-Helmrich, in Berlin. In the mid-1930s, after the Nazis enacted anti-Jewish laws, the couple tried to make life easier for their Jewish friends and neighbors. When the Jews were boycotted and Germans were forbidden to do business with them or purchase their services, the Helmrichs continued to go to their Jewish doctor and to employ Jewish tradesmen. When Jews were barred from entering German shops, Donata went shopping for her Jewish neighbors. She applied for new ID cards three times, telling the authorities that she had lost them, after giving them to Jews so that they could save their lives using her identity.

For Naftali, happening upon Eberhard Helmrich was like meeting an angel. Without him, it is doubtful that Naftali would have managed to keep his work team going. As the officer in charge of agriculture and supplies, with the rank of major, Helmrich was high up in the military administration in Stryj.

Naftali was adept at taking advantage of the rivalry between the military administration and the Gestapo. Once when he was in Helmrich's office, Tolle, the Gestapo chief, came in. Tolle asked what Naftali's profession was, and Naftali modestly said that he was a gardener. Tolle knew that Naftali had studied agriculture in France, and was aware that Naftali knew that Tolle knew it. They had a normal conversation in a friendly manner, as if there was no difference between them, a Gestapo chief and a forced laborer. Fifty years later, Naftali reconstructed the meeting: "Tolle said, 'I know France well, and I'd like to talk to you about it sometimes.' I agreed, and we chatted about Paris. Of course, I wasn't interested in what he thought about Paris. Only one thing was on my mind: how to survive, and how to expand the work group. I devoted all my energies to that."

Naftali took advantage of this amiable chat with Tolle to mention that many excellent skilled professionals and tradesmen, men and women, lived in Drohobych and that he had already recruited three hundred of them, mechanics, technicians, builders and carpenters, economists and bookkeepers, technical school graduates, and industrial workers. If they were properly organized, Naftali told the Gestapo commander, the Germans could derive great benefit from them.

The other Gestapo staff members acted respectfully toward Naftali when they saw Tolle speaking to him in a friendly way. When their long conversation ended, the German offered Naftali his hand. His aides bowed, as is the German custom. Tolle said, "Auf Wiedersehen, Herr Backenroth."

But Naftali did not take Tolle's outstretched hand.

"You are refusing to shake the hand of a Gestapo officer?" Tolle asked in wonderment. "My hands have not killed Jews."

Naftali replied, "Herr Hauptman [Mr. Officer], it is not for me that I refuse, but for you. What will the Germans here think if they see the chief of the Gestapo shaking hands with a Jew?"

"Thank you for worrying about me," Tolle replied. "If you need any aid, I would be happy to help."

Tolle had made an offer, and on the spot, Naftali decided to settle accounts with the Ukrainians who had killed fifty members of the Backenroth family in the first pogrom. Naftali guessed that the Gestapo officer would not be unduly upset by a tale about the killing of Jews, so he did not stress the massacre carried out by the Ukrainians, but rather the property that had been looted. He told Tolle that immediately after the Soviet withdrawal, Ukrainians had attacked his wealthy family in Schodnica and robbed it of its property. This was not accurate, as by that time the family was impoverished. The Soviets had seized most of their property. But Tolle believed the story. In his eyes, murdering Jews was less of a crime than robbery. He listened to Naftali attentively and promised that the perpetrators would be punished.

Indeed, before many hours had passed, Tolle had sent three of his men, led by Felix Landau, to Schodnica. They rounded up the few Jews who were left in the village and then congregated in the square in front of the municipal building. They sent a messenger to bring the mayor, a Ukrainian who had been employed by the Backenroth family before the war. After a while, Ukrainians and Poles gathered in the square and Landau addressed them. He spoke in German, and Naftali translated into Polish, censoring some bits and adding others at will. Then the messenger returned and reported that the mayor had run away. Landau was enraged and slapped the messenger, who fell to the ground unconscious. The German asked the Ukrainians, with Naftali interpreting, to give him the names of the leaders of the pogrom. They immediately revealed three names, including that of the Polish pork butcher. The Gestapo caught the three men and imprisoned them.[14] The butcher was interrogated for two weeks. The Gestapo used a vicious dog to attack him until he died.

Now that Naftali had succeeded in having the leaders of the pogrom, the sadistic butcher and his two henchmen, punished, his ties with the Gestapo commanders became even closer, especially with Landau and his superior officer, Tolle. Naftali suggested to Landau that he set up a technical office in Drohobych. "You give me all the instructions in writing, and I will distribute the work accordingly," Naftali told Landau. His aim was to expand the working groups. He had organized fixed employment for tradesmen, mostly carpenters and metalworkers, and women who worked at gardening, laundering, sewing and repairing clothes, and bookkeeping. But he had not found jobs for engineers, agronomists, and chemists. Landau was flattered by the idea of having a "technical office" under him, and he agreed. To broaden the employment possibilities, Naftali suggested building projects and set up an architectural department. Then he started a school for gardeners and a nursery, where many young people were employed. He also began an agricultural school and appointed the agronomist Rosenmann as its director.[15]

Once Tolle decided that Naftali looked ill because he had lost weight, and Tolle suggested that Naftali eat with the Aryan workers in Stryj. "They get our leftovers, but there's enough for you," Tolle said. Naftali turned down the offer, though.

"It's not appropriate for the team leader to eat separately, especially when there isn't enough food," he said, and suggested that Tolle help him set up a kitchen for the Jewish workers. Tolle agreed, and Naftali asked him for a written order that would be submitted to Helmrich. Without the Gestapo's permission, Helmrich did not have the authority to allocate food to the Jews, but on Tolle's orders, a separate kitchen was set up in Drohobych for Naftali's working groups. This was independent of the Judenrat, which received rations from the Germans for the Jewish population and maintained a kitchen where they were fed.

In order for Naftali to get rations for his teams, his office reported directly to Helmrich's supply department. The process was more complicated for the Judenrat's kitchen. The Gestapo had to cross-check two lists: the Judenrat's list of names of all the Jews, compared with the Gestapo's own list. This put the Jews in a bind. On one hand, they wanted to keep the list as short as possible, so that fewer Jews would be liquidated, but on the other hand, doing this meant that the amount of food supplied by the Germans would gradually decrease. For its part, the Gestapo aimed to demonstrate that the list was getting shorter and that fewer and fewer rations were being provided to the Judenrat. Naftali operated outside of this framework. His kitchen was well organized, and his friend Helmrich's supply department gave it generous quantities of food, right up until the Germans retreated as the advancing Soviets drew near during the summer of 1944.

"When the kitchen opened," Naftali recalled, "a group of educated and well-off Jews, some of them bookkeepers or engineers, came and complained to me. They demanded that they be separated from the manual laborers [at this point on the tape of Naftali's interview, he laughs loudly], but I never agreed. 'Everyone eats in the same place,' I told them. 'What I say goes. This isn't a democracy [another laugh].' My friends always respected my opinions and obeyed my instructions. It was a dictatorship, and they feared me more than Landau. I insisted on discipline from all, there was no other way. Life went on under constant fear. We had to pay attention to every detail, to be alert; any small mistake would cost us dear. I was careful that mistakes weren't made, but although I was always on guard, I could not prevent everything."

One day, three Gestapo officers were walking near a forced-labor unit, and three girls, named Sternbach, Kupferberg, and Zukerman, waved at them.

"They waved at them and smiled," Naftali related, "and the Gestapo officers killed them on the spot, wiped them out just because the girls had smiled at them." Leon Thorne wrote in his diary that the killer was an officer named Günter.[16] The father of the Kupferberg girl was a barber in the ghetto. Just after Günter killed the girl, he ordered the father to be brought to him. After demanding a shave from the man, Günter then bragged that he had shot the barber's daughter a half-hour earlier.

Naftali learned that Günter had killed the girls without getting permission from his superior officer. "I was told that Landau objected after the fact. He wasn't angry because three Jewish girls were killed, but because they were killed without his explicit instruction. After all, the Jews of Drohobych were his personal property, and only he had the right to determine their fate. Now the order of the hierarchy had been broken—he was the only one who was permitted to kill Jews! I understood that many of our young people had failed to grasp the extent of the danger, and I issued instructions not to go near the Gestapo, to avoid contact, no words and no gestures."

The year 1942 drew to a close. Of course, no one in Drohobych knew that on January 20 of that year, their fate had been determined at a conference in a villa on the banks of Wannsee Lake. In this wealthy Berlin neighborhood, the German administration in charge of dealing with the Jewish problem had decided on the "Final Solution" (Endlösung).[17] In practical terms, on the ground, this meant that in Nazi-occupied Poland, death camps were erected and equipped with the means to commit mass murder.[18] Thus, late in the winter of 1942, the Germans began to implement the Final Solution.

The first major transport of Jews from Drohobych took place in the beginning of March 1942, when fifteen hundred people were assembled at the high school on Mickiewicz Street and were told by the Gestapo that they would be resettled near the city of Pinsk, in Belarus. Instead, they were transported to Belźec's extermination camp, where they were gassed.[19] Another *Aktion* ("operation," in German, in which Jews were hunted to be sent to extermination camps) took place in the beginning of August, and six thousand Jews from Drohobych were transported to Belźec.

Until the mass murders began in Belźec, the Jews had been confined to ghettos. They were debased, starved, and tortured, but nevertheless, most were still alive.[20] In the winter of 1942, however, the SS began to systematically evacuate the ghettos and send the Jews to extermination camps. For the first time since Jewish settlers had arrived in that region hundreds of years earlier, most of the cities and the towns of Galicia were empty of Jews.

On the battlefield, too, the outlook was bleak. On the eastern front, the largest and bloodiest arena of the war, there was no sign that the Soviets would be able to block the advance of the German military machine. The Wehrmacht reached the gates of Moscow, then conquered Stalingrad, Sevastopol on the Black Sea shore, and Salonika in northern Greece. Although the United States joined the war in December 1941 after the Japanese attack on Pearl Harbor, this had no immediate impact on the battlefields of Eastern Europe.

In retrospect, we know that by mid-1942, one ray of light could be seen at the end of the dark tunnel. A major turning point in the war had occurred at El Alamein in Egypt, when the Wehrmacht's Afrika Korps, commanded by Erwin Rommel, was first stopped and then put to flight by the British Eighth Army, under Bernard Montgomery.[21] But in Drohobych, the Jews who lived under the Gestapo's brutal regime of terror were unable to link the triumph in North Africa with a possibility of defeating the Nazis in Galicia. Throughout their centuries-long history, the Jews had never experienced such a terrible nadir of suffering and despair as during 1942.

18

Parting

IT WAS NOT JUST IN DROHOBYCH, where Jews were tormented by the Gestapo, that circumstances had changed for the worse. On the other side of the Eastern Front as well, where Ullo Kahane was leading his small group of refugees, a period of distress had begun.

The four quiet months that passed since the group had reached the Caucasus and settled in the remote town of Armavir came to an end. Feder took ill with typhus. His body grew weak and skinny, and his wife, Lidka, the doctor, had no medications. Nushka became dejected: not a word had come from Siberia, and she feared for her parents and her young sister, Zhizha. Above all, Ullo was worried about the Germans' advance. He and his group had a roof over their heads, and they had all found work, but once again the Nazis were drawing close.

"Do you believe that Hitler would chase us to this dump, at the end of the world?" asked Feder, and Ullo taunted him, "One day you're optimistic and the next day you're pessimistic; we can't go on like this. You have to decide and let us know who'll win the war, the Russians or the Germans." Feder replied with a cynical laugh, "It doesn't matter who wins; we'll always be the losers."

As the German armies rolled eastward, the Soviets retreated. On November 21, 1941, the Germans seized the city of Rostov, the gateway to the Caucasus. This mountainous area between the Black Sea and the Caspian Sea separates Europe from Asia. Hitler's strategy was to take the range and then drive his Army Group South in a pincer movement to the southeast and conquer the Middle East. The armies, under the command of Field Marshal Gerd von

Rundstedt, forged ahead toward the Caspian, while the Soviets, led by Marshal Semyon Budyonny, fought bitterly to defend the strongholds on the Don River. But the German forces broke through the Soviet defense lines and were only a few dozen miles away from Armavir. It was time for the Galician refugees to pack their meager belongings and set off once again.

"There were six of us. Nushka and I, Lidka and her husband, Feder, the engineer Est and his wife, Clara. She was in the ninth month of pregnancy and they were both terribly scared about how she would give birth and what would happen to the baby," Ullo recounted forty years later. "Feder was the 'theoretician' of the group and I was called the 'practician.' Only months earlier, Feder had said, 'Germany will never attack Russia,' and when his theory collapsed, his spirit broke and he simply gave up. After that, he couldn't see the logic in anything. By his lights, the end had come. 'There's no chance of surviving,' he said. And so I remained the sole leader of the group, and now I had to decide quickly because the Germans had crossed the Don and were already at the gates of Armavir." (Actually, the German lines were overextended, and a Soviet counterattack successfully blocked the German offensive and forced the Nazis to retreat. It was the first significant German withdrawal on the Eastern Front, and it removed the German threat to the Middle East. Of course, Ullo and his group could not accurately follow and comprehend the battle's ebb and flow.)

Ullo gathered his group and led everyone to the train station. They boarded a cargo train, bound for the Caspian Sea. It was heavily loaded with machinery from factories that the Soviets were moving so that it would not fall into German hands, and between the machines huddled hundreds of refugees. They laid the feverish Feder down on a blanket in a corner of the car, and Lidka wiped the sweat from his forehead. Several days before they left, the communist governor of Armavir had presented Lidka with a certificate of excellence. "For your deeds in the medical service in the harsh days the nation is going through," the citation read. Indeed, she was a devoted and effective doctor. Everywhere they stopped, she reported to the director of medical services and went to work. She believed wholeheartedly that communism would save the world and, unlike her husband, put her trust in Stalin—and in the Soviet winter. "Together, they'll beat the Nazis," Lidka told her friends. ("Stalin saved us from death!" Lidka said into the tape recorder in Tel Aviv in January 1988. "And if you do not promise me that you'll put an exclamation mark at the end of this sentence, I'll cut off the interview," the aged physician teased me. Lidka remembered her years in the Soviet Union as the best of her entire life. "The challenges were enormous, but, you see, we achieved our goals," she said almost fifty years later.) Lidka was stubborn and had a sharp tongue, but she made do with little, volunteered to take care of anyone in need, and refused to take money from those who could not pay.

Two important cities lay on the west coast of the Caspian Sea: Baku, the capital of Azerbaijan, and Makhachkala, the capital of Dagestan.[1] Ullo prefered Baku. He wanted to head south. "The whole idea of traveling south was based on an attempt to reach Palestine," he related years later. If he and the group managed to cross the border from Dagestan to Azerbaijan, they would continue to move south, then would try to cross the border from Azerbaijan to Iran and turn east to Tabriz or Teheran. Almost all of the hundreds of thousands of refugees fleeing with them wanted to go east, farther into Soviet Asia.

The road south, to Baku, was blocked, and the cargo train they were on had stopped at Makhachkala. Its population was about 120,000 at the time, but refugees were streaming in, like swarms of ants. At least half a million had crowded into the old city, near the small port, and some even estimated their number at a million. They all wanted to catch a boat and cross the Caspian Sea, to Turkmenistan in Asia, or at least to sail along the shore south to Baku. It was the end of November 1941 and freezing cold; the situation was close to desperate. Refugees were sleeping in the streets and waking up covered with snow. Some did not wake up at all. Feder was as thin as a stick, Lidka was worried, Nushka depressed, Clara groaned as her pregnancy neared its end, and Est, her husband, was pale from fear.

"Makhachkala was our lowest point," Ullo recalled. "Nushka sold a ring she'd gotten as a present from my mother, and we rented one room for all of us with the proceeds. We had no food. Feder was half dead from the typhus he contracted in Armavir, and Lidka caught it from him, and all of us were in one little room, with Clara pregnant, and me trying to be encouraging and keep up an optimistic spirit. Over the official loudspeakers, they announced that the Germans were entering Moscow.[2] Feder said to me sarcastically, 'You, the optimist, what will you say now? That's it, the Germans have won,' and I replied, 'You have to admit, at least we're living at a historical moment,' and Feder went on, 'People, quiet! Don't disturb him please, now he's witnessing a historical moment.'"

At that exact second, Clara was seized by labor contractions and Est begged Ullo to do something. "I went out and walked down the street," Ullo recalled. "I didn't speak Russian. I asked passersby in Polish and German where the hospital was, but no one answered me. In front of me I saw a wagon harnessed to a horse and a donkey. Ever seen a wagon harnessed to a horse and a donkey? The driver asked me in Russian, 'Are you Yevrei?' [Jewish]. It turned out that he himself was Jewish, and I talked Yiddish to him, but he gestured to me that he didn't understand a thing, that he came from the mountains, from around the city Grozny in Chechnya, and he talked to me in a strange eastern language.[3] Nevertheless, I managed to persuade him, and we took Clara to the hospital on the wagon. In the evening, Matthew was born, a whole and healthy baby. For some reason, in the documents it said he was born in Kraków."

Things got still worse. Six worn-out adults and a newborn baby were crowded into one room, with no food or income. Ullo walked the streets in search of food. All of a sudden, a stranger grabbed his arm and pushed him into a public park. He found himself in a huge crowd with hundreds of young men. The park was an army induction center.

"I stood and waited, not understanding what was going on. Time went by, and when I never came back to our room, they sent Est looking for me. He stood outside the park, observing the place, and they grabbed him, too. The two of us sat there, on the sand, and waited. It was impossible to leave. We didn't know where we'd be taken to, and we began to worry that we'd lost contact with the group. Suddenly, I saw Nushka standing behind the fence. She waved to me and I went to her. There was a big hole in one of my shoes, and she asked me worriedly how I'd join the army with shoes like that. I passed her the shoe over the fence, and she ran to a shoemaker's shop and got it fixed. Now I had whole shoes, and I was ready to be a soldier."

And so the entire day passed, the evening and the night, too. In the morning, the officers called Ullo, "Hey, you, come here!" Ullo stood by the desk and presented his papers—a Polish identification card and a lawyer's diploma. One of the officers began to scream at him and Est, "What are you Poles doing here? Why are you here? We are drafting Russians here!" Ullo and Est were suspected of being spies. Luckily for them, there was a Caucasian present who had lived in Lvov during the Soviet occupation, and he explained to the officers that they were Ukrainians, the Soviet Union's allies. Had the Caucasian not explained, it is doubtful that Ullo and Est would have come out of there in one piece. In the end they were thrown out of the park, and the enlistment episode was over.

Out of fear of similar conscription operations, they all remained in the rented room. Lidka and Feder slowly regained their health, while Ullo looked for ways to get out of Makhachkala quickly. Three times they traveled south to a border crossing called Khajmas and endeavored to persuade the border guards to allow them into Azerbaijan, but they were sent back each time. There was only one way left—crossing the Caspian Sea eastward, to Asia Minor—but the sea had frozen and only icebreaking vessels could navigate it. The situation was complex, yet precisely at this nadir in their trek, as the Germans advanced from the northeast and the roads to the south were blocked, a ray of light shone through the darkness. East of the Caspian, in the Samarkand region of Uzbekistan, there was an urgent need for doctors. Tens of thousands of refugees were crowded there in dire unsanitary conditions, and many had contracted typhus, cholera, and diarrhea. The authorities gave Lidka, the doctor, official permission to cross the sea with her family, in a little military vessel, which plied the route between Makhachkala and the Turkmenistan port of Krasnovodsk, on the eastern shore.

What better solution could they ask for? The entire group would be allowed to get out of range of the German threat, under the auspices of the Red Army, in the only icebreaker sailing the Caspian Sea in the winter. Any refugee in Makhachkala would have paid a fortune to get onto that ship, but an odd spectacle now unfolded in the group's room. Ullo ruled the idea out, point-blank. He stubbornly insisted on not crossing the sea, and because of his adamant stance, a sharp dispute broke out—Ullo against the rest. They said, "Let's cross now," and he said, "Never." They said, "Hitler is getting closer," and he said, "Correct, but we will go south by land, I'm not going east by sea." They bellowed, "We tried to cross by land and failed!" but he persisted, "We will not sail into Asia. We have no money and no food. We will not cross the sea eastward with no money and no food."

"The whole thing sounded crazy," Ullo recounted years later. "We had only about a hundred rubles, and they were charging five for a glass of water. There were rumors in the city that many of those who cross the sea eastward, to Asia, die of thirst, hunger, and disease. I heard that near Samarkand sixty thousand Polish refugees had died of thirst and sicknesses.

'If we cross the sea, we'll die in the desert, that's one reason, but mainly traveling east distances us from the way to Palestine.' That's what I told them, and they replied, 'The roads by land are blocked.' We each stood our ground. 'You're right,' I said, 'the roads south are blocked, but we'll find a solution nonetheless.'

"They said to me, 'Hitler is getting close. Don't be stubborn; he's twenty kilometers [12.5 miles] behind us,' and I refused to listen. They fumed at me, 'You're alone against the rest of us, taking a grave responsibility on yourself. How dare you stand against reason—there is no way to go south, the roads are blocked, and everyone, all the refugees, is going toward Samarkand.' That's how they pressured me and I remained certain of myself, I didn't give up. Then they asked what would become of the baby Matthew, and I hardened my heart. I didn't budge. In the end they declared, 'We're going,' and Feder, who was nine years older than me and very persuasive, said to them, 'Let's go and don't you worry, he'll come after us.'

"And in fact, Lidka and Feder packed their bags, left the building, and marched to the port, and after them, Est, Clara, and the baby, and only Nushka remained in the room with me. She thought I'd gone mad. I explained to her that Feder was wrong: 'He managed to talk them into it because he's very persuasive and effective, but Feder is wrong! You're going to die. By no means can you go by sea.' I tried to change her mind, but nothing helped. Nushka kissed me and left, quite certain that I'd join her right away, and I was left alone in the room, equally sure that she'd come back to me right away. I had no doubt at all, I trusted her completely, in my mind there wasn't even a trace of a thought that she might cross the sea without me. And indeed, after a quarter of an hour, Nushka returned to the room, and after her came Lidka, mumbling, 'We didn't want to leave you alone,' and after them, Est and Clara came back with their baby, and finally Feder walked in. Now they all agreed with me, and the whole affair became much more serious. From that moment on, I was solely responsible for anything that happened; after all, I had prevented them from crossing the sea! I was doomed if I didn't come up with a solution."

The Caspian Sea incident epitomizes Ullo Kahane's life. From that point onward, he took pride that he had been so insistent in Makhachkala in the winter of 1941. In his eyes, no other fateful decision that he'd ever made, before or since, was as important as this one. He was not a stubborn man. On the contrary, he was moderate and easy to persuade with reasonable arguments; his leadership of the group of refugees was never questioned. They accepted it naturally right from the start, and all of the decisions that he made had seemed logical to them, until this dispute and the brief rift it caused. It was not out of obstinacy for its own sake that Ullo refused to cross the sea, but out of cold calculation. To his last day, he believed that his foresight saved their lives. He was proud that he had not been deterred from following his convictions, even though his loved ones and friends argued so strongly against him.

19

A Perfect Riding Hall

IN THE FINAL MONTHS OF 1942, the Nazis completed their preparations to annihilate the Jews of Galicia. The Gestapo followed their detailed master plan with exemplary organizational skill and first emptied smaller ghettos and Jewish neighborhoods, then transferred the inhabitants to ghettos in large cities. Next, they cleared out those ghettos, packed the Jews into cattle trucks, and consigned them to the death camps.

In October 1942, the mayors of small towns and villages were given written orders to make sure that there were no more Jews in their communities, that they were *Judenfrei* (free of Jews). "The exceptions," the order stated, "are people in essential occupations, such as doctors, pharmacists, garbage collectors, and agricultural workers."

In early November, orders were issued to separate these essential workers from their families. The workers would wear armbands with the letter R, for *Rüstungsarbeiter* (armament employee), or the letter W, for *Werhmachtsarbeiter* (military employee). These employee certificates would be valid until March 31, 1943. (Because expiration dates were marked on the armbands, the Jews called their employee certificates *Totenschein*, "death certificates.") The workers' wives and children would be taken away for immediate extermination.

At the end of November, Gestapo headquarters instructed field offices to prepare to dismantle the work camps for essential workers and to eliminate Judenrat members everywhere. As the number of Jews had been reduced to the minimum needed to maintain the last ghettos, Jewish council members were not needed anymore. They had been exploited to destroy their communities, and now it was their turn to be sent to the extermination camps.

In Drohobych, however, one group of Jews was overlooked by the Nazi Angel of Death, at least for the time being. This group numbered approximately seven hundred souls, all of them gathered around the imposing figure of the agronomist Naftali Backenroth, who stubbornly insisted on protecting them. He adopted creative methods to thwart Nazi logic, which was based purely on force and domination. In a series of well-planned maneuvers, Naftali contrived to make the Germans dependent on his work groups, and he succeeded in creating an upside-down world in Galicia, with Nazis defending Jews. He knew how to organize the forced laborers for the benefit of the German war machine, and he took pains to supply amenities to enrich the stark lives of Gestapo and Wehrmacht officers—for instance, fresh vegetables for their meals every day and fresh flowers in their quarters. He tried to improve their service conditions, elevate their standard of living, and provide them with as much comfort as possible. Naftali's teams of gardeners grew fresh fruits and vegetables to feed the officers. The carpentry workshop that Naftali set up now built office furniture. Officers' uniforms were washed, the rooms of the police and the military encampments were cleaned, broken machines were fixed, and army and police cars were maintained.

As absurd as it may sound, Naftali Backenroth and his teams of essential workers put a little color into the drab military lives of the Germans who lived in the desolation of conquered Galicia. He and his men served the Nazis, pampered them, and succeeded, to a certain extent, in suppressing their sense of obligation to carry out the explicit orders that they get rid of all the Jews. Some of the German officers and officials needed Naftali's people to get their own jobs done. Naftali gathered information about each of them and used it in a "divide and rule" tactic. He became friendly with certain officers and created friction between others. Some Gestapo officers assisted Naftali's Jews, calculating that this would serve as an insurance policy in the event that the Germans lost the war and they faced trial for war crimes. Naftali identified their insecurity and tried to cultivate this fear in them.

Most of the Gestapo personnel were Germans and Austrians who sprang from the lower levels of society, and in their eyes Naftali had the characteristics that they had been conditioned to attribute to the Aryan type: tall and strong, blue eyes, and a brilliant brain. Naftali never groveled, and he looked the Gestapo officers straight in the eye.

In the course of his extraordinary endeavor, Naftali came across some good Germans, and he gave them a chance to demonstrate their humanity. One of his benevolent Germans was mentioned previously, Eberhard Helmrich, who was in charge of agriculture in the region and who assisted and supported Naftali's crew in various ways. Naftali identified lofty qualities in Helmrich, not only compassion, decency, and courage, but also a gift for improvisation.

Helmrich and his wife, Donata Hardt-Helmrich, took advantage of the shortage of workers that developed in Germany at the end of 1941, after Hitler had mobilized its massive armies. Hermann Göring, the second in command of the Third Reich, decided to bring in people from Ukraine, called east workers, *Ostarbeiter*, to work in Germany. Ukrainian men were recruited to work in the war industries, and Ukrainian women were chosen to be domestic servants in German homes where husbands were away fighting and their wives were raising children alone.[1] The Ukrainian women had to pay for their own train tickets to their places of work in Germany.

Helmrich and his wife devised a daring plan to save Jews that exploited this arrangement.[2] Helmrich found fair-haired Jewish women in Drohobych, gave them fake Ukrainian ID papers, and sent them to Berlin, paying the fare out of his own pocket. In the capital, his wife, Donata, found them work in homes where they would not come into contact with Polish or Ukrainian women, whose suspicions might have been aroused. Among these Jewish women from Drohobych was Hansi Warner, who worked in Donata's own home. Other Jews, both men and women, hid for short periods of time in Helmrich's offices in Stryj until he could fix them up with counterfeit documents. One of these was Theodor Goerner, the owner of a printing press. Another was Irene Miszel, the young daughter of a doctor at the Jewish hospital. Helmrich drove her to a nearby town in his military car, and when the SS became aware of her presence there, he drove her back to Stryj. For two weeks, he let her hide in his office until he managed to get the counterfeit papers that made it possible for her to escape. If he had been caught, he would have paid with his life.[3]

There were times when Naftali was unable to supply every German unit with all of the fresh food that they needed because the amount that his team of gardeners could grow in the Gestapo vegetable garden was limited.

His aim was to expand the amount of land planted in crops and thus strengthen the Germans' dependence on his workers.

"We supplied the Gestapo with vegetables from the garden that we cultivated in their camp," Naftali explained, "but I wanted to avoid envy between the German units, so I saw to it that the army officers and the officials also got vegetables in the winter." In a conversation with Helmrich, Naftali proposed setting up an agricultural estate near the town, at a place called Hyrawka. Helmrich agreed, and a team of Jewish agriculturists started a farm to grow vegetables and flowers. About 250 Jews were employed at the farm, some of them women.

"There was a good fellow there, a little strange, an artist at planning gardens," recalled Naftali, "and he took pains to be sure that the army officers also had flowers in their quarters. I brought Landau of the Gestapo to show him the farm. We rode there on horses. That was the only time I rode a horse during the war." Naftali could move freely throughout the region. He held an armament worker certificate, which guaranteed his safety, and he was well known to the Gestapo and the army officers.

Then a group of six Jewish farmers came to Naftali and asked him to find jobs for them in agriculture. They owned about twenty-five acres of farmland on the outskirts of Drohobych. Naftali arranged a deal with Felix Landau from the Gestapo, who managed the Jewish labor assignments. Together, they set up an "Agricultural SS Unit" (called SS Landwirtschaft, in German), and the Gestapo issued a special SS stamp to distinguish it from the other SS units. Its duty was to supply the Gestapo headquarters with fixed quotas of agricultural produce, particularly butter, vegetables, and fruit.

Helmrich helped to create the farms. He was in charge of agriculture in the district, and all of the large estates were listed in the land registry. The registry was headed by a German named Foss, who was subservient to Helmrich. He lived in Drohobych with his lady friend, a Polish countess. It was difficult for Foss to extend his patronage over the Jewish farms because the heads of the villages in the district strongly objected to their existence. Naftali thus had to move them to a distant village called Mainitz, near the city of Sambor, about twenty miles to the west.

The move to the faraway village was carefully planned, and the Jewish farmers and their families settled there secretly. Helmrich told Naftali that the Gestapo chief in Sambor was not a hard-core Nazi, and Naftali believed that it would be good to locate the Jewish farmers near him. If necessary, the

Gestapo chief would intervene and give the farmers his protection, Naftali thought. Helmrich also allotted a plot of land in the same village to Naftali's family, and they all moved there. Fifty years later, Naftali described the creation of the new SS agricultural entity with relish: "It was a Jewish SS unit, can you believe it? Jewish SS!" (On the tape during his interview, he can be heard chuckling when he tells this story.)

Indeed, the Jewish farm was an extremely unusual situation because the Nazi laws forbade Jews from living in rural areas and working in agriculture. "Of course, we put more than those six families onto the farms, by combining families that were linked by marriage," Naftali recalled with amusement. He noticed that some of the Gestapo staff members became friendly with the Jewish farmers. Nazi propaganda had taught them that Jews were avaricious middlemen, speculators, merchants, and financiers. In the Nazi worldview, there were no productive Jews. And lo and behold, a new type of Jew had appeared, one who did not fit the mold they had made for him.

But Naftali was soon called back to the city because in Drohobych and its surroundings, the hunt for Jews was at its peak. The local Gestapo unit carried out one Aktion (the German word for operations that rounded up Jews for annihilation; the Jews called them *aktzias*) after another. The Gestapo used the Judenrat to supply them with lists of Jews and mobilized the Ukrainian militia and sometimes Wehrmacht units to round up the Jews. The Gestapo headquarters in Stryj coordinated the schedule that determined when people were evacuated and consigned to the death camps. The orders came from Lvov to Drohobych by telex, and when that telex machine broke down, Naftali made sure that it wasn't repaired for as long as possible. Even when it was working, he could exercise some control over the flow of messages because the operator was a member of one of his teams. In most cases, Naftali had prior knowledge of the times of the next Aktion.

One message to Landau that reached Naftali first said, "Following the decision on the 'Final Solution' it is inconceivable that you should be employing 700 Jews. We order you to recruit workers from the unemployed Ukrainian population, and to cancel the employment of those Jews who are not experts."

Naftali hid the message and began to improve the skills of his people. He called all the builders, put them through the German tradesmen's exams, and then gave them all experts' certificates, which entitled them to the status of "armament Jews," *Rüstungsjude.* He worked without rest to find things for his people to do that would make them indispensable to the army and the Gestapo, and Landau cooperated. He was eager to broaden his domain of control, but this led his colleagues to give him despotic nicknames behind his back, such as "King of the Jews."

Naftali was a creative thinker. "We knew that Landau was an inveterate horse lover, and we offered to build a riding hall for him," Naftali recalled. His engineers found a suitable spot, and a Jewish architect named Karol designed a big project: a well-equipped riding hall with offices and restrooms, all surrounded by gardens. The plans called for the Jewish writer and artist Bruno Schulz, a resident of Drohobych who enjoyed Landau's protection, to decorate the walls with paintings of riding scenes.[4] Landau was very enthusiastic. A date was set for the ceremony to lay the cornerstone, and in the commemorative scroll Landau was given all of the credit for the idea and its implementation. "We never mentioned the Jewish workers in that document, only the Germans," Naftali said.

A touching scene preceded the official ceremony. While the Jewish workers were waiting for the Germans to come and lay the cornerstone, Naftali suggested that each worker write a note saying what he felt at that moment and throw it into the foundation pit. Some wrote wills, others described their situation and their hopes and bade farewell to their families. Naftali's brother-in-law, the physician Schmer, threw his diary into the pit. Several workers wrote harsh critiques of the Judenrat's behavior. The most emotional note was composed by another Backenroth relative, Leon Thorne:[5]

> If somebody reads these words some day, it is important to proclaim that in the future and under normal conditions, no member of the Judenrat should be elected to a representative position. Most of them are scoundrels and corrupt, and have disregarded the miserable plight of their brethren, and if, by chance, one or two of them were more sensitive than others, they too soon changed their minds, and even when they acted on behalf of their brethren, they did so not out of the goodness of their hearts but for personal reasons.

Thorne addressed his message to any of Drohobych's Jews who might be saved from the Nazi hell, when and if the Third Reich collapsed. The message could explain why in June 1941 Naftali made his dramatic decision to depart from the Drohobych Judenrat's method of management and initiatives and go in a different direction. He would independently create an enterprise to rescue himself, his family members, his friends, and every Jew who was able to join him.

When the riding hall was completed, it was a great success among the Germans, and word of its existence spread. One of Heinrich Himmler's personal representatives in Galicia was sent to inspect it.[6] When he arrived in Drohobych, he asked to meet "the Jew Backenroth," but Naftali managed to avoid him. There were hundreds of Jews working for the Gestapo at the time, and Naftali feared that his meeting with a senior Nazi might jeopardize the lives of these workers.

"They took him to the riding hall that we built and gave him a horse," Naftali recalled, "and he rode around jumping over the obstacles. Landau was happy."

In the ghetto (which was a defined territory, but its area was not fenced), people were starving and dying of exhaustion, but Naftali's work teams had their food supplied by Helmrich.[7] "In our separate kitchen the food was divided into portions," Naftali said. "Those employed in hard labor received larger portions than the office workers, and sometimes we would switch jobs, in order to avoid grumbling."

One day Landau murdered a Jewish gardener. Naftali saw it happen. "It was a summer's day, and a certain German Jew from our gardening group, by the name of Fliegner, a very thoroughgoing man, rather slow, was working in the nursery. He was working seriously, planting saplings, slowly but very steadily, and Landau was there and watched him for a few minutes from the villa that he used for his residence, on the main square of Drohobych, next to the Church of the Holy Trinity. Villa Landau, they called it.[8] In Landau's opinion, Fliegner was too slow, so Landau stood there and aimed his pistol at him, pulled the trigger, and killed him on the spot. But that was an isolated incident. In our groups, there were two such events—Fliegner and the three girls."[9]

Leon Thorne described Fliegner's shooting in his diary. In his version, Landau was with his mistress, Gertrude Segel. She felt like trying out her shooting skills and took Landau's gun, fired a few shots at Fliegner, and missed. Landau took the pistol from her and shot Fliegner in the head. Naftali immediately went to protest to Landau, and his response was harsh: "What are you complaining about? Others are killing all the time, and I killed one Jew." Furious, Naftali traveled to Stryj to tell the new Gestapo commandant Hans Block about the killing. He responded, "Landau killed a Jew without an order, and that is a grave matter. I'll handle it."

Block disciplined Landau by banishing him to the Gestapo headquarters in Lvov. Then Naftali regretted what he had done because his enterprise had lost one of its most important channels of communication to the Gestapo office. Many years later, Naftali was still sorry for his mistake: "After all, I had tried all the time to make Landau feel important, and despite his lowly NCO's rank and the fact that he had no supporters in the Gestapo, they envied him—and I knew all this because I had organized constant surveillance of him and all the others, I surrounded the Gestapo personnel with chambermaids, and I saw to it that all the information they gathered came to me, the messages that arrived and scraps of gossip and in particular I followed the requests for workers—they came straight to me, and now with my own hands I had handed Landau's head to Block and eliminated the most important source of information."[10]

Having Landau removed from Drohobych was indeed a foolish act. Landau had been better than any other Gestapo man for Naftali's Jews, but Naftali realized this too late. Now he could do nothing to get Landau back to Drohobych from Lvov. "I parted with him cautiously," Naftali recalled. "I thought that he might acquire some power in his new job in Lvov and that he may be able to influence things in Drohobych."

Naftali was wrong because at that time the commanders of Lvov's security police (Sicherheitspolizei, SIPO), to which the Gestapo offices in the region were subordinate, was particularly interested in the Jews working for the Gestapo in Drohobych and Stryj and was pressing for them to be replaced by Ukrainians. Landau's successor as Gestapo chief in Drohobych, Karl Günther, came to Naftali and said, "Backenroth, we can't keep so many Jews at work here." Naftali began to look for other essential jobs. He assigned some of the people to set up a brick-making plant, but that wasn't enough, so he went to the German who was in charge of construction at the Kolomyya refineries and persuaded him to take over an entire Jewish technical team. Dozens of engineers, architects, and draftsmen moved over to the refineries.

While this was happening, the extermination process continued, and the *aktzias* became more frequent. The Drohobych Judenrat was ordered to come up with lists of "unessential" Jews, and for the time being, Naftali's teams were exempt from deportation. Now Naftali was working against the clock. If he could only manage to delay the plan to expel the Jews of Drohobych, he just might be able to save his people. Naftali was not indifferent to the fate of all the other exhausted and hungry Jews who still resided in the ghetto area, but he knew that he could not save everybody. His people were relatively young and well fed and held armament-worker certificates. He was sorry for the old and the unemployed but had to make a choice. The selection was rough, he knew it from the beginning, but his excuse was simple: in an insane situation like that, one has to give precedence to the individuals who have a better chance of surviving.

Meanwhile, on the front, events worked to Naftali's advantage because the German army's advance into the Soviet Union's territory had been blocked, and a decisive shift in the war was rapidly approaching. But the Nazis' drive to destroy the Jews knew no respite. Naftali realized that to save the handful of people who had gathered around him, he had to show the SIPO and the Gestapo that these Jews were indispensable to the German war effort. Most of his groups worked for the Gestapo, and he could see that the number of jobs at the Gestapo headquarters was limited.

Therefore, Naftali focused on the refineries. Oil was the Germans' top priority, and anyone working in oil could easily obtain essential worker status, like the "armaments Jews." They used to call an oil worker's certificate an "iron letter" (*Eisenbrief*, in German), and it was like an insurance policy. Some of Naftali's crewmembers had been among the top workers in the oil industry, and he had excellent connections with the managers of the Drohobych refinery. "I had placed the four senior engineers there myself, all Jews, of course," he recalled many years later. "I had an advantage there because I knew every nut and bolt in the place; after all, it had belonged to my family."

Naftali went to talk to the director of the Drohobych refinery, Haftsmann, and asked him to employ three hundred Jewish workers. "He was a member of the Nazi Party," said Naftali, "but a decent man, and he didn't turn me down. He just said he'd consult his engineers." After Haftsmann had discussed the request with his team, Naftali was told that a senior Jewish engineer, whose name he didn't want to mention, had said to Haftsmann, "What is with you? Before the war they [the Backenroths] never employed three hundred Jews at the refinery. Why do you need so many Jews?" That Jewish engineer, who is no longer alive, could have caused terrible damage, but Haftsmann did not listen to his advice. He took on 280 Jews, and many of them survived the war.

There were other oil plants spread over the oil belt area, among them the Galicia, Gross, and Polmin refineries, where skilled Jewish workers were employed. Many Jews also worked for the Carpathian Oil consortium, whose headquarters were at nearby Boryslav. Carpathian Oil was run by a German, Berthold Beitz, an exceptional German official whose sense of humanity was exemplary in Holocaust history.[11]

Naftali admired Beitz.[12] They bore an outward resemblance and had a similar way of thinking. Like Naftali, Beitz was authoritative, extroverted, sociable, and very open. Beitz was a handsome, strapping man. With his staccato, rapid-fire speech, he had an extraordinary power to sway people.

Born to a Protestant family in Pomerania in eastern Germany, Beitz had studied oil economics.[13] His father was a bank official. When the war broke out, young Berthold was working in the Hamburg office of the Royal Dutch Shell oil company.

In the summer of 1941, a short time after Germany invaded the Soviet Union, Beitz's grandfather, a Nazi Party member, invited him to a dinner at the Villa Hugel near Essen, the headquarters of the Krupp industrial concern.[14] Gustav Krupp, the owner of this company in Germany, helped the Nazis to reach power and then, during the war, was numbered among those closest to the Nazi elite.[15] The guest of honor at the dinner was Reinhard Heydrich, the deputy of Gestapo chief Heinrich Himmler. Heydrich reported to the guests that the German army had taken over the oil refineries in Galicia. The national war machine needed every drop of oil, he said, and to that end, skilled manpower was required to operate the refineries. Beitz responded eagerly. He was twenty-seven. Although Beitz had never joined the Nazi Party, the German administration of occupied Poland, known as the Generalgouvernement, appointed the young economist to a senior position: general manager of the Carpathian Oil Company in Boryslav.[16]

In July 1941, Berthold and his wife, Else, settled in Boryslav. The new manager's task was to step up fuel production. At that time, long columns of German troops were rolling into the Soviet Union, and the demand for fuel increased each week. The Carpathian Oil Company employed approximately thirteen thousand workers. About twenty-five hundred of them were Jews, a fifth of the workforce. Most of the Jews worked in marketing, administration, and some of the technical departments that specialized in chemistry and engineering.

That summer, under pressure from the Gestapo, the management of the company fired most of the Jews, but by October, fuel production was down, and without the Jews, it was doubtful that it could be brought back up. The Nazis therefore bent the rules, and most of the Jews got their jobs back. The Jewish neighborhoods in the towns of the oil belt had not yet been declared ghettos and had not been sealed off with fences and barriers. (As a rule, the Gestapo assigned the Ukrainian militia the task of ensuring that Jews never left their neighborhoods except to go to work.) There had not yet been any *aktzias.* But every now and then, groups of a few dozen Jews whom the Nazis said were intellectuals or communists were taken into Bronica Forest, where they were shot.

At first, Beitz was indifferent to the fate of the Jews, until the Gestapo began to organize transports by train to the Belźec extermination camp. The first such operation that the young refinery director witnessed took place in early August 1942. The Gestapo had ordered that the children, the cripples, and the ailing be shipped out. The Germans were extremely violent when evacuating the children of the Boryslav orphanage. Beitz watched children being thrown out of the windows and others forced to march barefoot down the street to the train station. He stood near the wagons and saw a woman clutching a little girl to her bosom. The child couldn't stop coughing. "I said to the SS officer who was guarding the group that he ought to find a doctor as quickly as possible," Beitz said after the war. "Where they are all going, they won't need a doctor," the officer replied with a guffaw.

The Nazis' brutality and victimization of the innocent appalled the young German, particularly one incident when an SS soldier shot a woman carrying her child. "We watched from morning to evening, as close as one can get, what was happening to the Jews of Boryslav," he recounted. "When you see a woman with her baby in her arms being shot, and you yourself have a child, then your response is bound to be completely different."

The military government gave Beitz wide authority to employ any worker who could help the war effort, and he decided to use that authority to save Jews. "I should have employed qualified personnel. Instead, I chose tailors, hairdressers, and Talmudic scholars and gave them all cards as vital 'petroleum technicians.'"

Indeed, many of the Jews whom Beitz recruited were unskilled. Some of them were incapable of working due to weakness caused by starvation. "I went every day to the station to grasp several young men from death. I could have selected a better-qualified force."

As time went by, the repulsion that Beitz and his wife, Else, felt at the Nazi atrocities only grew, as did their empathy for the victims. Unlike most Germans, they refused to turn a blind eye to the Nazis' cruelty. The Beitzes' world outlook was fundamentally humanist: in the presence of the Jews' suffering, they felt it was their duty to provide aid, comfort, and moral support, even in mundane matters.

In August 1942, Beitz granted armament-worker documents to some 250 Jews who were due to be transported to Bełźec. "Beitz saved them from certain death," said Naftali, "and many of them survived the war." In some cases, Beitz himself went to the train station and took Jews and Poles off trains that were about to leave for Bełźec. Once a Jewish woman who worked as a secretary in the oil company's administration and her elderly mother were put on a train heading to the extermination camp. Beitz climbed onto the train car and took them both off, but the Gestapo insisted that the old woman was not fit for work and put her back on the train. The daughter told Beitz that she wanted to join her mother. "We never saw them again," he said after the war.

Sometimes Beitz allowed fugitive Jews to spend a night or two in the company management's offices. In one case, he and his wife hid a Jewish child in their home.

"I had no intention of initiating resistance to the regime or helping the partisans," Beitz explained. He stressed that he had no desire to be a hero. But with the passage of time, he and his wife found themselves in situations in which they were compelled to break the Nazis' laws. Some German colleagues mockingly called Beitz a "Jew-lover" (*Judensfreund*) or a "Pole-lover" (*Polensfreund*) and threatened to denounce him to the Gestapo.

At the end of 1942, Carpathian Oil's Jewish forced laborers and their families were living in two special work camps. The one in Drohobych had about a hundred Jewish inmates, and in Boryslav there were about fourteen hundred. They wore armament-worker armbands bearing the letter R, which granted them a certain degree of immunity to the *aktzias*. Scores of the camps' inhabitants were not genuine armament workers and had sneaked into the camps illegally to avoid being selected for extermination. Beitz tried to provide them with essential-worker documents. He also helped many other Jews who lacked that document to hide during *aktzias*.

Beitz was in charge of both camps. In order to remove a Jew from one of them, the Gestapo needed his authorization, which made it easier for him to protect the workers. There was a constant struggle underway between him and the Gestapo chief in Boryslav, Lieutenant Friedrich Hildebrand, who demanded that Beitz employ fewer Jews.[17] Nevertheless, Beitz increased the number, but he also made sure to cultivate a friendship with Hildebrand. The two played tennis and hunted together. Their social camaraderie ended up benefiting many Jews. Sometimes sources inside the Gestapo informed Beitz in advance before an *aktzia* took place.

The Beitz family in Germany had connections with top Nazis, among them apparently Josef Goebbels, the Nazi propaganda chief and one of Hitler's closest associates. In Boryslav, it was rumored that these connections to the upper echelons protected Beitz from being harassed by the local Gestapo officers. (Beitz himself never confirmed these rumors in the interviews that he gave after the war.)

At the end of 1942, the *aktzias* and the selection procedures (*selektzia*) became more frequent, the latter process to determine which Jews the SS considered dispensable and which were still fit for work. Beitz was forced to make compromises. A few times he had to give up unskilled Jewish workers in order to hire skilled workers in their place.[18] He constantly walked a fine tightrope. On one hand, he was obliged to increase oil production, and on the other, he was trying to add Jews to the work roster. He effectively exploited the contradiction between the Gestapo's lust to destroy more Jews and the German army's thirst for fuel, in order to save Jews by using them to bolster the war effort.[19]

Once, in early 1943, the Gestapo summoned Beitz for an interrogation that could have cost him his life. A Jewish brother and sister had been caught on a train to Hungary, carrying the papers of an Aryan employee of Beitz's firm bearing his signature. The employee ID documents had been forged by a Jewish underground group (headed by a man named Zwi Heilig) on blank forms belonging to Carpathian Oil. Beitz was questioned at the Gestapo headquarters at Dessau and charged with assisting Jews, but in a stroke of good luck, the investigator turned out to be a colleague who remembered Beitz from his student days. The case was dropped.

In March 1944, Beitz was mobilized and sent to the Eastern Front. At that time, perhaps 800 Jews worked for Carpathian Oil. During the last months of the war, many of them were sent to the extermination camps, but at least 250 survived.

Just as Beitz departed, the Gestapo in Drohobych was ordered to complete the ghetto's liquidation and to send all of the Jews to the camps. At the last moment, Naftali managed to erase a hundred names from the list of those to be evacuated from the ghetto. By this time, his work groups numbered more than a thousand Jews. The Gestapo chief, Block, made a special effort to delay the transport of Naftali's people. When the last Jews of the ghetto were assembled for the final shipment to Belźec death camp, Block sent the officer Karl Günther to collect forty Jewish workers whose teams worked at the Gestapo headquarters. Then Block erased their names and their families' names from the liquidation lists.

At that time, Naftali's nephew George had been living with his family. He was twelve. When the Germans evacuated the ghetto in Kraków, Naftali's sister Sabina put her son in the hands of a gentile Polish friend and had him sent to her brother in Drohobych with a letter. "We are sharing the fate of all our brethren," she wrote before being transported to the death camp. "I pray to God that He will protect you and my son."

When the Gestapo, accompanied by a Wehrmacht unit, came to the ghetto to carry out the evacuation, Naftali's wife, Anna, told Günther that she had two children, Yehuda (her real son) and George. George had dark skin, however, and Günther doubted that he was her son. The brave boy understood the situation, and he said to Anna, "You go with Lucien [that's what they called her son Yehuda], I'll stay in the ghetto." Günther insisted that George was not a Backenroth. and Naftali rushed to the Gestapo office and told him the truth.

"George is my sister's son," Naftali said, "and he is more important to me than my own son." Günther agreed that George would stay with the family.[20]

All of the Jews in the Drohobych ghetto were sent to the death camps, but Naftali's group remained at their workplaces. The Germans invited Naftali to live in the Gestapo compound, but he preferred to stay with his engineers' group in a cellar at the Nafta company's oil fields.

"I preferred living in the Nafta area because that's where I was born, and I knew the territory. I could move freely between the refinery and the Gestapo headquarters. At that time a strange thing happened to me that shows how bizarre life was. Günther had a Polish woman friend who had a pedigreed bitch that was in heat. There were not many dogs of that breed in the area, and Günther came to me and asked me to find her a mate, in order to preserve the purity of the race [on the tape of his interview Naftali laughs]. I told him that Foss, the head of the land registry office, had a dog of that breed, and I tried to make the match, but Foss was insulted by the idea and said, 'You want me to bring my dog to the Gestapo? Never!'

"I tried to persuade him and told him that the bitch wasn't Günther's but his Polish girlfriend's and that she was kind to animals. She bred horses and dogs, I told him. But Foss was obstinate and refused point-blank. Then he changed his mind, but the dog wasn't interested. Nothing could be done. Two days later, Günther came to the cellar at Nafta at five in the morning and woke me up and said, 'My friend's bitch has disappeared. Go look for it at Foss's place.' I said, 'Wait until nine o'clock. There's no need to bother Foss at five A.M.,' but Günther ordered me to go and look for the bitch right away. I went to Foss's home. He lived in Schodnica, in the house that had belonged to the Gerstenberg family, Jews, relatives of ours. There was a guard at the gate. He let me in, and indeed I found the bitch there. After that, Günther looked upon me as a wizard, who had succeeded in mating the dogs and preserving the purity of the race."

20

Ullo's Best School

IN THE PORT CITY OF MAKHACHKALA, on the Russian part of the western shore of the Caspian Sea, the situation was grave. The icebreaker had weighed anchor and sailed eastward with hundreds of refugees on board. But Dr. Lidka Feder and her little band had remained behind, all because her brother, Ullo Kahane, stubbornly insisted on trying to find a way south to Azerbaijan. Then he could follow his plan of traveling to the Middle East.

Everyone in the group felt hopeless and miserable after the quarrel. Why had they given in to Ullo? The vanguard of the German forces was only 12.5 miles away. If the small group of refugees from Galicia didn't act immediately, they would fall into Nazi hands. What's more, a typhus epidemic raged in Makhachkala. Feder already had the disease, and Lidka had caught it from him. She lay feverish and groaning on the floor. The group made an urgent call to her colleague Dr. Davidson, also a refugee from Galicia, but he forbade them to take her to the hospital. "She's likely to die if she goes," he said. "She's better off here in this room." Yet they didn't have enough food with them. Clara and Est's baby, Matthew, was growing weak.

Ullo searched for a solution. Ever since he had adamantly refused to board the icebreaker and the group had reluctantly stayed with him, he felt responsible for finding a way out. For a whole week he vainly tried to find a crack in the Azerbaijani border to the south, but it was closed. Rumors in the city said that skilled applicants were being registered at the labor exchange for work at new industrial plants being built in the Caucasian Mountains. Ullo decided to check out the rumors, even though the mountains were not directly on the route to the Middle East he had laid out in his mind. There was no other solution on the horizon.

The exchange director, a Russian, judged from Ullo's dress and speech that he was an educated European. He asked Ullo to wait, and Ullo complied. He sat there for eight hours until the place emptied out, and then the director called him and told him not to go to the Caucasus with his group. "It's not for you," the Russian said. "It's a long, hard road, and the work is doubtful. Instead, travel south with the wounded soldiers."

Ullo knew nothing about this, and the director told him that a delegation of doctors from Azerbaijan had arrived in Makhachkala to pick up soldiers wounded in the fighting and take them to hospitals in the south.[1]

"This evening, the delegation will collect the wounded men in a convoy of wagons, and later tonight they'll leave by train for the south. Wait for the convoy near the main road," the official suggested. Ullo realized that a golden opportunity was at hand. Purely by accident, he had met a communist official, a man he had never encountered before, who had taken the trouble to steer him toward a lifesaving option.

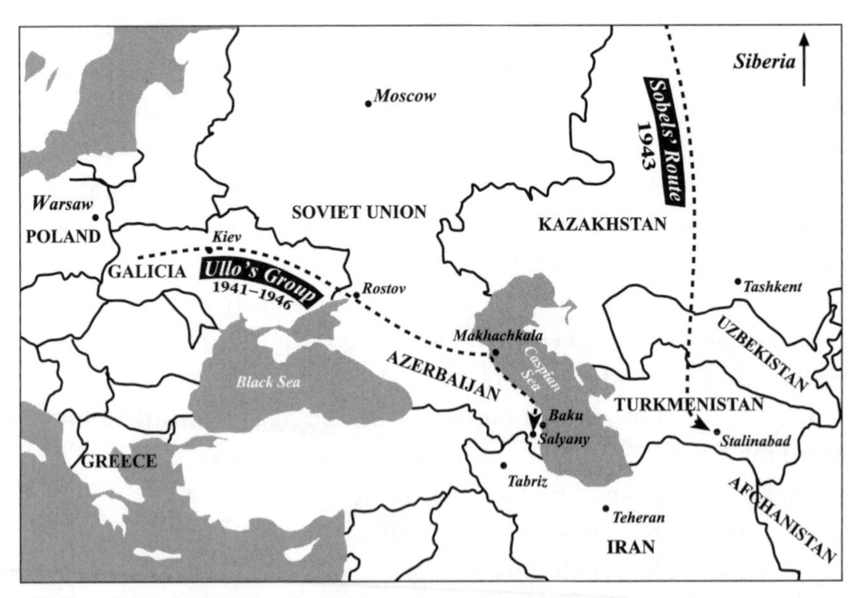

Ullo's and the Sobels' routes of flight during World War II.

"It was a pitch-black night," Ullo recalled fifty years later. They managed to get a wagon tied to an old horse and laid their two patients, Lidka and Feder, in it. Clara carried her baby, and they stood there waiting on the side of the main road for the convoy of wounded men. When Ullo saw it, he smoothly maneuvered their wagon into the line of vehicles, and they slowly made their way toward the train station.

When the convoy reached the station's yard, it turned out that the head of the medical team was looking for someone to be in charge of the travel arrangements. "It became a routine," Ullo recalled. "Whenever the communists were looking for someone to take charge, strangely enough, they always picked me." At the Makhachkala train station, the same thing happened. They pointed at him and put him in charge. Of course, now that he was in control, Ullo put his group on the train with the wounded soldiers. Then he wanted to go into the street and sell their few possessions, such as a gold watch and Lidka's suitcase with her nylon stockings and silk pajamas. Ullo wanted to sell everything to get some rubles so that they could settle down in Azerbaijan, but Lidka objected.

"We've still got hard times ahead," she said.

Ullo was angry, and he said to her sharply, "One day I'll sell the watch, along with the arm that's wearing it," but there was no time for quarreling, and in the end he gave in. When he put the suitcase on the overhead rack in the coach, he warned Feder, "Watch the case, don't take your eyes off it." Ullo immediately went out and sold the other stuff, clothing, shoes, everything they didn't need. He immediately came back to the train, but the case was gone. It had been stolen right from under Feder's nose, and Feder was so weak that he never noticed.

They left Makhachkala on that gloomy, depressing night and traveled south along the Caspian coast. After crossing the border into Azerbaijan, they passed through the capital city of Baku and in the morning stopped at the town of Salyany. And here a miracle happened. Right before their eyes, a new reality appeared, a wonderful world where people were vibrantly alive and could even laugh.

"It is impossible to describe the change that we underwent after that night. Things like that happen only in wartime," Ullo said. "A few hours earlier, we had been in the hell of Dante's Inferno, and now we'd arrived in Paradise."

The sun was shining, the sky was blue, and on the platform there was an apparent mirage: sandwiches, fruit and cakes, coffee with sugar, and a delegation of the town's citizens, embracing the wounded soldiers and their escorts and plying them with food and drink. The mayor made a welcoming speech and a small band played on lutelike instruments called *kubuz*.

"In a moment, the gloomy expressions had vanished from our faces," Ullo said. "We were smiling with happiness, and I said to myself, What luck that we never boarded that icebreaker in Makhachkala."

Although they had arrived at Salyany by pure chance, they decided to stay there. Their lives literally changed overnight. Salyany lay north of the border with Iran, far from the advancing German army. It was the capital of an undeveloped rural area that was crying out for expert economists.[2] The Soviet Union had mustered up all of its military power to block the Germans, and Azerbaijan was mobilizing to bolster the war economy. To increase production, the region desperately needed experts in economic planning. Ullo and Feder were welcomed with open arms.

Feder, whose health had improved, as did Lidka's, got a job in the economic planning department of the region's trade office (part of Azerbaijan's Trade Ministry), and Ullo worked in the municipal building department. He had landed in just the right place. The building department was responsible for allotting housing to the new refugees. They settled in homes that had been deserted by their occupants because of the war. Ullo obtained a large house with a plot of land. All six members of the group found jobs. They felt a deep sense of relief. There was a regular supply of bread, and they procured vegetable seeds for their garden. Life gradually took on a normal routine. Lidka worked at two jobs: for half of the week, she was at the Salyany hospital, and during the other half, she visited the clinics of the *kolkhozy* in the area.

Most of the doctors at the hospital were from Baku. It was clean and well run, although there was no heating and food was scarce. "We couldn't tell the patients to eat more to get well," said Lidka forty-five years later. "We just gave them whatever there was."

But the shortage of food was a minor worry. The epidemics that often accompany cold weather, poverty, and unhygienic conditions were a greater threat. There was malaria and dysentery, and typhus was the worst of all. It was transmitted from one person to another by the common body louse, *Pediculus humanus.* The louse moved from one person to another at random.

Simply being near another individual, especially at night, could result in lice migrating from one person to the other. During the war, typhus was widespread throughout Russia, mainly in the winters. More than twenty million people fell sick, and the death rate was between 10 and 15 percent.

In the course of the group's escape, Lidka had faced many types of illnesses as a physician, but in Azerbaijan she saw up close for the first time how the typhus epidemic was wiping out masses of people. "I saw a Russian wearing a *rubashka* with this creature crawling out of the pocket.[3] I asked the nurse what it was, and she replied in Russian, '*Shto eta?* [What is it?] It's a louse that carries typhus.' There's stomach typhus, which I knew about before, and there's lice typhus that is transmitted through the blood and which I had never seen. It begins with a fever and then trembling and then meningitis and pneumonia, and there's nothing more that can be done."[4]

No medications were available to treat typhus in Azerbaijan. Even the common drug pyramidon, for the relief of fever, was hard to get. In the *kolkhoz* clinics, Lidka worked standing up, to make it harder for the lice to get onto her clothing. Between the *kolkhozy*, she walked, sometimes as much as eleven miles a day. When the epidemic grew more deadly, she was given an old health department pickup truck. Thousands of people were sick with typhus in southern Azerbaijan in 1942 and 1943, and one tenth of them died. "It was a disease of the poor," said Lidka. "There were no rich people's ailments like heart or gall bladder disease in that region because people ate so little."

Lidka found great satisfaction in her work. With Ullo, Feder, and Est working in the economic departments of the district and the town, it was Nushka who took care of the home and helped Clara with the baby. The peace lasted four months. In the late summer of 1942, the German advance on the two main axes, north and south, had been blocked and the Russians were gearing up for two enormous efforts, at Stalingrad and in the Kursk region.[5] Everyone who was capable of contributing to the war effort was mobilized, young and old alike, men and women. Refugees from Nazi-occupied areas, including the Poles, were not exempted.

The Russian authorities didn't count on the refugees too much, though. They were not assigned to the front, only to construction work. Feder had recovered from typhus fever but still suffered from exhaustion, and he was exempted. Est and Ullo were called up. They rode hundreds of miles eastward on trucks that were stopped near the border of Georgia. Six thousand men had been assembled there, and chaos prevailed. Their heads were shaved, and they were sent to work in industrial plants. The conditions were harsh. The workers slept in an open field, and sometimes it rained at night or it even snowed. Most of the men had colds, and some got pneumonia.

After a while, the Caucasian Command planned to move the men to Sochi, a holiday resort on the Black Sea coast, where a canal was dug to obstruct the Germans. Before they set out, each man went through a medical checkup. A Jewish doctor from Poland found marks on Ullo's lungs and diagnosed pneumonia. He said, "Kahane, go home. Your life is in danger. You aren't capable of working, and there is a risk that you will infect others."

Ullo wandered along the road for six days. There were many floods, and he had nothing to eat. Kind people occasionally gave him a piece of bread or a potato. When he reached home, he stood outside and looked up at Nushka watching him from the window. His head had been shaved, and he was very thin. "I stood outside waving to her, and she didn't know who I was," Ullo said, recalling their reunion.

When Ullo was released by the doctor, Est was sent to Sochi to dig the canal. He was thirty-two. A year later he came back to Salyany, emaciated and mortally ill. Three months after his return, he caught dysentery and died from weakness. If Ullo had gone to Sochi, his chances of surviving would not have been any better.

Ullo now entered a highly productive phase in his years of working for the Soviets. "It was the most important school of my life," he repeatedly said. He described the industrial complex that he built in the winter of 1943, a network of factories and production workshops that the communists called a *promkombinat* (combine-corporation).[6] It was in the Salyany region, one of the remotest spots on the globe, five hours' drive southward from the Azerbaijani capital of Baku. The Red Army had rallied and pushed the German armies back on the two main eastern fronts in the central sector and the south. Now the Soviet Union called up its remaining strength in order to win the war. East of the Ural Mountains, the Soviets were rebuilding an armaments industry, and across the empire every fit woman and man had been harnessed to the war effort. The United States sent massive shipments of aircraft and other armaments and supplies to the Soviets, and in Baku, the deputy secretary of the Communist Party summoned the economic planner Ullo Kahane for a discussion.

"They say good things about you in the Salyany municipality," he told Ullo. "There is industrial potential in that region, and we want to exploit it.

Don't expect a steady supply of raw materials, though. And we don't know whether you will have enough manpower. We are at war; you will have to make do with substitutes."

"It was the most important school of my life," Ullo repeated proudly. When he began, there were fourteen functioning plants in the region; most were failing and the fifteenth was defunct. When he left years later, there were forty-eight, with production that increased each month.

In the beginning, Ullo's communist bosses requested him to supply the needs of the civilian population, but as time passed, their emphasis shifted to the military. "Top priority to the military," said the officials in Baku, and they never asked whether he had the raw materials. They wanted results, and Ullo came up with ideas to prevent production from coming to a standstill. "We had a proverb: 'In Russia, we never say no.' And in truth, everyone tried to say yes." Ullo described his enthusiastic approach to the task: "Today I look back and I can see clearly what a young man is capable of when he has no alternative. I always saw myself as an office person, a lawyer, an economic planner, in a white collar, but reality created challenges and we met them, met them very well."

Here's one example. Once Ullo was traveling to Baku, and the train stopped at a station. There were some neglected, broken-down trucks parked nearby. They were fully loaded, and a strange stench emanated from them. He stopped and could smell fertilizer. "It was not just any old fertilizer, but Argentinean nitrogenous fertilizer, produced by Kebrako," Ullo recalled. He recognized the fertilizer from Bolechow and also knew that it was excellent to use in tanning hides to produce leather. At Baku, he talked to the director of supplies at the industry ministry and mentioned what he had found at that station. The director agreed that Ullo should take some of it. ("I'm going into details to illustrate how it is possible to set up a factory from nothing," Ullo explained).

Upon returning to Salyany, Ullo spoke to his sister Lidka. She knew the *kolkhozy* from working in their clinics. Ullo said to her, "Go and talk to the head of the *kolkhoz* where they raise cattle, and tell him that your brother needs animals' hides for tanning."

Two days later Ullo received eighty hides, stripped off the cattle carcasses. The deal was for the *kolkhoz* to give him this number of animal skins and to get back forty processed hides. The rest would be sold.

"It's funny," laughed Ullo, "at home, in Bolechow, my father had a leather tannery, but I had never learned the process. Now I had the raw material and the tanning chemicals and even the manpower, but I was lacking an expert."

So he told the party chief in Salyany that he needed someone who knew how to process leather. The party official went to a prison camp and found an expert—"an excellent chap," recalled Ullo. The man was released from prison, and he taught the factory workers how to use the fertilizer to tan the hides and how to manufacture ink. Within a month, Ullo had opened ten shoemaking workshops, and they continued to expand quickly. They received supplies of rawhide from the army, from the government, and from several of their own *kolkhozy*. In each workshop they employed twenty workers. All of a sudden, an entire leather industry had grown up from nothing. Ullo became highly valued by the party bosses, and he regained his self-respect. Many years later, he described his feelings of happiness during that time: "Sometimes I stood there and chuckled about Ullo Kahane setting up factories for leather, ink, and textiles in that remote dump in Azerbaijan. All that was needed was initiative, and people were glad to work, proud to contribute to the war against the Nazi enemy. I, too, suddenly felt a great sense of patriotism and identification with the Soviet Union."

That was an exciting time, and Nushka was a wonderful companion. There was always something to eat in the house. She organized their home and cooked on a kerosene stove. When there weren't enough rations, they shared an egg and drank tea. She always kept a samovar ready to supply tea. Lidka devoted herself entirely to medicine, sometimes working twenty-four hours at a time as she looked after patients with typhus or those suffering from exhaustion because of hunger. All of them felt a sense of urgency and were ready to make a mighty common effort. Only Feder languished in despair. Something in his soul had died, beyond the devastation that typhus had wreaked on his body. "He was finished," recalled Ullo, and Feder's wife, Lidka, agreed.

Feder was depressed. He thought that the war would never end and didn't believe that Hitler would be defeated. Feder worked for Ullo's department, in planning. He did everything that he was told to do, and Ullo trusted him, but he had no enthusiasm. "In this, he was the exception," recalled Ullo. "Everyone else on my team was enthusiastic." Many refugees from Bessarabia, and locals as well, worked with Ullo.[7] "The party gave me a big title [on the tape of his interview he laughs again]—director of the industrial *promkombinat*—and treated me with great respect."

In the spring of 1943, a telegram arrived at the Salyany post office from Tajikistan. The postmaster himself knocked on Ullo's door. Ullo opened it and took the telegram, then read it out loud: "We are in Stalinabad [the capital of Tajikistan, today called Dushanbe], near the Soviet border with Afghanistan, not far from Tashkent [the capital of Uzbekistan]. Come and visit us. Sobel."

Nushka let out a screech of joy and excitedly jumped up and down. Her family had been released from the work camp in Siberia.[8] They had joined the stream of war refugees that was slowly spreading through the republics of the southeastern and south-central Soviet Union. The Sobel family was now camped near the junction of the borders of the Uzbekistan Republic and the Tajik Republic, very close to the ancient Silk Road along which merchants used to transport goods between the Far East and Europe and the Near East.

It was hard to picture the Sobels, authentic representatives of the Polish-Jewish bourgeoisie, being compelled to find refuge near Tashkent, in an oriental landscape that evoked the *Thousand and One Nights*, where time stood still and the climate was unbearably harsh. There among the Tajik, Uzbek, and Tartar tribesmen, with their foreign customs and tongues, hundreds of thousands of Russian, Polish, and Ukrainian refugees now filled the streets. Many were emaciated, exhausted, and sick with typhus. The death rate was phenomenal. Almost no medications were available, and even people who received shots and survived the disease were afflicted with large suppurating sores caused by unsterilized hypodermic needles. Food was scarce, and every drop of drinking water had to be boiled, but nevertheless, each refugee confessed that after Siberia, Tajikistan was like paradise.

The Sobel family rented a room from a Tajik family. The Sobels' daughter Sara, known in the family as Zhizha, enrolled in a nurses' course at a hospital. The father, Israel, soon found work because bookkeepers were in great demand. In the early summer, rumors spread that the Polish general Wladyslaw Anders had set up headquarters in Tashkent and was recruiting Polish citizens for an army that he was building.[9] Anders intended to take his battalions and join the British forces, and thousands of Jews were ready to enlist.

"I went there, thinking that perhaps they would let me join as a nurse," Zhizha recalled forty-five years later. It was not easy to travel on the roads. The authorities demanded official passes, but somehow she obtained one and journeyed alone on the train to Tashkent. The Tajik trains were peculiar, with the seats in two layers. Some passengers sat on the bottom layer, and others sat above them on the top one. Many traveled standing, and others sat on their luggage. Hundreds of young people joined up. It turned out that Anders did enlist Jews in his army, but Zhizha was refused.[10]

In the summer, Nushka and Ullo packed a bag and went to Tajikistan. They drove by jeep to Baku, crossed the Caspian Sea in a ship to Turkmenistan, and caught a train to Ashkhabad. This took them to Samarkand and Stalinabad, in the southernmost part of the Soviet Union. The family reunion was emotional. For two days everyone cried with excitement. They could hardly express their joy that they had all survived. For the next two weeks, day and night, while sitting in the courtyard of the Tajiks' house, they described their adventures and the ordeals they had endured since last being together in Galicia. Three years previously, Clara and Israel Sobel had objected to their prospective son-in-law because he was secular, and they had refused to come to their daughter's wedding ceremony. Now they warmly embraced him. The war had changed the way they looked at life and its priorities, and they were particularly grateful that Ullo had saved their daughter.

It was a special encounter, and everyone came out of it strengthened. Until a short time ago, they had not believed that they would ever see one another again. Now they knew in their hearts that their difficult trials had made them stronger. And in any case, the war was drawing to an end. At that family reunion in Stalinabad, euphoria prevailed and new bonds were forged among members of the two families. (On the tape of her interview, Zhizha is so excited as she talks about the meeting, it's as if it had happened to her the day before.)

The newfound acceptance that Nushka and Zhizha's parents felt for Ullo did not mean that they had abandoned their religious faith and become secular. On the contrary, in Tajikistan they wouldn't touch meat unless they were able to find a kosher ritual slaughterer (*shohet*) to kill a chicken or a lamb for them according to Jewish law. They observed the Sabbath and prayed three times a day, but they had nevertheless learned from bitter experience that religious faith was a personal matter and that there was no guarantee that a religious person would also be a moral one. Ullo was now an admirable person in their eyes, despite his secular beliefs.

When Nushka and Ullo returned to Salyany, something unusual happened. Before the war, people in Azerbaijan hadn't known what anti-Semitism was.

The Azeri made no distinction between the Europeans; Poles, Russians, and Jews were all the same to them. In the Red Army units that were stationed in the town, on the other hand, there were manifestations of Jew hatred. The commanders always suspected that spies had infiltrated their units, and they sometimes pointed an accusing finger at foreigners, the Jews among them. During the course of the war years, anti-Semitic expressions spread from the army into the parlance of the local population. In the Red Army they used the racist epithet *Zhid*, while in Salyany they had always called the Jews *Yevrei.*[11]

The incident was quite prosaic. Children throwing stones at old Jewish refugees became a common occurrence in the town. One rock hit a woman and wounded her, and she had to undergo surgery. Ullo was chosen to represent the Jews and to complain to the local party secretary. This official, however, considered the whole incident strange. He couldn't grasp why anyone would harm a Jew, Ullo recounted. "He asked me who had thrown the stones, and when I told him it was children shouting, 'Zhid, Zhid!' he said, 'What do you want from me? Go to the police.'"

Ullo insisted that it was a political problem, and he pressed the party to investigate the case, but the local secretary refused. In the end, the daughter of the injured woman complained to the Komsomol, the communist youth organization. She also wrote a letter to the general secretary of the party in Baku, Bagirov, who was very close to Stalin.[12]

A few days later, a delegation from the party headquarters was sent to Salyany to investigate the incident. Ullo was called to testify, and by chance on precisely the same day, Nushka got involved in a quarrel with a bookkeeper in the local bureaucracy, who refused to pay her for some translation work she had done for him. She went to demand payment, and he called her a Zhid. Ullo went to see the man and persuaded him to come to the session with the delegation from Baku. When Ullo was called upon to testify, he stood up and made a speech: "Do you want to see what an anti-Semite looks like? Look at him! He called my wife a Zhidovka" (the feminine of *Zhid*). The commission immediately ordered that the bookkeeper be arrested and prosecuted.

These anti-Semitic incidents occurred when the economic situation was at its worst. The supply of raw materials had ceased altogether, and for the first time there was hunger in the town. Children rummaged in garbage bins for food, and people grew weak and died. "You would see an exhausted person and go and try to hold him up, to straighten him, but if you only touched his shoulder, he would drop down dead," Ullo recalled.

Every day the *promkombinat*'s directors were required to send everything they produced to the front—food, clothing, boots. Everything that was manufactured went to the army, and very little remained for the civilians. Many people were in a state of exhaustion, and Lidka said that they looked like *musulmanner* (the concentration camp inmates' slang for emaciated prisoners who had given up the will to live).

One day in the winter of 1943, party secretary general Bagirov was driving through Salyany when he saw a soldier eating fish and throwing the bones away. Immediately, two ragged children pounced on the bones and licked the remaining scraps of flesh from them. Bagirov was shocked. He stopped the car, picked up the two children, and drove to the town's party secretary, Aliyev.

"I can see what's happening over here," Bagirov rebuked Aliyev. He demanded that Aliyev save the town's hungry children and dress them in a proper manner. Aliyev complained that his warehouses were empty, and Bagirov promised to send some basic foods to Salyany. "And all the rest you'll have to do yourself," he told the local party boss, giving him one month to complete the task. "I'll come back to check," Bagirov warned Aliyev, "and if I find one hungry or naked child here, I'll execute you myself."[13]

In the middle of the night, there was a knock on Ullo's door, and he was called to the party headquarters. Aliyev anxiously told him about Bagirov's visit and said, "Kahane, you're in charge of industry, you must clothe the children."

Ullo replied that he had no raw material because everything went to the army, and Aliyev said, "We are also at war, and this is an order. If you wish, Comrade Kahane, I'll call a meeting of the central committee for you, and we'll issue a directive."

Ullo agreed to help. He worked with his people day and night, and after two weeks, they had clothed all of the children in Salyany from head to foot. Ullo walked down the street with Nushka, pointed at the children, and said proudly, "There, look. I dressed those as well." Everyone in the city said that providing proper clothes for the ragged children was a big achievement, but shortly afterward it got Ullo into trouble.

There was a new wind blowing in the Soviet Union, and it soon reached Salyany. The amazing victory at Stalingrad had made the Russians stand tall. The Germans were finally retreating. Ullo Kahane was the head of a large industrial complex. He spoke Russian to the officials from Baku and Azerbaijani to the *kolkhoz* residents. His sister Lidka also spoke both languages. Azerbaijani doctors worked with her in the hospital, and she had a good friend from the aristocratic Babzade family. This woman was a young doctor, and her relatives and friends admired the Jewish refugees.[14] In the eyes of the Azeri intellectual elite, the refugees came from a civilized place, and Judaism represented wisdom and values. They had heard of Jews living in the West who were not like the Jews in the East, but they had never seen them until Ullo's group came to Salyany. The Babzades asked Lidka naive questions. "How can it be that a man is married to only one wife?" they wanted to know, and "How can it be that Jews do not drink like the other Europeans and why don't they behave like the Russians?" The Azerbaijani intelligentsia, which had absorbed its customs mostly from the conservative Persian culture, totally rejected the revolutionary communist avant-garde but was eager to encounter Western ways of thought.

In the hospitals and the clinics, young Dr. Lidka Feder was admired, and Ullo, too, did very well at his job. He developed and expanded the local industry, and the heads of the industry ministry in Baku urged him to join the party. Ullo turned them down, giving various excuses, because in his mind he was already planning to return to Poland. If he joined the party, it would be difficult for him to leave the Soviet Union, and that was why he refrained from identifying too closely with the party.

"When they suggested that I join the party," Ullo said, "I said that I wasn't able to because I was a member of the Polish Communist Party, and I didn't want to lose my seniority rights. They accepted that excuse." Luckily for him, the Salyany central committee never knew that the party in Moscow had declared that all Polish communists were Trotskyists and had thrown them into prison.[15]

The party leaders trusted Ullo, and he took part in their internal deliberations. KGB personnel were guests in his home. Ministry officials demanded more development, and Ullo learned the system very well. He was an excellent organizer and displayed leadership, but one thing posed an impassable obstacle for him: the entrenched corruption of the bureaucracy. Despite the constraints imposed by the war, communist society was already corrupt to the core. Managers and officials stole whatever they could lay their hands on. The party tried to combat it but sometimes picked the wrong cases to investigate.

Corruption was an ever-present temptation. Ullo managed dozens of plants, and stealing occurred at all of them. Ullo did not take part in the orgy of theft, not because he wanted to be a paragon of morality but out of simple fear. Even when he lacked food in his own home, he refused to take anything from the plants.

"I had many chances," Ullo said fifty years later, "but I never did anything because I was afraid of Russian prison. I knew that if they put me inside, I would never come out." For a foreign person, imprisonment meant death. Ullo was watched all the time because he was a foreigner and especially because he stopped the foremen from stealing, which made them resent him.

One day a *commissia* arrived from Moscow, an official inspection delegation. The inspectors were there to investigate why Ullo's administration had made clothes for the poor children, and they discovered that raw materials intended for military production had ended up in private hands. The *commissars* wrote a report and asked Ullo to sign it. He informed them that the party had decided to use the material for civilians.

"There is a written resolution of the local committee," he told the delegation.

They argued that the raw materials had not been local but had come from Russia. Therefore, the local committee had no authority to change its end purpose to civilian use. In the end, a terrible injustice was done. In their report, they accused Ullo of stealing military raw material. He consulted friends and lawyers, and all agreed that the situation was perilous.

The delegation traveled to Baku to report to the central committee, and in the middle of the night Ullo decided to follow them. Luckily, a friend had a jeep, and they drove there together. Ullo went straight to the minister of industry and told him what had happened. The minister said, "Kagane [the Russians can't pronounce the letter *h* and say *g* instead], you should have spoken to me beforehand!"

Ullo explained that if he hadn't carried out the party instructions and had refused to make clothes for the children, he would have been sent to prison.

The minister remained silent, and Ullo assumed that he would probably be spending the night in jail. After a few seconds, however, the minister suggested that they go to speak to another minister, who was in charge of inspection, a woman with whom Ullo was friendly. They went to her chamber, and Ullo told her what had happened.

She looked at him and said, "Kagane, you used military material, but because it was a for children I'll see what I can do to help you."

Suddenly, there was a knock at the door, and two members of the Moscow *commissia* entered. They saw Ullo in the minister's office and asked him what he was doing there. Ullo replied, "You came to accuse me, and I came to defend myself."

In the end, the minister said, "Leave it to me. I'll decide," and Ullo knew that he would not be prosecuted.

21

Stolen Identity

ON DECEMBER 24, 1943, the Soviets launched their first big offensive on the Ukrainian front.[1] At that time, about fifty Jews lived around the area of the Nafta refinery, which the Backenroths had once managed. Among them were Naftali's distant relatives Yaacov Avigdor, the chief rabbi of Drohobych-Boryslav, and his son, Isaac, along with ten other well-educated Jews—lawyers and rabbis who now specialized in forging documents.[2] Naftali assigned them the task of preparing the official documents that the work teams required to enable them to move around freely. They forged seals, German certificates, and Polish documents, and altered existing documents. The men had worked together for almost three years now, and their spirit was still strong. Naftali fully trusted all of them and was certain that they would be able to endure the hardship for three or four more months. He could not know that the Russians would need seven months to push the Wehrmacht another four hundred miles westward in order to liberate Drohobych.[3]

While working in the refinery, Rabbi Avigdor found a bundle of old documents marked "personal papers." Naftali leafed through them and found a letter that had been sent to his father in 1917 by his lawyer, Dr. Bergwald. The lawyer listed details about some financial deals and noted that he was sending Backenroth the sum of 2,000 crowns. The money was still in the envelope. An ingenious idea occurred to Naftali. "I said to myself that I could do something with this," Naftali recalled with evident enjoyment many years later, in describing how he had decided to become the bastard child of Katya Bronicki and Doctor Kozlowsky.

The story that Naftali invented was based in part on authentic data. In 1905, two babies, the Jew Naftali Backenroth and the gentile Mikola Bronicki, were born in Schodnica a few days apart. Naftali's mother was very sick after the birth, whereas Mikola Bronicki's mother was healthy and strong. She was a single parent. Her name was Katjina, Katya for short, and Naftali's wet nurse was also called Katya. All of these details were facts, but the other data were fabricated.

Naftali chose a father for Mikola from the community where they lived. There was a well-known non-Jewish Polish physician in Drohobych called Kozlowsky, an old bachelor and a very energetic person. He ran the hospital, and everyone knew that he was an anti-Semite. "I decided that I could not be just anyone's bastard," explained Naftali, "but that it would be respectable to be Kozlowsky's bastard."[4]

"We wrote up a contract. I still have a photograph of it," Naftali said. "Three people signed the contract: my father, Israel Backenroth; Dr. Bronislav Kozlowsky; and Katjina Bronicki—Katya, the single mother of the infant Mikola"—all of whom were dead when the document was forged. The forgers faked the Polish script that had been used in 1905, and Rabbi Avigdor prepared the lawyer's official stationery. Katya Bronicki had been illiterate, so the forgers put a cross for her instead of a signature. For Kozlowsky, they forged a real signature. The document looked like an authentic contract from 1905.

This was the story they fabricated: Backenroth's infant had died immediately after birth. His wife was very sick, and they did not tell her the tragic news. Several days later, Katya Bronicki gave birth to Mikola, Kozlowsky's bastard. With the consent of the doctor and of Katya, the infant Mikola was handed over to the Backenroth family. Kozlowsky agreed that the infant should be circumcised, but only on condition that no religious ceremony be performed. Katya Bronicki agreed to the circumcision and guaranteed not to reveal the identity of the infant. In return for her consent, she received a sum of money from Israel Backenroth. Another sum of money was entrusted to the lawyer Bergwald, and in the contract it was stipulated that it would be placed at Mikola's disposal when he grew up. If, for any reason, his identity was revealed before he reached adulthood, the money would be given to him immediately. All of this supposedly occurred in 1905. Subsequently, in 1917, during World War I, Dr. Bergwald left Drohobych and settled in

Vienna. From there, he dispatched the money to the child's father, Israel Backenroth, and this explained the envelope with 2,000 crowns that was found in the refinery.

Three of the forgers and the seal makers were made privy to the story: a lawyer, Dr. Gerstenfeld, who was an expert on Polish script at the turn of the century, and the two master forgers, Rabbi Avigdor and his son. (Several months later, young Avigdor was dispatched to a death camp where his skills saved his life: he forged English currency for the Germans.)

Rabbi Avigdor insisted on adding the signature and the seal of a notary. It was easy to forge the signature because the notary they chose was very old and his hand shook, but there was a problem with the seal because it was changed yearly and it was necessary to reconstruct the one used in 1905. Then the co-conspirators learned that a copy of every document that a notary approved was kept in his files.

"Of course, there was no copy of our contract," recalled Naftali, "but we solved the problem easily. We added a clause in which the notary declared that since the arrangement was not legal, he would not leave a copy in his files."

Naftali placed the forged papers among the heap of old documents found by Avigdor and told the refinery foreman, a Polish Catholic named Tomka, "If you need paper, come with me." Paper was a rare commodity during the war, and Tomka went with Naftali to the stack of papers. There, as if by chance, they found the bundle of documents with the forgeries. Naftali said to the Pole, "Look, Tomka, I've found my father's papers. Take them, and if you find anything interesting, show me."

Since everyone knew that Israel Backenroth was a wealthy man, Tomka and his wife looked for money and found the envelope with the 2,000 crowns and also the contract. The next morning, Tomka's wife asked Naftali to come and see her. She was a devout Catholic. "She curtseyed to me, embraced and kissed me," recalled Naftali. He asked her, "Why are you hugging and kissing me?" and she said, "Look, you are not a Jew, and we have been insulting you. We thought you were Jewish. You are the son of the doctor, Kozlowsky. I am going to the priest to show him the documents."

Naftali said to her, "Wait, wait, don't go, do you believe those letters? Do you really believe that I am not the son of Israel Backenroth? You knew my father."

She replied, "But it says so here. What shall I do?"

Naftali suggested that she take the money and the documents to the German director of the refinery, Haftsmann. He read the contract and said to Tomka's wife, '"You have found a pearl." He immediately gave her a reward: a liter of oil and a kilogram of sugar.

She was delighted and said, "Now we must go to the priest," but Naftali demurred.

"I still don't believe it," he said. "Don't take this to the priest; don't involve him."

At that time, the head of the SD (Sicherheitsdienst, or Security Police, the intelligence service of the SS) at the district headquarters in Stryj was a Prussian, Paul Lischkuss. He disliked Naftali intensely because Naftali had arranged for Jews to do clerical jobs, while Ukrainians were primarily doing manual labor. But Lischkuss could not change the situation because the heads of the Gestapo gave Naftali their patronage and protected him. "Haftsmann did not know that Lischkuss hated me," said Naftali.

Haftsmann telephoned Lischkuss and told him about the document, and Lischkuss said, "Backenroth did it. He is intelligent enough to forge a document." Lischkuss ordered Haftsmann to keep the Polish foreman Tomka with him to buy time. "Don't let the foreman contact Backenroth, and wait until I arrive," Lischkuss said to Haftsmann. "I will prove to you that Backenroth fabricated the document."

Lischkuss hurriedly went to the priest and interrogated him. The priest told Lischkuss that he had heard about someone called Naftali Backenroth but wasn't acquainted with him personally. Lischkuss wanted to know whether Naftali had ever been in the church, and the priest replied that he had never seen Naftali. Then the Nazi showed the documents to the priest and asked him whether the story seemed likely. The priest read the contract and told Lischkuss that Dr. Kozlowsky was not a devout Christian. Lischkuss requested that the priest keep the whole affair between them and asked him whether the infant Mikola had been baptized, but the priest refused to divulge any information. He explained that the Gestapo had forbidden him to issue documents without their prior approval.

Lischkuss gave a full account to his commanding officer, Captain Nicolaus Tolle, who proposed that the documents be sent for verification to Hans Block, the Gestapo chief in Drohobych. Lischkuss suspected that there was some connection between Naftali and Block, however, and preferred to send the documents to Lvov. He knew that nobody there was acquainted with Backenroth. When Haftsmann told Naftali about Lischkuss's actions, Naftali said to him, "I don't believe the whole story. I was a Jew and I'm still a Jew."

Then Tolle sent two Gestapo men to interrogate Naftali. They were told to clarify whether it was possible that he was a Christian. The first question they asked him was "Do you want to be an Aryan?" and Naftali immediately replied, "Do you think it's possible?"

They said, "Well, you know how the Jews kidnapped Christian children in order to convert them." Then they examined him closely, studied his profile, and scrutinized him from all angles, checking the shape of his head. Finally, they showed him the forged document and asked, "And what do you say about this?"

Naftali perused the document that he himself had written and said, "There are people who are fond of me, and they have done something interesting. I can tell you one thing, the copy of my father's signature is excellent, but I don't believe that it's real." The atmosphere was pleasant. Naftali joked with the Germans and treated the document with suspicion.

From the outset, Helmrich, the German director of agriculture and supply administration in the region, had been privy to the plot. Helmrich feared for Naftali's safety and tried to persuade him to escape. "Quick, pack your belongings and run," Helmrich told him, and Naftali replied, "You're the only one who knows. The whole thing will either succeed or fail. In any event, I feel that that is what I want."

Several days later, Helmrich telephoned him and said, "Come at once. It worked." Helmrich quoted SD chief Lischkuss, who had told him, "I have news. Backenroth is not Jewish; he did it so well that he deserves to be an Aryan." Lischkuss was not fooled by the letter. He was sure that it was a complete forgery, but he could not prove that his assumption was true.

Now that the ploy had succeeded with the Germans, Naftali set out to examine the reaction of the Poles. The greatest problem was that there were documents but no witnesses. All of the witnesses were dead. In order for the contract to be convincing, there had to be a witness.

By chance, Naftali met a Polish woman who lived in the neighborhood and had nursed him in childhood. Her son, who had been killed in the war in Italy, was Naftali's friend. She said to Naftali, "Tulek [Naftali's nickname], there is something I must tell you. I saw the priest, and he told me that you are Kozlowsky's son, and I am very happy."

Naftali was delighted but kept up the performance: "You knew my father, and I know that you don't believe the story. Do you really think that I am not a Backenroth?"

She replied, "Of course. It is written there."

The woman said that although the priest had been forbidden to see Naftali, he wished to meet Naftali secretly. They met that night on the path between the refinery and the labor camp. The priest said to Naftali, "Do you know who you are? The son of one of the most respected citizens in town, and you were even baptized. I have proof that you were baptized, and I am very happy that you are who you are, and I would like your wife and son to be baptized as well."

Naftali replied cautiously, "Sir, I am an honest man, and if I have my family baptized, people will think that I am planning to escape. After the war, if I have proof that the story is true, I will join your flock."

The priest said, "In my heart I had some doubts, but now I have none. You are one of us."

Nevertheless, Naftali felt that to round off the affair, he needed a living witness to substantiate the document. There was a gentile in Schodnica, a barrel maker to whom Naftali had once given a pair of horses as a present in return for a favor. They met by chance. "I'm so happy to see you," the barrel maker said to Naftali, and he told Naftali about his strange dream. "For some time, every night, I have been dreaming about your father. Why is that? Do you think I did something bad to make your father appear in my sleep every night?"

Naftali instantly realized that he had found a witness and said, "Go to the priest, he may tell you something that will explain the dream."

The Pole went to the church, and the priest told him that Naftali was the illegitimate son of Dr. Koslowski and Katya Bronicki. The priest persuaded the man to go to the Germans and tell them that he remembered the story of Naftali's sick mother and the substitution of the infant. The priest said that anyone who persuades a Jew to convert is doing a good deed, so the barrel maker immediately went off to give evidence to the Germans.

With all of the proof before them, the Germans organized a ceremony to mark Naftali's change of identity. The chief director of the oil industry in the Carpathians came to drive Naftali to the office of the district governor, where the Gestapo commandant Heck was waiting with five officers. They said to Naftali that he was 100 percent Aryan, his son was half-Jewish, and his wife would remain Jewish. "She will be protected to some extent," Heck said, "because Naftali is a well-known person, but she mustn't go to the market when the German women are there." Then the district governor asked him whether he had any relatives in the town, and Naftali said that his sister's son, George, was staying with them.

The district governor turned to the Gestapo commandant and asked cynically, "What's this? There's a sister in the story as well?" He tried in every possible way to get George away from Naftali and asked, "Why are you so concerned about the boy?"

Naftali said that he was learning interesting things about himself, and if he was really as talented as they said, then it was thanks to Israel Backenroth, who had raised him and educated him. And if Naftali was not Israel's son, then his nephew George was the sole descendant of Israel Backenroth, the man who had raised him. "You see that all this time you have respected me, even when you thought I was a Jew. Now you say that I am not a Jew. Does that mean that I must behave like a scoundrel?"

In the end, they agreed that George could stay with Naftali but suggested that the boy try to avoid being seen in public. The governor attempted several other delaying tactics, chatted a while, and made jokes, but in the end he gave Naftali a document stating, "The man known as Naftali Backenroth is Mikola Bronicki."

This was in the beginning of the summer of 1944. The governor informed Naftali that he was free to choose a place of employment, but the refinery director Haftsmann put his foot down: "I am keeping him. I found him and he is mine." Until then, Naftali had lived in the cellar of the refinery, and now he received an apartment with three rooms and a kitchen on the upper story. Helmrich was glad. He told Naftali how, behind the scenes, the entire Gestapo leadership in Galicia had been kept busy with his forgery.

One may assume with a high degree of certainty that Naftali Backenroth would have escaped the Germans even if he had not adopted Bronicki's identity. First, he was a champion at survival and was skilled at improvising under conditions where ordinary people suffer paralysis of the will. Second, he had a safety net, provided by the Gestapo officers. In his cunning, he succeeded in extracting from those criminals the drop of humanity that exists in even the most despicable of human beings, and thus he served as their life insurance. After the war, when the murderers were required to give an account of their actions at their war crimes trials, they summoned Naftali to tell their judges how they had helped him to save Jewish lives.

This suggests that perhaps Naftali had no real need to devise an additional safety net by changing his identity, since the one he had sufficed. But it is clear that Naftali prepared another line of defense for himself because he feared that something might go wrong at the last moment. At the same time, one should not overlook the fact that Naftali was an adventurer. The very prospect of deceiving the Germans brought a rush of adrenaline to his blood. He enjoyed toying with fate. Walking on the edge of the abyss was a way of life for him. When he told people how he had tricked them all, the Germans, the Poles, and the Ukrainians, his eyes lit up and he smiled. It was evident that this had been the most fascinating adventure of his life.

Perhaps that is why Naftali never reverted to his original name. He used his new identity to save not only himself but hundreds of other Jews as well, and Tulek Bronicki was what they called him. After the war, he took the name of Bronicki officially. Even his son, Lucien, adopted the name of Bronicki.

22

Phoenixlike

Every year on May 8, Ullo Kahane enjoyed reminiscing about his life. On this day in 1945, the day the war in Europe ended, crowds of jubilant people all over the world rejoiced together and danced in the streets. In the town of Salyany in Azerbaijan, however, it was a drab, ordinary day, made exceptional by only one unusual incident.

When the Germans invaded Russia in the summer of 1941, the Soviet government had ordered all citizens to turn in their radio receivers to the authorities, and people would instead receive radio sets that were tuned in to a single station, the official one. In Salyany, the private radio sets were stored at the post office. Feder had become friendly with the postmaster, and sometimes he was allowed to come in and listen to forbidden foreign stations. On the government station, only official news was broadcast, whereas foreign stations carried news that was not as highly censored. Feder, who knew several languages, often listened in order to keep his friends up-to-date.

On May 8, 1945, he went to the post office and heard a speech by King George VI of England, declaring that Germany "has been finally overcome" and the war was over. Feder ran home and broke the news. Yet the official station said nothing.[1] "Until then," Ullo related forty years later, "we had kept all the news that Feder heard at the post office to ourselves. We never told anyone that we had a private source of information, but this time we couldn't restrain ourselves. It was strange. We were spreading the news that the Nazis had been defeated and the war was over, but the official radio said nothing."

During the next twenty-four hours, the Soviets remained silent, and people in Salyany felt confused because of Feder's announcement. Citizens asked one another who was spreading rumors that could harm the Soviet war effort. The police started to make inquiries.

"It wasn't funny," Ullo said. "Babzade, Lidka's doctor friend at the hospital, said to her, 'You won't ever go home now. They'll take you straight to Siberia.' And it was really obvious that if they caught us, they would put us in jail. Because of this, Feder went into hiding."

But Ullo had to be at work that day. Fortunately, a Polish officer who had returned from Iran showed up at the office next to Ullo's. He knocked on the windowpane, and Ullo could see that the man was eager to tell him something. Ullo opened the window and the officer said, "Excuse me sir, there's something I don't understand. In Iran, everyone's happy and rejoicing, and no one's working, and no one's sleeping because the war's over, but here everyone's asleep."

"I don't know anything," Ullo replied innocently and immediately called the guard who was posted at the building's entrance. Ullo asked the officer to repeat what he had just said for the guard. That is what saved Ullo because the next morning, when officers of the NKVD (the Soviet secret service) came to question Ullo, he told them about the Polish officer who had come from Iran and he sent them to speak to the guard. They detained Ullo for two hours, and when they came back from the guard's post, they let him go. Feder stayed in hiding until the official announcement was broadcast.

Ullo and his friends remained in Salyany for another year. Only in April 1946 did the party leadership in Moscow allow the refugees from Poland to go back to their country. It was a difficult year. Nushka had become pregnant before the end of the war, but she miscarried early in the pregnancy, and after the war ended, she became pregnant again. She gave birth to their son Roman, but when he was three months old, he contracted severe blood poisoning and died.

Before Ullo and his group set out, the local Communist Party organized a farewell get-together for Ullo. The party chiefs were grateful to him. They drank a lot of vodka and got drunk. Ullo drank juice. The secretary Alayev made a speech about Ullo's valuable contribution to the economy. "Let it be recorded to your credit that you built an infrastructure for light industry, and when the youngsters come back from the front, they will have jobs."

Alayev wished Ullo a safe return to Poland and hoped that he would lead communism to victory there.

"They thought I was an orthodox communist," Ullo said. "They suggested several times that I join the party, and I evaded the issue. Then they suggested that I remain in Azerbaijan and take an important position in Baku, and again I managed to get out of it, telling them that I was needed in Poland to help the party. That was an excellent excuse, and they all believed that I was an important Polish communist. A friend of mine who worked in the mayor's office overheard Alayev saying, 'Just as Dimitrov has to go back to Bulgaria, so Kahane has to go back to Poland.' Giorgi Dimitrov was the head of the Third International, and I was an unknown youngster from the village of Bolechow.[2]

"The party heads ceremoniously bade us farewell and, as a goodwill gesture, gave us a special vehicle to drive home in. All of the other Poles went home on supply trains, and we returned in a party jeep. We took the few belongings we had acquired. We had a sack full of salt, and we put it in the jeep. On the way, at every stop, we exchanged some salt for food. After a twelve-day journey, we crossed the border into Poland and stopped at the city of Katowice. Our Russian adventure had come to an end. Only then we did realize that all of Poland had become a Jewish graveyard."

After five years of flight, Katowice was an ideal final stop for Ullo and his partners. It was conducive to reorganizing their lives and working out future plans.

But for Naftali Bronicki, the final phase of his risky adventures was still perilous. In August 1944, when the Red Army liberated Galicia, Naftali was living in Drohobych, near the oil wells and the refinery that had belonged to his family, the Backenroths. But now his new name, Bronicki, was that of the illegitimate son of a gentile woman named Bronicki who had become pregnant to a gentile doctor, Kozlowsky. Along with the rest of his family, Naftali helped the Jews who emerged from their improvised hiding places and the temporary shelters they had sought during the last months of the Nazi occupation. Among these survivors were several relatives, including Stella Backenroth (later Wieseltier), Leon and David Thorne, Dora Backenroth, Meir Weintraub, and others.

When the Germans withdrew, they demanded that Naftali come with them, but he refused. Most of the German soldiers and civilians ran away, along with a few Poles and Ruthenians who had cooperated with them.

Naftali was the only engineer remaining. Just one platoon of German soldiers was left in the town, and its commander told the director of the refineries, Haftsmann, that when they withdrew, the commander would take Naftali with him. The German command didn't want the Russians to benefit from Naftali's professional know-how, but Naftali succeeded in evading the order. While the soldiers were getting ready to go, Naftali distracted their officer's attention by giving him an expensive white jacket for a present. The officer became confused, and in the end the German platoon left without Naftali.

As the Germans pulled out, Red Army units moved into Drohobych. With them came some of the town's residents who had fled to Russia at the beginning of the German occupation. They came in military uniforms and immediately arrested the Russian manager of the refinery and accused him of collaborating with the Germans. Then they interrogated Naftali and arrested him.

"I was not surprised. I knew I would be arrested and interrogated," Naftali told his son many years later. Once, in the middle of the war, Dr. Mauricio Ruhrberg, who was the head of the Judenrat at the time, had asked Naftali what would happen when it was all over. Naftali answered, "We will be tried. I may get off, but you won't." Dr. Ruhrberg was shot by the Nazis at the end of 1942.

Every evening the Russians questioned Naftali, and during the day, they wouldn't let him sleep or sit down. The interrogators claimed that he had collaborated with the Gestapo by persuading the Nazis to punish the Ukrainians who perpetrated the pogrom in Schodnica, and Naftali told them the whole story. "I said that I had chanced upon the opportunity to settle accounts with Jew killers," recalled Naftali.

Then the Russian police arrested the mayor of Schodnica and put him in Naftali's cell. The next day the interrogators claimed that they had evidence that Naftali had been seen in the company of the heads of the Gestapo. "During one of the *aktzias*," they said, "you were seen talking to the Nazis." Naftali explained that during one of the horrible *aktzias*, he walked through the streets with the mayor, trying to save as many people as possible.

Some weeks later, a special commission to examine Nazi crimes came to Drohobych and conducted a thorough investigation. The commission gathered evidence from witnesses: Ukrainians, Poles, and Jews. It also asked to see documents. For that purpose, the commission dug up the letters, the

In the summer of 1944, following the liberation of Galicia from the Nazis by the Red Army, Naftali Backenroth-Bronicki was photographed with his son, Lucien, at Nafta's courtyard in Schodnica, where the family resided during the last month of the war.

notes, and the diaries that had been thrown into the cornerstone pit of the riding hall that was built for the Gestapo officer Felix Landau. One document that was found inside the pit was the diary that had been placed there by Naftali's brother-in-law, the physician Schmer. From that diary and other papers found in the pit and from testimony given by Poles, Ruthenians, and Jews, the truth about Naftali's project emerged.

Fifty years later, Naftali said that during the whole interrogation, he was relaxed and confident that the true story would come out. Only when the commission ordered people to dig up the riding hall's pit did he become concerned: "I didn't want them to open the pit because I feared that they would find incriminating evidence against Judenrat members, but they did dig it up and found the diaries, and then they called me to the commission and questioned me, and right away my conditions improved. The members of the commission called me 'comrade,' while the secret police investigators were still calling me 'citizen.'"

Then certain Jews told the authorities that Naftali had witnessed the Germans executing Russian prisoners of war. He did not deny it and gave a detailed account of the happening: "I told them the Germans had bound the Russian officers together with wire, in groups of four. They were all officers and they were slaughtered like sheep. The killers were Krause and Günther of the Gestapo, the same Günther who was made head of the Gestapo in Drohobych in Felix Landau's place. After the interrogation, one of the commission members told me, 'Don't worry, you'll get out,' and the priest sent me a cake with a picture of the Black Madonna of Czestochowa in it."[3]

Imprisoned with Naftali in his cell was a boy of about seventeen or eighteen from the Polish underground, Armia Krajowa (the Home Army).[4] "I taught him mathematics and physics, and I gave him the picture of the Madonna," recalled Naftali. "After all, my 'mother' Katya Bronicki was also a virgin [Naftali chuckled]. They let the boy go two weeks after me."

Toward the end of the interrogation, Naftali was asked about his identity. Was he a Backenroth or a Bronicki? He insisted that he was Bronicki, the son of the physician Kozlowsky. "They released me after someone who knew my father very well told them that there had been good relations between Backenroth and Kozlowsky. The witness sounded reliable because he knew the name of our family's wet nurse. He said they called her Kasha. Later, the town police chief told them that the doctor had illegitimate children. He also said that my father and Kozlowsky were friends, and that's the way the circle was closed."

The interrogation, the inquiries, and the identity check lasted five months. On being released from prison, Naftali told his friends that, ultimately, the testimonies of Ruthenians and Poles had helped him more than those of the Jews.

On August 8, 1944, when the Nazis retreated from Schodnica, the ordeal of Stella Backenroth was over. At exactly 7 A.M., Beneck, the sixteen-year-old son of the Pole Janiewski, opened the hatch that covered her hiding place and yelled, "The Russians are here already." Stella was the first to go out. Her legs were swollen; she blinked in the sunlight and she had lost her voice from excitement. For nine full months she had been imprisoned in the narrow shelter dug under the stables, its opening covered by a sliding board.

Stella's parents and her brother, Zygus, had been murdered in the nearby Bronica Forest in the summer of 1943. Stella's name had also been on the list of those to be killed that day, but at the last moment a member of the Judenrat had intervened and managed to get her off the truck. For six more months, she lived in the ghetto in Drohobych, and when it was liquidated in November 1943, she fled on foot to Schodnica, where she was hidden in the shelter under the stables on the Backenroth family estate, close to one of the oil wells.

Together with her in the burrow were two others who had escaped when the Nazis liquidated the ghetto, the young lawyer Isidore Friedman and Luisa Mahler, the widow of Dr. Mahler. In the beginning of 1944, two of Stella's relatives joined them in the hideout: Leon and David Thorne. Five people were crammed into the dugout. It was a very small place; they could not stretch their legs or stand up straight. There were two mattresses and wooden benches, and the only light was from a candle. A bucket in one corner served as a toilet.

The stable over the shelter was part of a small livestock farm, and it housed a pig, a goat, twenty rabbits, and a few chickens, raised by the families of Stanislav Nedza and Franz Janiewski, Polish gentiles from Schodnica. Before the war, the two men had worked for the Backenroths' oil company. The families hid the five Jews and provided them with food. They had taken a great risk upon themselves. They knew that the Germans had threatened to kill any Pole who helped Jews, and in one case a Polish woman was executed for hiding Jews not far from there. But more than altruism induced the Poles to help.

"Of course, we are grateful to them," Leon Thorne wrote in his diary, "but at the same time it should be noted that they are not endangering themselves solely out of idealistic motives. The Poles are hiding some of their Jewish acquaintances and employers from the Gestapo for materialistic reasons as well. First, we are paying them well for their cooperation and, in addition, we have promised them in writing that half of our oil-well assets in Schodnica, which we are sure we will get back after the war, will be theirs. The documents have been signed by us and are here with us in our hiding place."

Thorne kept his diary in the burrow out of a belief that he might be the only Jew left in the world, and it was his historical duty to record the events

The only existing photograph of Bruno Schulz.

for posterity. The diary opens with these words: "I am writing these lines with great difficulty, at a time when my life is at risk and I have little prospect of surviving these terrible years. But I must write, even if my words will be annihilated with me, because I feel that I must tell how the Jews lived, how they were liquidated and how they survived the Hitler years. The desperate weeping of my Jewish brethren in the ghettoes and the death camps is ringing in my ears. Their voices will not be silenced. Will one of them be left to record these events? Who will describe our sufferings to the coming generations? Or will posterity live in total ignorance?"

Thorne wrote that his fellow fugitive Isidor Friedman had been forced to work at sorting stolen books for the Nazis with the renowned Jewish writer and artist Bruno Schulz, who lived in Drohobych and whose tragic fate, when it became known after the war, touched many hearts across the world. Schulz's unique works inspired many intellectuals, so much so that he became one of the outstanding symbols of the cultural and artistic genius exterminated by the Nazis in Poland.[5]

Bruno was born in 1882, the younger of the two sons of Jakub and Henrietta Schulz, an assimilated Jewish couple whose family was blessed with talent and imagination but was fated to endure the torments of Job. Since childhood, Bruno had suffered from a severe heart condition and from unrelenting depression. His father was also chronically ill, and the mother had to run their business, a haberdashery store on the Rynek, Drohobych's main square. But she wasn't up to the task, and the store went bankrupt. Bruno enrolled twice at a university (in Lvov and in Vienna) to study architecture, but both times had to break off his studies due to illness. His older brother, Izydor, a senior clerk in the oil industry, died young of a heart ailment, and Bruno became the sole breadwinner for the rest of the family: a sickly widowed sister, Hania Hoffman, whose husband had committed suicide; her son, Zygmunt, who was also afflicted with depression; and a female cousin who lived with them.

When the Germans conquered Drohobych, Schulz was an art teacher at the Polish high school. The Jewish teachers were dismissed, so he gave private classes. The Germans then ordered the Judenrat to send two people to sort tens of thousands of books that they had looted and stored in a former home for the aged, and the Judenrat chose Bruno Schulz and Isidor Friedman. Most of the volumes came from the library of the Jesuit monastery of Chyrow, a nearby town. The two worked for months, separating rare works, which the Nazis shipped to Germany, and the less valuable books, which were destroyed.

By the time the war broke out, Bruno Schulz was already well known in Polish intellectual circles as a gifted poet, a short-story writer, and a painter. His prose style was dreamlike and enchanting, and his stories took place in a small town like Drohobych and depicted an imaginary world where spiritual values had been decimated by materialism and sadistic impulses. His drawings and paintings were of a similar ilk. They, too, were unique, both stylistically—in their eclectic use of the various "isms" of the era, particularly surrealism, expressionism, and cubism—and in the manner that the figures were drawn. Just as in his stories, Shultz's figure drawings were grotesque and erotic, with a clear element of perversion, particularly a series of drawings that portrayed sadomasochistic scenes of cruel women dominating submissive men.[6]

Friedman told Thorne that one day he and Schulz had watched from the window of the monastery as a convoy of Gestapo trucks pulled up in the street below. They saw Naftali Backenroth standing on the sidewalk talking to the SS officers who led the convoy, which was on its way to the town of Turka from the district capital of Stryj. The soldiers on the truck had been ordered to capture five hundred Jews and kill them. Naftali was trying to convince them to call off the operation. Some of the officers were drunk. They were discussing their drinking habits and laughing out loud, and they ignored Naftali's pleas.

One officer complained that the local brandy was tasteless. He said that he preferred Martell cognac from France. Naftali heard him and offered to get him a bottle. The Gestapo officers agreed to give Naftali an hour to get them the Martell, and he disappeared into the ghetto. When he came back, he was carrying two bottles of cognac, which had been stored away before the war. In appreciation, the Gestapo reduced the number of Jews they killed in Turka that day, from the planned five hundred to three hundred.

"One hundred Jews are worth one bottle of cognac," Thorne wrote in his diary.

Schulz was known to be a delicate man, and he suffered from bad dreams. His friends in the Polish underground prepared counterfeit papers for him and begged him to escape to Warsaw, but he lingered in Drohobych, perhaps because it was more important for him to save his family from starvation, or because he was too timid to venture to an unknown place.

Thorne related in his diary that some of the members of the Judenrat employed Schulz to paint their portraits and that Gestapo officers sat their sweethearts down in front of him and demanded that he paint them. But most of Schulz's artistic commissions were assigned by the Drohobych Gestapo commander, Felix Landau, who extended his patronage over Schulz and gave him food in exchange for paintings. Schulz decorated the riding hall that Naftali's work groups built for Landau, and he also painted frescoes of fairies from Grimm's fairy tales in the bedroom of Landau's five-year-old son in the villa where the senior Gestapo NCO lived with his family.[7]

But Schulz's outstanding talent did not save his life. Thorne described how the artist fell victim to the brutality of another Gestapo officer, Karl Günther. It happened on Thursday, November 19, 1942, exactly a month after the Nazis murdered the wife, the son, and the parents of Max Reiner, a pharmacist's assistant from the ghetto with whom Günther was friendly. Günther had made no effort to rescue the family, and Reiner evaded him. That morning, Günther came to the pharmacy, and Reiner stabbed him with a knife. Günther drew his pistol, shot Reiner dead, and left the shop in a fury. He summoned more Gestapo officers to the ghetto, and they went on a rampage of vengeance in the Judenrat offices and then in the streets. They stood on a corner on Mickiewicz Street (now Shevchenko Street) and shot everyone they encountered. Schulz happened to pass by on his way to see his sister. Günther was carrying a miniature pistol, and he used it to shoot two women and then, when Shultz walked by, Günther shot him twice, point-blank, in the head. Dr. Ruhrberg, the leading official in the Judenrat at the time, witnessed the terrible scene from his office window. Two hundred and thirty Jews were killed on that day.[8]

Isidor Friedman also witnessed the murder. It happened, he wrote after the war, on the corner of Czacki and Mickiewicz streets, where he and Schulz "happened to be in the ghetto to buy food [instead of at work outside] when we heard shooting and saw Jews running for their lives and we too took flight. Schulz, physically the weaker, was caught by a Gestapo agent called Günther, who stopped him, put a revolver to his head, and fired twice."

Friedman said that Landau, who was a rival of Günther's and hated him, had killed Günther's dental technician, a Jew by the name of Löw, and Günther's murder of Schulz was an act of revenge. "You killed my Jew, I killed yours," Günther said to Landau.

That night Friedman went back to the scene. "I searched his [Schulz's] pockets, and gave his documents and some notes I found there to his nephew Hoffman, who lost his life a month later. Toward morning I buried him in the Jewish cemetery," Friedman related.[9]

Later, in the hideout where Thorne composed his memoir, a crisis occurred. Luisa Mahler took ill and became so weak that she could not get out of bed. Stella Backenroth fed her carrot juice in a spoon heated over a candle and washed her, but her condition worsened until she could not move or speak. Then she lost consciousness.

Thorne left the hideout and went to consult a doctor. He described the symptoms, and the doctor said that there was no hope and that Mahler would die soon. The Polish farmers made plans to bury her at night, but a remarkable thing happened. A week after they had given up hope that Mahler would live, she suddenly woke up and asked for a glass of milk. There was no milk so they gave her carrot juice. An hour later, she asked for more. In the evening, the Poles brought her a little milk. She gulped it down and began to talk. After two weeks, she could get up and wash herself. "In another two weeks she had completely recovered," wrote Thorne in his diary, "thanks to Stella Backenroth's self-sacrifice."

More than being angry at the brutality and the cruelty of the German occupiers, Thorne was furious at what he described as the immorality and the corruption of his own community's leaders. As mentioned previously, in his diary, Thorne wrote a scathing indictment of the members of the Judenrat.

Forty-five years after Stella came out of the foxhole where she and Thorne had hidden during the last months of the war, she said that one should not envy either the members of the Judenrat or the community members whose lives they controlled on behalf of the Nazis. She admired her cousin Naftali, who had grasped this extraordinary situation from the beginning. "Naftali understood," said Stella, "that if he wanted to survive and help his family and his neighbors to survive, he had to find a way to avoid this tragic predicament."

Although the intentions of most of the Judenrat members were benevolent, some of them were submerged up to their necks in the quagmire of internal politics of their cities and towns, embroiled in favoritism and nepotism, and could therefore not withstand the pressure. They were given an impossible task: deciding who in their community would live and who would die.

In the summer of 1946, when Ullo Kahane and his group returned to Poland, the dispute about the role the Judenrat played in the extermination system had barely been articulated. After the survivors' emergence from their hiding places, most of them were occupied with searching for relatives, mourning the dead, and trying to establish new lives. Still, many survivors doggedly carried out one duty: giving their own testimonies and collecting others' stories. Calling themselves "the historical committee," they organized into groups of researchers who interviewed the survivors and put their statements in writing. That was the first thing that Ullo had done when the group made its final stop at the city of Katowice.

"I joined the testimony gatherers," Ullo recalled many years later, "to pay tribute to the victims before our memories drifted and vital material for official investigations was lost." These valuable early testimonies were incorporated into trial proceedings, including the 1945–1946 Nuremberg trials and also in numerous commission reports.

Ullo's assignment was to take down the statements of Jews from his hometown, Bolechow, and its surroundings. Some survivors felt a need to bear witness and be heard by empathetic listeners. Yet for others, the trauma was so severe that they couldn't reveal their horrific experiences even to compassionate people. Thus, it was difficult to conduct an accurate, systematic survey of the terror and the horror that Bolechow's Jews were forced to live through. Only years later when Ullo met some childhood friends was he able to grasp the whole picture after hearing their accounts of the shocking events.

Out of approximately three thousand Jews who had lived in Bolechow when the Nazis conquered the town, only forty-five were still alive after the war, including two children. One survivor was a close friend of the Kahane family, a woman by the name of Lusha Schindler. With her mother and two aunts, she had found refuge in the home of a Polish judge. They were in hiding for three years and received full reports of the *aktzias* and the massacres, of the dreadful crimes committed by her neighbors, the Ukrainians, and of Jews who had escaped. Although she was not an actual eyewitness to each of the stages, one can say that almost all of the information reached Schindler's ears in real time, and she mentally recorded the history of the liquidation of the Jews of Bolechow.

After the war, Ullo had written a letter to Schindler from Salyany asking for details about the fate of his parents, and she wrote back describing how they had been murdered and what had happened to some of his relatives. Following the Nazis' retreat, Schindler left Bolechow for Vienna, and many years passed before Ullo had a chance to speak to her.

Another important witness was Benno Reisman, the brother of Ullo's boyhood friend Gustav Reisman. Benno had remained in Bolechow throughout the Nazi occupation. He hid in the surrounding forests and on a nearby farm belonging to Polish farmers. His friend David Schindler had saved his life when they jumped from the same train that took Yerahmiel and Rachel Kahane to their deaths in the Bełźec extermination camp after the second *aktzia.* The torment had begun directly after the communists withdrew from the town, on July 2, 1941, as the German offensive advanced. On the very same day, the Ukrainian community set up a militia, whose members wore white armbands so that they would be easily identifiable, and went about wreaking their revenge on the communists (many of whom were Jews).

Apparently, the first incident occurred even before the Germans arrived. On a side street, near the bridge over the Sukiel River, a squad of militiamen caught two Jews and beat them. A Polish youth, Andrzej Lozinski, watched the incident from the window of his home. He saw the Ukrainians dragging the Jews to the river bank and tying them to logs. Although no one had ever suspected him of sympathizing with the Jews, he became infuriated at the Ukrainians' violence against the two passersby. In a rage, he went into the street and yelled, "Let them go! They didn't do anything to you!" Young Lozinski's intervention did not succeed. A bullet pierced his skull, and he dropped to the ground, dead. His mother saw the murder from the yard of their home. Immediately after that, the Ukrainians shot the two Jews dead and threw their bodies into the river.[10]

On that morning, the delicate balance that had prevailed between the Jewish community and the Ukrainian community since the Bogdan Khmelnytsky massacre in the seventeenth century suddenly tipped under the weight of anti-Semitism. The new reality for the Ukrainians was that Poland had been crushed by Germany and wiped off the map, and the Jews were apparently destined for deportation (at that stage, the Nazis had not yet hinted at plans to exterminate them). This fed the Ukrainians' nationalistic dreams that finally they would succeed in achieving independence. With this in mind, many Ukrainians made themselves available to carry out the agenda of the German conquerors.

Of course, Hitler never for a moment entertained the idea of granting the Ukrainians independence. According to the Nazi race theory, all Slavs—Poles as well as Ukrainians—were classified as slave peoples who were meant to serve the Aryans. The Slavs' status was only slightly higher than that of the Jewish race, whose destiny was total annihilation.

The Germans made very good use of their Ukrainian collaborators. Although many Poles mobilized to do battle with the Nazi occupiers, from the underground and in other ways, and a good number of them hid Jews, very few Ukrainians came to the aid of the Jews. Some of them even tortured and murdered Jews with no less zeal than that displayed by the worst SS officers.

As for the Jews of Bolechow, they were caught totally unprepared. Most of them never grasped how desperate their situation had become. On the eve of the communists' retreat, there were arguments in the community as to which of the conquerors were preferable, and many said they looked forward to the departure of the "crass Russians" so that the "cultured" Germans would move in and restore order to their lives. Yerahmiel and Rachel Kahane were among these advocates of the German solution. Exactly a week before the Red Army pulled out, when Ullo and Lidka were visiting their parents for the last time, Rachel was optimistic. "There'll still be a miracle," she told her children. On June 30, 1941, they had their last telephone conversation with their parents, and two days later they embarked on the supply train that took them to Russia with the retreating communists. Rachel and Yerahmiel lived in Bolechow for another full year, a year of unimaginable persecution and suffering.

The Germans took control of the Stanislaw region using units of the Hungarian and the Slovakian armies, and under their aegis, Ukrainian militiamen went out hunting for communists. Dozens of young people were caught, most of them Jews, and some were executed with guns, at night near the town. One group of communists was shot under the bridge over the Sukiel, where the Admor of Perlov had in better times held the Tashlikh service. One of the victims was Leah Schindler, a friend of Ullo's and Lidka's. Her father, Ben-Zion Schindler, had been the mayor of Bolechow in the 1930s.

A Nazi administration was soon set up in the town, and the race laws were promulgated on the billboards. The Germans selected a Judenrat and appointed Dr. Archie Reifeisen to head it. For several days, the German governor humiliated Reifeisen, sometimes slapping his face, until the head of the Judenrat could no longer stand it and hanged himself from a tree in the public park next to his home. He was replaced by Dr. Schindler. Advocate Pressler, his son-in-law, was made head of the Jewish police. Buma Krauthammer, a relative of Nunio's, the husband of Sonia Kahane, was an active member of the Judenrat.

Because of restrictions on the Jews' movements, the economic life of the town immediately ground to a halt, and most commerce and production ceased. Instead of citizens using money to buy and sell, a barter economy evolved. The Judenrat instituted food rationing, and the allocations to each family were small. Starvation set in among the poor, and a typhus epidemic broke out. Hundreds of women, men, and children with swollen stomachs knocked on the doors of the well-off and pleaded for alms. At the same time, some of the wealthier residents still employed household help and private tutors for their children. Personal security deteriorated, with Ukrainian militiamen breaking into Jews' homes to degrade them and plunder their belongings.

The first four months of the German occupation seem to have passed relatively quietly for Yerahmiel and Rachel, perhaps because they still possessed enough valuables to keep the wolf from the door. That lasted until Tuesday, October 28, 1941, when the shocking event that later became known as "the first *aktzia*" dealt a crippling blow to the Jews of Bolechow.

At approximately noon, German and Ukrainian troops went from house to house, following their lists, and rounded up hundreds of Jews. The victims were allowed to take one suitcase apiece. The troops assembled them in the market square, the Rynek, and told them that they were slated for resettlement (*Umsiedlung*, in German), then marched them over the bridge. The procession of Jews passed the public gardens and the Polish church and then turned right toward the Dom Katolicki, the Catholic Center. On each side of the building's entrance stood Ukrainian militiamen carrying metal-tipped clubs. Some of them beat Jews with the clubs until they lost consciousness.

Inside the building, one of the most horrifying atrocities of the Holocaust took place. Ukrainian militiamen and Gestapo officers, many of whom were drunk and bent on revenge for what they perceived as years of being exploited by the Jewish race, used the hundreds of Jewish men, women, and children to stage an enactment of Dante's Inferno. It was a depraved orgy of life and death, nudity and blood, music and dance, all mixed together.

"The hall filled up, and they forced us all to lie facedown on the floor," Benno Reisman recalled forty-seven years later. "They closed the windows and the doors, and then they lit the coal-burning heaters and blocked the chimneys. Ukrainians and the SS troops stood along the walls. The heat was unbearable, and the air stank."

The teacher Sabina Friedman was also there and was made to prostrate herself on the floor. "I wanted to take my jacket off," she recounted later, "but a policeman kicked me in the chest and told me that if I tried to take my jacket off again, he would beat me to death."

"One of the stoves was heated until the metal was red hot," Reisman said. "And then they made the Jew, a teacher, undress and get onto it. He roared with pain, and many people fainted." German soldiers stood in the gallery and fired into the crowd. Women screamed with fear, and some simply went mad. Rabbi Mendel Landau recited the prayer of confession.

In the evening, groups of Jews were taken onto a platform and shot to death. "Dogilewsky, the school principal, lost control, began shrieking and striking himself until he got a blow from a rifle butt that split his skull into two," Sabina said. The blind pianist Bruckenstein was told to play, and the Gestapo officers stripped girls naked and dragged them to dance the polka on the stage, among the corpses. One of them was named Perlstein, Lidka Kahane's friend. Rabbis Horowitz and Landau were shoved onto the stage and forced to make speeches rebuking the community and admitting that the Jews of Bolechow deserved to be punished for their sins. A cross was cut into Rabbi Horowitz's chest. In the evening, someone shouted out,

"Dinner," and everyone who got up was shot. Twenty-eight Jews were killed in the hall, and dozens were wounded.[11]

The next day at noon, the Jews were taken out into the yard, and names were called off a list. Most of the young, strong people who were fit for work were sent home. All of the others were put on trucks and taken to the nearby Tanyawa Forest. There, they were lined up. Six machine guns had been placed behind them, and the Germans opened fire at the ranks of Jews. Most of the victims were still in shock. Very few showed any reaction. Almost all went to their deaths silently and compliantly. More than a thousand Jews were murdered in the forest, and only a few survived. One of these was Duzio Schindler, a friend of Ullo's. He managed to climb a tree, and hid there, watching the massacre. In the evening he crawled out of the forest and returned to town. Sabina Friedman was saved from the slaughter by a Polish friend, Mariza, a fellow teacher, who managed to persuade an SS officer to let her off the truck taking the Jews to the forest.[12]

This first *aktzia* passed over Yerahmiel and Rachel Kahane. They were not taken to the hall to be tortured or to the forest. The next day they heard details about what had happened. Until then, Rachel had been sustained by hope that she had nurtured, but now her spirit was extinguished. The couple knew what was in store for them and from then on functioned like automatons, selling some possessions every now and then to buy food, sitting in their home, and waiting for death.

The second *aktzia*, on August 20, 1942, was much worse. For thirty-six hours Germans and Ukrainians gathered hundreds of people who were to be transported and made them run to the town hall square. Some were murdered on the spot, among them the Polophile Dr. Blumenthal, Yerahmiel's friend, who had come to the Kahanes' house to hear seven-year-old Ullo's *drasha* speech.

Most of the killers in the square were Ukrainians. They were commanded by Matovicki, who was the chief of the Ukrainian police and a pathological sadist. Two policemen named Luchov and Demanion also did their worst to abuse the Jews. According to various witnesses, the members of the Jewish police were unrelenting in their efforts to find Jews who had evaded the roundup and were hiding.

"Many of the victims died from the abuse, the beatings, the thirst," Benno Reisman observed. "The things they did were cruel beyond belief. Pregnant women were beaten without mercy. The devils kicked them in the stomach. Infants were grabbed from their mothers' arms, and their heads were dashed against stone walls or telegraph poles. I was an eyewitness to the atrocities in the town hall square, and I can therefore permit myself to describe it."

Rachel and Yerahmiel were also taken to the square and from there to the train station. Three hundred and fifty years after their forefathers had settled in the little house built for them by the Polish nobleman Gidzinski, in the new town of Bolechow, they and their fellow Jews were evicted by their Ukrainian neighbors, who, acting on behalf of the Germans, abused them, abased them, and murdered them.

On that day, four hundred Jews were massacred in Bolechow, mostly in the town hall square, in the marketplace, and in the Jewish cemetery. One of them was a niece of Feder's (Lidka's husband). A pretty, yellow-haired three-year-old, she had been hiding in the home of a Polish woman who worked in the post office. Someone informed on the woman, and the Germans came and took the little girl from her hiding place. In the Jewish cemetery, a Nazi with a pistol in his hand seemed to hesitate when he saw her, so a Ukrainian came up, drew his own gun, and shot her in the head. Her mother was with the partisans in the forest. Shortly afterward, she, too, was shot after being spotted as she went down to a river to wash. The little girl's father, the physician Meyer Feder, escaped to Russia and survived.[13]

The bodies of those murdered during the second *aktzia* were buried in the Jewish cemetery, and the rest, sixteen hundred souls, among them Yerahmiel and Rachel, were marched to the railway station. On the way, the terrified Jews were forced to sing the Yiddish song *"Mein Steteleh Belz"* ("My Small Town Belz").[14] At the station, they were crammed into cattle cars, 120 people in each compartment. Then the train took the Jews of Bolechow to the Belźec death camp, and in the coming months most of them were murdered in the camp's gas chambers.[15]

Yerahmiel and Rachel were imprisoned at Belźec for six months. There is clear evidence that Ullo's cousin, the lawyer Nunio Kahane, managed to get them released and transferred to the Stryj ghetto. No one knows how he managed to do it. They lived in the ghetto for six months, under harsh conditions, until June 4, 1943, when they were taken along with several hundred other Jews to a forest outside the city and murdered.[16] An eyewitness who stood near them and survived told Lidka after the war that just before they were killed, Rachel said to a German who was aiming his rifle at her, "And you belong to the same nation as Goethe and Schiller." She said it in German.

Ullo's friend Benno Reisman survived. He escaped from the train at Belźec after the second *aktzia.* He roamed through the Carpathian forests overlooking Bolechow and then with a friend, Munzio Turkel, a relative of the Kahanes, found a hiding place in the loft of a Polish farmer's barn. They hid there for twenty-one months, in exchange for money, until August 1944, when the Red Army came back.

After Ullo and his sister Lidka returned to Poland and realized what suffering their parents had undergone, they had qualms of conscience for having left them behind. They could not justify to themselves how they had abandoned their parents and allowed them to be murdered. Yet the children certainly had enough mitigating excuses. After all, before the German occupation, they never imagined what was going to happen. They didn't realize that the civilized Germans would become mass murderers and set up an industry of death such as the world had never seen, even though they knew what had happened to the Jews in Germany and they, along with thousands of others, had the prescience to flee. After all, their parents had taught them to identify with German culture, with its romanticism and its concepts of honesty and fairness. Their mother had guided their education in that direction and they could have used this as an excuse, but, nevertheless, along with their grief they felt a great sense of guilt. If only they had been more forceful in persuading their parents to leave Bolechow in time and to join them while they were living in Stanislav, and then had taken their parents on their journey to Russia.

But Ullo and Lidka's parents had insisted on remaining behind in Bolechow and, as hard as it may be to comprehend today, actually looked forward to the German occupation. They thought that the Germans would rescue them from the torments they had been subjected to by "the communist barbarians," as Rachel called the Russians. With hindsight, it is easy to ridicule their naïveté, but in those days it was difficult for the adult bourgeoisie to find their existential bearings. Strangely, at a time when most Jews in Galicia had been overcome by panic and hysteria, and many loaded their belongings onto their backs and fled eastward, Rachel and Yerahmiel had remained clear headed and composed. They were certain that everyone who fled would soon regret it, so they stayed where they were and paid for it with their lives.

And for that, Ullo judged himself harshly. On several occasions he told his sister that he had not done enough to save them. As their only son, he felt that he had a special responsibility and had let them, as well as himself, down. From the moment that he decided to get onto the train to Russia, he had sealed their fate. If he had stayed behind, he might have been able to save them. We cannot enter his mind, and we are certainly not entitled to judge him, whatever happened. Fortunately, when he returned to Poland, he did not lose his head, as happened to many other returning Holocaust survivors. He took stock of his situation and began everything anew. From the moment that he opened a new chapter in his life, he put the tragedy behind him.

Despite the deep grief the family members felt, it must be said that they came out of the Holocaust relatively well. Only two had died in the immediate families of Ullo and his wife, Nushka: Ullo's parents, Rachel and Yerahmiel. All of the others survived. Seven of them had left the area conquered by the Nazis in time and either willingly traveled to or were expelled into Soviet territory: Ullo and Nushka; Lidka and her husband, Feder; Nushka's parents, Clara (née Backenroth) and Israel Moshe Sobel; and Nushka's sister Zhizha. Two other relatives had emigrated from Poland to safe havens: Ullo's sister Sonia and her husband, Nunio Krauthammer, had settled in Brazil; and Nushka's sister Hella and her husband, Israel Horn, settled in Palestine.

On the other hand, in the extended family, the results were tragic. Hundreds of souls had perished. It was impossible to accurately calculate the numbers of those who died and those who lived because the branches of the family are complex and tortuous. Still, a detailed survey of the fate of Avrumche Backenroth's sixteen daughters and sons, from both of his wives, who were living when the war broke out revealed that out of a total of eighty-five of Avrumche's offspring, sons- and daughters-in-law, and grandchildren, thirty-five were murdered by the Nazis.

A more general survey of some of the other branches of the family tree shows that from both the Backenroth and the Kahane sides, about half of the members of the extended families perished, more than five hundred souls. (Their family names were Backenroth, Heller, Kuppelmann, Sobel, Weber, Kahane, Graubart, Feder, Krauthammer, Wickler, Silberstein, Greenwald, Turkel, Barsam, Schmer, Panzer, Weidmann, Weintraub, Weinberger, Tenzer,

Thorne, and Gartner.) If they had not been killed, many thousands of Avrumche's descendants would be alive today.[17]

Most of the family's survivors did the same thing as the other Polish Jews who came out of the Holocaust alive. They refused to allow despair to control their fate and with energy and determination built new lives for themselves. They chose new countries to live in, away from Europe, and built families and businesses and careers. This is the way that Jews have always behaved throughout their history, which has been so full of upheavals and tribulations. Many had lost their spouses, their children, or their parents. Some remained alone in the world, without even one relative. And nevertheless, they had a gusto for living and an optimism that made it possible for them to pull themselves out of the pit and climb to the peak of the mountain. These survivors were so determined to begin again and to succeed that for the first two decades of their new lives, many of them pushed the horrors of their past into the deepest recesses of their subconscious. They abolished their memories and never told a soul what had happened to them, not even their closest friends and relatives.

23

Interlude on the Way to Anchorage

IT WASN'T THE NAZIS WHO DEPRIVED LEOPOLD WEISS of his freedom, cut him off from his family, and tormented him, as had happened to others in the extended Backenroth clan. Rather, it was the British who imprisoned him in an internment camp in India for five and a half years, along with thousands of Germans, Austrians, Italians, and Japanese, all of whom were citizens of the Axis countries. Weiss had converted to Islam and changed his name to Muhammad Asad, yet he remained an Austrian citizen.[1] At the beginning of the war, he was living in India with his family, in Lahore, the capital city of the province of Punjab.[2]

Asad's passage to India had been forced upon him. In 1933, six years after he settled in the city of Medina and rose to the status of adviser to King Ibn Saud, he had to run away from Saudi Arabia with his wife, Munira, and their son, Talal, to save their lives. The details of the dispute that broke out between Asad and the House of Saud have never come to light, and Asad himself never revealed them. It seems that Munira's father, the head of a branch of the influential Shammar tribe, quarreled with the royal family about money matters, and as a result the Sauds accused Asad and his associates of treason.[3]

In his memoirs, Asad wrote that he never regretted being exiled from Saudi Arabia, because the Bedouin king had disappointed him by not creating a process of revival and renewal in Islam. Asad had hoped that Ibn Saud would impose the tenets of Wahhabism on the tribes of the Arabian

Peninsula.[4] Wahhabism, which asserted the superiority of the Sunni branch over the other trends in Islam, mainly the Shi'a and Sufism, caused the tribes to unite in the early twentieth century and established the political entity known as Saudi Arabia. It is a fundamentalist sect that places social solidarity at the top of its order of priorities; it prefers the simple, natural life over the materialist ways of the West; and it combats corruption and profligacy.

This emotional attraction to pristine purity, which had earlier found expression in young Leopold's attempt to grasp the essence of basic divine wisdom, led the adult Asad to the court of Ibn Saud. But his hopes were dashed. In his opinion, the king had no religious vision and had become a slave to materialism. Asad wrote, "Ibn Saud was no more than a king—a king aiming no higher than so many other autocratic Eastern rulers before him."

Muhammad Asad was therefore obliged to take his Bedouin wife and their son and set out for the next station in his life, the Indian subcontinent. The converted Jew wanted to be close to the poet Muhammad Iqbal, an Islamic politician from Lahore, who was famous across the Muslim world and whom Asad ardently admired.[5]

Iqbal's worldview suited the philosophy of Asad. The esteemed poet preached a return to the origins of the faith and a pure religion, and he opposed any innovation that could lead to assimilation. He deplored the secularism that had spread by government decree in leading Islamic states such as Turkey, Iran, and Egypt. Iqbal was also the first to advocate, in 1930, establishing a separate state called Pakistan for Indian Muslims. Asad became Iqbal's disciple and put his considerable intellectual powers at Iqbal's disposal.

In the mid-1930s, the Muslims' political struggle to separate from the Hindus in India and achieve independence gathered momentum. Asad was a member of the circle surrounding the founding fathers of the state-in-the-making. He moved with his family to Karachi, the future capital of Pakistan, became the editor of the Urdu-language journal *Islamic Culture*, and helped Iqbal to disseminate his religious and political vision.[6] Asad was convinced that Muslims felt a yearning for a spiritual revival, one that would unite Muslim communities all over the world behind an agreed-on ethical and political platform. It would pave the way for a renewal of the Golden Age of medieval times that had lasted for five hundred years, from the eighth to the thirteenth centuries. Asad believed that of the three monotheistic faiths, Islam had been corrupted and spoiled less than Christianity and Judaism had and that it was therefore capable of resurrecting the pure goals of its founders. In his mind, the poet Iqbal was the prophet whom fate had destined to realize the hopes that had earlier hung on King Ibn Saud.

Two years after fleeing to India, Asad renewed his correspondence with his sister and his father, who were still living in Vienna.[7] The frustrated banker Akiva Weiss, whose wife had died in 1919 and who had lost his assets, had remarried. Despite the bitter rift between father and son, in the face of the Nazi menace Asad was concerned about his family's fate and was prepared to do what he could to rescue them. A few months after Hitler carried out his Anschluss and annexed Austria to Germany in March 1938, Asad traveled to Europe to try to arrange for his relatives to leave Austria and relocate in England. In the spring of 1939 he visited Vienna and London, renewed ties with influential connections from his journalist days, and begged for their help in saving his family. But his efforts were fruitless, and he returned to India, frustrated.[8] In late September, after World War II had broken out, the British authorities in India declared Asad an enemy alien, and he was interned. If he had stayed in Saudi Arabia, which remained on the sidelines in the conflict, the war probably would not have affected him, but as happened so frequently to this eccentric and talented Jew, international conditions dictated a tortuous path for his life.

During the years of Asad's internment, his uncle in Jerusalem, the eye doctor Aryeh Feigenbaum, sent him food parcels, clothing, and money from Palestine and tried to get him released. In the 1920s, Asad had been living in Jerusalem as a guest of another uncle, the psychiatrist Dorian I. Feigenbaum, and traveling in the Middle East as a journalist. At the time, Asad had snubbed his uncle Aryeh because he believed in Zionism. Ultimately, however, the family connection was stronger than the insult, and Aryeh did what he could to help his sister's son, who was in dire straits.

After Asad's release from internment in the summer of 1945, his standing in the All India Muslim League grew stronger. He became well known across the subcontinent and even in Europe as a reliable representative of the voice of an independent Pakistan. When independence came in 1947, the first governor general of Pakistan, Muhammad Ali Jinnah, chose the former Jew to head the Department of Islamic Reconstruction, which was in charge of deepening Islam's control of the country.[9] After two years as a kind of commissar of religion, Asad was transferred to the Foreign Ministry and chosen to run the Middle East department. He worked to strengthen ties between Pakistan and the Arab world, which he knew well from his days as a peripatetic journalist in the 1920s and the 1930s. He wrote vitriolic speeches against the new state of Israel that were delivered by his boss, foreign minister Zafaruyllah Khan.[10] Some of the speeches included passages from the anti-Zionist articles that he had sent from the Middle East to his newspaper in Frankfurt when his name was still Leopold Weiss.

The course of Asad's life took another turn in 1952, when the Karachi government appointed him Pakistan's ambassador to the United Nations. To the surprise of his friends, Asad left his wife and son behind and went to New York City by himself. He lived in an official residence on Manhattan's Upper East Side and led an active social life. A friend introduced him to Pola Hamida, a Bostonian woman of Polish Catholic extraction, who had become a Muslim before she met him. Asad divorced Munira and married Pola Hamida.

At the same time, a man named Harry Zvi Zinder was serving as the spokesman of the Israeli delegation to the United Nations. His wife, Hemdah, was the daughter of the Jerusalem eye doctor Aryeh Feigenbaum, Asad's uncle. In the late 1930s and the 1940s, Hemdah Feigenbaum Zinder had been an announcer on the Voice of Jerusalem, the radio station that was established in Palestine by the British Mandatory authorities in 1936.[11] Her voice was heard across the Middle East, and her cousin Muhammad Asad had also heard it during his travels in Arab countries. The link between the cousins was renewed in New York in the 1950s, and they met often. Decades later, Harry and Hemdah's son, Professor Oren Zinder of the Rambam Medical Center in Haifa, recalled his uncle Poldi, as Leopold was known in the family back then, who had attended his bar mitzvah celebration in New York.

"He was an educated man, who spoke many languages, and a very friendly man," Professor Zinder said about his memories of Weiss-Asad, and added, "Poldi loved classical music and played the piano well." In his childhood, Leopold's parents had hired private teachers to teach him Jewish subjects and give him piano lessons.

The diplomat Zvi Zinder reported to the Foreign Ministry in Jerusalem on his meetings with Asad, and the Mossad, Israel's external intelligence agency, proposed that he try to recruit the Pakistani ambassador to its ranks. But Zinder had heard from his father-in law how extreme his wife's cousin was in his critique of Zionism, and he hesitated.[12] He feared that if he even hinted to Asad that he collaborate with Israel, the Muslim convert would break off relations with the family. If the Mossad had managed to recruit him as an agent, this could have been the spy story of the century, but Zinder never made the offer and Asad was not called upon to make the decision. In view of his life story and his personality traits, it's doubtful that Asad would have been ready to switch loyalties.

Or perhaps he would have been. Asad's abandonment of Munira and his marriage to the American Pola Hamida had angered his superiors in Karachi. Their relationship with him cooled to the point that he was dismissed from his diplomatic post. Asad remained in New York, and his links with Pakistan gradually dissolved. To earn money, he wrote an autobiography, *The Road to Mecca*, which won critical praise and became a best-seller.[13] Later, he and Pola Hamida moved to Geneva, where he worked on an English translation of the Quran.[14] In the 1970s, he taught Islam at Al Azhar University in Cairo. When he retired, he chose to live in Spain, where he died in 1992. Weiss-Asad was buried in Granada's Muslim cemetery.

In the annals of the Jewish people, many individuals have lived extraordinary, even wondrous, lives, because over the course of generations Jews have been "people of the world": polyglots, merchants, revolutionaries, innovators, and particularly creative and extraordinary inventors. Throughout the history of the Jews, there have been many apostates, most of whom became Christians. Some of the converts to Christianity became famous because they angered the Jews or because they pleased the gentiles. But there have been very few Jews who chose to become Muslims, made the pilgrimage to Mecca, and circumambulated the Kaaba. And no other Jewish convert ever led a life similar to that of Weiss-Asad, who became an adviser to the founder of the Saudi Arabian monarchy and a friend of his son Faisal; a disciple of the poet philosopher Muhammad Iqbal, who envisioned the new state of Pakistan; and then that country's ambassador to the United Nations. He even translated the Quran into English. Leopold Weiss was not the only Backenroth to lead an extraordinary life, but he certainly wandered the farthest from the clan's origins in Ashkenaz and Galicia.

Nushka and Ullo Kahane had also wandered far away from Galicia, but, unlike the eccentric Weiss-Asad, they had no desire to redeem humanity by reforming an alien and dogmatic doctrine. The Kahanes simply wished for peace and tranquillity; primarily, they yearned to have a child.

For more than ten years after the war, Ullo Kahane groped in the dark before finding the right path. He spent another ten years building up his business, along with his Brazilian partner, Kaxika Peris. Their labors bore fruit in the late 1960s, and if his wife, Nushka, had not been afflicted with an incurable disease, Ullo would have been happily sitting under his own grapevine and fig tree. To his business associates, he used to compare himself with the Good Soldier Schweik. When they tried to teach Schweik how to aim a rifle, Ullo said, he had trouble creating the imaginary straight line that connects the eye, the gun sight, and the target. "Schweik wasn't capable of seeing that line, but I am," Ullo said. He could indeed identify a target and focus on it. That was his advantage.

He started off on a small scale and, as was usual for him, first surveyed the terrain thoroughly. In a Rio de Janeiro neighborhood, he located a struggling tin sheet–processing plant by the name of Real and enlisted investors and partners to purchase it, guided them through the various business obstacles, and in particular was careful not to take superfluous risks.

The partners began with almost nothing, having a very limited amount of funding. Until they acquired the necessary goodwill, they had trouble raising capital. At first, they had to work with twenty-five banks simultaneously, juggling their accounts until their plant accumulated enough assets for them to get a substantial sum from one bank at a time. Sometimes they were stymied by high interest rates, or they purchased raw materials but couldn't immediately find a buyer for the finished product. Ullo had an excellent memory for figures, and he kept most of the facts in his head. Every day he wrote the bottom line on a slip of paper and put it in his shirt pocket. His partner, Kaxika, never checked up on him. Their business relationship was based on total mutual trust.

The purchase of Real was the auspicious final step on the winding path that had led from Galicia to Salyany in Azerbaijan, had passed through Katowice and Jerusalem, and had ended in Rio de Janeiro.

The Salyany period ended in the summer of 1946, when the Communist Party permitted Ullo's group to return to Poland and gave them a jeep to drive from the Caspian Sea to the coal-mining city of Katowice in southern Poland.[15] Ullo found work immediately as an economist in the Ministry of Industry and as a lecturer in the local university. Nushka wanted to have a child and to leave communist-controlled Poland as soon as possible. Her goal was to get to Brazil. Ullo's sister Sonia bombarded them with letters about Rio de Janeiro being heaven on earth. "Living in Rio is inexpensive, comfortable, and pleasant," she wrote, "and the view from our apartment is stunning."

The balcony of the Krauthammers' luxury apartment on Avenida Atlantica overlooked the long, wide strip of beach known as the Copacabana and the mighty rocks that lay off the coast. "Five o'clock coffee in the Copacabana Palace Hotel will make you forget what you went through in Europe," Sonia wrote. Like her and her husband, Nunio, most of the Jews in Rio had fled there from the Nazis. They were able to apply their business talents because of the easygoing Brazilian mentality and the fact that democracy had returned to the country in 1946, which stimulated its economy after a decade of dictatorship.[16] Most of the Jewish men were merchants, and some of them made fortunes. The women enjoyed cheap household help and spent their time at card parties or in coffee shops, chatting in Polish. "The precious metals business," as Sonia described her husband's occupation, supported them very comfortably. Nunio rented a small office in Rio's business district, where he dealt mainly in gold. He had given up the medical profession even before the war broke out.

Nushka persuaded Ullo to apply to the Interior Ministry in Warsaw for permission to emigrate, although the chances of getting it were slim. The Cold War between the East and the West was intensifying, and the Communist government in Poland allowed only a few citizens to leave for Western countries.[17]

Ullo's sister Lidka and her husband, Feder, had also settled in Katowice. She ran a clinic in a hospital, and he was a lecturer in economics at the university. Both still had faith in communism's ability to bring prosperity to Poland. They never went back to their native town of Bolechow. "What was left for me there? Nothing! Not one Jew was left in Bolechow, and the Ukrainian murderers were still there," Lidka said with a grimace of disgust forty years later, as she remembered the neighbors who had tormented her parents before the Nazis murdered them.

Nushka's parents, Clara and Israel Moses Sobel, and her younger sister Zhizha, made their way to the United States in 1947. The immigration quota that the U.S. Congress had set for Holocaust survivors was very low, but the Sobels were helped by the Rescue Committee founded by Orthodox Jewish communities in the United States. Two New Yorkers arranged entry visas for the Sobels outside of the regular official quota. These men were among the most active members of the committee: Herbert Tenzer, who was part of the Backenroth clan, and Stephen Klein, who was sent to Europe to help the survivors.[18]

The Rescue Committee also organized the Sobels' escape from Poland to Czechoslovakia. They were told to join a group of Jews that was about to set out on foot from the city of Waldenburg in southern Poland. A guide took them to a point on the border where they crossed into Czech Sudetenland, and on the other side a truck waited to take them to Vienna. There, they were housed in the Rothschild Hospital with hundreds of other Jewish refugees. The overcrowding and the living conditions were tough, but for the first time since 1939, their mood lifted. After more than seven years of hardship and wandering, they were finally on the way to freedom.

In late 1949, when Nushka opened the letter from the Ministry of the Interior giving her and Ullo permission to emigrate from Poland, she let out a shriek, and even though she was pregnant, she jumped in the air. The authorities' compliance with their request was unusual; the Polish government didn't allow most Jews to leave until 1957. Why had they agreed to let the Kahanes go, at the same time that they turned down a request from the Feders? Ullo did not know. "Very rarely, the bureaucrats make a mistake to your advantage, and that's what happened here," he told friends. He immediately applied to the U.S. and Brazilian consulates for entrance visas, but he was turned down. One state, however, was prepared to admit any Jews and even give them citizenship immediately, and that was Israel.

The couple planned to leave for Israel right after the birth, but their plans went awry. Nushka bore a son, but he died shortly after birth. This death was caused by an unfortunate accident. "The baby was born with a birthmark on its head," Ullo said in Rio forty years later, "and an inexperienced doctor pressed on it with his fingers, trying to push it into the skull. The baby died immediately. It was a terrible thing, to lose a second child after it was born."

The couple shut themselves up in their house and sat and wept. They refused to see the friends who came to console them. "It was one of the worst times of our life, you know, to lose a second child like that. I consoled her and she consoled me. We searched our souls, we'd lost two children. . . . I thought a lot about myself and my family during those days. Together with Nushka, we went back to our childhood days in Bolechow, to our families. We tried to work out where we had come from and where we were going."

The couple left Poland and embarked for Israel. On a spring morning in 1950, the passenger ship that had brought them from Europe docked in Haifa. The Graubart family, close relatives of Ullo's mother, Rachel, came to meet them. When they went ashore, Ullo was as excited as a small boy. He recognized the views of Haifa and Mount Carmel from the pictures he had seen as a child. Everyone around them was speaking Hebrew or Yiddish. He was well aware that it wouldn't be easy to settle down in the new state, but he was ready to make whatever effort was necessary. The Middle Eastern climate never bothered him, and he knew that he would soon overcome the language barrier by attending a Hebrew *ulpan* (an intensive course in Hebrew).

Ullo was no stranger to the culture and the religion. He knew the fundamentals of the language and could read the prayer book. He knew how to crack jokes in Yiddish. He had relatives and friends from Galicia scattered all over the country. He had planned to travel to Eretz Yisrael once before, in 1936, at the time of the Arab revolt against Jewish immigration, when scores of Jews were being murdered. His parents had objected strenuously, however, and his mother, Rachel, had told him, "Don't forget, Ullo, you are our only son, and Palestine is a dangerous place. In Hebron they massacred Jewish children like you." For the sake of keeping peace at home, he had agreed to give up on the idea. At the time, he was still in his last year of high school, and his parents' opinions were important to him. He had never been a rebellious son.

But now he was here, and it was better late than never. The young country needed him, and he needed it. After all, that's why it had come into being, as a refuge for Jews and a place where they could feel at home. In Azerbaijan Ullo had acquired experience in planning industries under very difficult conditions, and later, in Katowice, he had managed a division of the Industry Ministry, specializing in mines. True, there were no coal mines in Israel and no steel mills, but he knew the fundamentals of economics very well. And Israel also had a socialist government, with a bureaucracy headed by people like him, primarily natives of Eastern Europe: immigrants from Galicia, Poland, Austria, and Russia. If he had to improvise, he was an expert at it, and if he needed to teach, he was an experienced teacher. In brief, after ten years of wandering from one place of refuge to another, this was the first time that Ullo had changed addresses with a sense of enthusiasm.

Many years later, Ullo told some of his friends that during his first weeks in Israel, he had walked around as if in a dream. Often, tears of joy filled his eyes. This happened when he and Nushka traveled to Jerusalem for the first time. They rode in a heavily loaded bus on a narrow road that wound between the hills. The bus groaned and the engine overheated, the bends were sharp and frightening, but Ullo felt elated. Hella, Nushka's older sister, who had come to Palestine in 1938, was waiting for them at the bus depot. Hella's husband, Israel Horn, had died in the battle defending Jerusalem. He was one of approximately 6,400 Israeli dead in the War of Independence, a full 1 percent of the Jewish population. When Israel was declared a state in May 1948, all of its Arab neighbors had attacked it, and some of the bitterest battles had been fought in Jerusalem.

The day after Ullo and Nushka arrived, they joined the line at the Ministry of the Interior, received identity cards, and became citizens. Then they began to renew old acquaintanceships. They met relatives, friends, and neighbors from Galicia and never stopped talking. Everyone they met demanded a full account—what had happened, what they had done, and how they had been saved from the Nazis—and people told Ullo and Nushka their own stories. Some had immigrated to Palestine in the 1930s and had been pioneers in the *kibbutzim* (collective communities) that played an important role in the establishment of the state). Others, who like them had survived the Holocaust, had come to Palestine right after the war as illegal immigrants on ships that broke through the maritime cordon that the British had deployed along the coast. Many of them said that the independent Jewish state symbolized a victory over Hitler's murderous anti-Semitism. Some of their friends were officers in the military. Others worked in the government. One had died in the war with the Arabs, and another was an inmate in a mental asylum—the scenes from the death camps had taken over his mind.

Ullo was amazed at the miniature dimensions of the new state and at the difficult living conditions. Signs of the 1948 war were still visible everywhere: shell-damaged buildings, guns installed on roofs, and high sandbag barriers at the entrances to buildings. Jerusalem was divided, and every second person was in uniform. Masses of refugees, who had been gathered from displaced persons camps in Europe after the war, poured into the country. Oriental Jews were airlifted in on special flights from Muslim countries. Almost the entire Yemenite Jewish community had been taken in, and the Jews of Iraq had begun to arrive. Tens of thousands of destitute immigrants lived in tents and huts in transit camps.

The state coffers were empty and so were the shelves of the stores. Warehouses still held small quantities of basic foods. The black market was thriving. The administration's bureaucracy was no smaller than Poland's, and one of its tasks was to oversee the food rationing and austerity program. People used coupons for shopping. Coffee and meat were unavailable. Nevertheless, Ullo was impressed by the energy and the optimism of the Israelis. The young ones seemed especially enthusiastic and reminded him of characters in the films that were made in Russia after the revolution.

The couple settled in quickly. There were plenty of jobs, and professionals were snapped up by the government. A friend offered Ullo a position as an economic planner in the ministry that oversaw the austerity program, but he chose instead to attend an *ulpan* to improve his command of the Hebrew language. Nushka found work as an auxiliary nurse at the Hadassah Hospital

Nushka and Ullo Kahane in Haifa, Palestine, with Hella's son, Arie Horn, in 1950.

in the center of town. She had picked up a little practical experience in Azerbaijan and a great deal of theoretical knowledge from her sister-in-law Lidka, the physician. The exhausting Middle Eastern summer and the strenuous work in the hospital didn't help to make her happy with her new home. She had not yet recovered from the tragedy of her baby's death, and Israel was far from being her ideal place to live. The couple stayed in Hella Horn's apartment, in the Kiryat Moshe neighborhood of Jerusalem. Hella herself went to the United States to complete her doctorate in biology.

Three months of *ulpan* were enough for Ullo, and he took a temporary job as a planner in the Austerity Ministry in Jerusalem. On his first day of work, he felt as if he were in a government office in Poland. Half of the workers spoke Polish, the office equipment was elementary, and a heavyset woman served pale tea in glasses. Within days, Ullo had spotted the weak points and identified the challenges. "There is a great deal to be done here," he announced excitedly to Nushka, but she remained silent. Ullo was ready to sacrifice his comfort in order to integrate rapidly into the spartan, pioneering society, but she was visibly reluctant. His experiences as a child and a young man in the Zionist youth movement had inspired him, and he completely identified with what Israelis used to call the "national goals." He felt that he had succeeded in proving his abilities and achieving a respectable status, but Nushka regarded Israel as an interim stopover. "Either America or Brazil," she told her husband. For a while, Ullo could put off the move because neither country opened its doors to them.

Ultimately, what tipped the scales was Nushka's third pregnancy and Sonia Krauthammer's efforts to get a Brazilian visa for her brother and sister-in-law. Precisely when Nushka told Ullo she was pregnant, they heard from Sonia that she had succeeded in her quest. Ullo decided to concede. After the two tragedies, the baby in his wife's womb was too precious to risk. He would do everything to ensure that his wife's soul abided in ultimate peacefulness so that she could give birth to a healthy baby.

What would have happened if Ullo had insisted on staying? It was people like him who built the state up from almost nothing and filled the senior posts in the government, the economy, and the defense establishment. Most of them accomplished significant things and reached positions of influence. If Ullo had remained an Israeli, he might have gone into politics. He had the leadership abilities and the charisma, and people considered him an example. His political beliefs were compatible with the platform of the socialist party that ruled Israel for its first thirty years. It was a pragmatic, liberal, and moderate social-democracy, and Ullo was nothing if not pragmatic, moderate, and liberal. He could have run for Parliament. Or he might have risen to the top levels of the bureaucracy or gone into academic life.

But it was Sonia who dictated the Kahanes' future. She wrote them a letter with exact instructions: "Go to Milan and check into the Duomo Hotel. A man by the name of Samuel Morgenstern will come. He'll pay for the hotel and arrange the visa. I gave him money and he has connections. I promise you that everything will work out for the best."

And that is exactly what happened, Nushka and Ullo left Israel at the end of November 1950, and early in December they met Morgenstern in the hotel in Milan. Thirty-seven years after that, in his apartment in Rio, Morgenstern recalled the encounter: "We met and shook hands. I told Ullo, 'Sonia instructed me to pay for the hotel, to give you a thousand dollars, and to buy clothes for you. Sonia's paying for everything. Your visa will be ready next week.'"

An immigrant visa to Brazil was a very valuable document, and to obtain one, connections and money were necessary. Sonia told Morgenstern to spend as much as was required. He had his own good connections. The mediator in the deal was the police chief of Milan, through whom Morgenstern reached the Brazilian consul in the city. Why did the chief of police agree to help, and was he paid anything? Morgenstern's lips were sealed. All he would say was, "I paid whom I had to pay, and the visa was stamped and signed."

Morgenstern was the embodiment of the Wandering Jew: rootless, unmarried, educated, a hedonistic bargain seeker, a trader who bought cheap and sold dear and who smuggled currency. He admired Il Duce and believed that because of Mussolini, he had not been handed over to the Germans.[19] Morgenstern was born in Drohobych, the hometown of the Backenroths. His father was a food merchant, and Nushka's grandfather, Avrumche Backenroth, had dealings with his company, Pod Karpaczka. During the war, Morgenstern had hidden in Milan.

Nushka and Ullo went to Paris for a week, and when they got back, there was a lavish dinner for them at the hotel. The Brazilian consul himself came to present them with the visa. The chief of police cabled his congratulations.

Then Morgenstern handed them the key to his Copacabana apartment and escorted them onto the ship bound for Brazil.[20] Nushka was in the seventh month of pregnancy.

Ullo's heart was heavy when he and Nushka disembarked in the port of Rio de Janeiro. He was still excited over his brief stay in the independent Jewish state, and here he was cast into a new, different world. But Nushka was content. From the first moment, she knew she was where she wanted to be. The broad white beaches, imposing Sugarloaf Mountain, the tempo and the music, the bright colors, the economic opportunities, the cheap servants, the exotic fruits—all at once, she threw off the cloak of depression she had wrapped herself in while living in Israel. No more tension about shooting and border incidents. No more austerity, rationing coupons, or the heavy heat of the *hamsin* winds blowing in from the desert. No more

Ullo Kahane in São Paulo, Brazil, at the end of the 1950s.

of the congestion, the noise, the feverishness, and the lack of privacy that marked the early years of the new state. Now Nushka could give birth at ease, and if Ullo managed to achieve only a tenth of what he had organized and initiated in the Azerbaijan economy, they could look forward to a wonderful life. She had faith in him, and he relied on the wealth of his sister and her husband. From the start he zeroed in on his goal: private business. He would make the most of the experience he had gained in Azerbaijan and, with the assistance of Sonia and Nunio, he would become an industrialist.

Ullo spent the first years in Brazil reconnoitering the terrain, studying Portuguese, getting to know the business community, and becoming used to the city's special tempo of life. He became popular in the Jewish community and learned to respect the natives. The conclusion that he came to was unequivocal: Brazil was the ideal country for private business. It was crying out to be developed and industrialized, and labor was cheap. There was much scope for corruption, but he tried to remain the epitome of honesty. While most of the Jews were in commerce, he preferred to go into industry. As was his wont, he set himself a goal: to reach economic independence—that is to say, make his first million—in ten years.

Ullo and Nushka had an easy time settling down in Rio, mainly because Nunio Krauthammer provided them with what they needed. After the Kahanes' son, Allan, was born, Nunio rented an apartment for them, furnished it, and kept them supplied with food. Sonia told her husband, "We owe Ullo everything."

She was indeed indebted to her brother for her marriage and indirectly perhaps even for her life: it was Ullo who had rescued her from her humiliating isolation in Bolechow and from the death trap that Galicia became shortly afterward. As was mentioned previously, Ullo had been a boy of only eighteen when his parents sent him by train to Paris to demand that the young physician Nunio honor his promise to Ullo's sister and make her his wife. The dramatic meeting between the brothers-in-law-to-be at the Gare du Nord railway station in Paris had cast a deep shadow over the relations between the two men that lasted more than thirty years, until Krauthammer passed away.

It was Sonia who served as the connecting link between the two, and her husband did as she bade. Nunio tried to persuade his brother-in-law to join him in his gold-trading business, but Ullo refused. "I don't have the nature of a trader," he explained. "In Azerbaijan I learned how to build up industries from nothing, and that's what I'll do in Brazil."

Nunio was reluctant to become a partner in an industrial enterprise, but when he was asked to invest in Ullo and Kaxika's first venture, the Real tin plant, he did it out of obligation, to please Sonia. He charged high interest, a little more than 1 percent a month, pegged to the American dollar. Nushka urged Ullo to break off the partnership with Nunio. "He's taking an appalling rate of interest," she said. Ullo knew she was right, but he continued to delay ending the business relationship because of his difficulties in raising credit from other sources. After all, Krauthammer had never wanted to be the owner of fixed property. He had a peculiar compulsion, a kind of pogrom phobia that made him want to keep all of his wealth in cash, gold, and silver, in his pocket. Ullo knew it would be better to pay Nunio off and end the partnership. When he finally did it, he used the utmost tact and delicacy toward his sister and brother-in-law.

In the beginning, Real was nothing more than a small, unsuccessful tin-processing plant, a family business that was losing money. Ullo had heard that it was nearing bankruptcy and that its owners, the Peris brothers, wanted to resuscitate it. Nunio warned him that it was a doubtful prospect and that he should be careful because a group of family members was involved who could not get along well together. But Ullo was not deterred. In Azerbaijan he had specialized in exactly this area: helping failing factories to recover. "This is just what I'm looking for. A firm that is in trouble but is economically viable," he told Nunio. He invited the head of the Peris family, Kaxika, to dine at the Russian restaurant near the beach.

Kaxika's grandfather had migrated from Spain to Argentina, and his father had moved from Argentina to Brazil. Kaxika was born in Rio, in a *favela*, a shantytown at the edge of the city where there were no sidewalks, the sewage ran in open conduits, and holes in the ground served as toilets. There was no phone line in the *favela* until one was installed in the 1960s, no buses entered its precincts, and the railway station was nearly a two-mile walk away.

Kaxika and his brothers had inherited Real from their father; it covered some 650 square feet and had a hundred workers and a deficit that was rolled over from month to month. Kaxika had no problem with working from dawn to dusk. His diligence was unbounded, but one of his brothers, Limeiro, was uncooperative, and when the creditors started banging on the door, the elder brother realized that the enterprise needed professional economic guidance. "I wanted to work, and I wanted to grow, and Ullo's seriousness impressed me," Kaxika said thirty years later.

That's how the partnership between the immigrant's son and the new arrival was formed. Ullo was the brains, a tough, centralized manager, who planned the expansion and took care of getting the credit. Kaxika was the brawn, an outstanding get-the-job-done person, effective and determined to succeed. Within a few months, it was obvious that the two complemented each other perfectly, and the accounts went from the red into the black. "The growth in activity was optimal," Kaxika recalled. "If Ullo had been more aggressive, the pace of growth might have been even faster, but the danger of collapsing would also have been greater. I urged him to give old customers more credit, but he balked."

At the start of every negotiation, Ullo displayed tenacity, but when he was satisfied with the deal, he compromised. Profitability continued to improve, and obtaining credit ceased to be a problem. The plant worked well, the products were good, and 90 percent of the customers became regular buyers.

Right from Ullo and Kaxika's first meeting, both a successful business partnership and a firm friendship flourished between the two men. Kaxika Peris, the Catholic son of a family from Spain, became a close friend of the Jew Ullo Kahane from Galicia for the last three decades of his life. How do two opposites unite? Of course, it was an exceptional relationship. For thirty years they addressed each other using honorifics and family names: Dr. Kahane and Mr. Peris, never Ullo or Kaxika. But they loved each other. In Ullo's eyes, Kaxika's diligence and energy and his highly developed commercial and political instincts more than made up for his lack of formal education. In Kaxika's eyes, Ullo was his guide.

"I owe Ullo everything good that happened to me," Kaxika said, not hiding his emotions. He spoke without stopping, and sometimes tears welled up in his eyes. "Ullo helped me to get ahead, without making me feel lower than him. On the contrary, we were equals and we respected each other. I could guess his reactions, and he knew what mine would be. We fitted like gloves. It was an amazing relationship from the start. From the very first deals I felt that we suited each other, although our temperaments were so different. And he knew everything about me—brothers, children, wives, everything, we were open with each other. Ullo was the story of my life for thirty years, and from the first I knew it would be a great friendship and success. Everything that I lacked, Ullo had, and since he died, he's been right next to me."

Kaxika could no longer hold back his tears, remembering Ullo in his villa, hidden behind huge old trees on a hilltop in Tijuca National Park, overlooking the ocean. He got up and left the room.

In 1965, Ullo had a brilliant idea. Until then, customers had purchased crude tin sheets from Real, roughly three feet by three feet in size, and then took them to another plant where the brand and the details of the contents were printed on them, and then to a third plant where they were cut into strips to be manufactured into tin cans. Ullo suggested that alongside Real, a production line be set up that would include the entire process: printing, cutting, and the manufacturing of cans. The idea caught on immediately because it saved money and time, especially for the medium-size customers.

Within two years, the partners had set up a modern plant called Litografia Volta Hedonda in the Hamassa neighborhood. In the years to come, they installed ten advanced production lines that processed sheets of galvanized tin. The printing press was purchased from the German Milander company, and between $500,000 and $600,000 was invested in each production line. In 1968, the plant was inaugurated. Customers waited in line, and the machines worked three shifts seven days a week. In the early 1970s, Ullo and Kaxika owned the largest production line of its kind in South America. In 1976, they were the target of a takeover bid by their largest competitor in Brazil, the Matrasso company, which was a partner of Continental Can Company, the world's largest tin can manufacturer at that time. They decided to sell.[21] Their enterprise had been launched with almost no money, and they left it wealthy men. They invested a large portion of the sale price in an international commodities trading company, Emesa, that they had started years earlier.

Ullo had by now reached a stage of peace and plenty. He invested his money wisely and knew that he would never have to start again from nothing. Although he and Kaxika had sold their factory, they were still partners, both in the old tin-processing plant Real and in Emesa.

But just as Ullo was realizing his dream, Nushka discovered that she had cancer. A few years prior to that, her sister Hella had died of the disease in Israel. "Their saga during the war had united them so closely that when Nushka got sick, he completely lost his balance," said Kaxika. Nushka knew that her disease was terminal but pretended that she didn't know it, and

Ullo knew that she knew but still denied to her that her condition was grave. Outwardly, she played the part of a tough fighter, but inwardly she crumbled. "He knew she was very ill but didn't believe that she could die," said Kaxika, and his eyes once more filled with tears.

During those years, progress was being made in cancer research, and the media frequently reported medical breakthroughs. Ullo consulted experts and called researchers all over the world, asking them to send him the latest drugs. He asked his sister Lidka (who had left Poland in 1957 with Feder and settled in Tel Aviv) to put a brain trust together. At times, it appeared that their fight was succeeding. Nushka's body strengthened and her mood improved, and Ullo was happy until the next decline. Cancer is an insidious enemy, and Nushka had been a heavy smoker. Ullo had also smoked, and when Nushka took ill, his own heart let him down and he had to undergo open-heart surgery, the first of three such operations.

Ullo's heart operation took place in 1971, in a hospital in São Paulo. The whole family accompanied him, the ailing Nushka and their two children, Allan and Alice; and Kaxika and his wife, Elanita, a former Rio beauty queen. Before Ullo went under the anesthesia, he called his partner and said, "I am giving you my family; take care of them if something happens to me."

But there was no need. Thirty-six hours after the operation, Ullo was on his feet and raring to get back to work. After the second operation, he also recovered rapidly. Each of the operations gave him seven more good years. It was only in the last two years of his life that he grew tired easily and weakened. On the eve of his third operation, in 1986, in Montana, in the United States, he spoke to Kaxika on the phone. "Ullo wanted to tell me that his journey in this world was over," said Kaxika in a hoarse voice. "He took his leave from me, but I knew he wanted to speak more. He ended the conversation at his initiative. He knew that I was sensitive and he took pity on me." Kaxika said that he had never seen Ullo cry. "He had great self-control." The next day, Ullo was wheeled into the operating room, and he died in surgery.

One night, Kaxika saw Ullo in a dream. It was in 1988, apparently in the late summer. Ullo was walking toward him, wearing a black suit and a narrow tie with a conservative pattern, in the fashion of an earlier era. Kaxika said that he smiled in his sleep because Ullo looked great. "He had not aged since he died, and he was very happy. I sensed that he was there with Nushka and I knew that there, where they were, things were very good for him." It had been a short dream, and Kaxika awoke and remembered every detail. He usually slept heavily and did not remember his dreams, he said, "but that night Ullo came and told me that he feels good and knows that the things that he left here are in good shape." Kaxika got up and left the room, his eyes wet with tears.

One scene from his dream replayed in Kaxika's head. "Nushka and Ullo spoke to me in Portuguese, like natives," Kaxika said proudly, "as if the whole Polish experience had been erased from their memory. In Rio they were born again."

Indeed, since they had left Poland, Ullo and Nushka never expressed any desire to visit their Galician native land. At any rate, as long as Ukraine was part of the Soviet Union, the Galician Jewish *shtetls* were practically out of bounds for tourists. The situation changed in 1991, however, when the communist empire collapsed and Ukraine declared its independence. Tourism focusing on Jewish roots in Eastern Europe became very popular.

Lucien Backenroth-Bronicki (Naftali's son) in the winter of 1945.

One of the first family members who traveled to Galicia was Lucien, the son of Naftali Backenroth-Bronicki. In the summer of 1992, he visited the neighboring towns where he spent his childhood, Drohobych and Schodnica.

When the war ended, Lucien was eleven years old, and one very clear picture remained in his mind from his life in Schodnica: relatives and neighbors, men and women, members of the work groups that his father had led, some of them family relatives, all coming out of the makeshift hiding places and temporary shelters where they had hidden on the refinery grounds during the last months of the war, and his parents helping them to stand on their feet.

Now, the physicist Lucien Bronicki, age fifty-eight and a citizen of Israel, is finding his roots. He is an expert in constructing geothermal power plants to produce "green" electricity. He is a tall, solid man, with a round face and a shy smile.

Professionally, Lucien is engaged with the same business that his forefathers were dedicated to: using the earth's raw materials to produce energy. Their professions differ only in the measure of sophistication. Lucien's ancestors had developed methods to use common minerals from the earth, whereas he invented tools and procedures to use environment-friendly natural substances, such as geothermal and solar energy, and to recover heat that is normally wasted in factories during the production process and convert it into additional electricity.

In 1965, along with his wife, Yehudit Bronicki, Lucien founded Ormat Industries Ltd., whose principal activities are constructing, maintaining, and operating "green" power plants. The company's headquarters are located in the small city of Yavne, fifteen miles south of Tel Aviv, and in the United States it operates through a subsidiary, Ormat Technologies Inc., which is registered in Nevada and is traded on the New York Stock Exchange.[22]

The company grew out of a pioneering invention that Lucien developed in the early 1960s: a turbine that converts solar energy into electricity. The small plant that Lucien and Yehudit established in Israel in the mid-1960s has matured into a giant international industry that uses its own advanced technologies.[23]

For the last ten years, Ormat Technologies has developed, built, and operated geothermal and recovered energy–based power plants. It sells its electricity in the United States (in Alaska, Nevada, Hawaii, and California),

Guatemala, Kenya, Nicaragua, and the Philippines.[24] Facilities and technologies that were developed by the company are used in dozens of other countries across the globe.[25]

The company's breakthrough occurred at the beginning of the twenty-first century, after seventeen U.S. states legislated regulations that oblige electrical companies to gradually increase their production capacity of green energy. Since then, Ormat Technologies has become the third-largest producer of geothermal energy in the United States.

In the 1970s and 1980s, successive mayors of Schodnica had invited Lucien's father, Naftali Backenroth-Bronicki, to visit his town of origin, but he always firmly refused. In 1945, after the communists had released him from prison, Naftali headed with his family toward Paris because he was a fervent Francophile. He had graduated from the University of Nancy and during the late 1920s had been a lecturer at the elite scientific institute the Ecole Polytechnique. The Bronickis had settled in Paris, where Lucien completed his engineering and physics studies. In 1958 Lucien emigrated to Israel.

In the beginning of the 1990s, drawing near the age of sixty, Lucien felt that his memories from Galicia had faded. He decided that he wanted to see his childhood haunts, mainly so that he could connect the stories he had heard to real places. He had no intention of creating new links with the oil belt's towns, many of whose citizens had collaborated with the Nazis.

Lucien visited his childhood home without his father. A professional camera team accompanied him to make a documentary movie of his return visit.[26] In the film, he stands on a hilltop in Schodnica and surveys the landscape. The camera pans to a residential neighborhood that the Backenroths had built. Ukrainian families are living there now. The villas, which were renovated and enlarged by his family during the roaring 1920s, have fallen into disrepair and neglect. The neighborhood looks squalid. Lucien stares long and hard at a rusting grasshopper oil pump standing near his relatives' old house. One of his escorts remarks, "It's all exactly like it was, only without Jews." The melancholy of a graveyard permeates the area.

Then the camera is placed exactly opposite the entrance to a building that housed the synagogue that Avrumche Backenroth, the brother of Lucien's grandfather, established. A number of elderly countrywomen come out of the nearby houses and gather around the visitors. Forty-six years after he left Schodnica, Lucien asks whether anyone remembers the Backenroths. At first, the women look at him in surprise, but after a few moments of silence, a tall old woman points at a row of houses. "That's where all the Backenroths lived," she says. She is wearing a simple gray cotton dress and a black headscarf.

"Of course, this is where they lived," chimes in another old woman, smiling at the camera. "I remember well," she says. "A girl that I went to school with used to live here." She furrows her brow as if trying to remember. "Hella, Hella Lewkowitz was her name."

"And over there lived Leib Backenroth," a third woman says, "the son of the old Backenroth. He lived over there." She is wearing a light housecoat and a transparent yellow headscarf.

A short woman is standing nearby and listening quietly. Suddenly, she perks up and says proudly, "You know, the Backenroths drilled in our land and they found oil."

"Leib had an oil well on the way to the compressor," says the woman with the black headscarf.

"That's right, he owned the well," the first woman fills in.

"And there was also Stella, tall and very pretty." (She meant Stella Backenroth-Wieseltier.)

"Leib's daughter, Stella."

"His wife was short."

"Feige, Leib's sister, I remember her well."

"She was tall."

"He was a good man, Backenroth. Poor Jews would come to him twice a week, and he would feed them. In the times of the Poles, there were poor people here, and they all went to their father, Leib was their father, they went to him, fifteen poor women went to Backenroth, and he gave them lunch."

Later, the rumor spread that the son of Tulek (Naftali's nickname) had come back. Within half an hour, the mayor showed up and presented himself to the guest, his hand outstretched. Lucien hesitated for a moment but then shook hands. The mayor smiled.

In the afternoon, Lucien went to the outskirts of the town, to Bronica Forest. There, local Ukrainians had carried out a pogrom against the Jews on July 4 and 5, 1941, immediately after the communists had withdrawn and the first German units were already visible on the horizon. Lucien was seven when the slaughter was carried out. On that day, his family was in Stryj, the regional capital, but Stella Backenroth-Wieseltier had told him what happened. She had been an eyewitness. The pogrom began on a Friday, and by the next day three hundred men had been killed. Many of the killers were their Ukrainian neighbors from Schodnica and the surrounding villages, among them some employees of the Backenroths. At that time, many of their relatives had gathered in Schodnica, to take courage from one another and to be close to Lucien's father, Naftali, upon whose strength everyone relied. Later, during the Nazi occupation, Gestapo officers and German policemen and soldiers, assisted by local Ukrainians, murdered groups of Jews in the forest almost every month.

On the second day of his visit, Lucien and his entourage met with civic dignitaries in the town hall of Drohobych. Most of the time, the guest kept silent while the Ukrainians did their best to display friendliness and outdo one another in verbiage. They spoke scathingly of the Nazis and the communists and in particular praised the Jews' contribution to the development of their town and its environs. It was evident that the imprint the Backenroths had made on the annals of Drohobych and Schodnica had not faded, especially the myth that developed around the figure of Naftali, despite the fact that the last members of the family had left the region almost fifty years previously.

Lucien listened and now and then asked a question. His face remained frozen. He never reacted, even when the mayor let it be known that a donation from the wealthy family would not be unwelcome. Lucien brought one present with him. His father, Naftali, had commissioned an Israeli sculptor to make a bust of Drohobych's best-known personality, the author Bruno Schulz, to stand as a monument in his native city. At the time, it was believed that no photographs of Schulz had survived the war. So Naftali gathered in his Paris home the few living people who had known Schulz, and they reconstructed his face from memory for the Israeli sculptor to work from.[27]

When the reception was over and everyone had dispersed, Lucien's thoughts had already moved elsewhere. This tall scion of Elimeilech Backenroth—the man who had been among the first to sink an oil well in Schodnica, probably in 1817—was focused on the future. The following day Lucien was scheduled to fly to Berlin and from there to Toronto, so that he could reach

Anchorage, Alaska, by the next morning. They were expecting him at a remote site along the eight-hundred-mile-long Trans-Alaska Pipeline project, where the Ormat group had built fossil fuel–powered turbo-generators, which operate unattended in extreme climate conditions.

On leaving his ancestors' homeland, Lucien said that he felt no hatred toward the people of Drohobych. "Just look where they are and where we are," he said softly with a smile.

Notes

1. Transfer

1. Ashkenaz was the name for Germany in medieval Hebrew. The Jews had used the name Ashkenaz since the year 800, when Jewish settlement spread in the valleys of the Rhine and the Main and in Flanders (today, parts of Belgium, France, and the Netherlands).
2. In the olden days, the Hebrew name Elimeilech—which means "God is king"—was widely used in the family, although more recent generations have dropped it because it sounds old-fashioned to the modern ear.
3. At that time, Yiddish was the primary language that Ashkenazi Jews spoke. It was a Germanic dialect that later had developed into a full-fledged language, incorporating idioms and words from Hebrew, Aramaic, Slavic, and Romance languages.
4. The first Jewish uprising against the Roman Empire in Palestine, called the Great Rebellion, lasted seven years, from 66 to 73 CE.
5. The demolition of the Second Temple by Titus Flavius took place on the ninth day of the Jewish calendar month of Av. It was one of the most important defining events in Jewish history, denoting the destruction of the homeland and the start of the two-thousand-year exile. Herod was a Roman client king of Judaea (southern Israel of today) between 37 and 4 BCE. He started to build the Second Temple on Mount Moriah around 19 BCE. It was one of the biggest construction projects of the first century BCE.
6. Around 1200 CE, Kiev had a population of fifty thousand, while London, the most populated city in Anglo-Norman England and one of the most advanced cities in Europe, had only around twelve thousand inhabitants.
7. Today, it is believed that the epidemic broke out in the Crimean peninsula, and soldiers of the Mongolian army contracted the disease while they were besieging the city of Caffa, which had been established by Genoa in Crimea.

The Mongols flung the bodies of those who died of the disease into the city, and its inhabitants were infected. In October 1347, a fleet of merchant vessels sailed from Caffa to the port of Massina in Italy, and when they anchored, it transpired that all of their crew members were suffering from the plague or had already died. From Massina, the disease spread to Venice and Genoa and then to all of Europe and the Middle East, including Jerusalem (1348) and Mecca. The last places that it reached were Yemen and northwestern Russia, in 1351.

8. There had been similar invitations, such as the one issued by King Idris II of Morocco, for Jews to come to Fez, a community that produced many famous learned Jews, but there was no precedent for a ruler issuing an open invitation for masses of Jews to settle in his realm. Prince Boleslaw Pobozny (1221–1279) was the first Polish nobleman to grant security and privileges to Jews. In 1264, he issued the famous "Statute of Kalosz," guaranteeing protection to the Jews and granting them the right to be businessmen and moneylenders. King Casimir the Great (1310–1370) extended this charter.

2. The Tavern Keeper

1. The first appearance of the Lubomirski family in Polish chronicles comes at the end of the thirteenth century. Its members were Roman Catholic nobles from the city of Lubomierz, in southern Poland. At the beginning of the seventeenth century, the family's political and economic influence grew significantly after Stanisław Lubomirski married Zofia Ostrogska, the daughter of the richest family in Poland. Together, they owned 18 towns, 313 villages, and 163 farms.
2. The rabbinical rulings of the day, including those of the leading authorities, Rashi, his grandson Rabenu Tam, and many others, reveal much agonizing over issues relating to established communities' right to prevent newcomers from joining them. In the main, the rabbis ruled that it was not permitted to bar newcomers, but certain limitations were laid down. Sometimes, different rulings were made in different localities.
3. Eastern European Jews usually called the descendants of the Mongol invaders "Tatars" (a reference to the ancient Turkic-Mongols who were from the Gobi Desert in northern China and Southern Mongolia of today and who mingled with inhabitants of Eastern Europe during the Middle Ages). For Eastern European Jews, "Tatars" became a synonym for persecutors and brutes, and the warning "Tatars are attacking" was heard in Jewish neighborhoods during pogroms.
4. The first was Prince Roman the Great Mstislavich (1199–1205), who united Galicia and Volhynia in the mighty principality of Halych-Volhynia and captured Kiev in 1202. Upon Roman's death, his four-year-old son, Danylo (1201–1264), was forced into exile by the boyars (the ruling nobility), but with help from the Polish and Hungarian monarchs he returned and in 1219 was proclaimed king of Galicia. Danylo founded the city of Lviv (Lvov), and his son, Lev (c. 1228–c. 1301), moved the capital to the city (from

Halych). Lev's son, George, known as King Yuriy I (1252–1308), enlarged the principality through three marriages to noble families, and when he died, his sons, Andrew and Leo II, ruled the kingdom together. In 1323, when they both died together battling the Mongols, this broke the direct line of descendants from Roman Mstislavich, and Galician boyars unsuccessfully attempted to hold onto power. In 1340, a tense period of uncertainty ended when Galicia was annexed to the kingdom of Poland.

5. Battles between the private armies of the Ruthenian aristocrats and the Polish army continued intermittently for more than twenty years until, in 1366, the Poles occupied all of Galicia. The Halych-Volhynia principality ceased to exist, and Galicia became part of Poland.
6. The union between Poland and Lithuania was achieved through the marriage of the Grand Duke of Lithuania, Jogalia, to Queen Jadwiga of Poland, who was known for her beauty. The result was the coronation of Jogalia as king of Great Poland and the creation of the Jagiellon Dynasty of Polish kings (1386–1572).
7. Practically, Galicia had never been an integral part of Poland, but on the joyful occasion of the previously mentioned marriage, both sides apparently felt comfortable in putting this spin on Poland's historical narrative.
8. In 1365, King Casimir put the Magdeburg Rights Treaty into effect in the cities of Galicia. This treaty applied the most advanced Germanic laws of the Middle Ages and set a high degree of internal autonomy. According to the treaty, most city issues were to be solved by a city council, which would be elected by the wealthy citizens.
9. This analysis is based mainly on a study written by a Polish scholar, Magdalena Opalski. She examined the portrayal of the Jewish tavern keeper in 120 literary works published in Poland between 1820 and 1905 and focused on the stereotype in provincial towns and villages. The study reveals that Polish literature reserved a particular place for the Jewish tavern keeper and that a mythology was created around his representation. I emphasize Opalski's findings because of the lack of detailed family records of the daily life of Shmuel Leib and his relatives.
10. Opalski quotes from a ballad written by the great Polish poet Adam Mickiewicz, "Pani Twardowska." In the ballad, the Devil appears at the bottom of a drunkard's glass in a tavern. The Devil is dressed like a German. According to the ballad, the tavern is the only place where satanic forces are permitted to enter, and within it, incredible events occur.
11. Jews are strictly prohibited from drinking wine or brandy made by gentiles, for fear that it has been produced for purposes of idol worship.
12. When King Casimir the Great and then the Jagiellon Dynasty forced their rule on Galicia, most of the Ruthenian aristocratic families joined the Polish nobility and adopted Polish coats of arms. They were officially integrated in 1569, and henceforward there was a rift between the Ruthenian people and most of its aristocratic houses.

13. *The Deluge* is a famous historical novel, written by the Polish writer Henryk Sienkiewicz, that dramatically portrays this period. *Potop*, a Polish film directed by Jerzy Hoffman, was based on Sienkiewicz's book and was nominated for an Academy Award in 1974 for Best Foreign Film.
14. During the uprising, the Cossacks stormed the city of Lvov and its cathedral. Local Poles, as well as people belonging to minorities that were members of Eastern churches (which were in full communion with the Holy See of Rome) and many Jews, were murdered. Some managed to survive in the bell tower, which was not seized in the raid. Jews had participated actively in Lvov's defense and paid part of the ransom that induced the rebels to end the siege.
15. Over the years, a different interpretation took root in Jewish consciousness, in which the national element in the wretched downtrodden Ruthenians' uprising was downplayed, and the anti-Jewish element was stressed. Particularly because Zionism's ideology condemns the Jewish Diaspora, the historical perception that is prevalent among Jews today is that the Khmelnytsky "pogroms" were in the main an anti-Semitic phenomenon. The concepts of "Khmelnytsky" and "Cossack" are associated in Jewish consciousness with pogroms and anti-Semitism.

3. The Miracle

1. Retroactively, Rabbi Tzvi Hirsch Eichenstein became a family relative of the Backenroths. Tzvi Hirsch's father, Yitzchak Isaac Eichenstein, was the great-grandson of Yom Tov Lipman-Heller, whose history and family relations to the Backenroths are detailed in chapter 5.
2. On Saturdays, the Hasidic rabbi sits at the head of his *tish* while his followers sit around him, and together, they sing their court's songs. The rabbi is honored with slicing the Jewish Sabbath bread, the challah, and then he makes the blessing over the bread, eats one slice, and hands out the rest of the slices—which are called remnants—to his followers.
3. Rabbi Tzvi Hirsch lived from 1785(?) to 1831.
4. A Hasidic court is named for the locality where it is first established. Today the Zhidachov dynasty is active in Brooklyn, New York; Monticello, New York; Chicago, Illinois; London, England; and Israel.
5. The spread of anti-Semitism is excellently portrayed in *On the Edge of Destruction* by the American historian Celia Heller, who is herself a descendant of the Backenroths. (See especially the introduction.)
6. The Council of the Four Lands started at a Lublin fair in 1580, when a group of rabbis formed a central rabbinical court, and developed into a social central institution and a political lobby that was granted an official status by Polish kings and nobility. The "four lands" were Greater Poland, Little Poland, Volhynia, and Ruthenia. Galicia was part of the fourth land, Ruthenia.

7. Poland's Jewish communal organization constituted self-governed educational, judicial, religious, and charitable institutions. In each community, the *kahal* administration was democratically elected. The leadership's functions included supervision of schools, communal taxes, and charitable institutions, while rabbis were in charge of religious and judicial affairs.
8. Anthony Radziwill was the son of Lee Bouvier Radziwill Ross, the sister of Jacqueline Kennedy Onassis. His Polish title was Prince Stanislas Radziwill. He died in 1999. For the Radziwill dynasty, see also notes in the Backenroth family tree in chapter 4.
9. Another story tells of two Jewish land leasers who cheated the Radziwills out of some property and then went to the Baal Shem Tov, the founder of Hasidism, and begged him to pray for them, but he refused and they were apparently arrested and imprisoned.
10. From the book *Tiferet ha-Maharal* (Maharal's splendor), a collection of legends about Hasidic rabbis that was compiled and published by Y. Rosenberg in 1914. These stories of landlords tormenting their estates' Jews should be seen as folk tales that portray the tense relationship between the Polish landlords and their Jewish money collectors and not be taken as certified historical facts.
11. During the Thirty Years, War in Germany, Jews sold supplies to both sides, and many fortunes were made. The Industrial Revolution resulted in a similar scenario. "Court Jews" appeared who acquired palaces, titles, and even hunting licenses, and who drifted away from religious observance but remained part of the community.
12. In 1096 as well, when the first crusade embarked from Clermont in France, in an undertaking that slaughtered thousands of Jews, kabbalists of the time predicted that that year would be the year of redemption.
13. In Lvov, there appeared at the same time a self-proclaimed prophet who announced the coming of the messiah. His name was Nehemiah ha-Kohen, and Shabbetai Tzevi's followers considered him a dangerous rival. In September 1666, ha-Kohen was summoned to meet Shabbetai Tzevi in Turkey, and immediately after their meeting ended, fanatical Shabbateans murdered ha-Kohen.
14. The belief in the apocalyptic year 1666 among Jews and Christians alike was so strong that the Portuguese Jewish rabbi and scholar Menashe ben-Israel (known also as Manoel Dias Soeir) sent a letter to the English political leader Oliver Cromwell, requesting him to use the coming millennium for readmission of the Jews into England. "The opinions of many Christians and mine do concur herein, that we both believe that the restoring time of our Nation into their native country is very near at hand," wrote ben-Israel (the entire Jewish community had been expelled from England in 1290).
15. Hasidic Judaism had penetrated into Western Europe during the last two decades of the nineteenth century. It was carried to the United States by huge

waves of Jewish immigration. Today, the largest denomination of Judaism in the United States is the Reform branch, which was established in nineteenth-century Germany in response to the Jewish enlightenment movement and to Jews' emancipation, while Hasidism is the smallest branch.

4. Oil Fever

1. Tsiril gave birth to seven children: Sara (married to a son of the Libermann family), Shmuel Leib, Zvi Hersh, Jenta (married to a son of the Koppelmann family), Rabbi Berl, Yitshak (nicknamed Itsig), and Vove (which is a nickname that usually stands for the Hebrew name Ze'ev, or Wolf).
2. *Ozokerite* means, in ancient Greek, "odor's spreading." Its common name is "natural wax," and in Polish it is called *wosk ziemny*—"soil wax."
3. As early as the 1400s, in some places in Galicia but not in Schodnica, ozokerite was used to light torches and for softening raw leather. Natural (unrefined) ozokerite could not be used for indoor lighting or even for street lamps because it gave off quite a lot of smoke and an unpleasant odor. In ancient times, olive oil, beeswax, animal fat, fish oil, and whale oil produced less smoke and a better smell and were preferred for indoor lighting.
4. The refining process of crude oil developed in stages during the second half of the nineteenth century, as demands for various kinds of fuel grew. Distilling crude oil is a process of separating the substances present in it and dividing it into fractions by boiling. The crude oil is heated and changed into a gas. As the compounds boil at different temperatures, they each become a gas at a different stage. The gases are passed through a distillation column, which becomes cooler as its height increases. When a compound in the gaseous state cools below its boiling point, it condenses into a liquid and is removed from the distilling column and is ready to be used. Lubricating oil (the one that Shmuel Leib Backenroth produced from the crude oil in his plot of land) boils at 572–698 degrees Fahrenheit; heating oil at 482–572 degrees; kerosene and jet fuel at 392–482 degrees; gasoline at 104–392 degrees; and petroleum gas at 104 degrees. Higher-octane substances, such as gasoline or diesel, which are lighter types of oil, were successfully distilled many years later. The first commercial oil refineries were constructed in Romania, the United States, and Galicia in the beginning of the second half of the nineteenth century.
5. According to Swiss and German chronicles, a wick that draws up liquid by capillary action and is used in oil lamps was invented in 1783 by a Swiss chemist, Ami Argand. He was the first to sink a circular wick inside a small glass filled with kerosene, surrounded by a glass chimney, and thus created the first modern oil lamp.
6. In the second half of the nineteenth century, prospectors searched for oil and sank wells in dozens of other settlements throughout Galicia and southern Poland, but it turned out that the main oil field lay under the Schodnica–Boryslav–Drohobych strip.

7. Many years later, Ruthenian farmers filed lawsuits against noble families or Jews, whom they accused of seizing control of their lands and profiting from oil that should have been theirs. The Ruthenian farmers lost still more money in costs for legal procedures that dragged on for years without ever being decided.
8. It is accepted by historians that the first oil wells in history were dug in China in the fourth century CE, to a maximum depth of some 787 feet. The Chinese used the oil to manufacture sugar. The first oil well of modern times was apparently dug in Baku, Azerbaijan, in 1848.
9. In 1772, when Galicia became part of the Austrian Empire, it had been divided into administrative districts (*Kreise*, in German), and one of them was Drohobych.
10. *Naphtha* was the term used by Austrians and Germans for crude oil. Poles used *nafta*. Americans used the term *oil*.
11. The first map of the oil field, as sketched by the committee, is still to be found in the government archives in Vienna.

5. Backenroth the Hasid

1. Rital was born in 1579 in Wallerstein, Bavaria, and died in 1654 in Kraków, Poland; Rital is the Hebrew acronym of his name: Rabbi Yom Tov Lipman. Rital's grandfather was Moses Heller, the chief rabbi of the German communities (1520–1580).
2. The Maharal was born in 1525 in Posen, and died in 1609 in Prague. MaHaRaL is the Hebrew acronym of Moreinu ha-Rav Loew, Our Teacher the Rabbi Loew. The Maharal's descendants originated in Worms in Germany, one of the first Jewish comunities to be established in Central Europe during the era of the Roman Empire. His uncle Jacob was Reichsrabbiner (Rabbi of the Reich) of the Holy Roman Empire of the German Nation—a confederation of loosely bound principalities and territories with strong ties to the Roman papacy, which, between the end of the ninth century (Treaty of Verdun in 834) and the middle of the seventeenth century (Peace of Westphalia in 1648), encompassed the territories of most of Western and Central Europe, including parts of Poland and Italy.
3. On record since the 1870s, the legend says that the Maharal created the Golem—a being made of clay and brought to life by magical spells, based on his knowledge of how God created Adam—in order to defend Prague's Jewish community against anti-Semitic attacks. The Maharal placed the Golem in the attic of the famous Altneuschule, Old-New Synagogue, in the city's Jewish quarter, the Josefov, near the Jewish cemetery. During World War II, as an addition to the legend has it, a Nazi officer climbed to the attic and tried to stab the Golem. The Nazi immediately perished. Another later addition relates that a rabbi visited the attic in the late twentieth century and "came down white and shaking." The legend of the Golem of Prague has inspired numerous literary, theatrical, television, and film works.

4. Ganz traveled across Europe and wrote historical works that included treatises in Hebrew about the rise of Europe and the fall of Islam, as well as a book on Jewish history. He was also an expert on the natural sciences and was the first systematical astronomer among the Jews of Ashkenaz. Luanz's grandfather, Rabbi Yossef of Russheim in Germany, is regarded by historians as the most influential Jewish leader in the Holy Roman Empire of the German Nation in the first half of the sixteenth century and the greatest intercessor in jewish history. He left an intriguing daily diary. His son Eliyahu Luanz served as a rabbi in the city of Frankfurt on Main and in Worms on the Rhine River and was known as a miracle worker and a kabbalist. He wrote two well-known commentaries on the *Book of the Zohar* (*Aderet Eliyahu*—"Elijah's Cloak"— and *Tzofnat Paanah*—"Revealer of Secrets"—in Hebrew; both manuscripts are now located in Oxford, England). Shlomo Efraim became known for his sharp criticism of Jews who entered the service of Polish noblemen as land leasers and debt collectors, under the system of *arendas.* His classic commentary on the Torah, *Kli Yakar*—"Precious Vessel," in Hebrew—was written in the popular style of a preacher and appeared in many editions.
5. Emperor Rudolf II von Hapsburg was born in 1552 in Vienna and died in 1612 in Prague; he was emperor of the Holy Roman Empire, king of Bohemia, and king of Hungary. He was the oldest son and the successor of Maximilian II and Maria of Spain (a daughter of Charles V and Isabella of Portugal). Rudolf was tolerant toward Protestants and gave shelter to Counter-Reformation activists. He suffered from melancholy and was insane at the end of his life.
6. The Maharal showed up with his elder brother, Sinai; his son-in-law Isaac Cohen; and his student Shlomoh Efraim.
7. The explanation by the Ari, Rabbi Yitzhak Luria Ashkenazi, of how divinity functions is irrational and esoteric, of course, as are the concepts of kabbalah as a whole. They are unexplainable in logical terms, but inside the mystical structure there is reasoning because each of its components is based on a model of a conventional earthly hierarchical authority and therefore is explainable in terms of rational logic. Kabbalah researchers indicate that the Maharal's "rational-abstract approach" to questions about the creation and the definition of life was a revelation for his era. He is considered a mystic but is also counted as the creator of a rational system of explanation.
8. The Maharal was lauded in his time as the best of Jewish thinkers, but after his death, his writings fell out of print and his philosophy lost currency. He was rediscovered in the eighteenth and nineteenth centuries by some Hasidic groups (in the beginning, mainly in Belarus and by the Lithuanian Lubavitch court) and also by some leaders of the Mitnagdim (the opposition to Hasidism). Each sect found that certain parts of the Maharal's thoughts supported its credo.
9. Moses Maimonides (in Hebrew, Moshe ben Maimon), 1135–1204, was a Spanish rabbi, a physician, and a philosopher, whose work established the fundamental principles of Jewish religious law (*halakha*) and is accepted by

the Orthodox branch of Judaism. Maimonides wrote the basic commentary of the Mishna in Arabic and, in Hebrew, wrote the most comprehensive and authoritative code of Jewish law, called *Repetition of the Torah* (*Mishne Torah*, in Hebrew).

10. The Maharal influenced the outlook of two religious leaders, both of whom were regarded by their followers as supreme mentors: Simha Bunem of Przysucha (1765–1827) in Poland and Avraham Yitzhak HaCohen Kook, the first Ashkenazi chief rabbi of Eretz Yisrael (1864–1935). Kook wrote that the Maharal was "a cabbalist of philosophical style" and, unquestionably, the Maharal's methods blended general philosophical concepts with a kabbalist outlook.
11. The mainstream of kabbalist thought, that of the Ari of Safed, Rabbi Yitzchak Luria Ashkenazi (1534–1572), emerged only a few years before the Maharal's interpretations appeared, and in people's minds, the holy scriptures could not yet encompass mysticism.
12. The Thirty Years' War was a series of long battles fought in Central Europe with the involvement of most of the major European powers. It started as a religious conflict between Protestants and Catholics and developed into a bitter quarrel between the Hapsburg dynasty and most of the other Central European powers. Historians refer to the Peace of Westphalia that ended the long war (1648) as the beginning of the modern era because it recognized the fundamental right of all nations to have self-determination, recognized the sovereignty of states, and declared that all nations are legally equal. Ferdinand II was born in 1578 in Graz, Austria, and died in 1637 in Prague. He was the son of Charles II of Austria and Maria Anna of Bavaria and was a Holy Roman Emperor from 1620 to 1637. He was also a warrior, who was one the initiators of the Thirty Years' War, and was an absolutist and a devout Catholic who was extremely intolerant of other religions, including Protestantism and Judaism. By strengthening the Catholic Church in Bohemia, forcefully converting Protestants, and pressing Jews to abandon their scriptures, Ferdinand II acted exactly opposite to his previously mentioned predecessor, Ferdinand I.
13. From the mid-eleventh century to the mid-seventeenth century, almost every pope ordered the burning of Hebrew books. The first was Pope Gregory IX, who in 1243 initiated a special ceremonial in Paris for burning the Talmud. Almost every subsequent pope followed his lead. The last and one of the most ruthless despisers of anything Jewish was Pope Clement XXII (1592–1605). Nevertheless, the invention of the printing press by the German Johann Gutenberg in the mid-fifteenth century made it henceforward impossible to totally destroy all Jewish books.
14. The essay was printed for the first time in 1818 in Breslav and later published in German and Yiddish in at least three editions, in Prague, Vienna, and Warsaw. The date of Rital's imprisonment, the fifth of Tammuz in the Hebrew calendar, was declared a fast day by his family. I questioned several of his descendants but have not found even one who observes this fast today.

15. There is a tale about the rabbi, in the 1920s, taking an elevator on the Sabbath. A rumor quickly spread from synagogue to synagogue in Galicia that rabbis had ruled that riding on elevators on the Sabbath was permitted. It later emerged that there was no such new ruling, but Schreiber had simply been accompanying a mortally ill patient to the hospital and rode the elevator on the Sabbath because the necessity of saving a life takes precedence over the Sabbath laws. But his authority was so powerful that the common people had been convinced that his act meant that the rabbis had implemented a historic change in those laws.
16. Hatam Sofer means "Seal of the Scribe"—a rabbi who has the authority to reply to letters that have questions on *halakhic* (Jewish law) issues and then interpret the law for the petitioner; if the rabbi cannot find a solution, he sends it to a more authoritative rabbi, and so forth, until a new rule is created. That's the way rules are created in Judaism, as it has no single supreme authority.
17. Moses Sofer-Schreiber was born in 1762 in Frankfurt, Germany, and died in 1839 in Pressburg, Hungary. He sharply attacked the reformers and forbade congregations to allow mixed choirs to perform in their synagogues. His saying "Anything new is forbidden by the Torah" is quoted by many important Orthodox rabbis to this day. Sofer was the most important figure in the development of ultra-Orthodox (Haredi) Judaism. His influence is still felt today.
18. The official investigation of the conflagration revealed that the management and the professional inspection of the development of Boryslav's new oil city had been inadequate. Inquiry commissions published long lists of recommendations. According to local press reports, neither the empire's control nor local regulation were truly enhanced.
19. Galicia's Provincial Diet was established in Lvov in 1861. Its legislative power was restricted to local affairs in the economic, educational, and cultural spheres. The laws passed by the diets had to be approved by the emperor.
20. Szczepanowski's most well-known publication was his 1888 book *The Poverty of Galicia*, a brilliantly written analysis of the quality of life in Galicia compared with other European countries, including Italy and England. He claimed that the principal purpose of his political and economical activities was "to make our [Galician] society equal to the civilized nations."
21. Szczepanowski came to a bitter and cruel end. The company that he founded went bankrupt, and he died a young man, penniless and grief-stricken (see the excellent depiction of his rise and fall in Alison Fleig Frank's book *Oil Empire*).
22. Tzvi Hirsch Eichenstein, the miracle worker who had predicted the oil riches, was a straight-line descendant of Rital. His father, Yitzchak Isaac, the founder of the Eichenstein dynasty, was Rital's great-grandson, and Haya Heller was a great-great-grandchild of Rital, so the two were actually fourth cousins (see also chapter 3).

23. The Jerusalem Hasid Arieh Backenroth said that it had been Avrumche's father, Shmuel Leib, who initiated the departure from the Zhidachov court. "It was not Avrumche who left Zhidachov but his father, Shmuel Leib," Arieh Backenroth told me, but I could find no supporting evidence for this claim.
24. The rabbi was accused of ordering the murder of two Jewish informers, and he spent almost two years in prison. He was released in 1845, and the Austro-Hungarian authorities permitted him to settle only in the remote town of Sadigora in the region of Bukovina, the easternmost crown land of the Austrian Empire. Today, Bukovina is divided between Romania and Ukraine.

6. Ecological Disaster

1. In synagogue services, the *shaliah tzibur* leads the ordinary prayers, while the cantor (*hazan*, in Hebrew) conducts the more significant liturgical parts of the prayers. For each day, there are three prayer services, and the Musaf ("addition," in Hebrew) is a fourth prayer service that is added by Orthodox and Conservative congregations on the Sabbath, during New Moons, and on major holidays (holidays that are mentioned in the Pentateuch). Each holiday has its own version of that prayer. Some American Reform Jews omit the Musaf prayer.
2. The Mazurians originated in today's east Ukraine and Belarus territories. During the eleventh century, many of them settled in northeastern Poland, in a region that is now called Warmian-Mazurian Province and is famous for its beautiful lakes.
3. Ignacy Daszynski (1866–1936) was a leader of the Polish Socialist Party. In 1897, with the support of workers, peasants, and left-wing Jews, Daszynski was elected to the Viennese State Council. Between November 1918 and January 1919, he was prime minister of the Polish Provisional Government (known as the Lublin Temporary Popular Government). Ivan Franko (1856–1916) was a political activist and one of Ruthenia's most influential writers. Lvov State University, one of the oldest in Europe, bears Ivan Franko's name.
4. One of Franko's novels that depicted the oil workers' hardships, *Boryslav Is Laughing*, had been published by a Lvov magazine in serial form during 1881 and 1882.
5. Eighty percent of Galicia's breadwinners were peasants. In Germany and France, the figure was only 40 percent.
6. In the middle of the first decade of the twentieth century, most of the production from the wells of Boryslav no longer consisted of paraffin taken from shallow pits, but instead was crude oil that came from depths of around 656 feet at a rate of more than half a million tons a year, or some 40 percent of the entire Galician output.
7. During the 1860s and the 1870s, MacGarvey made Canadian drilling technology famous around the world. In 1883, he drilled holes two thousand feet deep in Galicia. By 1904, thirty drillings in Boryslav were more than three thousand feet deep.

8. The wide-gauge railroad was inaugurated in 1883.
9. The Austrian bank of the federal states (Bundeslander).
10. Today, economists estimate that between 1885 and 1905, the average annual economic growth of the Galicia Oil Belt was around 15 percent. In comparison with the rest of Galicia, the average salary in the oil belt was very high, and over the years the gap between the rich and the poor increased even more. At the end of the 1880s, 6.4 million inhabitants lived in Galicia, and two-thirds of them were peasants. Only 0.8 percent of the households paid luxury tax in Galicia, compared with 2.8 percent in the Bohemian region and 10 percent in Lower Austria.
11. Between 1880 and 1914, Drohobych's population almost tripled, from eighteen thousand to forty thousand.
12. At the center of Boryslav, four roads form an intersection: to the north stretches Drohobycka Ulica, leading to the city of Drohobych; to the south, the main street of Boryslav, Kosciuszki Ulica, leading to the rural neighborhood of Mraznica; to the west, Lukasiewicza Ulica; and to the east, Wolanka Ulica, leading to the spa town of Truskawiec.
13. A huge fire broke out in one of Boryslav's most productive wells in July 1908 and lasted until November. A blaze in another well broke out in November 1902 and was extinguished in January 1903.
14. Boryslav's population had increased fourfold between 1880 and 1914, from seven thousand to twenty-eight thousand (although its Jewish population declined dramatically).
15. Barrels were filled with crude oil for the first time in Pennsylvania during the 1860s. By 1866, one oil barrel was standardized at 42 gallons, from which 19.5 gallons of gasoline were produced. Since the introduction of oil tanker ships, oil is not stored and shipped in barrels any more, although the 42-gallon size is still the unit for measurement, pricing, and taxation.
16. Through its daughter company, Schodnica Actiengesellschaft for the Petroleum Industry.
17. Once the drill reaches an oil reservoir, the oil is forced upward to the surface by pressure from dissolved gases or from water that is lying beneath the oil. Sometimes the pressure is so powerful that even a sturdy plug at the upper end of the pipe is shot out.
18. Schodnica's annual crude oil production in 1883 was 10,000 tons; in 1894, 21,000 tons; in 1895, 84,000 tons; and in 1896, 190,000 tons. A careful estimate assesses that the Backenroths' share was approximately 10 percent of that.
19. Bergman, J; Birmbaum, E; Brzozowski & Winiarz Co.; Hauptman, A; Helfer, S & Silberberg, M; Leichtmann, J & Ambach, M; Spitzmann & Kamermann Ltd were some of the Jewish companies that were active at the beginning of the twentieth century. While around one-quarter of Schodnica's population was Jewish, more than 60 percent of the village's businesses were owned by Jews, even after many Jewish small oil producers abandoned the industry.

20. In the nineteenth century, U.S. oil prices were lower than those of oil produced in other places in the world. Since 1869, U.S. crude oil prices (adjusted for inflation to the end of 2006) have averaged $20.71 per barrel at the wellhead, compared to $21.57 per barrel for world oil prices. At that time, the average break-through price for revenues was $17 (based on WTRG Economics' data—London, Arkansas).
21. Two refineries were built in Schodnica, one was built in the tanning and leather-making center of Bolechow, and the fourth was in the village of Krosno on the San River. In Schodnica, one refinery was built inside the village and the other close to the village of Urycz, at the very spot near the strange outcropping of rocks, crannies, and caves where the Backenroths' ancestors, led by Elimeilech, had settled in 1350.
22. Because of the division into subsidiary companies, and because the Backenroths had accounts in various banks in Vienna and Lvov, it is apparently impossible to calculate the annual revenue and profits. This figure of $1.5 million is based on an estimate supplied by Avrumche's two grandsons in the early 1990s. According to Samuel H. Williamson's exchange rate that is based on the U.S. Consumer Price Index, in the 1900s $1.5 million was equivalent to $36 million in 2005 (see "How Much Is That," http://eh.net/hmit/, accessed April 2, 2008).
23. A close friend of Avrumche Backenroth, Lipa Schutzman, started as a wagon driver working for a paraffin-digging company, then was promoted to become an office administrator. He later became the company's owner and bought oil companies and refineries. Schutzman was Boryslav's mayor between 1906 and 1917. Binyamin Mermelstein's son, the writer Avigdor Mermelstein, was known in Galicia in the 1880s as the first teacher who taught Hebrew in the "Hebrew by Hebrew" method.
24. Ivan Franko described what he called the "Brazilian Fever" in magazine articles and short stories. Many other Polish and Ruthenian writers extensively documented the Ruthenian emigration to Canada.
25. Boryslav's Jews were dependent on decisions made for them in Drohobych because, until 1929, Boryslav's Jewish *kehilla* ("community," in Hebrew) was not autonomous.
26. At the end of the nineteenth century, one Austrian gulden was the equivalent of 2 Austrian kroner, which equaled forty U.S. cents, or $9.20 in 2005 (using the U.S. Consumer Price Index). Half a million Austrian gulden equaled approximately U.S. $4.6 million at 2005's value (see "Six Ways to Compute the Relative Value of a U.S. Dollar Amount, 1790 to Present," http://eh.net/hmit/compare, accessed April 2, 2008).
27. Between 1880 and 1910, the Jewish population in Boryslav decreased by more than one-third. In 1880, Jews in Boryslav numbered 7,400 (80 percent of a total population of 9,300); in 1890, there were 7,800 Jews (75 percent of 10,400); in 1900, they numbered 6,000 (56 percent of 10,700); and in 1910, there were 5,800 Jews (45 percent of 12,800).

28. ICA's organizational management was handled by Maurice's wife, Baroness Clara Hirsch (neé Bischoffsheim, 1833–1899), the daughter of the principal partner of the Bank of Bischoffsheim and Goldschmidt and a wealthy woman in her own right.

7. A King Is Born

1. In Bolechow, some people used to pronounce the family name Kohane because the source of the name is *Kohen* or *Cohen*, which means "priest" in Hebrew, but over time, people became accustomed to the easier pronunciation of Kahane.
2. Two children born after Ullo, Frida and Hanna, also died of illnesses. Infant and child mortality was high in those days. In 1902, 25 of every 1,000 Eastern European Jewish infants were born dead and 50 to 60 children of every 1,000 perished before the age of five from illness (mainly dysentery, diarrhea, typhoid fever, smallpox, diphtheria, and influenza). For an infant born in 1900, the average life expectancy was 47 years (men, 46 years; women, 48). A peasant's life expectancy in 1900 was 35 years.
3. Emperor Franz Josef was born in 1830 and died in 1916. He was crowned emperor of Austria in December 1848, at age eighteen, and reigned until his death in November 1916.
4. The most important Jewish prayer, which starts with "Hear, O Israel, the Lord is our God, the Lord is One"—Deuteronomy 6. These verses are also written inside the *mezuzah*, which is a small box that hangs on the doorposts of many Jewish homes.
5. *The World* was the official publication of the World Zionist Organization, which was created in 1897 in Vienna by Theodor Herzl, the founder of modern Zionism.
6. The Napoleonic Wars occurred from 1803 to 1815. They were a series of conflicts initiated by France's ruler, Napoleon Bonaparte, who subdued a large part of the European continent and established the ideals of the French Revolution there. One of Bonaparte's new undertakings was to grant emancipation to the Jewish minority, and after he lost power, in some places in Eastern Europe nationalist political parties became prejudiced against the Jews.
7. Hauptmann was the first Jewish mayor of Bolechow. Local tales relate that when Kaiser Franz Josef came to the region for a hunting trip, Hauptmann represented Bolechow in the welcoming ceremony. Traditionally, Bolechow's residents take tourists to see an oak tree that is called "the Kaiser Aiche"—"Kaiser's Oak," in German. According to the story, the kaiser and his entourage rested under the tree during that visit.
8. The largest leather plants were those belonging to Kurts and Eisenstein, Goldschlag, Kaufman, Kimmel and Roseboim, Kurtser, Rechter, Weissbart and Frey, the German Pfeifer, and the Pole Lubashevsky.
9. See the Hebrew weekly *HaMagid* (published in Berlin, Kraków, and Vienna), issue 44, November 13, 1878, pp. 379–380.

10. Two skin dealers, the brothers Israel and Josef Berger, were known in Bolechow for their skilled work.
11. This was very similar to the forest railroad, which was used to bring timber to the sawmills of Schodnica. In Bolechow, Griffel owned the largest sawmill and employed hundreds of lumberjacks. He developed the first railroad. In Schodnica, it was reported that Griffel's train was the first, but it turned out that in the middle of the nineteenth century, similar trains had been built in other places in the world, to carry tree trunks from the mountains to the river valleys, using the force of gravity.
12. In other places (Victorian England, for example), the hides were soaked for several weeks in pools full of the excrement and the urine of dogs and fowl. The bacteria in the solution softened and tenderized the leather (there are still factories in England that process leather using these methods).

8. For God, Emperor, and Homeland

1. Historians mark the beginning of the Great War two days earlier, on Saturday, August 1. At that time, a local European war between Austro-Hungary and Serbia that had begun on July 28 was transformed into a general European struggle when Germany declared war on Russia.
2. The emperor's residence in Vienna's First Quarter was called the Hofburg ("fortress' courtyard" in German). Today, the Burg houses the Austrian president's residence.
3. The last German emperor, Wilhelm II von Hohenzollern of Prussia, ruled from 1888 to 1918. Born in 1859, he died in 1941.
4. The state-of-the-art carriages were constructed by the Wagon and Tender Company, Franz Ringhoffer & Smichow of Prague. All of the train's carriages were destroyed during World War I, except one that is exhibited in Prague's Technical Museum.
5. A threat by Austro-Hungary to join the Ottoman side caused the czar to evacuate territories in Romania that had been conquered by Russia from Austro-Hungary in August 1854. The czar refused to forgive the kaiser for that act.
6. The emperor himself planned to grant self-government to the Slavs, but under German and Hungarian pressure, his bureaucracy opposed his policy.
7. Franz Josef's younger brother, Maximilian, had been shot in Mexico in 1867. Franz Josef's son, Rudolf, committed suicide in 1889. Franz Josef's brother Karl Ludwig died in 1896 from drinking infected water, during a pilgrimage to the Holy Land. Franz Josef's wife, Elisabeth, was assassinated in Geneva in 1898 by an Italian anarchist.
8. Austro-Hungary declared war on Serbia on July 28. Russia ordered a general army mobilization to the Austo-Hungarian border on July 30. Having vowed its support for Austro-Hungarian, Germany declared war on Russia on August 1. On August 2, Germany delivered an ultimatum to Belgium demanding free passage for its armies to France. The Belgians refused. Germany declared war

on France on August 3 and invaded Belgium on August 4. Britain was committed to defend Belgium and declared war on Germany on August 4.

9. Theodor Herzl, 1860–1904, was the founder of modern Zionism.
10. Pilsudski had founded the Polish Socialist Party in 1892. Before the war started, he created a private army of ten thousand men who were supposed to fight against Russia for Poland's independence. In August 1914, Pilsudski joined, with his legion, the Austro-Hungarian army in the battle against the Russian army.
11. The two German generals Paul von Hindenburg and Erich Ludendorf were known for their successes in World War I and symbolized what were then known as "Prussian values": stiffness and strictness. Hindenburg became the last German president before the beginning of the Nazi era, and he was the man who swore Hitler in as chancellor on January 30, 1933.
12. Today, the Sudetens region is the mountainous northeast of the Czech Republic.
13. Mozart was born in 1756 and died in 1791. Mozart's *Ave Verum*, written to oblige Anton Stoll, a friend of his who was a priest in Baden, was first performed at Stoll's church on Corpus Christi day in 1791.
14. The Somme River in northern France was the site of a famous battle fought in 1916.
15. By the end of August 1914, the German army had continued to advance victoriously westward through France, while the French and British armies were forced to retreat. It seemed that Paris would soon be taken by the Germans. But from September 9 to 13, the French and British armies conducted a superb defense on the Marne River, and the Germans retreated. Their commander, von Moltke, suffered a nervous breakdown and sent a message to Kaiser Wilhelm: "Your Majesty, we have lost the war."
16. In the trial, the main witness for the prosecution, a lamplighter, confessed that he had been misled by the Russian secret police, and his testimony resulted in Beilis's acquittal. In 1920, Beilis and his family immigrated to the United States. He died in 1934. Bernard Malamud's book *The Fixer* tells the Beilis trial story. The book was adapted into a film of the same name, starring Dirk Bogarde and Alan Bates, in 1968.

9. Crime and Punishment

1. He was the last emperor of Russia. Nicholas II ruled Russia (and the annexed territory of Poland) from 1894 until his forced abdication after the 1917 Bolshevik Revolution.
2. Congress Poland was the popular name of the Kingdom of Poland that was created when Europe's map was reshaped by the Congress of Vienna, in 1815, following France's defeat in the Napoleonic Wars. Between 1815 and 1832, Congress Poland was a puppet state under Russian rule, and after 1832, it was fully integrated into Imperial Russia.
3. In the opening battle, Przemysl's fortress was besieged by the Russian army, and the Austro-Hungarians succeeded in lifting the siege for a while, but in

October, the Russians again cut the fortress off from the Austro-Hungarian lines. Then, on March 22, 1915, a shortage of ammunition and a lack of food caused the Austro-Hungarians to surrender, and 125,000 of their soldiers were taken prisoner by the Russians. On June 3, 1915, the Austro-Hungarians counterattacked and recaptured the fortress. The battles for Przemysl's fortress cost more than 110,000 lives.

4. Moye, Arie's son, remembered only that his name was Israel and his nickname Srull. He could not remember what his family name was.
5. His stepmother was Avrumche's second wife. Arie was born to Avrumche's first wife, Haya Heller.
6. Kaddish is a blessing in Aramaic for the sanctification of God's name. Part of the general Kaddish is called the Orphan's Kaddish and is recited by mourners at funerals, memorial ceremonies, and the three daily synagogue services. Following the death of a parent, it is customary for the firstborn son to recite the Orphan's Kaddish at the three daily synagogue services for eleven months and then on every anniversary of the parent's death.
7. The mourner's Kaddish may be recited only when a *minyan* is available. It is customary in many synagogues to arrange two or even three *minyans* for morning prayers: one for early birds, one for regulars, and sometimes one for late risers.
8. This cooperation can be explained by the very strong family bonds among the Backenroths. The intensity of the love and the interdependence that prevailed among members of the family is rare among modern, educated families. I have interviewed several older members of the family on this phenomenon of concealing the death of a son, and not one of them uttered a word of criticism.
9. When the war ended, the American-Jewish Joint Organization and the organization of Krosno's former Jewish inhabitants in the United States (the U.S. Krosner Landsmanschaft) financially aided the process of revitalizing Krosno's Jewish community.
10. Rosh Hashanah, the Jewish New Year, is a two-day celebration. The extra day is added because the Jewish calendar is lunar, that is, each month begins when the new moon is seen and ends after twenty-nine or thirty days when the next moon rises. In ancient times, when a new moon was observed, the beginning of a new month was officially declared, and messengers were sent out to tell people that a new month had begun. The Jewish New Year holiday occurs on the first day of the first month (Tishrei in the Jewish calendar), and messengers were not dispatched because of the holiday's sacredness, so people did not know whether a new moon had been observed; they knew only that the old month would be either twenty-nine or thirty days long but could not decide what the exact first day of the first month was. In order to prevent mistakes and to be on the safe side, everybody celebrated for two days. This practice continues even today, although the Jewish calendar is calculated mathematically and is not established upon observation anymore, because there is no authority in Judaism that is entitled to change ancient customs.

11. On Rosh Hashanah, work and travel are forbidden (although food preparation and moving or adding to the cooking fire are permitted). Much of the day is spent in the synagogue, where a special prayer book is used, the regular daily liturgy is expanded, and a *shofar*—ram's horn—is blown.
12. In prewar years, Russia had targeted much of its political propaganda toward Galicia's Ruthenian people, trying to reinforce their national aspirations. From the other side, Vienna's bureaucrats also tried hard to win the Ruthenians' loyalty.
13. Between September 1914 and May 1915, Russian army units demolished and burned around two-thirds of Galicia's oil derricks. In many places, the Russians set fire to oil wells, but, surprisingly, in Boryslav all the wells and most of the refineries were left untouched.
14. Judaism prizes nothing more than human life, and *pikuakh nefesh* (which means "lifesaving" in Hebrew) is the obligation to sanctify and preserve life, but not property.
15. Galicia's oil fields provided more than 60 percent of the Central Powers' oil supply.
16. Oskar Kokoschka was born in 1886 and died in 1980. In the beginning of his artistic career Kokoschka, a Czech, was a frequent guest in Viennese salons and painted many famous personalities. In World War I, he served in the Austrian army and was wounded. Alban Berg was born in 1885 and died in 1935. Berg was part of Vienna's intelligentsia. He served in the Austrian army from 1915 to 1918.
17. Karl Seitz was born in 1869 and died in 1950. He was known as a liberal and a pacifist. Following World War I and the empire's dismantlement, Seitz headed the Social-Democrat Party and was elected to be the first president of Austria. Then, as mayor of Vienna, his education programs earned him popularity. In 1944, the Nazis put him in the Ravensbruck concentration camp. He was released and returned to Vienna in May 1945.
18. Robert Stricker was born in 1879 and died in 1944. Stricker, a Czech, was a journalist and an editor of the official Zionist newspaper *Die Judische Zeitung* (The Jewish Newspaper). Stricker and his wife were sent to Auschwitz by the Nazis and were murdered there.
19. "Beloved of the soul, compassionate Father; attract Your servant to Your will, then Your servant will run like a hart, to bow before Your Majesty" is a famous Sabbath hymn that was written by a sixteenth-century kabbalist and is sung by Hasidic Jews.

10. The *Drasha* Speech

1. In 1256, King Danylo of Halytz, the head of the Ruthenian duchy of Halych-Volhynia, founded the city and named it in honor of his son, Lev. Lvov means "Lev's city."
2. Jan I Olbracht was born in 1459 and died in 1501. Jan Olbracht (John I Albert) was known as a brave warrior but an inadequate politician.

3. King Jan's relations with the Jews had their ups and downs. On one hand, he granted asylum to hundreds of Lithuanian Jewish families who were expelled by his brother, Alexander Jagiellon. On the other hand, in 1495, Jan transferred Kraków's Jews to the neighboring city of Kazimierz, establishing the first Jewish ghetto in Poland's history (in the course of time, Kazimierz was annexed to Kraków and is known today as the historical Jewish district).
4. Many Jewish craftsmen who were not members of the guilds managed to carry out their occupations clandestinely, however, and some could obtain the right to engage in their professions from Lvov's guilds, for money.
5. He was known as John II Casimir, the great-grandson of Gustav I, the king of Sweden.
6. The figures for Jewish citizens are based on the Polish census of 1921 (between 1918 and 1939, two censuses were held, the second one in 1931). In 1921, the city's entire population was around 215,000.
7. Betar was a Revisionist Zionist movement founded in 1923 in Riga, Latvia, by the journalist and author Ze'ev Jabotinsky (1880–1940); he claimed that the Jewish state's territory should include both banks of the Jordan River (comprising the territory of Israel, the Palestinian Authority, and part of the territory of the Kingdom of Jordan of today). Betar's main support base was located in Poland and Galicia. Hashomer Hatzair means "the Young Watchman" in Hebrew. The movement was founded in Lvov in 1911, and its main support base was in Galicia. In 1920, it began to establish *kibbutzim* (communal farms) in Palestine.
8. The Bund party was a secular Jewish socialist party operating in Eastern European countries between the 1890s and the 1930s. The party was called the Bund and its members Bundists. They preached internationalism, opposed Zionism and emigration to Palestine, and promoted the use of Yiddish as the Jewish national language. *Karaites* means "readers of the scriptures" in Hebrew. They were a small ancient Jewish sect. Karaites believe that the written Torah (Pentateuch) is the only source of Jewish law, and they reject the Oral Law (*halakha*). Shabbateans were believers in the sixteenth-century false messiah Shabbetai Tzevi (see details in chapter 3).
9. According to the report of the official commission of inquiry, 72 Jews were murdered and 443 wounded. Many homes were looted and vandalized; 38 Jewish houses and flats were completely burned.
10. *Haynt* means "Today" in Yiddish. It was the leading Jewish daily published in Warsaw between January 1, 1908, and September 1, 1939 (the day Germany attacked Poland).
11. JTA is the Jewish Telegraph Agency. PAT was Polska Agencja Telegraficzna, the Polish Telegraphic Agency. In 1944 PAT was replaced by PAP—Polska Agencja Prasowa, the Polish News Agency.
12. According to some sources, on November 17, a Jewish militia unit was attacked by Polish Legion soldiers inside the boundaries of the Jewish Quarter, and

a Jewish officer was killed. Another report described an incident in which Poles confused Jewish militiamen with Ukrainians. The Poles opened fire, but nobody was injured.

13. Emperor Franz Josef died on November 21, 1916, at age eighty-six. His successor, Karl I (1887–1922), was Franz Josef's grand-uncle and the last monarch of the Hapsburg dynasty. The cease-fire was declared on November 3, 1918. On the same day, Poland proclaimed its independence from Russia.
14. On November 12, Emperor Karl abdicated the Austro-Hungarian Empire, and Austria became a republic.
15. An independent Ukrainian state was declared at this time; thus, from this point on, the term "Ruthenian" will be replaced by "Ukrainian" in this book.
16. The account of the pogrom is based, among other sources, on the report that was published by the official Polish investigation committee. It is kept in the archives of the YIVO Institute for Jewish Research in New York City.
17. The United States declared war against Germany in April 1917.
18. *Gazeta Polska* is a daily newspaper expressing the ideas of the Polish right wing.
19. Nevertheless, a pogrom did take place in 1644, when Ruthenians murdered a hundred Jews—but Poles were not involved. Then, after sixty-four years, two Jews were burned at the stake after being accused of reconverting a Jew who had become a Christian. Since 1728, there had been no record of the murder of Jews due to national or religious reasons.
20. *Havdala*, which means "separation" in Hebrew, is the rite that marks the end of the Sabbath and the start of the new week. At nightfall, when three stars are visible in the sky, the head of the family lights a candle, hands it to one of the family's children to hold, and reads a blessing. Some believe that the height at which the candle is held is the height of the holder's future spouse.
21. Jewish religious texts from as early as the twelfth and thirteenth centuries mention this tradition. It seems that during the Middle Ages, one of the customs was to carve certain Hebrew letters on a cake and to have the celebrant lick them off. The *drasha-shpruch* ceremony commemorates the revelation on Mount Sinai in which the Ten Commandments were given to Moses (see Exodus 19–20).
22. The Allied victors negotiated peace with the defeated Central Powers from January 1919 to January 1920. These series of international meetings, known as the Paris Peace Conference, concluded with five treaties that redrew the map of the world. One of them was the Treaty of Versailles, which granted Poland complete independence.
23. As the frontiers between Poland and Soviet Russia had not been defined in the Treaty of Versailles, in February 1919, a war broke out between the two countries. Throughout 1918, while Pilsudski's Polish Legion took control of much of Ukraine, the Bolsheviks gained the upper hand in the Russian Civil War and advanced westward into Ukraine in order to expand the communist

revolution. The Polish-Russian war lasted until March 1921. When it ended, both states proclaimed victory, but history's conclusion is that Poland won. Soviet Russia was not able to reach its main aims and annex the entire Ukraine territory, and the losers were the Ukrainians, as their country had been divided between Poland and Russia.

24. In 1787, the Austrian kaiser established a Jewish elementary school network in forty-six Austrian Jewish communities, including Bolechow. In the schools, the language of instruction was German. All of the teachers were Jewish, and the curriculum was mainly secular. The chain's superintendent was a Czech Jew, Hertz Homburg. The school network existed until 1806 and then collapsed because of community intrigues, but its name survived.

11. Pilgrimage to Jerusalem

1. Moye Backenroth-Heller named his diary *The Insane Journey*. It was privately published and distributed among friends.
2. The description of the Polish Legion's preparations for the pogrom in the early hours of November 22, 1918, are based on the report of the official commission of inquiry, on Ronald Sanders's book *Shores of Refuge: A Hundred Years of Jewish Emigration*, and on Moye Backenroth-Heller's diary and oral descriptions.
3. Other machine guns were stationed in Kraków Place, near the State Theater, in Theodora Place, and on Boznicz and Cebulna streets.
4. Not all of the family members whom I spoke to knew what to make of Moye. Was he a daring and gifted man of deeds or, on the contrary, was he a loafer and a clown, a spinner of yarns that were full of charm and color but had little to do with reality? Some described him as a "fantasizer," "a storyteller," and "a person with an enormous imagination." Others swore that all of his amazing stories actually happened. The details of his journey to Jerusalem, as recorded in his diary and as he recounted to me at our meetings, have been examined and found reliable.
5. The idea of recruiting young people in the Diaspora for a Jewish legion that would occupy the land of Israel to prepare for a future independent Jewish state had been proposed during World War I by Ze'ev Jabotinsky. He became known in 1903 when he formed self-defense units to protect Jews across Russia from pogroms and then, in 1914, when he suggested forming a Jewish unit that would be integrated into the British army and would take part in the battle to wrest control of the land of Israel from the Ottoman Empire. In 1923, Jabotinsky founded the Revisionist Betar Youth Movement (see chapter 10).
6. The Balfour Declaration of November 2, 1917, was a formal statement that the British government supported Zionist plans for creating a Jewish "national home" in Palestine. It became the essence of the political campaign that the Zionist movement carried out between 1917 and 1948.

7. By 1924, reacting in response to a growing anti-immigration mood, the U.S. Congress legislated the National Origins Quota, which severely restricted immigration from Eastern Europe and Russia and blocked the huge wave of immigrants that was streaming to the United States. (Between 1880 and 1924, approximately two million Eastern European and Russian Jews had immigrated to the United States, part of the thirty-five to forty million Europeans who had settled in the United States since 1820.)
8. In 1918, the Austrian currency was still legal tender in Galicia (the successor states of the Austrian Empire started to limit the krone's validity in their territories during 1919). Under the Gold Standard, $1 U.S. was equal to 5 Austrian kroner in 1918 and had the same buying power as $14.16 in 2006, which means that in 1918, the value of 5,000 Austrian kroner was equal to $14,160 in 2006. (For more information, see www.dollartimes.com/calculators/inflation.htm, accessed April 3, 2008.)
9. During the war (from the summer of 1914 to the autumn of 1918), money steadily lost value as prices of basic food products rose between 3,000 and 6,000 percent, and other consumer goods, such as clothing and shoes, rose between 1,000 and 2,000 percent.
10. The demand for oil increased, and in some regions of Austro-Hungary, a shortage of oil led to rationing. The shortage had stemmed from the bureaucracy's inefficiency and not from a real deficit of crude oil. During all of the war years, the Austro-Hungarian administration lacked the ability to properly arrange the supply of oil for army and civil needs (see Alison Fleig Frank's analysis in her book *Oil Empire*).
11. Historians emphasize that despite the deep historical dispute between the two sides, the 1918–1919 Polish-Ukrainian war was conducted by disciplined and obedient politicians and generals on both sides, resulting in relatively few civilian casualties and little destruction (approximately ten thousand Poles and fourteen thousand Ukrainians, primarily soldiers, lost their lives in the war).
12. President Wilson propounded his Fourteen Points policy in Paris on January 8, 1919. Point No. 13 stated, "An independent Polish state should be erected which should include the territories inhabited by indisputably Polish populations." The majority of Galicia's population was Ruthenian, not Polish. Point No. 14 stated, "A general association of nations must be formed under specific covenants for the purpose of affording mutual guarantees of political independence and territorial integrity to great and small states alike." The Ukrainian delegation was confident that this point would be implemented with regard to Ukraine's demand for independence.
13. Except the city of Lvov, which had a Polish majority.
14. On June 16, 1919, the Western Ukrainian People's Republic officially had given up both Lvov and the oil strip and signed an armistice with Poland. A week later, the Allies approved the Polish occupation of Eastern Galicia. Then Ukrainian troops withdrew east of the Zbruch River.

15. At the end of the war, the newly independent country of Poland actively engaged in exploiting the oil fields of eastern Galicia. Poland conducted a systematic geological survey of the Carpathian region and established new wells.
16. Ford's mass-production methods made it possible to manufacture a Model T every three minutes.
17. One *funt* (a Russian unit of weight) equals 0.9 pound.
18. The Passover Haggadah is a book that is read during the traditional ceremonial dinner that is called a seder. The Haggadah specifies the order of food courses served at the dinner and tells the story of the Exodus of the Children of Israel from ancient Egypt. *Haggadah* means "narration" in Hebrew and *seder* means "order"—the order of the food served at the ceremonial dinner.

    Six symbolic food items are placed on the Passover seder plate, all related to the Exodus from Egypt. The seventh item is a stack of three *matzoth* that is placed on its own plate. *Matzo* is the special bread that the Children of Israel baked before they rushed to escape Egypt, having no time to wait until their dough rose (Exodus 12:39).
19. During the Haggadah reading, the youngest participant in the seder asks the head of the ceremony four questions about the differences between seder night and all other nights of the year, and the head of the ceremony answers by narrating the story of the Exodus from Egypt.
20. At the beginning of the seder, the head of the ceremony sets aside a piece of *matzo* called the *afikoman*—a Greek word that means "dessert"—and when he leaves the table to wash his hands, the children steal and hide it. Because the *afikoman* is the last item that is eaten in the seder and without it the ritual cannot be finished, the head of the ceremony pretends to search for it. When his efforts fail, the children negotiate its price with him. Only when the price for handing back the *afikoman* is settled does each guest eat a small piece of it, and by that act, the seder is completed.
21. Munkach is located in the valley of the Latorica River in western Ukraine, close to the border with Slovakia. At that time, Munkach was part of Czechoslovakia. Since then, it passed to Hungary and then back to Czechoslovakia. Today, it belongs to Ukraine.
22. *Yishuv* means "settlement" in Hebrew. The Jews in Palestine were referred to collectively as "the Yishuv."
23. Jewish farmers preferred to hire Arabs as agriculture and construction workers because they were cheaper than the newcomers and more used to hard manual labor.

12. The Road to Mecca

1. The Austro-Hungarian, Ottoman, Czarist Russia, and German empires, and the Hapsburg, Ottoman, Romanov, and Hohenzollern dynasties.
2. The expression is ascribed to the American writer Gertrude Stein and was popularized by Ernest Hemingway in the epigraph to his novel *The Sun Also Rises.*

3. Owen's poem was written in 1917, when he was in a hospital in Edinburgh, recovering from shell shock.
4. Jaroslav Hasek was born in 1883 and died in 1923. (Svejk, pronounced "shvake," is often spelled Schweik.) Ernest Hemingway was born in 1899 and died in 1961; he was an American novelist and a journalist and the 1954 Nobel laureate in literature. Erich Maria Remarque was born in 1898 and died in 1970; he was a German novelist and a teacher, and was wounded several times in the war.
5. Called Czernowitz in German and Yiddish, the city is the regional capital of Bukovina in western Ukraine, on the northeastern side of the Carpathian Mountains. According to the census of 1900, the city's 21,600 Jews were the largest minority.
6. According to *halakha* (Jewish law), a deserted woman, *agunah* in Hebrew, is forbidden to remarry because of the strictness of the biblical command against adultery and the possibility that the disappeared husband might reappear. The woman needs a religious divorce, but this can only be granted by the husband. No religious court will grant it to her, and she cannot marry unless her husband is proved to be dead. Cases of deserted women are regarded by rabbis as the most difficult to resolve, and even the enormous number of missing individuals in the Holocaust did not influence twentieth-century rabbis to modify the rule.
7. Aramaic is the original language of two books of the bible, Daniel and Ezra, and is the main language of the Talmud. It was probably the native language of Jesus Christ. The Bible, the Mishna, and the Gemara contain the entire body of Jewish law. The Mishna and the Gemara are the Talmud's two main components.
8. The two versions were produced by two different groups of Jewish scholars. The Jerusalem Talmud originated in Tiberias, and its final redaction was done in the fourth century CE. The Babylonian Talmud was written during the Israelites' exile in Babylonia (which started in 586 BC) and was compiled in the sixth century CE. The Babylonian Talmud is regarded as more precise, and therefore its influence has been far greater. *Talmud* means "study" in Hebrew.
9. See a later version: D. C. Lau, *Lao Tzu: Tao Te Ching* (London: Penguin Classics, 1963).
10. The Romanische Café was a well-known artists' café (in 1925, the café moved to Budapester Street). Among the regular guests were the dramatist Bertolt Brecht, the Dadaist painter George Grosz, the poet Else Lasker-Schüler, the authors Alfred Kerr and Erich Maria Remarque, and many others (most of the regular guests moved to the Romanische Café from the famous Café des Westens when the latter ceased to exist in 1915).
11. At that time, Leopold Weiss had another uncle in Jerusalem, Aryeh Feigenbaum (1885–1981), an ophthalmologist, who had immigrated from Lvov to Palestine in 1913 and lived at 3 Ethiopia Street (where the Jerusalem branch of the British

Council was located in the 1990s). Aryeh Feigenbaum was a leading authority on trachoma whose Jerusalem clinics treated Arabs and Jews alike. For thirty-two years, from 1922 to 1954, he headed the ophthalmology department of the Hadassah-Rothschild Hospital and was elected to be the first dean of the Medical School of Hebrew University and Hadassah. Aryeh Feigenbaum was a fervent Zionist, and Leopold Weiss omitted all mention of Aryeh from his writings in order to distance himself from any links to Zionism.

12. Before he immigrated to Palestine, Dorian Feigenbaum (1887–1937) had practiced under Julius Agner-Jauregg in Vienna and Emil Kreapelin in Munich; he was a member of the Swiss Psychoanalytic Society and one of the founders of Berlin's Psychoanalytic Institute.
13. Two Jerusalemite psychiatrists, Kalian and Witztum, have summarized the syndrome's signs: "The psychiatric hospitalization of tourists in Jerusalem is uncommon (around fifty patients per year, from among almost two million tourists). In our view, perhaps Jerusalem syndrome should be regarded as a unique cultural phenomenon because of its overwhelming theatrical characteristics. Such dramatic qualities have been reported by various biographers since the establishment of pilgrimage and tourism to the Holy City. Jerusalem syndrome should be regarded as an aggravation of a chronic mental illness, and not a transient psychotic episode. The eccentric conduct and bizarre behavior of these colorful yet mainly psychotic visitors became dramatically overt once they reached the Holy City—a geographical locus containing the *axis mundi* of their religious belief." See M. Kalian and E. Witztum, "Comments on Jerusalem Syndrome," *British Journal of Psychiatry* 176:492.
14. In 1925, Dorian Feigenbaum was accepted into the New York Psychoanalytic Society, the oldest psychoanalytic organization in the United States. From the society's foundation in 1932 until Feigenbaum's death in 1936, Feigenbaum was one of the editors of the prestigious *Psychoanalytic Quarterly*. Only in 1933 did psychoanalysis begin to thrive in Palestine when Max Eitingon (1881–1943) emigrated from Berlin to Jerusalem following Hitler's rise to power.
15. Jacob de Hahn was born in 1881 and died in 1924. The author Arnold Zweig wrote a novel based on de Hahn called *De Vriendt Comes Home*. De Hahn's sister was the well-known Dutch writer Carrie de Hahn. She was married to a non-Jewish writer, Kaes Van Brigen, and was a vehement opponent of Zionism.
16. An acronym of *merkaz ruhani* ("spiritual center," in Hebrew).
17. Hussein bin Ali was born in 1852 and died in 1931. He proclaimed himself king of the Hejaz in 1917 and received international recognition. In 1924, he was defeated by Abdul Aziz al-Saud, who established Saudi Arabia and was its first monarch.
18. Emir Abdallah was born in 1882 and died in 1951. Between 1949 and 1951, he was the king of the Hashemite Kingdom of Jordan. In 1951, he was assassinated while visiting the Al Aqsa Mosque in Jerusalem, and his grandson

Hussein succeeded him. Weiss's only son was named after King Hussein's father, Talal.

19. De Hahn was murdered in Jerusalem in June 1924, apparently by activists of the Haganah, the Zionist paramilitary organization that was created in 1920 to protect the Jewish community in Palestine. This murder is regarded as the first political assassination in Zionist history.
20. *La Chanson de Roland*, the oldest known French epic, was composed by the Norman poet Turold, probably at the end of the eleventh century. It deals with the historical Battle of Roncesvalles (Roncevaux) in the year 778 and narrates a tale of heroism, faith, and human suffering during the reign of King Charlemagne, in which the valiant Roland, a tenth-century knight, helped to halt the advance of the Saracens (Arabs who invaded Europe from North Africa) from Spain into France. The last part of the long tale relates how the Christian fighters destroy the Muslim army and King Charlemagne defeats Baligant, the emir of Babylon, in personal combat. Then the Christian army swarms into Saragossa, destroying synagogues and mosques and baptizing a hundred thousand Muslims and Jews. *La Chanson de Roland* is one of the *chansons de geste* ("songs of heroic deeds"), French epic poetry of the twelfth through the fifteenth centuries, some of which relate to the events of the First Crusade and the establishment of the kingdom of Jerusalem. The original *Chanson de Roland* manuscript from 1080 is now at the Bodleian Library in Oxford.
21. Tents of the pastoral Shammar tribe were spread throughout the Middle East, from Mesopotamia in the north through Syria to the Arabian Peninsula and Aden. The tribe's main settlement was located in central Saudi Arabia along the rocky plateau area of Najd, east of the Hejaz. The tribe's leaders resided in the oasis town of Hail. Munira Asad belonged to the Rashid clan of the Shammar tribe.
22. Ibn Saud (1880–1953) was the founder of Saudi Arabia.
23. The orientalist Dr. Martin Kramer, who directed the Moshe Dayan Center for Middle Eastern and African Studies at Tel Aviv University and who is a Wexler Fromer Fellow at the Washington Institute for Near East Policy, presents in his blog (see www.martinkramer.org/, accessed April 3, 2008) an intelligence report that was submitted in late 1928, by an Iraqi named Abdallah Damluji (an adviser to King Ibn Saud), to the British Consul in the Hejaz. The report's title was "Bolshevik and Soviet Penetration" and referred to "Asadullah von Weiss," which meant Leopold Weiss (Public Records Office, London, FO967/22). It says,

> I must bring attention to the person known as Asadullah von Weiss, formerly an Austrian Jew, now a Muslim, who resides presently near the holy shrine in Mecca. This Austrian Leopold von Weiss came to the Hijaz two years

> ago, claiming he had become a Muslim out of love for this religion and in pure belief in it. I do not know why, but his words were accepted without opposition, and he entered Mecca without impediment. He did so at a time when no one like him was allowed to do the same, the Hijaz government having recently passing a law providing that those like him must wait two years under surveillance, so that the government can be certain of their Islam before their entry into Mecca. Since that time, Leopold von Weiss has remained in Mecca, wandering the country and mixing with people of every class and with government persons. He then traveled to Medina, and stayed there and in its environs for several months. Then he was able—I have no idea how—to travel to Riyadh with King Ibn Saud last year, and he stayed in Riyadh for five months, seeing and hearing all that happened, mingling with the people and speaking with persons of the government. He does not seem to me to be a learned or professional man. His apparent purpose is to obtain news from the King, and especially from Shaykh Yusuf Yasin, secretary to the King [and editor of the official newspaper *Umm al-Qura*]. Asadullah uses this news to produce articles for some German and Austrian newspapers, in reply to the distasteful things written by some European newspapers on the Hijazi-Najdi court. This is the occupation of the Austrian Jew Leopold von Weiss, now Haj Asadullah the Muslim. What is the real mission which makes him endure the greatest discomforts and the worst conditions of life? On what basis rests the close intimacy between him and Shaykh Yusuf Yasin? Is there some connection between von Weiss and the Bolshevik consulate in Jidda? These are mysteries about which it is difficult to know the truth.

It should be pointed out that the Iraqi informant Abdallah Damluji didn't know that Weiss had proved his support to the Arab cause during his journalistic work in Jerusalem and that he had excellent credentials in the eyes of Arab political and religious leaders.

13. A Love Story

1. That is also true today. When I interviewed religious family members in New York City and Jerusalem and the name of Weiss-Asad was mentioned, each man immediately spat to the side and a repugnant expression appeared on his face.
2. It is also called the battle of Tannenberg, in which Poles and Lithuanians defeated the Knights of the German Teutonic Order in 1410. The battle was fought in Prussia, between the villages of Grunwald and Tannenberg.
3. Frederick Chopin (1810–1849), a Polish-French pianist and a composer from the Romantic era, is widely regarded as one of the most prolific and celebrated composers of piano music. Johannes Brahms (1883–1897), a German composer, is often described as the greatest Romantic composer.

4. Meir Hazanovitz (1890–1913) was a Russian-born member of Hashomer, the Jewish defense organization that was founded in Palestine in 1909. *Hashomer* is Hebrew for "the guard." The organization ceased to exist in 1920, and part of it was integrated into the Haganah. Hazanovitz is buried at Israel's Pioneers cemetery in Upper Galilee. Joseph Trumpeldor (1880–1920), a Russian-born, one-armed Zionist activist, died together with five other men and two women in 1920 while defending the small settlement of Tel-Hai in Upper Galilee against an attack by local Arabs. His reputed last words were, "Never mind, it is good to die for our country," and his personal bravery made him possibly the most important Zionist icon in Israel's history. His memorial day is officially marked in Israel every year.
5. Thomas Masaryk was born in 1850 and died in 1937. The founder and the first president of Czechoslovakia, he is regarded as one of the most influential liberal statesmen of the twentieth century.
6. "I gratefully thank Thee" (*Modeh ani* in Hebrew) is a short prayer that is said every morning immediately after awakening. It does not include God's name, and Jews are allowed to recite it at any time and under any circumstances.
7. In Yiddish, these dumplings are called *kreplach*. Polish Jews usually fill *kreplach* with chopped meat and serve them in soups. Poles usually stuff *pierogi* (plural of *pierog*) with a variety of fillings—cheese, potatoes, and chopped meat. They are served with homemade *kielbasa* (sausage) and sauerkraut. Jews skip the *kielbasa* because it is not kosher.
8. In the mid-1930s, U.S. $1 equaled 5.18 zlotys; 80 zloty's were worth U.S. $15.4, with a purchasing power of approximately U.S. $172 in 2006.
9. A few names of rich Jews were well known in West Galicia: Streiman and Bodek, the owners of the flour mills; Bencher, who owned a foundry; Michael Katz, the owner of a chemical factory; and the Zalman brothers, who were furniture manufacturers.
10. *Kugel* is a baked noodle cake traditionally eaten on the Sabbath. *Fresser* in Yiddish and German is "a greedy eater."
11. It is considered immodest for an Orthodox married Jewish woman to have her hair uncovered in the presence of men. Women cover their heads with hats or kerchiefs. Some prefer to shave their hair off and wear wigs. In Galicia, wigs were worn by upper-class women.
12. Podolia lies southwest of the Kiev region in the western part of present-day Ukraine. From 1921 to 1939, Podolia was part of Poland.
13. Buma Krauthammer was Nunio's uncle, and Bronia was his relative.

14. Deceptive Fate

1. The idea of the "Final solution to the Jewish problem" (Endlösung der Judenfrage) by systematic genocide against the European Jewish population began to be implemented by the Nazi regime during the second half of 1941. Until then, the Nazi authorities were ambiguous about their real plans regarding the Jews.

Before 1941, Nazi Germany formulated vague plans to deport German Jews to Palestine and then to deport all European Jews to the island of Madagascar.

2. Kristallnacht, "Night of the Broken Glass," was a government-directed pogrom in which dozens of German Jews were beaten to death; 30,000 Jewish men and boys were imprisoned in concentration camps; and 1,668 synagogues, many Jewish cemeteries, and 7,000 Jewish shops and department stores were ransacked or set on fire. The Jews who had been sent to concentration camps were released over the next three months, but by then, more than 2,000 of them had died.
3. According to the secret part of the treaty, Nazi Germany seized the western part of Poland and the Soviets controlled the areas east of the Narev, Vistula, and San rivers, which included Galicia. The nonaggression treaty lasted until Nazi Germany invaded the Soviet Union in June 1941.
4. Stella now lives in Brighton Beach, New York. Her son is Leon Wieseltier, the literary editor of the *New Republic.* Her husband, Mark, who is mentioned further on, died in March 1996, and Leon described his mourning for his father in his book *Kaddish* (New York: Knopf, 1999).
5. Nikita Sergeyevitch Khrushchev was born in 1894 and died in 1971. From 1958 to 1964, Khrushchev was the first secretary of the Communist Party of the Soviet Union. In February 1956, in a secret speech delivered to the 20th Party Congress, Khrushchev accused Stalin of committing crimes during the period of the Great Purge. In 1964, Khrushchev was removed from power by his party colleagues and replaced by Leonid Brezhnev.
6. Naftali's brother, Leib, committed suicide while studying chemistry at the University of Vienna. In his short story "Backenroth," the Nobel laureate in literature Elias Canetti penned a unique profile of some aspects of Leib's personality (for more information, see E. Canetti, *The Torch in My Ear* [New York: Farrar, Straus and Giroux, 1982], p. 182).
7. International stamps were special postage stamps issued by the Universal Postal Union that were affixed to letters mailed to enemy countries.

15. The Wedding

1. Stanislav was a rail junction and an industrial center seventy miles south of Lvov and forty miles southeast of Bolechow. Before World War II, more than fifteen thousand Jews dwelled in the city (about 50 percent of the city's inhabitants).
2. The American historian Celia S. Heller, a Backenroth scion (a descendant of Yom-Tov Lipman Heller), wrote that between 1921 and 1937, some four hundred thousand Jews left Poland, about a tenth of the total Jewish population. Most of them settled in the United States. A few went to Palestine. About 3.5 million Jews remained in Poland. Those who left were saved from the Holocaust, but almost all of those who remained were murdered, with only a few survivors (see *On the Edge of Destruction: Jews of Poland between the Two World Wars* [New York: Columbia University Press, 1977]).

3. In this context, an Orthodox family member, Avi Backenroth, a lawyer who lives in Brooklyn, New York, told me (during an interview in 1988) that even before Hitler's arrival on the historical scene, assimilation had destroyed the Jewish people. "The Nazis annihilated the body, but the soul had been attacked long since." Avi Backenroth was implying that the spiritual annihilation of the Jewish people in Eastern Europe had begun around the turn of the century when secular culture infiltrated the Jewish ghetto with great impact.
4. See also chapter 7 in Celia Heller's book *On the Edge of Destruction: Jews of Poland between the Two World Wars.*
5. Jewish dietary law (*kashruth*) determines whether something is kosher (clean or fit) to eat. Eating pork is forbidden. Eating meat and dairy products at the same time is also forbidden.
6. In 1927, 29 percent of Jewish students were forced to study abroad, and once they returned, the government did not recognize their diplomas, and they had to wait five years to take their examinations.
7. Vyacheslav Mikhailovich Molotov (1890–1986) was the premier from 1930 to 1941 (the weapon the Molotov cocktail was named after him). The peace treaty between the victorious Allied powers and defeated Germany was signed at the Palace of Versailles near Paris on June 28, 1919. The Versailles Treaty formally ended World War I.

16. The Communist Train

1. On November 20, 1940, Hungary signed the Tripartite Pact and joined the Axis—Germany, Italy, and Japan. On July 1, 1941, the Karpat Group—the Hungarian army's best-equipped unit, consisting of around forty-five thousand troops—had been attached to German general Carl Heinrich von Stülpnagel's 17th Army, and it attacked the 12th Soviet army. The Hungarians' task was to drive the Soviet troops from the Carpathian Mountains and pursue them east to the Dniester River.
2. A klezmer band is made up of musicians who use violins, clarinets, and flutes to perform Jewish folk music that originated in Eastern Europe.
3. *Kishke* is an Eastern European Jewish sausage made of mincemeat, *matzo* flour, schmaltz (chicken fat), and onion. *Tzimmes* is a Jewish dish of carrots and raisins cooked slowly over very low heat and flavored with honey and cinnamon. *Tzimmes* is traditionally served at the New Year's meal, as well as on other occasions.
4. In the ritual of casting sins upon the waters—in Hebrew, Tashlikh, or "cast out"—worshippers place small pieces of bread in their pockets and walk to a place of flowing water such as a creek, a river, or the seashore and empty their pockets into the water, symbolically casting off their sins. In the ceremony, Psalms are read, along with lines from the kabbalah and the last verses of the book of the prophet Micah (7:19): "He will take us back in love; He will cover up our iniquities, You will cast all their sins into the depths of the sea."

5. Juliusz Slowacki (1809–1849) was a Romantic Polish poet and playwright, who immigrated to Paris and died there.
6. Vladimir Ilyich Lenin (1870–1924) was the founder of Bolshevism and the leader of the Bolshevik Revolution. *One Step Forward, Two Steps Back (The Crisis in Our Party)* was published in Geneva in 1904.
7. Karl Radek (1885–1939) and Nikolai Ivanovich Bukharin (1888–1938) were Bolshevik thinkers and international communist leaders. Radek was born in Lvov to the Jewish Sobelsohn family.

17. Judenrat

1. In the months following the German invasion, Khrushchev had been responsible for coordinating the defense of Ukraine, but he was recalled to Moscow after Kiev was conquered by the Germans. In 1944, when Kiev was liberated by the Red Army, Khrushchev was back in Ukraine.
2. In 1939, about 14,000 Jews dwelled in Drohobych; they were the largest ethnic group in town (of the entire population of 34,600, 40 percent were Jews, 33 percent Poles, and 26 percent Ukrainians). There were 13,000 Jews in Boryslav and about 1,500 in Schodnica.
3. Sixty years of Jewish emigration from Galicia, mainly to the United States, but also to Palestine, South America, and Western Europe, had dramatically reduced the size of the lower class. A higher proportion of poor people emigrated from the oil belt than from other Galician regions.
4. In neighboring Boryslav, the head of the Judenrat was Michael Herz. Schodnica's Jews were regulated by Drohobych's Judenrat.
5. In practice, Felix Landau was a member of Drohobych's Security Police (Sicherheitspolizei, or SIPO in German) unit, but during the German occupation and also after the war, when war criminals were brought to trial, everyone referred to him as a Gestapo officer. The assignments and the activities of the SIPO units and the Gestapo were similar, and most of the time both units operated together. Naftali Backenroth also referred to Landau as a Gestapo man.
6. At the same time, the NKVD also shot dozens of Jewish, Polish, and Ukrainian detainees in the prisons of neighboring towns, including Stryj and Stanislav.
7. Leon Thorne, *Out of the Ashes: The Story of a Survivor* (New York: Rosebern, 1961), p. 108. From the beginning of 1944, the last year of the war, Thorne and four other Jews, among them Stella Backenroth-Wieseltier, were squeezed into a musty hiding place that had been dug out beneath a stable in Schodnica, near an oil well that had belonged to the Backenroth family. See the detailed story of the hiding place and Thorne's diary in chapter 22.
8. In 1941, the German occupation authorities established central Gestapo offices in Lvov, Stanislav (Ivano-Frankivs'k), Ternopol, Kolomyya, and Drohobych. The offices were active in the cities themselves and the environs. The Gestapo office in Stryj was smaller than in Drohobych, and later on, Gestapo officers were sent from Drohobych to assist with the liquidation of Stryj's Jews.

The officers from Drohobych who actively participated in the murder of Stryj's Jews were Landau, Ebenrecht, Dengg, and Gabriel. The Gestapo office in Drohobych was also in charge of the Jewish population in the town of Boryslav and the surrounding villages, including Schodnica.

9. Before the war, the building housed the Jewish orphanage.
10. In his book *Drohobycz, Drohobycz and Other Stories: True Tales from the Holocaust and Life After*, Henryk Grynberg wrote, "When twenty Jews didn't show up for work out of fear, Landau ordered twenty to be shot, pointing at them himself with his finger, *'Du, du und du!'*. . . (You, you and you!)."
11. After the war, Landau was arrested by the Americans and held at Glasenbach prison. He escaped, changed his name, and built a new life as an interior decorator in Bavaria, West Germany. In 1959 he was identified and arrested again. In 1961, a German judge in Stuttgart convicted Landau of committing two "extermination crimes" and sentenced him to life imprisonment. One was the case of "killing 20 Jews, captured at random in the office of the Jewish council, as a reprisal for the escape of 17 Jewish forced laborers from a labor commando"; the other case was the murder of the forced-laborer gardener Fliegner (see the detailed story of Fliegner's murder by Landau in chapter 19).
12. The committee was established by the communist liberators a few days after the Germans had retreated from Drohobych in the summer of 1944.
13. In March 1933, Dollfuss suspended Parliament in order to prevent the Austrian Nazi Party from gaining a majority in future elections. In June, he banned the Nazi Party and turned to the Italian fascist ruler Mussolini for support against Hitler's plans to annex Austria to Germany. On July 25, 1934, Austrian Nazis assassinated Dollfuss in his office. The assassins were caught and jailed. Dollfuss's successor, Kurt Schuschnigg, was imprisoned by the German Nazis during the Anschluss (annexation) in 1938.
14. See also Harry Zeimer, "Report from Drohobych, Fall 1942," Yad Vashem Archives (YVA), M20/136, p. 1—"The Wehrmacht executed several Ukrainians for looting during the pogrom in Drohobych."
15. Today Rosenmann is a resident of Jerusalem. Before his retirement, he was the head of the Judean Mountains Development Administration.
16. In November 1942, the same Günther murdered the author and painter Bruno Schulz (see chapter 22).
17. The conference's chairman was Reinhard Heydrich, the deputy head of the Nazi Security Service, and the participants were fourteen high-ranking Nazi officers and German government officials, including the secretaries of the Foreign Ministry and the Justice Ministry. It was the first time that the Final Solution plan was formally revealed to non-Nazi government officials. One of the participants was Dr. Josef Bühler, the deputy to the head of the Generalgouvernement (Nazi-occupied Poland), Hans Frank.
18. At that stage, four extermination camps were established, in Belźec, Sobibor, Treblinka, and Majdanek.

19. Bełżec's gas chambers began to liquidate masses of people in March 1942. Jews from Drohobych were among the first to be murdered in Bełżec. This was also the place where the poison gas Zyklon B was tested for the first time on three thousand Jewish prisoners on August 19, 1941.
20. In Drohobych the Jewish ghetto was not fenced, but German Gestapo officers and members of the Ukrainian militia were stationed there twenty-four hours a day to ensure that Jews would not leave. The Jewish police, established by the Judenrat according to German Security Police orders, also took steps to prevent Jews from escaping the ghetto's territory.
21. Winston Churchill was convinced that the battle of El Alamein marked the turning point in the war, and he ordered that church bells be rung all over Britain. He said later, "Before Alamein we never had a victory, after Alamein we never had a defeat."

18. Parting

1. Dagestan is in the southernmost part of Russia and is bordered on the south by Azerbaijan, which was then part of the Soviet Union.
2. In the middle of November 1941, the Germans formed a ring around Moscow and ten days later got within twenty miles of its center. The Soviet defense was strong, however, and in the beginning of December the Soviets halted the German attack. In fact, at the exact time when Ullo believed that "Makhachkala was our lowest point," the Red Army had succeeded in forcing back the Germans on the Eastern Front.
3. Chechnya is located in the mountains of the Northern Caucasus. Until 1991, it was part of the Soviet Union, and today it is part of Russia.

19. A Perfect Riding Hall

1. The German propaganda machine published ads in Ukrainian newspapers calling on the local population to cooperate. On March 3, 1942, a Kiev newspaper printed this ad: "Germany calls you! Go to Beautiful Germany! 100,000 Ukrainians are already working in free Germany. What about you?"
2. Cornelia Schmalz-Jacobsen, the daughter of the Helmrichs, was born in Berlin in 1934 and as a child witnessed her parents' courageous rescue efforts. She described their activities in her book *Zwei Baume in Jerusalem* (Two trees in Jerusalem) (Hoffmann and Campe, 2002, in German).
3. The friendship between Naftali and the Helmrichs lasted until Naftali's death in 1993. Both Eberhard and Donata were separately recognized by Yad Vashem as "Righteous among the Nations"—the title bestowed on gentiles who helped to save Jews during the Holocaust. After the war, the couple separated, and Eberhard emigrated to the United States. In 1968, Eberhard came to Israel and met Jews whom he and his wife had helped to rescue. Speaking about their motives, Eberhard said, "We were fully aware of the risks and the clash of responsibilities, but we decided that it would be better for our children to have

dead parents than cowards as parents. After that decision, it was comparatively easy." And Donata added, "We figured that after we had saved two people, we'd be even with Hitler if we were caught, and with every person saved beyond that, we were ahead."

4. Bruno Schulz's life and tragic death in Drohobych's ghetto are described in detail in chapter 22.
5. See Leon Thorne, *Out of the Ashes: The Story of a Survivor* (New York: Rosebern, 1961).
6. He was one of the deputies of Otto Waechter, the governor of Galicia District. The witnesses to the event could not remember his name.
7. Drohobych's ghetto included Chary, Sienkiewicz, Gabarska, Ribia, Kowalska, and Schonica streets. Watchmen were posted by the Judenrat and the Ukrainian militia to see that no Jew left the area without authorization.
8. It was from the roof of that villa that the thief Schloma sent out pigeons in Bruno Schulz's story "The Age of Genius." The story was part of a novel that Schulz was writing in the middle of the 1930s, titled *The Messiah.* He was murdered before he completed the book (see chapter 22).
9. The girls' last names were Sternbach, Kupferberg, and Zukerman. They waved and smiled at three Gestapo officers, and for that, the officers shot the girls on the spot. See the details of this story in chapter 17.
10. In 1961, Landau was put on trial in Stuttgart, West Germany, for war crimes. Naftali Backenroth was called to testify about the murder of Fliegner. Landau was sentenced to life imprisonment (see also chapter 17).
11. In 1973, Yad Vashem recognized Berthold Beitz as one of the Righteous among the Nations.
12. Three of the 427 Germans who were recognized by Yad Vashem as "Righteous among the Nations" were involved in rescuing Naftali's labor groups: Eberhard and Donata Helmrich and Berthold Beitz. The total number of gentiles thus recognized is 21,310, among them 5,941 Poles and 4,726 Dutch (the numbers were accurate at the end of 2006).
13. Today, Pomerania is divided between northern Poland and Germany on the south coast of the Baltic Sea.
14. The famous and luxurious 1873 mansion was home to the industrialist Krupp's family until the end of World War II.
15. In 1948, Alfried Krupp (1907–1967) was sentenced by the Nuremberg Tribunal to twelve years in prison for war crimes. He served seven years and was released in January 1951. His steel company, along with his private wealth, was returned to him. In 1952, Krupp hired Beitz to manage his company. Beitz ran the Krupp firm until 1990. In 1993, in an extravagant and well-attended eightieth birthday celebration, Beitz summarized his Holocaust experience: "As I look back, I can now say that I did something in my life. I am proud of what I did out of a sense of humanity. I passed through that period, as you cross through a dark forest with self-assurance and with incredible luck."

16. Immediately after the German occupation, the plant was named Beskiden Erdöl AG, and then the name was changed to Karpathen Öl AG.
17. In 1966, during Fritz Hildebrand's trial in the city of Bremen, West Germany, Beitz testified in his favor, claiming that Hildebrand "shut both his eyes" to the forbidden employment of Jews. Beitz's testimony angered Boryslaw's forced-labor camp survivors. In 1953, Hildebrand was charged in Bremen with responsibility for the mass killing of Jewish inmates in the forced-labor camps of Drohobych and Boryslav, which he commanded between February 1943 and June 1944. He was sentenced to life imprisonment.
18. After the war, Beitz was criticized by relatives of workers whom he had been compelled to hand over to the Gestapo, which had sent them to the death camps. But an examination of his actions led to the conclusion that he had functioned in an ethical manner. Researchers for Yad Vashem reached the same opinion when in 1968 they recommended that he be given the Righteous among the Nations award.
19. In the "new" postwar Germany, Beitz's activities on behalf of the Jews were widely publicized, and he became known as a man with a conscience who had very adroitly identified a weakness in the Nazis' racist system and had succeeded in penetrating it.
20. George died in Paris in September 1987.

20. Ullo's Best School

1. From 1920 to 1991, the Republic of Azerbaijan was part of the Soviet Union. It had been briefly independent from 1918 to 1920. Azerbaijan is bounded by the Caspian Sea to the east, Russia to the north, Georgia to the northwest, Armenia to the west, and Iran to the south. The majority of the population are Azeri Muslims; Russian and Armenian Christians make up sizable minorities. The Azerbaijani language is part the Turkic family of languages. Since the collapse of the Soviet Union in late 1991, Azerbaijan has been independent.
2. The Mugano-Salyan region in south-central Azerbaijan lies south of the Kura River and specializes in light industry and agriculture, particularly cotton growing. At the beginning of the twentieth century, Azerbaijan was the world's leading petroleum producer and was the birthplace of the oil-refining industry. In 1901, Azerbaijan produced 11.4 million tons of oil, more than half of the world's production and more than the United States was producing. As the twentieth century progressed and the oil industry developed in other regions of the world—the Soviet Union, Romania, Galicia, and the United States—Azerbaijan's oil production decreased.
3. A *rubashka* is a full-cut, embroidered shirt made of heavy white linen, worn outside the trousers and extending to the hips.
4. A safe vaccine against typhus was mass produced in the beginning of the 1940s but was not available during the war in Eastern Europe.

5. The battle for Stalingrad at the end of January 1943 was the war's decisive turning point. After the Germans' defeat at Stalingrad, their troops began the long retreat westward. The battle of Kursk in the summer of 1943, which has been described as the biggest tank battle of all time, finally exhausted the Germans. It was a defensive success for the Soviets, although at a heavy cost. The German losses of more than five hundred thousand troops and a thousand tanks hindered any initiative they might have attempted to start a new offensive on the Eastern Front.
6. *Promkombinat* was a term used in the Soviet Union and other Eastern European countries denoting a large industrial complex that usually combined several plants and workshops.
7. Bessarabia was a region in Eastern Europe, between the Dniester and Prut rivers, which was annexed by the Soviet Union in the beginning of World War II. When it was conquered by the German army, many of its residents fled to the east. Today the land is divided between Romania and Moldavia.
8. After the German invasion of the USSR (Operation Barbarossa), Stalin recognized the Polish government in exile and ordered the release of all Polish citizens from the Siberian camps.
9. Wladyslaw Anders was born in 1892 and died in 1970. After the Germans invaded the Soviet Union, General Anders had been authorized by his government in exile to establish a Polish military force in the USSR. Anders's Army Corps was transferred (along with a large number of Polish civilians) to Europe through the Middle East and fought with the Allies in Italy.
10. Later, the recruits headed off in the direction of the Middle East, and when they reached Palestine, many of the Jews deserted and stayed there.
11. In Russian, *Zhid* (Jew) is disparaging; *Yevrei* (Hebrew) is politically correct. *Zhid* was officially replaced by *Yevrei* in the late 1700s by Catherine the Great (1729–1796).
12. Mir Jafar Bagirov ruled Azerbaijan with an iron fist from 1928 until Stalin's death in 1953. He was a protégé of Lavrenty Beria, the chief of the NKVD (the secret service, the KGB's predecessor), and was Stalin's closest confidant.
13. During the early 1930s, when Stalin implemented the forced collectivization of agriculture, Azerbaijani farmers rose up against it and were brutally suppressed. By 1940, during the Great Purge era, when Stalin executed Communist Party officials throughout the Soviet Union, an estimated 120,000 Azerbaijanis were killed. The purges were directed by Bagirov. In 1956, Bagirov was executed by Stalin's successor Nikita Khrushchev, who purged what was called "Beria's Gang."
14. After World War II, the communist regime executed many upper-class Azerbaijanis and confiscated their property. Communist apparatchiks accused numerous Azerbaijani intellectuals of adopting a nationalist, anticommunist ideology. Azerbaijani works of oral and written literature were denounced as "bourgeois" and banned.

15. Trotskyism differed from Stalinism mainly in its adherence to Karl Marx's idea of a permanent international revolution, in contrast to the Stalinist doctrine of endorsing political deals with imperialist powers and bourgeoisie parties. Leon Trotsky (1879–1940) was born in Ukraine to the Jewish Bronstein family. He was a Marxist theorist and one of the leaders of the 1917 Communist Revolution. In 1928, Stalin expelled Trotsky from the Soviet Union and then sent an assassin to murder him in his exile in Mexico.

21. Stolen Identity

1. Kiev, on the northern edge of Ukraine, was captured by the Red Army on November 6, 1943, as part of the Battle of the Lower Dnieper. It was one of the bloodiest battles in history. On both sides, approximately four million soldiers took part and more than half of them were killed or injured. Only when that battle had been won did the Red Army begin to invade Ukraine.
2. In 1946, Rabbi Yaacov Avigdor immigrated to the United States and served a Jewish community in Brooklyn, New York. In 1950, he became chief rabbi of Mexico's Jewish community, where he served until his death in 1967. His son, Rabbi Isaac C. Avigdor, serves today as the spiritual leader of the United Synagogues of Greater Hartford in West Hartford, Connecticut.
3. Drohobych was liberated from the Nazi occupation on August 6, 1944.
4. Nothing in this book is exaggerated or fictitious; everything is true. I emphasize this because, upon reading the story of Naftali's change of identity, some readers may suspect that I have taken poetic license to exaggerate, add color, or touch up the facts, in order to create a new myth. Certainly not. Once again, I want to stress that all of the facts in Naftali's story have been checked and found true. He did not invent anything.

22. Phoenixlike

1. The Wehrmacht's chief of staff signed the surrender documents for all German forces to the Allies in Rheims, France, in the early morning of May 7. On May 8, the German surrender became effective and King George delivered his victory speech in London. Also on May 8, shortly before midnight, German officials in Berlin signed similar surrender documents before the head of the Soviet forces. Because of the time zone difference between Berlin and Moscow, in Russia the German military surrender became effective only on May 9, which is why Eastern European countries commemorate Victory Day on May 9.
2. Giorgi Dimitrov (1882–1949), a devoted Stalinist, became the head of Bulgaria's Communist Party and the state premier in 1946. The Third Comintern was one of seven World Congresses held by the International Union of Communist Parties, which was founded by Lenin in 1919.
3. The Black Madonna of Czestochowa (Czarna Madonna Czestochowa, in Polish) is an icon that, according to the Eastern Church tradition, was painted by St. Lucas the Evangelist and was carried from Jerusalem via Constantinople

to the monastery of Jasna Gora in Czestochowa; it miraculously saved the monastery from being destroyed during the seventeenth-century Swedish invasion.

4. Armia Krajowa (the Home Army) was the Polish resistance movement in occupied Poland.
5. Bruno Schulz (1982–1942) wrote two famous books of short stories: *The Street of Crocodiles* (also known as *Cinnamon Shops*) and *Sanatorium under an Hourglass*. Intellectuals such as the Nobel laureate Isaac Bashevis Singer compared Schulz to Franz Kafka and Marcel Proust (see Singer's interview of Philip Roth, *New York Times Book Review*, February 13, 1977). Cynthia Ozick's novel *The Messiah of Stockholm* (New York: Knopf, 1987) was about a lost manuscript that Schulz was writing before his death that he planned to call *The Messiah*.
6. In the beginning of 1942, Schulz succeeded in saving some of his drawings by entrusting them to friends who resided outside of the ghetto. Approximately three hundred of Schulz's drawings and caricatures are on display in the Warsaw Museum of Literature.
7. These murals, illustrating Grimm's fairy tales, were the last known works painted by Schulz. In 2001, they were rediscovered by a German documentary producer, Benjamin Geissler. A few months later, agents for Yad Vashem removed the murals from the wall in Drohobych and transferred them to Jerusalem, apparently with the permission of local authorities—an act that ignited an angry international dispute.
8. Other versions of Schulz's murder had stated that SS officer Karl Günther also kept a Jew under his protection, either a dentist named Löw or a furniture maker, Hauptman. Out of jealousy, Felix Landau shot and killed Günther's protégé (either the dentist or the furniture maker), and in return Günther murdered Bruno Schulz on the street. Nevertheless, Leon Thorne's version is supported by the official inquiry that was conducted by Drohobych's Holocaust survivors. According to that inquiry, on November 18, 1942, "the Jewish pharmacist, Reiner, attacks a member of the Gestapo," and on November 19, "The Germans take revenge on Reiner's action by shooting 230 people. Among those shot is Bruno Schulz, the writer and artist who taught in the Jewish High School in Drohobych. . . . Schulz was killed by Günther, a member of the Gestapo. When Landau discovered this, he killed the dental technician Löw, the Jew whom Günther protected, in revenge. Upon hearing this, Günther stormed into the Judenrat claiming that he had killed Schulz in revenge" (for more information, see www.shtetlinks.jewishgen.org/drohobycz/history/WWII.asp, accessed April 7, 2008).
9. In 1944, soon after being liberated by the Russian army from the group's hideaway beneath the stable, Friedman was murdered in Lublin. His version of the burial was accepted by the Schulz biographer Jerzy Ficowski. Another author who wrote about Drohobych's history during the Nazi occupation, Henryk

Grynberg, had considered Friedman's version doubtful and accepted another version, told by a pupil of Schulz's, Dr. Leopold Lustig, who was at that time eighteen years old and who claimed that he was the one who had buried Schulz. Grynberg wrote the book *Drohobycz, Drohobycz and Other Stories: True Tales from the Holocaust and Life After* (New York: Penguin, 2002), which is based on Lustig's account. Lustig was part of the Jewish Agricultural SS Unit that Naftali Backenroth established with the help of Eberhard Helmrich in a place called Hyrawka, close to Drohobych's new Jewish cemetery (see chapter 19). Along with another digger, Lustig was called from Hyrawka to bury "two men that lay on the ground near the Cemetery's entrance, just to the right of the gate." According to Lustig, the two were Schulz and Günther's protégé, the cabinet maker Hauptman, and both had been shot in the head. Lustig said that he and the other man buried the two corpses in one grave "right there where we found them." After the war, Lustig immigrated to the United States. Often, visitors to Drohobych try to find Schulz's grave, but the exact location of his remains is unknown.

10. See a detailed account of the incident in Anatol Regnier's book *Damals in Bolechow* (Once upon a time in Bolechow) (Goldman Publishing House, in German), p.83. Almost identical accounts were given to the author of this book by two of Bolechow's Jewish inhabitants of that time.
11. Benno Reisman remembered the names of some of them: Yizhak Landes; Jagar's son-in-law Zimmerman and his son Julek; Baruch Pepper; Ben-Zion Schindler and his son David.
12. A year later, in the second *Aktion*, in August 1943, Sabina Friedman was murdered along with her husband, the retired school director Josek Friedman.
13. Later, he returned to Poland and became a well-known physician in Warsaw.
14. *"Mein Steteleh Belz"* was a popular Yiddish song expressing longing for Jewish life in that Moldavian town (now called Beltsi): "Belz, my little town Belz, my little home where I spent my childhood years, in that poor little house where I laughed with all the children. Every Sabbath I'd run to read by the river. Belz, where I had so many beautiful dreams."
15. The Bełżec death camp was in southeastern Poland, between the cities of Zamosc and Lvov. It was the first place where, in August 1942, the Nazis tested Zyklon B cyanide gas on a large number of Jews.
16. According to research conducted by Stryj's Holocaust survivors, the ghetto was reduced in size at the beginning of 1943, and in May a few thousand Jews were killed in the city's Jewish cemetery, while another seven hundred were taken away to Bełżec (for more information, see www.shtetlinks.jewishgen.org/Stryy/stryj-history.html, accessed April 7, 2008).
17. Of all the Jews who lived in Poland before the war, 89 percent were murdered by the Nazis. One Polish Jew out of 10 survived the Holocaust. The following figures are accepted by most historians: There were 3,351,000 Jews in Poland in 1939, of whom 370,000 were still alive when the war ended. Of

this number, 300,000 went to the Soviet Union before the Nazis reached them and some 15,000 managed to emigrate to safe places after 1939. Only 55,000 remained in Poland and survived.

23. Interlude on the Way to Anchorage

1. Following the annexation (Anschluss) of Austria to Nazi Germany in 1938, Asad automatically became a German citizen.
2. Until 1947, India was a Crown colony of Great Britain's. In 1947, the Indian subcontinent was divided between Hindus and Muslims, and Punjab became part of Pakistan.
3. In the late nineteenth and early twentieth centuries, under the leadership of the al-Rashid dynasty, the Shammar were inexorable opponents of the al-Saud family. In 1921, Ibn Saud brought the Shammar under his control by sending preachers to their tents, who taught the doctrines of Muhammad ibn Abd al-Wahhab (known as the creator of Wahhabism) and convinced many of Rashid's loyal families to betray their chieftain.
4. Wahhabism is the path of Islam that was preached by the eighteenth-century religious reformer Muhammad ibn Abd al-Wahhab, whose interpretation of the *sunna* (custom) of the prophet Muhammad was the foundation for the alliance that the tribal leaders formed with the al-Saud family. The Wahhab–al-Saud treaty was the cradle of modern Saudi Arabia.
5. Muhammad Iqbal (1877–1938) was known as *Shair-e-Mashriq* ("Poet of the East," in Arabic), mainly for his classical poetry written in Persian and Urdu. His most important political message was published in his 1930s book of six lectures in English, *The Reconstruction of Religious Thought in Islam*.
6. *Islamic Culture*'s first editor was Marmaduke Pickthall, a British convert to Islam, known for his English translation of the Quran. Many years later, Asad published his own English translation of the Quran (see further on).
7. In his biography *The Road to Mecca*, Asad wrote that his relations with his father were renewed due to the fact that his father "understands and appreciates the reasons for my conversion to Islam," but no family member could confirm his assertion, and it is almost certain that although Leopold visited Vienna in the beginning of 1939 and made an effort to obtain exit permits for his relatives, only his sister was ready to meet him; Asad's father continued to ostracize his Muslim son. But according to Asad, in 1942, his sister's and father's letters ceased to arrive at his detention camp.
8. Asad's sister, father, and stepmother were exterminated by the Nazis, probably at the end of 1942.
9. Muhammad Ali Jinnah (1876–1948) was the founder of Pakistan; he was known as Quaid-e-Azam, "Great Leader" in Arabic. In 1947, upon the separation of Pakistan from India, Jinnah was nominated to be the first governor general of the country and the president of its constituent assembly.

10. Zafaruyllah Khan (1893–1985) was Pakistan's first foreign minister. In October–November 1947, as chief representative of Pakistan to the UN General Assembly, he was very active regarding the Palestinian issue and made a huge effort to prevent the division of Palestine between Arabs and Jews. Some of his declarations and speeches about the Middle Eastern conflict were written by Asad.
11. Its official name was the Palestine Broadcasting Service.
12. Many years later, Asad wrote that the Arabs would never reconcile themselves with Jerusalem being the capital of Israel. "In a conceivably free Palestine—a state in which Jews, Christians and Muslims could live side by side in full political and cultural equality," Asad wrote, "the Muslim community should be specifically entrusted with the custody of Jerusalem as a city open to all three communities." See *This Law of Ours and Other Essays* (Gibraltar: Kazi Publications, 1991).
13. Published by Simon & Schuster (New York, 1954).
14. King Faisal of Saudi Arabia (Ibn Saud's son), along with the Muslim World League and many personal friends (among them, one of Asad's closest friends, Ahmad Zaki al Yamani, the famous oil minister of Saudi Arabia during the Arab oil boycott of the 1970s, whose family also has Jewish roots), financed Asad's seventeen years of work on the translation. It was published in 1980 and was titled *The Message of the Qur'an* (Gibraltar: Kazi Publications, 1980). It was dedicated to "people who think." Asad's translation is considered the best in the English language, but it was not accepted by the Muslim establishment. Conservative scholars found the translation "advanced" and "too liberal" and blamed Asad for trying to bring the spirit of the Jewish Reform movement, in which he had been tutored as a young man in Vienna, into Islam. Asad himself often said that his translation is much more related to the original than Pickthall's is. In the introduction Asad wrote,

    > Familiarity with the Bedouin speech of Central and Eastern Arabia, in addition, of course, to academic knowledge of classical Arabic, is the only way for a non-Arab of our time to achieve an intimate understanding of the diction of the Qur'an. And because none of the scholars who have previously translated the Qur'an into European languages has ever fulfilled this prerequisite, their translations have remained but distant, and faulty, echoes of its meaning and spirit.

    It was known among experts that Pickthall's knowledge of Arabic was limited.
15. Some 160,000 Jews returned to Poland in 1946, mainly from the Soviet Union, and many of them left the country by the early 1950s, most of them illegally by crossing the border at night to Czechoslovakia. They then traveled by train

to Vienna, where half of them emigrated to Palestine and half to countries in the West, mainly the United States. Another 50,000 Jews emigrated from Poland to the United States and Israel between 1957 and 1959. This was during Wladyslaw Gomulka's reign as prime minister, following the Eastern Bloc's de-Stalinization process and the liberalization of the Polish Communist Party (that wave of immigrants was called the "Gomulka Emigration").

16. After more than a decade of dictatorship, Brazil declared a new democratic constitution in 1946, and a sense of optimism stimulated its economy.
17. Exactly at the same time (1948–1949), the Soviet Union blocked Western access to West Berlin, while the United States maintained supply lines to the city by flying food and goods over the blockade.
18. Herbert Tenzer (1905–1993) of Lawrence, Long Island, served two terms of office in the U.S. House of Representatives (1965–1969). He was a founding partner of the New York law firm Tenzer, Greenblatt (which merged with the Blank, Rome firm in 2000). Stephen Klein was the owner of the Barton's Candy chain in New York, selling kosher chocolates and kosher ice cream, which were very popular among Orthodox Jews. In 1981, the Klein family sold Barton's Candy, and the chain was closed.
19. Mussolini was in conflict with Nazi Germany regarding the fate of Jews. Although his regime initiated an extensive anti-Semitic campaign in 1938, with the aim of pleasing Hitler, most of Mussolini's bureaucracy opposed Nazi Germany's policies toward the Jews and obstructed the deportation of Italian Jews to the death camps. After Mussolini was overthrown, in 1943, Germany occupied north and central Italy. SS units, supported by passionate Italian fascists, rounded up eight thousand Jews and deported them to extermination camps in Eastern Europe, where almost all of them were murdered. Nevertheless, many other Jews succeeded in finding hiding places in Italy, and more than forty thousand survived the Holocaust.
20. Morgenstern was the only person whom the author of this book encountered who hated Ullo Kahane. "Ullo owed me a lot, and when he ruled against me, I couldn't remain indifferent," Morgenstern declared in his tape recorded interview, thereby opening up a little Pandora's box. "I attacked him and he boycotted me, just like that, and threw me out of the community." The conflict had occurred in 1965. Ullo agreed to be the arbitrator in a financial dispute between Morgenstern and a prominent and wealthy Jewish merchant in Rio de Janeiro. If Morgenstern had been a stranger, there would have been no problem, but it was he who had arranged for the Kahane couple to obtain their visas to Brazil, through his contacts in Italy, and then, when they reached Rio, they lived in his apartment for several months until Nushka was rushed to the hospital to give birth to her son. Ullo ruled against Morgenstern, and Morgenstern was deeply wounded. He voiced his complaints to his acquaintances, questioning Ullo's integrity. They never made peace with each other.

21. After that, Continental Can Company went through a few takeovers and changes. Since 1998, Viatech Continental Can Company, Inc., has been a wholly owned subsidiary of the Dallas-based firm Suiza Foods Corporation.
22. NYSE quote stock ORA.
23. Since 1991, Yehudit Bronicki has been the chief executive officer of Ormat Industries Ltd., and Lucien is the firm's chairman and chief technology officer. At gas-fired electricity plants in North and South Dakota, Ormat has installed systems that recover heat that is normally wasted in production and convert it into additional electricity. Similar projects are under construction in Washington State and Canada. Another technology that was developed by Ormat for producing oil from shale is being used in the tar sands of Canada's Alberta province in a project run by Opti Canada.
24. In mid-2006, Ormat and two partners—Japan's Itochu and Indonesia's Medco Energi International—won a bid to construct a new 340-megawatt geothermal power project on the island of Sumatra, the largest such facility in the world.
25. In August 2007, Ormat Technologies' market capitalization was $1.6 billion. For the second quarter of 2007, Ormat Technologies' total revenues were $84.1 million, as compared to $64.1 million for the same period in 2006 (31.2 percent growth). Net income for the second quarter of 2007 was $8.5 million, up from $8.4 million during the same period in 2006. Total sales in 2006 were $269 million.
26. The documentary *Arbeit Macht Frei* (Work Liberates) was directed by the Israeli Mordechai Kirshenbaum.
27. One of them was Erwin Schenkelbach, a Drohobych-born photographer who lives in Jerusalem today. Bronicki and Schulz were friends of his father's. Schenkelbach was thirteen when Schulz was murdered, and almost at the same time, the Nazis took Schenkelbach's parents. Gestapo officer Karl Günther, Schulz's murderer, was ready to save Erwin's father, Bertold, but the father would not be separated from his wife, and both were sent to be exterminated.

Bibliography

Books

Asad, Muhammad. *The Road to Mecca.* New York: Simon & Schuster, 1954.

———. *This Law of Ours and Other Essays.* Gibraltar: Kazi, 1991.

Avigdor, Dr. Isaac C. *Faith after the Flames: The Story of Rabbi Dr. Yaakov Avigdor.* New Haven, CT: Rodgiva, 2005.

Avigdor, Jacob. *From Prison to Pulpit: Sermons for All Holidays of the Year and Stories from the Holocaust.* New York: Shengold Books, 1975.

Benz, Wolfgang. *Überleben im Dritten Reich: Juden im Untergrund und ihre Helfer* (Survival in the Third Reich: Jews in Underground and Their Helpers). Munich: C. H. Beck, 2003 (in German).

Birkenthal, Dov Ber (Ber of Bolechow). *The Memoirs of Ber of Bolechow (1723–1805).* New York: Arno Press, 1973.

Brecher, Elinor J. *Schindler's Legacy: True Stories of the List Survivors.* New York: Plume (Penguin), 1994.

Canetti, Elias. *The Memoirs of Elias Canetti: The Tongue Set Free, the Torch in My Ear, the Play of the Eyes.* New York: Farrar, Straus and Giroux, 2000.

Davis, Joseph M. *Yom-Tov Lipmann Heller: Portrait of a Seventeenth-Century Rabbi.* Oxford: Littman Library of Jewish Civilization, 2005.

Ficowski, Jerzy. *Regions of the Great Heresy: Bruno Schulz, a Biographical Portrait.* New York: W. W. Norton, 2002.

Fleig Frank, Alison. *Oil Empire: Visions of Prosperity in Austrian Galicia.* Cambridge, MA: Harvard University Press, 2007.

Gelber, Dr. N. M. *Memorial Book of Drohobycz, Boryslav and Surroundings.* Tel Aviv: Association of Former Residents of Drohobycz, Boryslav, and Surroundings, 1959. (This *yizkor* book contains academic and historical eyewitness accounts in Hebrew and Yiddish. It is one of the richest available sources for the history of the Jews of Drohobycz and Boryslav.)

Gilbert, Martin. *The Holocaust.* New York: HarperCollins, 1989.

———. *The Righteous: The Unsung Heroes of the Holocaust.* New York: Henry Holt, 2003.

Grynberg, Henryk. *Drohobycz, Drohobycz and Other Stories: True Tales from the Holocaust and Life After.* New York: Penguin, 2002.

Halter, Mark. *Stories of Deliverance: Speaking with Men and Women Who Rescued Jews from the Holocaust.* Chicago: Open Court, 1998.

Heller, Celia. *On the Edge of Destruction: Jews of Poland between the Two World Wars.* New York: Columbia University Press, 1977.

Klee, Ernst, Willi Dressen, and Volker Reiss, eds. *The Good Old Days: The Holocaust as Seen by Its Perpetrators and Bystanders.* New York: Konecky & Konecky, 1991.

Lau, D. C. *Lao Tzu. Tao Te Ching.* London: Penguin Classics, 1963.

Litman, Jacob. *The Economic Role of Jews in Medieval Poland: The Contribution of Yitzhak Schipper.* Lanham, MD: University Press of America, 1984.

Opalski, Magdalena, and Bartal Israel. *Poles and Jews: A Failed Brotherhood.* Waltham, MA: Brandeis University, 1992.

Palmer, Alan. *Twilight of the Habsburgs: The Life and Times of Emperor Francis Joseph.* New York: Atlantic Monthly Press, 1997.

Regnier, Anatol. *Damals in Bolechow: Eine judische Odyssee* (Once Upon a Time in Bolechow: A Jewish Odyssey). Munich: Wilhelm Goldmann Verlag, 1997 (in German).

Rolnik, Eran J. *Freud in Zion: History of Psychoanalysis in Jewish Palestine/Israel 1918–1948.* Tel Aviv: Am Oved, 2007 (in Hebrew).

Rottenberg, Dan. *Finding Our Fathers: A Guidebook to Jewish Genealogy.* New York: Random House, 1977.

Sanders, Ronald. *Shores of Refuge: A Hundred Years of Jewish Emigration.* New York: Henry Holt, 1988.

Schmalhausen, Bernd. *A Man of Courage in an Inhuman Time: Berthold Beitz in the Third Reich.* Jerusalem: Yad Vashem, 2006.

Schmalz-Jacobsen, Cornelia. *Zwei Baume in Jerusalem* (Two Trees in Jerusalem). Hamburg: Hoffmann and Campe, 2002 (in German).

Stasiuk, Andrzej. *Tales of Galicia,* translated from Polish by Margarita Nafpaktitis. Prague: Twisted Spoon Press, 2003 (in Czech).

Thorne, Leon. *Out of the Ashes: The Story of a Survivor.* New York: Rosebern, 1961.

Trials of Nazi Criminals: Felix Landau's Life Sentence. Justiz und NS-Verbrechen, Vol. XVIII, Case No. 531, Stuttgart's Court, Germany.

Watt, Richard M. *Bitter Glory: Poland and Its Fate 1918–1939.* New York: Simon & Schuster, 1979.

Windhager, Günther. *Leopold Weiss alias Muhammad Asad: Von Galizien nach Arabien 1900–1929* (Leopold Weiss alias Muhammad Asad: From Galicia to Arabia).Vienna: Böhlau-Verlag, 2002 (in German).

Yad Vashem ASIN B0007C502O. *Love Letters of a Nazi Murderer in Lemberg and Drohobycz, Written by Felix Landau.* Jerusalem: Yad Vashem, 1987.

Articles and Essays

Avigdor, Jacob. "Questions and Answers 'Abir Yacov' "; autobiographical essay as preface. New York: publisher unknown, 1949 (reprint of 1934 edition).

Kalian, M., and E. Witztum. "Comments on Jerusalem Syndrome." *British Journal of Psychiatry* 176:492.

Kramer, Martin. "The Road from Mecca: Muhammad Asad (Born Leopold Weiss)." In *The Jewish Discovery of Islam: Studies in Honor of Bernard Lewis.* Tel Aviv: Moshe Dayan Center for Middle Eastern and African Studies, 1999, pp. 225–247.

Saebo, Morten. *The Oil Fields of Galicia.* Walnut Creek, CA: *Petroleum Philatelic Society International,* Quarterly Publication, winter 1998, pp. 5–7.

Sandkuehler, T. *Endloesung in Galizien. Der Judenmord in Ostpolen und die Rettungsinitiativen von Berthold Beitz, 1941–1944.* Arbeitsgemeinschaft kirchlicher Zeitgeschichtler (Association of Contemporary Church Historians), Newsletter 3, no. 11 (November 1997).

Web Sites

http://srbmods.dnsalias.org/grantville/1632Slush_200411/msg00045.html.

www.jewishgen.org/yizkor/Drohobycz/Drogobych.html.

www.shtetlinks.jewishgen.org/drohobycz/history/WWII.asp.

http://eh.net/hmit/.

www.jewishgen.org/Yizkor/Bolekhov/bol057.html.

www.geocities.com/martinkramerorg/WeissAsad.htm.

www.martinkramer.org/.

www.deathcamps.org/reinhard/finalsolution.html.

www.brunoschulz.org/.

www.benjamingeissler.de/ENGLISH/index-EN.htm.

http://motlc.learningcenter.wiesenthal.org/text/x00/xr0072.html.

www.motl.org/resource/curriculum/curriculum_10.htm.

Index

Page numbers in italics refer to illustrations.